Revolution and Reality

Revolution

Bertram D. Wolfe

Introduction by Lewis S. Feuer

The University of North Carolina Press   Chapel Hill

and Reality

Essays on the Origin and Fate

of the Soviet System

© 1981 The University of North Carolina Press

All rights reserved

Manufactured in the United States of America

Cloth edition, ISBN 0-8078-1453-9

Paper edition, ISBN 0-8078-4073-4

Library of Congress Catalog Number 80-16178

Library of Congress Cataloging in Publication Data

Wolfe, Bertram David, 1896–1977.
  Revolution and reality.

  Includes bibliographical references and index.
    1. Communism—Russia—History—Addresses, essays,
lectures. 2. Russia—Politics and government—1917–
—Addresses, essays, lectures. I. Title.
HX313.W64 1981   335.43'0947   80-16178
ISBN 0-8078-1453-9
ISBN 0-8078-4073-4 (pbk.)

To
the scholars and travelers—and those
who have lost their way—on the journey
to Utopia

Contents

Introduction: By Lewis S. Feuer
Bertram David Wolfe,
1896–1977

I

That Bertram D. Wolfe had written an enduring classic *Three Who Made a Revolution* was recognized as soon as it was published in 1948. Isaiah Berlin judged it as having "a degree of authority" unmatched by any similar book; William Henry Chamberlin said that it was "by far the best history of the Russian revolutionary movement available in English" while Edmund Wilson declared it "the best book in its field in any language." Now that Bert is no longer with us, the story should be told of how this gentle, courteous, and warm-hearted man became the penetrating student of the revolutionary spirit.

Bert Wolfe's formative years recapitulated those of Lenin and Trotsky. From the time he became a radical socialist in 1917, thereupon losing his post as a teacher in the Boys' High School in Brooklyn, New York, Bert lived for most of the next thirteen years the fitful, tangential existence of an underground revolutionist. He was familiar with the faction fights, the agitation of party conferences, the wanderings in foreign capitals, the tactical duels with the secret police, the camouflage of false names, the sparse rations of food and shelter. Together with John Reed, Bert wrote the Manifesto of the National Left Wing of the Socialist party, which in his old age he still characterized proudly as "a document of largely native American radicalism." In 1924 he worked his way on a ship to the Fifth Congress of the Communist International, bearing a Mexican passport and his credentials as a representative of the Mexican party. In the United States he had previously edited (under a pseudonym) a newspaper in San Francisco that was jointly financed by a curious directorate drawn from

Adapted with permission from *Survey*, vol. 23, no. 1 (Winter 1977–78).

trade union leaders, the Irish Republican Movement, and the Hindu Gadir party, the latter being mostly made up of revolutionary Sikhs. Chance and the "dialectic" intervened, however, so that he spent most of the early twenties working in the Mexican Communist party and serving on its Central Committee. The party, as Bert later wrote, was "a party of vaguely revolutionary painters." During these years Bert became the close friend and later co-worker of the painter Diego Rivera, who deeply influenced Bert's outlook toward art and nature. Meanwhile something of the political doubter emerged in Bert, for he persuaded Diego Rivera to resign from the Communist party. He felt that membership was helping neither Diego as an artist nor the party as an organization, and he actually won the Mexican comrades, at least temporarily, to his non-Leninist standpoint. Deported, however, from Mexico under some comic trumped-up charge, Bert was soon directing the American Communist campaign that was mounted on behalf of the Italian anarchists, Sacco and Vanzetti, then awaiting execution in Massachusetts. In later years he was to feel keenly that those like Carlo Tresca and Upton Sinclair who were skeptical of Sacco's innocence should have spoken out honestly. Soon the hectic years of the "faction" struggle within the Communist party began; Bert, at the time in charge of the party's educational activities, also became editor of its official magazine *The Communist*. He supported the party secretary and his fellow City College alumnus, Jay Lovestone, in advocating the so-called theory of "exceptionalism," according to which the strength and prosperity of American capitalism, together with its democratic political constitution and traditions, precluded the application in the United States of a revolutionary "line." Indirectly, the relative moderation of the Lovestone-Wolfe leadership made them sympathetic to the right-wing "deviation" that was arising in the Soviet Union around the figure of the cultured and ill-fated personality of Nikolai Bukharin. It was probably during this time that Bert came to realize that his own personality was not adaptable to the dishonesties and intricate maneuverings of international communist politics. In December 1928, he went to Russia as the American representative on the Executive Committee of the Communist International. Despite his collapse under the strains of physical illness, Bert fought with all his resources to induce the Comintern to allow the American Communist party to go its own independent way. Stalin, however, remained adamant in demanding the ouster of the Lovestone-Wolfe leadership. Bert, still trusting in the power of logic and fact then cabled Lovestone advising that an American delegation should come to Moscow to argue face to face with the Bolshevik chiefs. Bukharin by this time had been removed from fulfilling any functions as chairman of the International; he had been declared sick by a vote of five to four, as he told Bert. Thus Bert and the Americans fell into Stalin's trap. Stalin met with the Comintern's "American Mission" and laid down the condition of the Americans' capitulation; not satisfied with the simple acceptance of party discipline, he demanded that Lovestone and Wolfe be removed as leaders, and that they then stay on indefinitely in Moscow. Stalin's outburst against the Americans during the main session was so violent and threatening that Bert never forgot it. The memory of it hovered over the pages that he later wrote concerning the social system of Soviet despotism. The Americans, shunned by the Russians, and always under surveillance, kept sending back cables to their American supporters (using all sorts of code names like I. M. Shmendrick, a Yiddish combination for "I am a fool") in an endeavor to retain their control of the party "institutions" and press. But it was to no avail against the combined force of Stalin's apparatus and the pusillanimity of the comrades at home. Lovestone and Wolfe were fortunate to escape from Moscow two months later without the knowledge of the Comintern. Whereupon the Russians called upon the American Communist party to condemn these disrupters. Bert came alone to a meeting of the Political Committee and gave a speech that "absolutely astounded" those present with its defiance. He was the only one, as Theodore Draper recounts, who voted against the expulsion of Lovestone—who had enjoyed, half a year earlier, the support of 90 percent of the party. Shortly afterward, when Bert refused to make a speaking tour on behalf of the party's new "line," he was expelled from its membership.

During later years, I used to observe that the cardinal sin in Bert's eyes was "to run with the pack." He had seen the pack running in the Communist party in 1929, and how the pack could be led. Slowly, as he said, he began to turn the "searchlight" on himself and his comrades to understand the laws of ideological commitment, the laws of the pack, for only by such understanding could he achieve freedom.

Bert seems to have reacted to the debacle of his Communist experience by finding wisdom in the study of Spanish literature. Earning his living as a highly effective teacher at the Eron Preparatory School, he took a master's degree in Spanish literature in 1931 at Columbia University with a thesis *The Mexican Ballad*, and he became an authority on *Don Quixote*. The great translator, Samuel Putnam, has paid tribute not only to Bert's personal chivalry but to his magisterial judgment on questions of Cervantes scholarship. In Don Quixote Bert seems to have found the symbol of the intellectual's tilting at the windmills of history. Bert did not like to discuss religious-philosophical questions and seemed devoid of any religious longing. However, the Spanish language and literature somehow provided him with the words in which such feelings could be voiced. He could quote the lines of Calderón, *La vida es sueño*, but not stopping there, would recite whole passages. He later translated the poems of León Felipe, the poet of "Spain's exodus and tears," in whom he found, besides tragedy, the "thunder of the biblical prophets." He estimated Felipe's creed as "not unworthy of the vision of the mad Knight of La Mancha," citing his *Death's Calendar*:

> The pendulum has broken . . .
> Here let me sleep
> in nothingness. The nothingness that is
> the clock of the universe
> stopped forever.

The course that Bert gave at Stanford University in 1949 on *Don Quixote* during a year as lecturer on Spanish Culture must have contained the essence of his personal philosophy.

The fulcrum of Bert's political activity during the thirties was the "Communist Party of the USA (Opposition)" or the "Lovestoneites," as they were called in that era when proper names became the signposts of movements. In the nineteenth century, movements named themselves mostly after doctrines, with such words as "impossibilists," "maximalists," and "reformists"; then later came the Russians using such procedural words as "Mensheviks," "Bolsheviks," and "Liquidators." In the thirties, however, proper names that became hyphenated, obscure, and sometimes allegedly illegitimate were introduced. Bert as director of the New Workers School was in charge of educational activities. A big sign on a small building on 14th Street blazoned forth TRAINING FOR THE CLASS STRUGGLE; no school has ever summed up the philosophy of its curriculum so succinctly. Diego Rivera covered its dingy walls with murals on the history of the workers' movement, giving a notable place to Bert's meditative face. The "Lovestoneites" remained influential in New York's garment workers' unions, but among the intellectuals of the thirties they made little impression. For, as Bert once said, the leftist intellectuals of that decade tended to become Trotskyists; the severity of the American depression seemed to confute the notion of American "exceptionalism," while Trotsky's stirring, dramatic, personal brilliance made him an embodiment of the will to fashion a new world and to withstand the Nazi barbarism. During this decade, Bert's creative energies were chiefly devoted to the writing of his book *Diego Rivera, His Life and Times*, and to the texts that accompanied the plates of Rivera's murals in *Portrait of America* and *Portrait of Mexico*. Bert thus virtually wrote a brief history of the American radical movement and a volume on the social history of Mexico that ended with an augury of the socialistic labor movement that would carry matters far beyond the Cárdenas compromise. In addition, Bert published several memorable political essays, an incisively written pamphlet *What is the Communist Opposition?*, a booklet *Marx on America*, a pioneer essay in Marxist scholarship that blended with Bert's interpretation of American "exceptionalism," a book *Civil War in Spain* (1937), based on his visit to Loyalist Spain, and which included an introduction by Will Herberg, a translation of and introduction to Rosa Luxemburg's classic critique, *The Russian Revolution*, and then most important in 1939, *Keep America Out of War*, a book written with Norman Thomas, the leader of American socialism, which admonished *This Is Not Our War!* and warned that if America entered the war, "decency, tolerance, kindliness, truth, democracy, and freedom will be the first victims" and that in the name of stopping totalitarianism, we would in fact be installing it in America. This book was scarcely being sold when Bert decided he had gone so essentially wrong on political fundamentals that he must start anew to reexamine his political postulates. Why had his political intelligence culminated in epochal blunder? How had he been misled by Marxist shibboleths to misunderstand American and world political realities?

Laboriously and courageously Bertram Wolfe undertook to study the whole significance of the Russian revolutionary movement and the Soviet state. He worked hard in middle age to master the Russian language, helped by the tutoring of Vera Alexandrova. He could never learn it as he knew Spanish; he said he never acquired a feeling for Russian poetry. But he made himself capable of using the language for original historical research. He acquired the tools of the historian's craft. He learned, as he said, how the sources should be used and how the evidence should be impeccably marshalled. Through the war years and afterward, Bert wrote and completed his masterpiece *Three Who Made a Revolution*. He had found his vocation; the ordeals of his own life imparted to his political knowledge the ingredient of human wisdom that gave a timeless aspect to this work. In its pages, the "truth of the defeated" stood alongside and was indeed superior to the "official truth" as truth itself emerged.

Books and numerous articles then followed one another. With *Six Keys to the Soviet System* and *Khrushchev and Stalin's Ghost* Bert became America's leading political analyst of the Soviet Union. For four years Bert also served as chief of the Ideological Advisory Staff of the State Department and the Voice of America, greatly enjoying the intellectual companionship he found in these circles. He liked to tell of the several instances in which his advice had helped to shape the decisions of national policy. Then came the opportunity to serve as a Visiting Professor of History at the University of California at Davis in 1961–62. It also brought Bert an honorary degree, so that he joked that having never taken a doctor's degree, he had now gained an honorary one. He was given the degree because one day a member of the Board of Regents heard Bert lecture on the role of the Lysenko affair in Soviet genetics, a theme especially pertinent to the agricultural and biological faculties at Davis. The regent was so impressed that he nominated Bert for the honor. Bert was a natural teacher; in fact, he enjoyed it so much that he wrote very little that year. He could have become a permanent member of the Davis faculty, but he decided that with his advancing years, and the books he wished to write, it was wiser for him to accept an offer to become a Fellow of the Hoover Institution.

When his colleague, Boris Nicolaevsky, died in 1966, Bert was asked to speak at his funeral. He told movingly how the old Menshevik had finally found at the Hoover Institution a center where he could continue the studies that would be his contribution to the flame of freedom and truth. I felt that this was also true for the last phase of Bert's life. He published his large work *Marxism: One Hundred Years in the Life of a Doctrine*, a careful, definitive study with much new material on such subjects as Marx's relations to the Paris Commune. Its critical acumen and scholarship were not welcome, however, to a generation that had become ecstatic over the word "alienation." Then came *The Bridge and the Abyss*, a study of the Lenin-Gorky friendship that illumined the psychological dualities of revolutionary intellectuals. Finally, he wrote what may be the crowning work for his many friends and future students, forty-one chapters of his autobiography, *A Life in Two Centuries*.

Bert Wolfe's work is placed among the highest achievements of American political thought; nonetheless, he was not an ambitious man. When he took his bachelor's degree in 1916 at the City College of New York, the respected chairman of the Department of English, Professor Lewis Freeman Mott, offered Bert a "tutorship" and the virtual assurance of an academic career. Bert chose instead to teach at a school where the higher salary enabled him to marry his beloved Ella. He was singularly indifferent to prestige and pomp. When a friend of his was deciding whether to leave Berkeley in 1966 for a lesser university in Canada, Bert advised him to go wherever he could get the most done of what he wanted to do; everything else, Bert felt, was relatively trivial. In later years, Bert read comparatively little (he did not read Solzhenitsyn, with whom he had so much in common, until he was called upon to review *Lenin in Zurich*), for he had to husband his slender and failing physical resources. Nonetheless his spirit never flagged; he was much amused when I said he would keep on living so long as he had "unfinished business." That was true, he said.

Bert remained skeptical, however, of the prospects for Soviet-American détente, and no doubt he saw the new Euro-communism as an attempt to do all over again, and probably with equal futility, what he had tried to do with American "exceptionalism." A couple of years ago he and Ella happened to encounter in Mexico City the American secretary of state, Henry Kissinger. The Mexican police became agitated when they saw this tall, thin, wan, old man, with a smiling countenance, wending his way toward Kissinger, but the secretary of state, hearing who he was, said: "I want to meet that man. I've read every one of his books." So the Mexican police let Bert pass, and he told Henry he admired him, but that his détente policy was "for the birds." But no one would have been happier than Bert if for this once he had been proven wrong and that Don Quixote might on some rare day find the dream coinciding with reality.

The human drama of the participants in communist movements characteristically fascinated Bert. The book of collected sketches *Strange Communists I Have Known* was thus a complement to the more formalized essays collected in *An Ideology in Power*. Its title was a whimsical adaptation by Bert of the title *Wild Animals I Have Known*, a book by the Canadian naturalist, Ernest Thompson Seton. He hoped to add further chapters in political "characterology" in a later edition.

In all these personal essays, Bert preserved an almost Victorian sense of decorum. I think he was glad, for instance, that he could suggest that Inessa Armand had not been the "mistress" of Lenin, even though he differed on this point with other biographers. He was mindful of the unconscious, irrational motives that moved people, but it was a region which out of a sense of chivalry he preferred not to explore himself. In his second book on Diego Rivera, for example, he wondered as to the causes that could lead people who prize freedom to join a movement that would destroy it. Marx had no answer, "perhaps Freud does though: he called it the death wish," wrote Bert, but that was all he would say.

Perhaps his spirit remained so serene because there was almost nothing in Bert of the sense of guilt that characterized so many of his former comrades. When Arthur Koestler met Bert, he asked him what manner of guilt-feeling had led him to become a Communist. Bert replied that it was no guilt motive in his case, but that rather as an opponent of the World War in 1916–17, he had evolved toward left socialism. And indeed there was always a sense of moderation, of proportion in Bert even during his Communist days. He believed in reasoning with men. When Diego Rivera clashed publicly with Nelson Rockefeller because Lenin's head was prominently placed high in his Radio City mural, Bert advised him to yield on Lenin's head and save the rest of the large painting. Diego, however, was persuaded by others to stand uncompromising and to trust in demonstrations by the "masses"; six months later the mural was torn from the walls. But then, as Bert noted, the Soviet bosses minced matters even less when it came to Diego's art; they looked at his sketches, and heard his talk, and then decided they wanted none of his work on any Moscow wall.

By Bert's side throughout his life was his wife, Ella. He always carried with him a photograph of Ella in her girlhood beauty. She shared his activities, accompanied him to Moscow and Mexico, shared his San Francisco underground days. In his ailing years, she enveloped him with her love, patience, and understanding.

Listening to Ella and Bert in the evenings telling stories, and arguing affectionately over the variants, was to experience the art of storytelling as it must have been practiced in Cervantes's time. One evening in a delicatessen store they narrated how the poet Vladimir Mayakovsky had stayed with them for several months in Brooklyn (the poet particularly liked Ella's mother's cheese blintzes). But when the Soviet authorities ordered him to come home he had no money with which to travel. The Wolfe family thereupon came to his rescue with their meager savings. Back in Russia, the poet decided to cancel his debts to capitalist America; not until Bert complained of this uncomradely behavior to the Soviet party did the poet repay them. Then by way of self-exculpation, the poet invented the story that he had spent the money to support an illegitimate child in America. Though wholly imaginary, the story was duly incorporated into learned books. Then too there was the story of the love letters of Leon Trotsky to Frida, Rivera's wife, which Frida in her sorrows confided to Ella; when Frida asked for them to be destroyed, Ella loyally carried out her wish.

Bert, it should be mentioned, tried his hand during the melancholy thirties at a work of science fiction, whose theme was the consequence for humanity of its mastery of the secret of prolonging life indefinitely. Although the publisher's bankruptcy led to the scrapping of the book, a Spanish translation did appear in Chile in 1942 under the title of *Mundo sin muerte* [Deathless days].

Perhaps nothing illustrates better the substance of Bert Wolfe's insight than these words: "We might do well to remember that the human spirit is fearfully and wonderfully made, and that . . . in things of the spirit more can be accomplished by coals of fire than by bullying."

II

Bertram D. Wolfe was never a purely academic writer. The political and historical writings of the present collection were meant to contribute toward reversing the totalitarian drift in the modern world. His ideas would appear first in journalistic articles, then would grow with documentation into articles for scholarly quarterlies; some finally entered his books. Whatever he wrote bore the imprint of that sensitivity to word and logical order that had won him the Ward Medal in English at the City College of New York. Wolfe tested the Marxist and Leninist hypotheses in his lifework; in this respect he differed from the purely academic scholar who is only marginally affected by the fate of his hypotheses and for whom a contrary consequence may involve only a slight alteration of text and footnotes. Perhaps the academic bias, if there is one, is to justify those who have abstained from any "involvements," or to project a resentment against those who were involved in historical conflicts. Marxist scholars have their own a priori postulate; they regard the significant historical truth as that of the victors, even though it takes the direction of the totalitarians who are shaping the world.

The standpoint of Wolfe, on the other hand, was to articulate "the truth of the defeated." Not that he believed, as Henrik Ibsen did, that the majority is always wrong, for the majority too can be broken and defeated. Rather Wolfe saw that, from Thucydides to Trotsky, defeat has induced some statesmen to analyze and see more clearly what in the workings of events consigned their standpoint to rejection. The statesman in defeat might understand how his very gifts of thinking and foresight separated him from the masses whose leader he had aspired to be. "The truth of the defeated" can unfold strange perspectives. A Tory Loyalist might have had a dim perception in 1776 that an Anglo-American empire could constitute the world's bulwark of peace and make possible the emancipation of black slaves without sectional warfare. "The truth of the defeated," making victors humble, reminds all men of visions lost and repudiated in the quest for power. Thus Bertram Wolfe wrote: "It is always the historian's duty, too often neglected in our craft out of worship of the bitch-goddess Success, to seek out the truths of the defeated along with the truths that get published by the victors."

Unlike the political scientists of the present generation who are restive with the concept of totalitarianism, Wolfe continued to identify "the most important problem of our time" as that of "democracy versus totalitarianism in a world that is moving everywhere towards greater collectivism and greater state intervention." He turned from literature and art to the study of the history of communism because he sought an answer to the question: how and why does the totalitarian tendency triumph? He felt that American liberals were yielding to their longings when they told themselves that the "cold war" was ending because Soviet society was presumably evolving along a liberal path. Wolfe drew a crucial distinction between "within-system changes" in contrast to "changes in the system." Like the pre-modern Chinese despotism, the Soviet totalitarian system, he argued, had a "tendency to conserve itself," availing itself of literacy, education, and technology to heighten its control over people's thoughts and activities; Genghis Khan could return, as Herzen had said, but with the accoutrements of electronics and nuclear forces. Western intellectuals, reluctant to recognize the durability of the Soviet system, persisted in misreading maneuvers of the Soviet rulers as portents of a new era of understanding: the NEP, Socialism in One Country, the Popular Front, Collective Security, the Grand Alliance, One World, Peaceful Coexistence, the Geneva Spirit, Détente, were signposts of illusion substituted for the realities of forced collectivization, the purges, the labor camps, the Gulag Archipelago, the occupations of Czechoslovakia and Hungary, the missiles in the Cuban satellite, the grasp for African power.

The question, however, remained: what is the explanation for the rise of the totalitarian potential in modern times? The youthful Trotsky had perceived in 1904 that a centralized, dictatorial party would make for a personal political dictatorship. But why had Soviet society remained riveted in centralism and dictatorship? Why had the hegemony of the "mediocrities" such as Stalin seemingly taken on the aspect of an inevitable sociological law? Was a totalitarian society the inherent outcome of any effort to achieve a centrally planned socialist economy? If so, did this trend derive from the requirements of economic planning, as Friedrich Hayek believed, or was it founded rather on the psychological recalcitrance of personalities to a socialist order? Wolfe never dealt fully with these questions; he felt, however, that Trotsky had failed to comprehend that the rise to power of the "mediocre" Stalin was more than the consequence of Russian backwardness abetted by a postrevolutionary weariness. "If a Stalin, cruel and paranoiac," can in such a society terrorize a whole people, "is there not something paranoid about the system itself?"

Lenin's technology of party organization, his invention of a "party of a new type," one composed of professional revolutionists, was, in Wolfe's judgment, a cardinal source of the Soviet totalitarian society. Lenin's defenders argued that such a party organization, required by the conditions of tsarist repression, was the necessary instrumentality for the Bolshevik revolution of 1917. Wolfe replied that same party organization failed in the Revolution of 1905 to give Lenin any significant role, while in October 1917, Russia was enjoying, under the provisional government, as Lenin conceded, the most freedom in the world. Lenin's political technology, Wolfe finally asserted, was psychologically grounded: "his centralism sprang from the deepest necessities of his temperament, his confidence in himself, and his pessimistic view of his fellow men." Lenin's character reveled in secret, dictatorial organization, as had Blanqui and Nechayev before him, despite the fact that Karl Marx had repudiated secret, conspiratorial politics, regarding them as essentially bound up with dictatorship. Lenin's character became Russia's fate, a strange perversion of Heraclitus's saying that "man's character is his fate." Because Lenin called this party structure a "bureaucratic centralism," some political scholars have related his doctrine to Max Weber's concept of bureaucracy. But the source of Bolshevik power had nothing to do with the paraphernalia of bureaucracy—red tape, files, records, and rules and regulations. Rather, the Bolshevik power acted arbitrarily, without rules, and leaving no records. The party potentate, even on the district level, had a totalitarian drive not associated with the bureaucratic file clerk, the *chinovnik* of the Russian bureaucracy. Moreover, Lenin, in Wolfe's view, was "the organization man"; he also metamorphosed when dominant power was denied him into a disorganization man ordering "unconditionally and in the most resolute fashion, force splits, splits, and again splits."

The entropic evolution of Marxism into the political doctrine of a totalitarian society has not diminished its appeal to many of the world's intellectuals. Wolfe puzzled long over the problem: why, despite the fact that its predictions have been so largely falsified, does the attraction of Marxism for intellectuals remain so powerful? Part of the answer, he believed, was that "Marxism's staying powers lie in the fact that it is also an *ism*," that it is not a science, but "an ideology in the precise sense in which Marx himself used the term." Presumably, too, it projected the unconscious thought processes of the intellectual class. Wolfe was probing at the source of the modern distemper, the propensity of intellectuals to apocalypticism, indeed, their oscillations between cruelty and self-immolation. But at this point Wolfe's inquiry usually ended. He did not feel at home with psychological inquiry, though he felt that his analysis pointed in that direction.

Wolfe, above all, took note that Marx, who presumably made national economic motives the basis for historical evolution, invariably turned to war as the agency for human advancement. As against the customary view of Marx as the proponent of historical materialism and the economic law of capitalism, Wolfe brought into relief Marx the advocate of war. When history lagged, and economic forces seemed too inertial for evoking a revolutionary change, Marx would call, as he did repeatedly in 1848, for a "war of the West against the East" that would "wash away the sins of the past," making "manly" the German people. Wolfe documented the record of Marx and Engels as "war-mongers." They had urged, for instance, that the Crimean War be prosecuted by Britain and France with vigor, and in 1860 hoped for a war of Prussia against France that would catalyze a German revolution. Their military historicism, noted Wolfe, led Marx and Engels to view the extermination of peoples with a certain equanimity as the verdict of history. History, wrote Engels, required "crushing many a delicate little flower." Retrograde races and peoples "have as their immediate task the mission of perishing in the revolutionary world storm." "The coming world war will cause not only reactionary classes and dynasties to disappear from the face of the earth, but entire reactionary peoples, too. And that also will be progress." "These remains of nations, . . . this ethnic trash always becomes and remains until its complete extermination or denationalization, the most fanatic carrier of counterrevolution, since its entire existence is nothing more than a protest against a great historical revolution." Marxism was almost transmuted into an ideology of genocide. Such "ethnic trash" as South Slavs, with "their right to cattle-stealing" (in Engels's words) and "lazy Mexicans," had small claim to existence, according to the world-historical judgment as rendered by the clerks of its court, Marx and Engels.

For Marx and Engels the cause of civilization was wrapped up with the maintenance of the privileged status of German socialism; as the world's largest and most theoretically advanced movement, it seemed to them the bastion that above all had to be preserved. As Wolfe wrote, every socialist international has foundered on the rock of nationalism; later the Communist International came to regard the function of all other nations' movements as subservient to the Russian. Thus, too, Marx and Engels felt that a German defeat would be far worse for socialism than a French defeat. That a Berlin Commune, arising out of a German defeat, might have been even more of a milestone for socialism than the Paris Commune that they extolled was a notion they never would entertain. Meanwhile, as Wolfe pointed out, "the death of Lassalle (in 1864) had assured the gradual predominance of Marxism in Germany." The truth of the defeated comes to mind once more: if Lassalle had lived, and not ended his life in a miserable duel, German socialism might then have been spared the Marxist domination; the world's socialist movements might all have evolved in a liberal, reformist manner, and European history would have followed the road of a rational evolution.

Always in his work Wolfe had an eye for those aspects in the history of Marxism, the Communist party, and the Soviet Union that their official annalists wished to repress. Every society has what we might call its "unproblems," the questions it forbids to its scientists and scholars. The more repressive a society is, the more "unproblems" will it decree. Wolfe observed, for instance, that Soviet historians are not allowed to inquire into "the Bolshevik hold-ups" of 1905–7, or the Moscow Trials, or Trotsky's leadership in the 1905 Petrograd Soviet, and his crucial role in the October Revolution. He regarded it as a crime against the human intellect that the materials for knowledge were destroyed or concealed from men. Therefore he spoke with fervor against the actions of Krupskaia, Lenin's wife, in promulgating directives for the purging of the people's libraries of much of the world's greatest literature. Krupskaia had planted "the tree of unknowledge"; here was the unpardonable sin of bolshevism. Wolfe remembered what books and libraries had meant to his own spiritual life: "Nor could I fail to think of my own personal fate, born into a poor family in a Brooklyn slum, none of whose members before me, neither mother nor father nor older brother and sister had gotten more than an elementary education." Had it not been for the public libraries whose collections "did not exclude Plato, nor Aristotle, nor Herbert Spencer, nor any of the other difficult writers I struggled with as a little boy," wrote Wolfe, he would not have learned to write, and he would not have persevered for a higher education. America had been spared a Krupskaia to declare such works "senseless" for the children of the poor. It was the ideal of the freedom of the human spirit that first led Wolfe into the Communist movement; it was that same ideal that led him inevitably to separate himself from it. He became its deepest historical and political analyst, working upon the moral postulate that "the truth of the defeated" might contribute to a later chapter of victory.

I
Russia before the Revolution

1

Backwardness and Industrialization in Russian History and Thought

> When all other countries are crisscrossed by railroads and are able rapidly to concentrate and to shift their armed forces, Russia must necessarily be able to do the same. It is difficult, it is expensive, but, alas, inevitable. . . . With regard to railroads, as in many other things, we are particularly fortunate; we did not have to expend energy on experiments and strain our imagination; we can and shall reap the fruits of others' labor.
>
> A. K. Khomiakov

Before World War I most critics of Russia's condition, particularly Marxists and liberal Westernizers, held in varying degrees four propositions: (1) their country was backward; (2) while the West was advancing in seven-league boots, Russia remained stagnant; (3) her progress was blocked by removable obstacles; (4) once these were removed, Russia would follow the path already traversed by the West, although on this fourth proposition all who longed for a shortcut entertained reservations, their favorite shortcut running through the peasant "commune."

But what was this "West" which Russia was predestined to follow? When Russian intellectuals looked for an industrial model, "West" meant the England of the Industrial Revolution. Or Germany, which had followed England's example and was beginning to overtake her. When they concerned themselves with political obstacles to "modernization," "West" meant France, the France of a century of uprisings, barricades, coups d'état, the France in which the great broom of revolution had swept away the ancien régime in one dramatic decade, and with it, supposedly, all hindrances to progress.

To be sure, there was a catch. If all that was needed to unleash economic progress was a "Great French Revolution," why did the French economy limp so haltingly behind those of England and Germany?

There being no political answer to this question in their formulas, it

Reprinted with permission from *Slavic Review* 26 (June 1967).

was better not to ask it. Nor to ask whether the year of the Terror, with its forty thousand victims, was necessary to progress. Better to glorify the "Great Revolution" than to question its methods or its outcome.

French insurrectionary spirit and verbal audacity captured the imagination of the powerless Russian intelligentsia. Since in old Russia one could only dream, and since in dreams one is not responsible for consequences, there was no reason to put prosaic limits on their dreams. In the midst of oppression, the intelligentsia developed their ideals in freedom— freedom from reality, from practical activity, from roots in society, from tentativeness, shading, or self-questioning, from any limits on speculation and asseveration. "In all things I go to the uttermost extreme; my life long I have never been acquainted with moderation," wrote Dostoevski. His words could serve as the device of most of the intelligentsia. And, in a different fashion, of the peasantry as well.

Liberals might prefer the ordered progress of England. But the autocracy, as extreme as the Revolution, left little room for autonomous liberalism. One school of Social Democrats, of which Axelrod was an example, because of their concern for the *self*-activity of the working class looked to Germany's great mass organizations and German Social Democracy as its model. But *self*-activity was the last thing which either Lenin or the government wanted of the working class. The ideologues of the autocracy and the ideologues of bolshevism alike felt that it was their mission to be the guardians of, and do the thinking for, the people. If "spontaneous" is normally a good word in our vocabulary, it was an evil one in the vocabulary of both tsarism and bolshevism. Nay more, "spontaneity" was a thing of evil to the greater part of the entire spectrum of Russian thought. *Stikhiinost'*, which means both elementality and spontaneity, suggests the stormy, uncontrollable, unpredictable character of the elements. Both the thin layer of the Russian intelligentsia and the bureaucracy tended to fear and oppose it, seeking to contain or channel it into the ways of order, direction, and "consciousness." In moments of illumination the Russian intelligentsia felt that it was suspended over an abyss which at any moment might open and swallow it. Pressed down from above, sucked down from below, many nineteenth-century revolutionary intellectuals appealed to tsar and nobles and to their fellow intellectuals to transform Russia by a planned revolution from above lest they and all they valued be wiped out in an elemental storm arising in the depths. In the twentieth century Gorky often admonished Lenin not to stir "the dark people" to deeds of violence and blood. Our word *spontaneity* has no such stormy reverberations.[1]

Worshipers of the poetry of the machine and technology might look to Germany as the "West," as earlier Germany had looked to England, and as later many lands, including Russia, would look to America. But when it came to revolution, France was the land to follow. In the workshop of French history there was a model for every taste: 1789, 1793 and 1794, 1799, 1804, 1830, 1848 (with its February and its June), and 1870. The France they dreamed of and lived by was a France seen through the prism of the writings of Marx, more real to them than the France of history. Almost every figure on the Russian stage wore a costume tailored in Paris.

Tsarism was the ancien régime. Vyshnegradskii, Witte, and Stolypin were the Necker, Turgot, and Calonne. Lenin was a Jacobin, a Robespierre—both he and his opponents agreed on this. In a gentler mood he called his rivals Girondins or the swamp; when harsh, Cavaignacs.[2] Trotsky dramatized himself as the Marat of the Revolution, later as its Carnot. To the sailors of Kronstadt, whose hands were stained with the blood of their officers, he said in 1917 that they were "the flower of the Revolution," whose deeds would be copied all over Russia until every public square would be adorned by a replica of that famous French invention "which makes the enemies of the people shorter by a head." Trotsky and Stalin in their debates hurled at each other the epithet "Bonapartist." Stalin's regime was branded by Trotsky as "Thermidor." When Tsereteli in 1917 proposed to disarm the Bolsheviks lest they overthrow the Provisional Government, and Lieber supported him (Mensheviks both), from his seat the Menshevik Martov hurled the epithet *versalets* (Versaillist).[3]

As the French revolutionaries had donned imaginary togas and fancied themselves ancient Romans, so Russian revolutionaries sought to reenact the scenes and roles of revolutionary France. Much ink would be spilled, and in the end much blood, to determine Russia's place on the French revolutionary calendar (was she on the eve of her 1789 or 1793, her 1848, or her 1870?). The Soviets were pictured by Lenin as an enlarged replica of the "Paris Commune type of state."[4] After the Bolsheviks took power, the ink and blood would be poured out in combat with the ghosts of "Bonapartism" and "Thermidor," while the real problems were those arising out of an entirely new formation, totalitarianism, which had no exemplar in French revolutionary history.

Whether "following the path taken by the West" meant the political-social revolution of France or the Industrial Revolution of England, the underlying proposition that there was a single path for all lands moving from "backwardness" to "modernity" does not bear examination. According to this theory, there is but one line of progress along which all nations are marching at various points and at various speeds. The locus classicus for this widely held nineteenth-century view—at least for Marxists—is a passage in Marx's Introduction to the first edition of *Das Kapital*, where he acknowledges that he has "used England as the chief illustration in the development of my theoretical ideas" but admonishes his countrymen not to shrug off his conclusions as inapplicable to them: "*De te fabula narratur.* . . . The country that is more developed only shows to the less developed the image of its own future."

More scrupulous than the dogmatists he was to beget, more troubled by the recalcitrance and complexity of history, Marx had reservations concerning the universality of this unilinear picture. If he suggested that feudalism was pregnant with the "modern bourgeois" order, and capitalism with the "socialist" mode of production, he did not, like so many of his latter-day disciples, see "feudalism" in every land where there were latifundia and bondsmen or peons. Insofar as his schemata were unilinear, they pictured feudalism, where it existed, as destined to be ended by the despoiling of the small proprietor, so that the latter would be "thrown on the labor market." But this pattern did not obtain everywhere nor at all times in history. In his well-known listing of "progressive epochs in the economic formation of society" he included not only "the feudal and modern bourgeois modes of production" (which were steps in his inevitable march to socialism) but also the "ancient" and "Asiatic" modes.[5]

Like "Asiatic despotism" with its long ages of persistence of the same basic structure ("millennial slumber"), Russia, too, troubled the simplicities of Marx's formulas. His schema had been derived from his study of the social and economic history of England, where the enclosures and the Industrial Revolution despoiled the tillers of the soil, separated the artisans from their ownership of their own means of production, and turned them into propertyless "proletarians." Though this process "has taken place in a radical way so far only in England," Marx never doubted that "all the countries of Western Europe will go through the same development."[6]

But of Russia he was not so certain. On the one hand, Russia was "semi-Asiatic." Marx here was not talking geography but institutional structure. Russia had known prolonged and universal bondage but not feudalism. Its supercentralized "Oriental despotism" was built on a foundation of a dispersed and backward agriculture and village handicraft in isolated and powerless villages, each self-sufficient and each lacking connection with the others—in their economy, in awareness of common interests, or in the physical connection of a network of roads. Moreover, those villages possessed their peculiar institution, the *obshchina*, with its communal title to the land that it partitioned and repartitioned, its communal dictation of the methods of agriculture, its power over the freedom of movement of the villagers, and its collective responsibility to the state. Was this only a negative phenomenon, a source of despotism and stagna-

tion? Or was it also true, as the *narodniki* believed, that the "communal village" fostered unconscious socialist feelings and relationships and
might enable "the Russian people to find for their fatherland a path of
development different from that which Western Europe has followed and
is following"?[7]

To answer this question Marx studied Russian, as did Engels. They
read all they could lay hold of by way of official reports and controversial
literature. Yet, to the end of his days, Marx's voice faltered when he tried
to answer. For he and Engels were ambivalent concerning the "class
nature" of the Russian state, the meaning of the communal village in
general, and the Russian village in particular. On the one hand, as Engels
put it succinctly in his *Anti-Dühring*, it was clear to them that "where the
ancient communes have continued to exist, they have for thousands of
years formed the basis of the cruelest form of state, Oriental despotism,
from India to Russia."[8]

On the other hand, Marx was more than a little seduced by the *narod-
nik* idealization of the "socialist spirit" of the *obshchina*. Would "the
revolution," antisarist in Russia, socialist in Europe, take place before
the *obshchina* had too far disintegrated? Or would the Russian peasants
be fated "first to transform their communal property into private property,"[9] then be expropriated and turned into proletarians on the English
(and "inevitable" West European) model? If the second occurred, which
seemed likely unless "the revolution" came quickly, Russia would be
"giving up the best chance which history has ever given to any people,
and would suffer all the fated vicissitudes of the capitalist regime."[10]

The alternatives thus posed by Marx were false, since the basic feature
of the *obshchina*, which caused the government to enforce its existence
and even continue it after the Emancipation, was the obligatory collective responsibility of the village for recruits, redemption payments, and
taxes.[11] But the fact that Marx, unlike his Russian disciples who called
themselves Marxists, should have raised the possibility of these alternatives showed that he was not as dogmatic as they concerning a fated unilinear path for Russia, on the model of his schemata in *Das Kapital*. For
Marx, not only was Russia's past different, but its present—tentatively—
was open.

In his letter to the Russian journal *Otechestvennye zapiski*, written
in November 1877, Marx still left this troubling question unanswered.
Moreover, he warned his Russian readers not to take the schemata drawn
up by him for Western Europe as "a historico-philosophical theory of the
general march imposed by fate on all peoples, regardless of the historical
circumstances in which they find themselves." He instanced the case of
the ancient Roman peasants, expropriated and turned not into wage-

workers but into the "idle mob" of the Roman proletariat, to show that often "strikingly analogous events, taking place in different historic surroundings, bring about totally different results."[12]

That he could give such a warning shows the superiority of Marx to those who call themselves Marxists. But, of course, there were limits to how far he would allow that history was open, for in the next breath he made it clear that if the *obshchina* should disintegrate much further, Russia too must enter on the same and single path on which the West European lands were, inexorably in his opinion, following England.

Two years before Marx died, Vera Zasulich once more besought him to fit the Russian village into the schemata of *Das Kapital* and settle the "life and death" question of Russia's destiny. Again he hesitated, then, after a number of discarded drafts, replied with curt brevity that his book had spoken of the historical inevitability of the English road only "in the lands of Western Europe. . . . Hence the analysis present in *Kapital* does not give any conclusions either for or against" a special fate for Russia's peculiar institution.[13]

At the very moment when Marx was wrestling with these thin and indecisive drafts, a writer in *Narodnaia volia*, without benefit of Marxist orthodoxy, was working out a more realistic conception of the nature of the Russian state and its relation to agriculture and industry than Marx and Engels or Plekhanov and Lenin were to formulate. The state, said the anonymous author in a series of articles published in 1880, was not an executive committee of any ruling class or combination of ruling classes but in fact an independent organization, hierarchical, disciplined, and despotic, based upon brutal police power and the absorption of most of the population's income by heavy exactions:

"Our state owns half of Russia as its private property and more than half of the peasants are tenants on its lands." Political and economic power were inextricably interwoven in its fabric. In addition to being the greatest landowner, it was also "the greatest capitalist force in the country." It had set up much of Russian industry and had put up a tariff wall so high that the most backward industry could survive and make a profit. "Whole sets of feudal prerogatives have been created for those who own the mines. For centuries the peoples of the Urals have been handed over like slaves to the capitalists." "The building of railways in Russia provides a spectacle that is unique anywhere in the world; they are all built with the cash of the peasants and the state which, for no apparent reason, hands out hundreds of millions to the various business men." "The pennies of the peasants flow into the pockets of stockbrokers and shareholders by means of the state treasury." Russia was in its stage of primitive accumulation "in which wealth comes less from *production* than from more or less outright pillage." The state was an autonomous organization, the only autonomous organization in Russia, and it "would hold the people in economic and political slavery even if there were no privileged class in existence."[14]

Today historians have come to recognize the pluralism inherent in the variousness of the human spirit, the uniqueness of each country's history, each epoch, and social scene. But, as often happens when the specialist is having second thoughts, the doctrine of unilinear development lives on, simplified, vulgarized, all-pervasive, in journalism and popular thought. Today the Communists apply Marx's unilinear doctrine concerning Western Europe not only to Russia—even as it follows a path manifestly so different from England's—but also to Asia and Africa.

Thus in their comments on the Chinese Revolution, both Communist and non-Communist writers have spoken of traditional China's land system as "feudal," the term *feudal* having become in modern journalism not a precise term for a definite system of relationships but a mere pejorative for any noncapitalist or nonsocialist landowning system. It is more than doubtful that a Chinese feudalism ever existed at any time. In any case, one of the essential prerequisites for such a system, namely primogeniture, was abolished in China in the third century before Christ. It was the consequent lack of "strong property" which prevented the landowners and tillers of China from setting up a counterweight against centralized bureaucratic despotism. The resultant subdivision of the land and the pressure of population upon it made not the large landed estate but the "pocket handkerchief farm" the key agrarian problem of early twentieth-century China. If there are good reasons for not calling Russian bondage "feudal," there are still better ones for not using the term in connection with China.

Because of the uniqueness of each country's history, when nations borrow from one another—and in the age of world wars and world communications such borrowing has become well-nigh universal—what is borrowed suffers a change as it is transplanted.

To take a familiar example, how different is America's Congress from Britain's Parliament, whose offspring it is. How different from these two —and from each other—are the French Chambre, the German Reichstag, the Russian Duma. How remote from these are their offspring, the parliaments of the new nations of Asia and Africa. Until, at last, the very word *parliament* seems to be stretched beyond the breaking point when it is made to cover Franco's Cortes and Sukarno's handpicked council, or when a meeting of the Supreme Soviet is headlined by our press as a "session of the Soviet parliament." Of course, in this case "borrowing," to paraphrase Pascal, is the tribute which dictatorship pays to democ-

racy. But quite frequently a borrowed institution may alter, even profoundly, the course of the life stream into which it enters. Yet even more
profoundly is it transformed by the life of which it becomes a part.

Not institutions alone, but ideas and doctrines suffer a radical change
on transplantation. Most of Russia's nineteenth-century ideas were imported from the West, as in the eighteenth century Peter imported techniques and institutions. But what was taken and what ignored or rejected
from the variegated Western intellectual scene, and how these ideas were
utilized, held, and built into all-embracing systems or exclusive means
of salvation were things characteristic of the borrower rather than the
source.

Ideas tended to be borrowed without the long history that begot them,
without any of the qualifications, shadings, offsets, interplay with opposing and contrary ideas characteristic of the more pluralistic West. The
borrowed ideas were made characteristically Russian in that they quite
literally possessed those who thought to possess them. Each doctrine in
its turn tended to become mutually exclusive of its predecessor, and all-
embracing. One lived by the ism of the moment and felt moral scorn for
those who had not seen the light. "I become terrible," wrote Belinskii in
a moment of penetrating lucidity, "when I get some mystical absurdity or
other into my head." Each in turn, Fichte, Schelling, Hegel, Feuerbach,
Marx, Darwin, to mention only a few, for a moment utterly possessed
Belinskii, or some other of the succession of prophets. Even Westernism
itself, as Chaadaev showed, could become a peculiarly un-Western religious tenet. Even "scientism" became a quasi-religious creed. "When a
member of the Russian intelligentsia became a Darwinist," wrote Berdiaev, "to him Darwinism was not a biological theory subject to debate
but a dogma, and one who did not accept the dogma . . . awoke in him
an attitude of moral suspicion."

Marxism was held by Russian Marxists in ways which amazed those
of the land of its origin, not excluding Marx himself. Thus N. I. Sazonov,
landowner from the Russian steppe, who became one of the world's and
not merely Russia's first Marxists in the 1840s, said to Marx: "I, a
barbarian . . . love you more than any of your fellow-countrymen do."
Marx was astonished, even embarrassed, that his first disciples should be
Russian and use the un-Marxian language of love and veneration.

As Russia came to reject Byzantium, yet made of Byzantine orthodoxy
the orthodoxy of "the Third Rome," so Marxism was nationalized, the
Marxism of the West was rejected as heretical and revisionist, and Marxism became a Russian church. It became not merely a theory of economics and history and sociology but the basis for a total rejection of all
existing institutions (a rejection, incidentally, that formed a genuine con-

stituent of Marx's own complex and ambiguous doctrines). It was held totally and exclusively, and totally applied like all the isms that preceded it. In power, it became a totalitarian system of thought and life, embracing absolutely everything and employing total force and total control of the means of communication to prevent any other ism from succeeding it, as had been customary every half decade with the earlier isms. Lenin made of it a "profession" in both senses of the word, a profession by which and through which one lived and made one's living, and a profession of faith. It was Russian religiousness turned inside out and intended to end the long pursuit of a faith which had occupied the intellectuals for a century. As Dostoevski could proclaim that the Russians knew and loved Christ more than the Christians of any other land—indeed, were the only ones truly to know and love Him and must therefore teach the true faith to the world—so Lenin could persuade himself that all Marxists were lukewarm or apostates save only those who hearkened to him. Thus intellectual borrowing could become not so much appropriation as expropriation, even as the borrowing represented a terrible simplification and impoverishment.

Technological borrowing is simpler than the borrowing of institutions and ideas; it is more direct, more mechanical. Yet even technological borrowing has its institutional prerequisites and possesses aspects involving the subtle world of the spirit.

The industrially less developed country cannot begin to implant the structures and techniques of modern industry until, by methods engendered in its own history, it has overcome certain obstacles in its own life. Thus Germany could not become a great industrial land until it had put an end to its fragmentation into petty principalities, and Russia could not begin its industrial advance until it had abolished serfdom.

With centralization achieved in Germany's case and emancipation in Russia's, there still remained the problem of the accumulation and concentration of investment capital. This problem had been solved in England over centuries. Germany and Russia would take but decades, for often they borrowed only end results without the profound spiritual and cultural development which had engendered them. And each would meet the problem differently, by inventing and mobilizing its own characteristic institutional devices and rallying the spiritual energies for the great sacrifices and expenditures of industrialization under its own distinct ideological banner.

To overcome its particularism and fragmentation, Germany required a series of wars. These made Germany not more like the England it was "imitating" but less like it than before. Out of Bismarck's Blitzkriege came the strengthening of Prussian militarism, Prussian Junkertum, and imperial power; the predominant emphasis on heavy industry; and the close tie-up of militarism and industrialism—so characteristic of post-industrial Germany and so alien to the England of the Industrial Revolution.

Once unified, Germany had to find some fiscal device which would permit the concentration of huge sums of money for investment in industry, not over centuries but within a few decades. The device Germany adopted, as did a number of other late industrializing continental countries, was the industrial investment bank. While English banking, though growing ever bigger, still continued to be a traditional commercial banking system, Germany developed her "universal banks" to found huge industrial enterprises and cartels. This type of bank was, as Gerschenkron has put it, a "specific instrument of industrialization in a backward country." Within a few decades, however, indeed before the turn of the century, German industry became big enough to outgrow the tutelage and control of these banks. Enterprises broke the monopoly of a single bank by working with several, or grew strong enough to switch banks, while the mightiest giants, like the electrical industry, established banks of their own. Though a close relationship continued between banking and industry, industry was liberated from tutelage and control; "the master-servant relation gave way to cooperation . . . and sometimes was even reversed."[15]

In Russia, after Emancipation, the financial situation was so much worse, capital so scarce, standards of honesty and competence in business so low that no banking system could attract the huge sums needed to finance industrialization. Hence, Russia reverted to the ancient institutional device so deeply ingrained in her history: compulsory exactions by government. Taxation; tariffs; loans; government-guaranteed orders, often paid for long in advance of manufacture; abnormally high prices for domestic production and rejection of lower foreign competitive bids; concessions; subsidies; direct government ownership, construction, control, and investment—such were the devices employed. Thus did the Russia of Alexander III use the mighty machine of a "state stronger than society" (Miliukov) to undertake from above what the feeble, government-dominated society could not undertake from below.

Since the beginning of the seventeenth century, and especially since Peter I's day (1682–1725), moved by the needs of war and power, the Russian state had several times "modernized" the industries necessary for war with the technologically more advanced armies of the West. Now again in the last decade and a half of the nineteenth century—as so often in the past—"the state swelled up, while the people shrank" (Kliuchevskii). And so it would be again under Lenin, Stalin, and Khrushchev.

As the alliance between industrialism and militarism and a close fusion of banking and industrial capital distinguished the industrialization of backward Germany from its English model, so the fusion of statism with industrialism distinguished the Russian model from the German and the English.

Modern socialist theory was grievously derailed by a misunderstanding of industrialization. It was Rudolph Hilferding's attempt to generalize the investment banking system as it developed in Germany into a "universal" institution proper to "modern capitalism" in general that constituted the fundamental error in this serious Marxist thinker's Finanzkapital, an error that led Marxist theoreticians to misunderstand the whole process of modern banking and "monopoly capitalism." Lenin, for his part, his grasp of economics being largely limited to the illustration of accepted dogma by the culling of suitable examples, compounded Hilferding's error when he turned it into the formulas of his Imperialism: The Highest Stage of Capitalism. From this error, too, he derived his simplistic, utopian schemata for the economics of the seizure of power in his fantastic recipes of the year 1917. For his October coup he pictured "a single bank—mightiest of the mighty—with branches in every district, every factory" as the simple institutional means for the seizure of economic power and the administration of the new economy. It was, he declared, "already nine-tenths of the socialist apparatus . . . something in the nature of the skeleton of socialist society. This 'state apparatus' . . . we can 'take over' and 'put in motion' with a single stroke, by a single decree."

Four years later he wrote ruefully: "On the state bank, a great many things were written by us at the end of 1917 . . . which turned out to be no more than mere words on paper."[16]

In 1931 Joseph Stalin told a conference of Soviet managers:

> The backward are beaten. . . . The history of old Russia . . .
> consisted of the fact that she was always being beaten because of her backwardness. She was beaten by the Mongol khans. She was beaten by the Turkish beys. She was beaten by the Swedish feudalists. She was beaten by the Polish-Lithuanian gentry. She was beaten by the Anglo-French capitalists. . . . All of them beat her—because of her backwardness, because of her military backwardness, cultural backwardness, governmental backwardness, industrial backwardness, agricultural backwardness. They beat her because it was profitable and could be done with impunity.[17]

Stalin's test is a simple one—victory or defeat in war is the measure of the level of civilization. Yet his history is strangely one-sided, for it can as well be read in the opposite direction. Russia in time beat the Mongol khans, the Swedish feudalists, the Polish-Lithuanian gentry, the Turkish beys. For every "beating" Stalin cited—with the exception of the Crimean War ("the Anglo-French capitalists"), which ended without advantage to either side—there was a subsequent Russian comeback and ultimate triumph. It was these beatings and counterbeatings which form so much of the pattern of Russian history and have contributed so much to Russian institutions and the shaping of the Russian spirit.

When Peter I, still far from being "the Great," fled from Narva in 1700 and his armies melted away before those of Charles XII of Sweden, this "beating" became the spur to the first great modernization of Russia's army, navy, and war industries, under the ruthless hand of the greatest of all industrializers of Russia prior to the days of Witte, Stalin, and Khrushchev. By 1721 Peter's refurbished armies had broken the power of the "Swedish feudalists" and sent their king flying. And so after him, Russia would annex the Kingdom of Poland and Lithuania. And this same backward Russia, which Stalin pictured as forever being beaten, would crush Frederick the Great of Prussia and disperse his armies, then defeat the still greater Napoleon and occupy Paris.

In his own day Marx, too, regarded Russia as backward, but this did not prevent him from noting that backwardness had never precluded Russia's sudden stormy advances in military technique for the purposes of equipping mighty armies and turning defeat into victory and ultimate conquest. The once obscure Duchy of Muscovy had been expanding for the better part of the last three centuries, to north, south, east, and west, becoming in the process the world's greatest land empire. "Since Peter the Great," he wrote in the *New York Tribune* on June 14, 1853:

> The Russian frontier has advanced:
> | | |
> |---|---|
> | Towards Berlin, Dresden, and Vienna about | 700 miles |
> | Towards Constantinople | 500 miles |
> | Towards Stockholm | 630 miles |
> | Towards Teheran | 1000 miles[18] |

Marx's picture is, as he intended it to be, frightening. The expansion of Russia did not cease in his lifetime, nor after his death, nor has it ceased in our time. At the beginning of the century in which Marx lived, one European in seven was under Russian rule; at its end, one in four. By the middle of our century, when Stalin died, one European in every two— either directly or through puppet regimes—was under Stalin's control.

Far from testifying to Russia's progress, this immense expansion of the Duchy of Muscovy into the greatest empire in the world was one of the causes of Russian backwardness. "It might be said," writes Berdiaev, "that the Russian people fell victim to the immensity of its territory." Almost continuous warfare over centuries, the maintenance of huge armies, the forced development of war industries and military service strained to the utmost the poor country's human and material resources. She was forever spending beyond her strength to maintain and extend her illimitable bounds. The Eurasian plain was an armed camp, living under the harsh and autocratic laws of war. The social function of the autocrat was an important one: to "gather in" the Russian (and not only Russian) lands, to raise, equip, and lead her armies, hold the empire together, drive back the Mohammedan, Mongol and Turk, the Roman Catholic Pole and Frank, to defend Russia's wide boundaries and freedom—the only freedom autocracy and unending war permitted—freedom from the foreign invader, from foreign ways and foreign faiths.

Little wars were always being waged somewhere on the empire's metes and bounds, and in nearly every generation a great war that strained Russia to the utmost, leaving her exhausted, in a mood for stagnation and reaction against the excessive strain and the forced military-technological disturbance of her traditional life.

Every such effort imposed an intolerable burden upon the generation whose life span coincided with the crisis. To extract from that generation the manpower, wealth, and energies for so great a struggle, an already over-powerful government had further to expand its powers and its exactions, subjecting the people to yet more severe measures of oppression and coercion, curtailing the right of each crisis generation to live for its own purposes, or any purpose save service to the state and its monstrous growth.

Peter's industrialization may well serve as a paradigm of this process. What he sought in Europe, as Kliuchevskii said, was "Western technique, not Western civilization." To be able to fight the two-decade-long Northern War, he wanted Russia to become a shipwright building men-of-war; an iron miner and smelter casting cannon and forging barrels and bayonets; a weaver of woolen cloth, to uniform regiments.

If he cut off his nobles' beards with his own shears, it was not merely to humble them but to make them look like officials of the West. Like Ivan the Terrible, but on an all-embracing scale, he created state-service nobles who held their *pomest'e* at his will and as a reward for service to him, not by virtue of absolute hereditary right. The long struggle between the crown and the independent hereditary nobility, which began as the power of the prince grew in the fourteenth century and became a furious war on the boyars in the time of Ivan IV, was brought to an end when Peter reduced the free nobles to the status of state-service gentry. Therefore the old nobility continued to exist only in a residual sense, as a memory of aristocratic descent, a feeling of personal dignity and noblesse oblige, an awareness that there were still some high callings like top diplomatic and administrative posts which even a Peter hesitated to fill with parvenu "service people."

Peter completed the humiliation of the boyars so ruthlessly initiated by Ivan the Terrible. From now on, at least until 1762, the gentry, to use the apt words of Martin Malia, were bound to serve the state in the same way that the peasants were bound to serve their masters—as "serfs, although highly privileged serfs, of the autocrat." By ukase, or by direct command, Peter made nobles into industrialists, made technicians of their younger sons, made merchants into serf-owning manufacturers, and created a laboring class, not of wage earners but of serfs from the crown lands adscripted to factories, to be bought and sold along with the plant. Thus, in Ivan's as in Peter's Russia, it was the state that created the classes, rather than—as Marxism asserted—classes that created the state. The state "belonged" to no class, but all classes belonged to and owed service to the state.

Peter's barbaric cruelties to his subjects, the thousands of his tortured and slain, were in part a product of the caprice and anger that only those whose power knows no limit can indulge. But as often as not he was punishing men for resistance to his innovations, offering them up as a sacrifice to the Moloch civilization of war and despotism. His secret police spied out their unfavorable opinions of his deeds and innovations and their "treason" in seeking to evade state service. His exactions rose annually from some million and a half rubles at his accession to eight and a half million at the end of his reign. He and his advisers showed positive genius for inventing new taxes on everything, from rents paid on "corners" of rooms to private bathhouses in peasant huts, from marriage outside the church to the wearing of mustaches and beards.

But the heart of the reaction, which was the reverse side of Petrine "progress," was the systematizing and universalizing of bondage. The mines and smelters he founded in the Urals, like the city he laid out on the marshes to be a "window on Europe," were constructed and manned by assigning bondsmen—and not only bondsmen—to these tasks. He ordered nobles to open and run factories, ordered wealthy merchants to reside and trade in his new city.

It would take two centuries for the town thus founded to become a potential locus of countervailing power comparable to the fortified and charter-possessing towns of the West. Instead of Russian cities being a refuge for those who fled in search of freedom, it was long the case that strict government measures were necessary to prevent flight *from* the Russian cities.

When the nobility did not suffice to create a manufacturing class, Peter gave merchants the privilege of purchasing and owning serfs, with the proviso that when a factory was sold, the serfs were to go with it. As there was no *soslovie* of manufacturers, the decree of January 18, 1721, authorized merchants to share the hitherto exclusively noble privilege of purchasing and owning serfs. Here the state created not a new "estate" but, out of some merchants and nobles, a new "class."

Peter's endless wars, his servile-labor factories, his systematic endowment of officers and bureaucrats with land and serfs as compensation for their service to him, his great constructions, and the very energy and sweep of the reforms thus enforced—all combined to universalize and systematize bondage. In the century when feudal serfdom was being uprooted in the West, Russia, though it had no feudalism, developed a harsh and universal serfdom, destined to retard development and inject its evils into the social life of the next century and a half.

Russia's bondage had neither the contractual mutuality, nor the comparative autonomy, nor the natural foundations, of Western feudalism. In the kingdoms of the West, nature and society imposed limits on the flight of the serf by the absence of unoccupied land. In the ever-enlarging lands of the Russian giant there were forest, steppe, river bottom, and shore, deserted or laid waste by war or newly conquered, to which the peasant reduced to serf might flee, unless he were riveted to his place. The purpose of bondage was literally to establish fixity (*krepost'*) so that tax collector and recruiting sergeant would know where to find every soldier who dropped out, whether by reason of desertion, illness, injury, or death, so that the Russian soldier, as Florinsky has written, was "immortal."

The Petrine reforms were genuine, as his "Westernization" was genuine, but autocracy was their driving force, war and the power of the state their objective, subjection of society and the binding of everyone from serf to serving noble their method. "Peter did not hesitate," wrote Lenin admiringly, "to use barbarous methods in fighting barbarism."

What Lenin did not note was that technological progress and social reaction, the "civilization" of ironworks and the "barbarization" of bondage, were two sides of the same coin. And so it would be again under Lenin and his successors. The decreeing of technological advance from on high for the purposes of war and power and the social retrogression implicit in absolute power, absolute servility, and universal bondage were two sides of one and the same process, by virtue of which autocracy grew and Russia itself expanded. Paradoxically, as Russia became more "Western" in her war industries, she became more "Russian" in her despotism, her universal statism, her rural bondage, her servile factory labor, her subordination of society and all its members, high and low, to the omnipotent state.

The appearance of stagnation in nineteenth-century Russia, what was it but the persistence of serfdom until 1861, of absolutism until 1905, and of collective village responsibility until the Stolypin reforms loosened the bonds that tied the peasant to the *obshchina*? In the nineteenth century the earlier autocratic industrialization in the fashion of Peter, with its all-pervading serfdom, was to prove the chief obstacle to the development of a "modern" industry and state.

A word should be said here about Professor Gerschenkron's illuminating analysis of the *ideological banners* under which industrialization has been undertaken, justified, and exalted in various types of backward countries. To Saint-Simon and his disciples in France he traces the glorification of the investment banker as a "missionary" ushering in a golden age of flourishing industry and "happiness for all." In Germany, which lacked France's political revolution and national unification, ardent nationalism was the ideological banner. But "in conditions of Russian 'absolute' backwardness, a much more powerful ideology was required to grease the intellectual and emotional wheels of industrialization."

Though the main impetus for industrialization came from the Russian government, which needed no banner other than that of military might and governmental power, there was a notable change in the attitude of the intelligentsia toward industry in the course of the 1880s and 1890s. Earlier they had opposed industry and its values, seeking their justification in the will of the peasant, agriculture, and the commune. The switch from regarding nonagricultural activity as unnatural and unworthy to exaltation of industry came under the banner of "orthodox Marxism."

It is this that explains the sudden rise of "legal Marxism," the government's toleration of it, and the fact that for a moment Marxism took possession of such liberals as Peter Struve and such profoundly religious spirits as Bulgakov, Berdiaev, and Frank. It seeped into the university departments of history, economics and law, affecting to some degree even men like Miliukov.

So, too, Professor Gerschenkron suggests some insights into present-day Soviet ideological banners. In Russia's long-delayed industrialization and long-perpetuated serfdom he sees two of the causes "responsible for a political revolution in the course of which power fell into the hands of a dictatorial government to which in the long run the vast majority of the population was opposed." Since power cannot be retained exclusively by force regardless of the sweep of terror, the Soviet government has sought to make "people believe that it performs an important social function which could not be discharged" without it or by using other than its methods. By these methods, "by reverting to a pattern of economic development that should have remained confined to a long-bygone age, by substituting collectivization for serfdom, and by pushing up the rate of investment to the maximum point within the limits of endurance of the population"—by doing these things "the Soviet government did what no government relying on the consent of the governed could have done." As a result, muted opposition and "day-to-day friction" are inevitable. The banner under which the government seeks to make its harsh course less unacceptable bears two simultaneous devices: *nationalism* and *socialism*. To rally nationalism behind it the government has need of a military menace from abroad, so that it may pose as the indispensable form in which the country-in-danger can be defended, the sole guarantee that Russia will not be "beaten." The socialist device on its banner is "the promise of happiness and abundance for future generations." This is the meaning of the endless scholastic exercises in analysis of the road from socialism to complete communism. Thus, writes Gerschenkron, "economic backwardness, rapid industrialization, ruthless exercise of dictatorial power, and the danger of war have become inextricably intertwined in Soviet Russia."[19]

The reforms forced upon the people by Peter, like the bondage imposed on them, had met with sullen resistance. Thus a split began between people and state, between the masses and the bureaucrats, between the state church and the Old Believers, and later between the masses and the intelligentsia—a split which would prove fatal in Russia's "Time of Troubles" in the twentieth century. After such a "reform" the people were not better but worse prepared for initiation of reforms themselves.

Moreover, until the twentieth century all important reforms came from on high, from the tsar and his advisers. Peter's military industrialization, Catherine's Rescript (which remained largely on paper), Speranskii's administrative reform proposals (some of which Alexander I and Nicholas I introduced, others remaining on their desks, while the most important of them—a constitution and a reign of law binding on rulers as well as ruled—have not been realized to this day), Alexander II's emancipation of the serfs in 1861, and, finally, the great industrialization at the end of the nineteenth century under Alexander III and his son, Nicholas II, the last of the tsars—all these assaults on backwardness, indeed, the very consciousness of backwardness, came largely from the throne and its chosen advisers.

The greatest of these reforms was the emancipation of the serfs by Alexander II (1855–81) in the year 1861, two years before Lincoln emancipated America's slaves. Once more, as with Peter, it was the ineffectiveness of Russia's serf armies in war which brought home a sense that Russia must be "modernized" from above.

Unlike Peter's reforms, which have been overpraised, Alexander's have been overcriticized. Since the landowners still constituted the chief support of the throne, he had perforce to make some concessions to them, but he forced the liberation upon them by reminding them of two centuries of peasant mutinies. "It is better," he said, "to abolish serfdom from above than to wait until it begins to abolish itself from below." The chief defect of this complex of measures was not that the serfs got less land than they had expected and had to pay for it and for their own redemption in a long series of annual installments. Nor was it the fact that the nobles had to give up privileges they were reluctant to part with, receiving payments that were not large enough to enable them to enter industry or trade. The root defect was the ancient evil characteristic of Russia from before Peter's day: the tying of the peasant into his village community by constant communal repartition of the land, by village dictation of agricultural methods, and by collective responsibility for taxes and recruits. The peasant's tax ruble and the peasant soldier continued, as before, to be "immortal." At long last, in the brief period from 1907 to 1917, this burden of collective responsibility and bondage to the *obshchina* was removed, only to be restored in altered, more sweeping, and more exacting form in the Stalinist kolkhoz.

Whatever its defects, we need only remember that Alexander's emancipation endowed the peasants with most of the land they had been tilling as serfs, and compensated the landowners, while our emancipation left the slaveowners ruined and the freed men without farms. In the light of the history of agrarian reform in Western Europe and in our own South, there is much justice in Professor Karpovich's verdict that the emancipation of 1861 was "the greatest single legislative act in the world's history."

Moreover, it made necessary four other great reforms from above: rural self-government by zemstvos (county councils), 1864; a reform of the law courts, 1864; municipal self-government (the municipal dumas), 1870; and a reform of the army, 1874. At the moment he was assassinated in 1881 by revolutionaries who found his reforms inadequate, Alexander II was working on the outline of a shadowy semiconstitution.

The cutting of the bonds of forty million peasants led to a general loosening of the bonds that constricted Russian society. The subject was in a fair way to becoming a citizen. The army ceased to exempt the nobility from conscription and made the obligation to serve equal for all, at the same time shortening the term of service from twenty-five years to six (later reduced to four years), with strikingly shorter terms for students and with exemption for each family's breadwinner. The reform of the courts did away with class privilege before the law, made the courts independent of the bureaucracy, provided for qualified, irremovable judges, not subject to political dictate, and set up trial by jury and an autonomous bar. Though in time of stress the police sought to bypass them by administrative exile and court-martial, the Russian courts remained a shield against injustice, inferior to no other in the modern world—until the Bolsheviks returned to removable judges, subservient bar, political dictation of judicial decisions, and summary judgment by bureaucracy, party, and dictator.

It was the zemstvos that proved to be the greatest step forward in the awakening of an articulate "public" in rural, and not only in rural, Russia. However limited their budgets and their powers, they introduced into Russian life the principle of self-government and of nongovernmental, nonbureaucratic public initiative. They constituted the beginning of a multicentered society, a school of administration, a means of initiating, and gaining social assent to, social action. The zemstvos and the city dumas provided the foundations for a new representative system, foundations which seemed to the Russian intelligentsia to cry out for a national parliament and responsible cabinet "to crown the edifice."

Though the bureaucracy was jealous and suspicious (by 1914 only forty-three of Russia's seventy provinces had been permitted to set up rural self-governing institutions), yet by that date the zemstvos, led by the enlightened gentry, had in their employ some five thousand agronomists, had made significant strides on the road to universal education, had trained most of the men who were to be the leading liberal spokesmen of the Duma, and had built up a veritable army of new plebeian intellectuals: doctors, nurses, teachers, agronomists, veterinarians, engineers, statisticians, economists. It was these whom the peasants returned in overwhelming numbers to the Duma as their representatives. In World War I Nicholas's best generals and ministers, and Nicholas himself, turned to the zemstvos and the city dumas for help in mobilizing the country's agricultural resources, industry, and transport for war and for aid in caring for the refugees and the wounded. When, in 1917, the Russian people for the first and only time in their history were given the opportunity to choose their representatives freely by universal suffrage, it was the Socialist Revolutionary party, led by this rural plebeian intelligentsia and expressing above all the aspirations of the peasants, who received the overwhelming majority of votes throughout the nation.

Thus to the consciousness of Russia's backwardness on the part of Peter, Catherine, or Alexander was at last added a consciousness of backwardness arising from below—in that new social formation of the nineteenth century, the intelligentsia, and what they themselves called "society," that is, literate public opinion. Conditioned by all the past, even in the early twentieth century they still turned to the sovereign for reforms. But to give their opinions and petitions force, they strove to inject their ideas, necessarily coarsened and simplified, into the masses of peasants and, later, into the masses of peasants and workingmen. Thus were born the revolutionary parties.

The peasants had been there from time immemorial, as peasants, then as serfs, then as freedmen. But before there could be workingmen, the peasants had to be free to go to the cities, and the cities themselves had to become centers of industry. The last "reform" to come from the sovereign and his ministers without pressure from below was the great wave of industrialization in the last decade and a half of the nineteenth century and the first decade of the twentieth.

Emancipation had been a necessary condition, but by no means a sufficient one, to start this stormy upsurge. The merchants, small manufacturers, and nobles were too poor in capital and in spirit to undertake vast enterprises. An unstable ruble, a low state of credit, private and public, a corrupt officialdom, the lack of an adequate internal market were barriers to an influx of any significant foreign enterprise or capital. From the Emancipation to the middle of the 1880s the rate of industrial growth continued to be low. For the first few years after the Emancipation industrial production even dropped because the serfs bound to factories were free to abandon them, and many works simply shut down.

But from the middle of the 1880s the state itself once more assumed the task of building up the industry it needed most. To be able to cope with the technologically changing and rapidly moving armies of the West, to be able to bring its vast reserves of manpower to bear on any point of its far-flung boundaries, to connect distant parts of the empire for rapid transport of reports, officials, supplies, troops—the government undertook the construction of a railroad system of unprecedented proportions.

Railroads required iron and steel, rails and locomotives, coal and wood and ties, stations, telegraph lines, engineers and trainmen, miners and machinists and steelworkers, and enormous quantities of capital. To borrow capital abroad, the government had to strengthen its credit, firm up its ruble, and purify in some measure the economic and bureaucratic life of the country. Railroad building became the lever of an industrial upsurge so great, and an inner market so much wider than before, that in the end industry and finance developed a momentum of their own—a *self*-propulsion quite new in Russia's long history. When the state under Nicholas II lost much of its interest in the great enterprise, industry and finance continued their growth, from 1907 to 1914, without massive government aid. Thus there was every prospect—had it not been for world war and revolution—that the "modernization" of Russia might have continued on its own, not from on high, as under earlier tsars and later commissars, but from below; not for the purposes of war and the power of the state, but for the purposes of the market, the profit of the entrepreneur, and the satisfaction of the consumer.

If industrialization in and of itself is to be regarded as a "progressive" achievement, as Marxists tend to regard it,[20] then credit for Russia's industrial upswing at the turn of the century must go to Alexander III (1881–94) and to his successive finance ministers, to whom he gave unstinting support. N. Kh. Bunge, a former university professor, was Minister of Finance from 1881 to 1886. I. A. Vyshnegradskii, also a university professor and a successful businessman, held the post from 1887 to 1892. Then followed S. Iu. Witte, a professional railroad man who worked himself up in sixteen years of railroading from the post of stationmaster to director of the Southwestern railways, to Minister of Transport, and then served as Minister of Finance under both Alexander and Nicholas II, from 1892 until his opposition to Russian imperial adventures in the Far East caused him to lose favor with Nicholas in 1903.

Bunge introduced the first serious labor legislation as a paternal activity of the autocratic state. He abolished the hated poll tax, appointed tax inspectors to see what burdens the people could bear, encouraged the export of grain "even though Russia starve," increased substantially the burden of indirect taxation upon the masses, curbed the ruble-printing presses, and began the slow accumulation of financial reserves which would encourage foreign investment, increase the investment resources of the Russian state, and enable Witte, at long last in 1897, to tie the ruble to the gold standard.

The 1890s were the beginning of the golden age of Russian industrialization. Vyshnegradskii introduced a high tariff to encourage domestic industry; under him Russia's tariff became, and after him remained, the highest in the world. He continued the struggle for a balanced budget, a stable currency, an inflow of foreign capital for both investment and government loans, and a great increase in indirect taxation, which by 1892 provided for 72 percent of Russia's rapidly mounting public expenditures.

The chief stimulus to economic growth in the 1890s was the intense activity of the government in railroad building. Under Bunge and Vyshnegradskii a number of shorter lines were built by the state, while others were purchased by it and operated under state management. By 1894 the government had taken over twenty-four lines with an aggregate length of

8,000 miles. But the grand enterprise of the period was the Trans-Siberian Railroad, begun under Vyshnegradskii in 1891 and pushed steadily to completion throughout Witte's term. It had just come into operation as a single-track line when the Russo-Japanese War broke out in 1904.

The climax of Russian railroad building came in the five years from 1896 to 1900, when over 10,000 miles of road were built. No five-year period before or since, not even under the Bolsheviks, has equaled it. Here is a general picture of the rate of railroad construction:

1886–90	1,898 miles
1891–95	4,403 miles
1896–1900	10,035 miles

By the end of the 1890s the total investment in railroads was estimated at 4.7 billion gold rubles, a huge sum by any standard. The government's direct share was 3.5 billion; private interests and foreign companies provided the rest. The state was the owner, the great builder and railroader. It willingly paid domestic iron- and steelmakers from 110 to 125 kopeks per pood (36 pounds) of rails, while private buyers were paying only 85 to 87 kopeks. When the construction of the great Trans-Siberian began, the British offered rails at 75 kopeks a pood delivered, but the government decided to stimulate domestic production by giving long-term orders and huge cash advances at the rate of 2 rubles a pood. When the Bolsheviks decided to develop autarky by big subsidies to, and big losses in, heavy industry at the expense of the population, they were not introducing an altogether new principle into Russian life.

But autarky in the modern totalitarian fashion was not the aim of Alexander III and his finance ministers. They aimed at the development of domestic metallurgy, wisely welcoming foreign capital to share the heavy burdens of industrialization. Encouraged by the stabilization of the ruble and the enlargement of the domestic market, the inflow of foreign capital increased more than sixfold in the course of the 1890s, mainly in the last five years of the period. Nearly half the new foreign money went into mining in the new Don metallurgy and mining area, but something like 16 percent went into machine building. By 1917 the total foreign investment in Russian banking, commerce, and industry was 2.24 billion rubles. Mining came first, metallurgy second, banking third, and textiles fourth.

The respective national shares of this investment have been computed as: France 33 percent, England 23 percent, Germany 20 percent, Belgium 14 percent, the United States 5 percent, and the rest shared by Holland, Switzerland, Denmark, Austria, Italy, and Norway. But ownership by the Russian state and Russian investors exceeded all of these added together, while the state or crown was also the largest landowner in Russia.

In their development of the "Leninist" notion that foreign investment enslaves the recipient and renders the latter "semicolonial," Bolshevik writers have been hard put to specify which of these investing countries did the enslaving or on whose behest this huge imperialistic "semicolony" got into the "imperialist war."

The notion, at least as applied to Russia, is "Leninist" rather than Lenin's, for he regarded Russia as an imperialist power, not a semicolony, and was convinced of Russia's responsibility for the outbreak of the war, which she entered for her own "imperialist aims."

M. N. Pavlovich set Russia down as a semicolony of France, which dragged her as a vassal into the war for France's imperialist aims.[21] Pokrovskii denounced Russia as chiefly responsible for the war, and even the assassination at Sarajevo, and pictured the French government as headed by politicians who had been bought by Russian landowners. Later he changed his picture and had Russia playing a dependent role, "a reflection of the interests of stronger imperialist powers."[22] Stalin began in 1924 by describing Russia as "an immense reserve of Western imperialism" (in *Ob osnovakh leninizma*) and ended by picturing her (in *Kratkii kurs*) as being weighed down with the golden chains of entente capital and government loans from Britain and France. These "chained tsarism to British and French imperialism and converted Russia into a tributary, a semicolony of these countries." This decline of "tsarism's independent role in European foreign policy" he dated from Russia's having been "beaten" by the "Anglo-French capitalists" in the Crimean War![23]

Latterly, Soviet writers have come to acknowledge the absurdity of the whole notion of complete dependence—for Russia! This has solved for them the problem of picturing tsarist Russia simultaneously as an imperialist and an enslaved power. *Voprosy istorii* in 1956 published an article entitled "Byla li tsarskaia Rossiia polukoloniei?" which answered the question in the negative:

> Capital from various imperialist groups was ensconced . . . in all kinds of industries . . . primarily [sic!] to obtain maximum profits and not always [sic!] with the direct aim of accomplishing general political state purposes. Exaggerating the political role of foreign capital in Russia, some research workers turned "the complex intertwining of finance-capital relationships" and purely commercial deals "into a dramatic episode of a conscious patriotic struggle of various groupings of foreign capital, allegedly acting as agents of the respective foreign governments."[24]

Concerning tsarist Russia's industrialization, also, Soviet writers have attempted to prove two inherently contradictory things. On the one hand, they have pictured tsarist Russia as backward, stagnant, virtually devoid of industry, and incapable of industrialization. On the other, they have sought to show that Russia had a great enough industry, a large enough working class, and an industrial tradition sufficient in 1917 to make the country "ripe" for a "socialist" revolution. Without our trying to decide what "ripe" for socialism means, we can recognize that neither side of this dilemma will stand up under examination.

From 1885 to 1916 Russia was industrially backward. Yet her industry, in terms of percentage of increase per annum, grew faster than that of any other great power.[25] Only in the stormy period from 1900 to 1906 (a world depression, the Russo-Japanese War, the Revolution of 1905) did the rate of increase falter. If we take the growth by five-year periods, as became fashionable with the five-year plans, Russia's annual percentage of industrial increase was higher than Germany's in every period but that of 1901–6, higher than that of France, of England, and—except for the two periods 1885–89 and 1901–6—higher than that of the United States. For the whole three decades from 1885 to 1914 Russia's average increase in industry was 5.72 percent per annum, America's 5.26, Germany's 4.49, the United Kingdom's 2.11.[26] From the Emancipation to 1900 Russian industrial productivity increased more than seven times, German almost five times, French two and one-half times, English a little over twice.

Thus did Russia begin her giant strides toward "catching up with and surpassing" (*dognat' i peregnat'*—the phrase is Lenin's) the industrial countries of Western Europe. The secret behind the big percentage increases is twofold. On the one hand, it is a matter of simple arithmetic: the lower the base from which you start, the smaller the quantitative increment required to double, treble, or quadruple it. On the other, there is a real advantage in backwardness, once industrialization has begun, for the more backward an industrializing country, the greater is the backlog of technological innovations that it can take over from the more advanced countries. The larger the imports of foreign machinery, foreign know-how, foreign capital, the faster industrialization can proceed. The industrializing country sets up only the latest type of plant; it is not burdened by a wide range of obsolescent and semiobsolescent factories as is the older country from which the latest models only are borrowed. That is why "German blast furnaces so very soon [became] superior to the English ones, while in the early years of this century blast furnaces in still more backward southern Russia were in the process of outstripping in equipment their German counterparts."[27] Indeed, we can lay it down

as a general law that if a country is of the critical size and can summon up
the institutional and economic resources to begin general industrialization, the later this begins in history and the more backward the country
is, the faster its industrialization will proceed.

There was something in the lateness of her development, as there was
something in Russia's statism and in her physical size and natural extrem-
ism of spirit, which combined to reinforce the tendency toward bigness
of plant which both Germany and Russia manifested, and the tendency
of Russia's bureaucratic industrializers to concentrate on heavy industry
to the detriment of the lighter consumer goods industries. The very shortage of skilled labor is an incentive to introduce the most modern, large-
scale, labor-saving machinery.

In Germany the banks had been attracted to coal mining, iron- and
steelmaking, electrical and general engineering, and industrial chemistry,
to the neglect of textiles, food producing, shoes, and leather goods. In
Russia, too, the government of the 1890s showed no interest in light
industry. Railroads, iron, steel, oil, coal—these were the industries which
were government constructed and operated, or which received the subsidies, the long-term orders, the generous credits, the guaranties.

From 1890 to 1899, during the greatest period of Witte's railroad
construction, Russian industry as a whole increased annually at the formidable rate of 8.03 percent. (Compare this with the rate of 5.44 percent
in Germany and 5.47 in the United States during the same decade!) Most
of this increased national produce was in heavy industry.

This upsurge was cut short by the world depression in 1900. (In Russia
the depression was cushioned, and a slow rate of increase kept up, by
railroad building.) Then came war with Japan, the massive unrest of
1905, the peasant jacqueries of 1906. But in 1907 there began a transformation in the economic rhythm and structure of Russia, and the pattern of thought and life of Russia's intelligentsia, which seemed destined
to change the course of her history.

The state continued its railroad building, on a more modest scale:
about 4,700 miles in the nine years from 1905 to 1913, as compared
with the 10,000 miles in the last five years of the 1890s. But this cutback
did not cause industry to falter.

On the contrary, in place of stagnation there was a new upsurge,
primarily on the basis of autonomous, that is, nongovernmental, financing, for a nongovernmental or free market. This time the expansion
included textiles. For the first time in Russia's history the sphere of
operations of the managerial state began visibly to contract, and the
sphere of operations of nongovernmental society to expand. To reverse
Kliuchevskii: the state shrank, the people grew healthier. "Industry,"

Gerschenkron writes, "had reached a stage where it could throw away the crutches of government support and begin to walk independently."

To be sure, it still needed the protecting wall of a high tariff. But this cannot be compared to the outright refusal of the government of the 1890s to purchase English rails at less than half the price of Russian rails, and still less to the absolute exclusion of cheaper and better competitive products by the autarkic Soviet economy. A protective tariff is a common feature of all newly industrializing lands, though Russia, in this as in so many things, exceeded the common magnitude.

What was most strikingly new was large-scale financing by private banks. Just as Germany was beginning to outgrow the early stage of industrialization by investment banks and shake its industry free from control by bankers, Russia began to enter the stage in her development which Germany was leaving. Until then, since the government had performed the functions of investment banking, there had been room in Russia only for deposit banks, resembling the English commercial bank system.

But as the government withdrew, as businessmen became more trustworthy and enterprising and as independent sums of capital accumulated, the Moscow deposit banks began to be overshadowed by the development of St. Petersburg banks conducted on principles already familiar in German rather than in British banking. To follow Professor Gerschenkron's phrasing, financing of industry by investment banking instead of the government represented "a new and higher stage in Russia's backwardness."

What of the workingmen and peasants during this quarter century of stormy growth of industry? During the first fifteen years, from 1885 to 1900, it was from them that much of the "primitive accumulation" came, to enable the government to finance industry. The high protective tariff, the rising prices, the great leap in indirect taxes, the higher tax on village lands than on those of the large landowners, the export of grain, the heavy taxes on such articles of common use as matches, alcohol, and tobacco, later the rising sale of spirits by the government alcohol monopoly, all served to shift much of the cost of the great enterprise to the peasantry and the rapidly developing working class.[28] The wages of workers in textile and other light industries did not rise at all during that period. Wages in metal factories, though still very low, were about double those in textiles, and rose another 10 to 15 percent during the 1890s. Since prices also rose, the standard of living of the metalworkers increased slightly, while those of the textile workers deteriorated.

But here, too, the years between 1907 and 1914 showed a change for the better and demonstrated that, under conditions of relative freedom from state financing and state controls, industrialization—once it had gotten over the first hurdles—could produce a more favorable market for the peasant's product and begin to raise the workingman's wages and living standards.

The worker now acquired some, albeit much harassed, freedom to organize nongovernment unions, there was much more freedom for the press and for political parties, as well as complete freedom to form cooperatives and insurance and benefit societies. Factory legislation was better enforced. Studies of real income for the period are confusing, since wages now rose rapidly (in textiles, too, which tended to catch up with the wages of metalworkers), while agricultural prices rose 41 percent between 1900 and 1913 and general prices some 28.7 percent. Such studies of real income as have been made indicate that there was a genuine rise in the standard of living of the working class as a whole, and a greater rise in the case of the poorly paid, between 1907 and 1913.

Improvement in the village was even more marked. After the catastrophic decline of the 1890s there was a rapid recovery, until the village was better off than it had been at any time since the Emancipation. Redemption payments and poll tax had been canceled. Collective responsibility for taxes was abolished in 1903. The umbilical cord which bound the peasant to the village was cut by the Stolypin reform of 1906–7 (confirmed by Duma legislation in 1910). The village starosta's power over passports and free movement to the towns was taken away. The towns, free to invest in what the market required, began to turn to the manufacture of things the peasant needed. The growing and more prosperous urban population created a better market for what the peasant produced. The terms of village trade with the expanding industrial centers improved by some 25 percent between 1900 and 1913. The cities drained off some of the rural overpopulation, while continuing to send devoted technicians and teachers to assist the countryside. By January 1915 (although it was less than a decade since the Stolypin reform and he himself was assassinated in 1911) about 33 percent of all peasant households had withdrawn from the hitherto obligatory commune, to become independent farmers.

The freedoms granted by the Tsar's Manifesto of October 1905, although they were applied unevenly and grudgingly, presented no limitations to the burgeoning of peasant cooperatives. By 1914 nearly half of the peasant households of Russia had joined the cooperative movement. Their total capital rose from 37.5 million gold rubles in 1905 to 682.33 million in 1916. Government banks, in disregard of sound financial principles, lent up to 90 percent of the value of their land to the peasants who left the communes. The governmental Peasant Land Bank bought millions of acres of land from the gentry and resold them to the peasants. By

1914 over 75 percent of all the arable land of European Russia was held by the peasants. No wonder Lenin thought that if the agrarian reform should continue to operate for another decade, the possibility of a revolution such as he envisaged would vanish and he would never live to see it.[29] Indeed, it would take a world war, and a widening whirlpool of folly at court, to reverse the trend toward a more open and independent society that was at long last beginning to develop in Russia.

2

The Reign of Alexandra and Rasputin

All tyrants, isolated in dangerous eminence—especially if they are fundamentally weak men—require confidants whom
(perhaps wrongly) they suppose to be
outside the vortex of political power
around them; court fools, astrologers,
priests, mistresses . . .
H. R. Trevor-Roper

Hemophilia, the dread "bleeders' disease," which in the first years of our century was fatal in 85 percent of the cases, was also known as the disease of kings. It was hereditary in the House of Hesse—one of Alexandra's uncles, one of her brothers, and two of her nephews had died of it. Since hemophilia is sex-linked and congenital, women of a hemophilic family do not develop the disease but may be bearers of the recessive X-chromosome, which is transmitted from the generation of father and uncle to grandson through a daughter of the house. From her childhood Alexandra had brooded over this dread ailment that was congenital in her family, against which medical science was powerless.

With all her intense and brooding nature, Alexandra had longed for a male heir. Now she tried in vain to deceive herself as to her son Alexei's condition, but there was no mistaking it. The victim of hemophilia may start bleeding without the rupture of his skin: a fall, a bruise, a tiny cut might start the bleeding. Even the sudden movement of an arm or leg might result in internal bleeding in a joint. They would never be able to permit a dentist to pull a tooth; an operation of any sort would be fatal; from July 30 to September 10 the doctors had not been able to stop the bleeding which began in the infant with the severing of the navel cord. The Heir to the Throne could never lead a normal life: run, play freely, climb, fall, ride a horse, wield a sword. Death would attend his every step, the chances being eighty-five to fifteen that he would not reach manhood.

Alexandra consulted doctors, surgeons, specialists in blood and vascular diseases, but remembering the deaths of so many close members of her family, she knew their answers before they spoke. Doctors were always kept near (one of them, Doctor Botkin, followed them into their last imprisonment); two sailors were appointed as bodyguards to watch the boy's every step and to carry him when, as was true for long periods, he could not walk.

The illness of the tsarevich cast its shadow over the last thirteen years of Nicholas's reign. It made the empress fanatical about delivering the autocratic power, undiminished, to the royal heir toward whom she felt such love and such unconscious guilt. Whenever some minister was about to succeed in persuading Nicholas to make some sensible concession to public opinion, always her hysterical voice or unceasing pen would reach him with the admonitory words, "Remember Baby! You have not the right . . ." Because of Baby's hopeless illness she surrounded herself with quacks and charlatans and hearkened to their advice on affairs of state. The fatal isolation in which the sovereigns lived deepened steadily. More and more they lived in a world apart, a world created by her fantasy and fanaticism, her ministerings to the needs of the boy and their hangers-on. They were wholly absorbed in the tragic anxiety for the heir. In the end even the alienation of the sovereigns from the grand dukes became complete while they lived their private tragedy alone, and, as a more and more motley crew of charlatans and adventurers surrounded them, worse than alone.

Whatever gaiety may have won for Alix in her girlhood the name of *Sunny* now departed completely. Anxiety and dread were in her face. A sense of guilt took its toll in neurotic illnesses. (From this moment Anna Vyrubova dates the empress's constant heart attacks.) At the slightest sound from the heir's room she would run terror-stricken from any company, returning to resume her courtly mask and force herself to deal civilly with people for whom, even earlier, she had conceived distrust and dislike.

For days on end minute foci of internal bleeding would cause little Alexei's temperature to rise as high as 105 degrees. At times his legs were distorted from bleeding in the joints and he had to be carried in the arms of his sailor attendants wherever he went. When the illness was severe, on rare occasions, Count Fredericks, the Minister of the Court (Master of Ceremonial, Protocol, and the like), was permitted to issue vague bulletins about the health of the royal heir, but the sovereigns felt that they dared not tell the populace the real nature of the ailment of the boy who was supposed one day to rule Russia.

Since the doctors were honest enough to tell the empress that their science was of little avail, she turned in her fashion to God. He alone could help her. He alone could work a miracle, and His anointed rulers over Holy Russia had need of a miracle. She must make herself worthy of that great favor, build chapels, perform good works, spend endless hours in tearful and comforting prayer, seek out His saints and holy men who might work miracles. Her naturally intense religious piety tinged with superstition began to assume morbid forms. So great was her longing to believe that her credulity grew with the longing. She could not bear to consort with the frivolous and the worldly. Her favorite topics of conversation were the miracles reputed to have been performed by this or that wonder worker, the ever-present possibility of miracles in our century as in times past, the omnipresence and mercifulness of God, the power of prayer.

The boy's tutor, the Frenchman Giliard, the best source of information about the tsarevich and the princesses, his sisters, writes:

> Between each of the attacks, however, the boy came back to life, recovered his health, forgot his sufferings. . . . At these times it was impossible to credit that he was the victim of an implacable disease that might carry him off at any moment. Every time the Tsaritsa saw him with red cheeks, or heard his merry laugh, or watched his frolics, her heart would fill with an immense hope, and she would say, "God has heard me. He has pitied my sorrow at last." Then the disease would suddenly swoop down on the boy, stretch him once more on his bed of pain and take him to the gates of death.[1]

It was her desperate need of a continuous miracle which brought Rasputin into her life, and into the life of Russia. He came as a *strannik* (wanderer, pilgrim) and a *starets* (venerable holy man), one of those self-appointed holy pilgrims and religious teachers whom no one had ordained but whom the Russian peasants reverenced, fed, believed in. And not only Russian peasants, for members of high society were often as devout or as credulous and there were many churchmen who did not frown upon them nor deny their vocation. At every stage Rasputin would find such churchmen to encourage him, instruct him, proclaim his holiness, further his fortunes, until his fortunes waxed so great that he was in a position to further theirs. A *starets*, writes Dostoevski in *The Brothers Karamazov*,

> was one who took your soul, your will, into his soul and will. When you choose a *starets*, you renounce your own will and yield it to him in complete submission, complete self-abnegation . . . in the hope of self-conquest, of self-mastery, in order, after a life of obedience, to attain perfect freedom, that is, from self; to escape the lot of those

who have lived their whole life without finding their true selves in themselves. This institution of *startsy* is not founded on theory, but was established in the East from the practice of a thousand years. The obligations due to a *starets* are not ordinary "obedience" which has always existed in our Russian monasteries. The obligation involves confession to the elder by all who have submitted themselves to him, and to the indissoluble bond between him and them.[2]

The boundary between wanderer and elder was not a clear-cut one. As often as not the *starets* was the *strannik* grown old and, ceasing to wander, settling down in some monastery where men came from afar to consult him and learn from him the wisdom he dispensed. Rasputin had several times settled in monasteries, but strong, restless, and driven by who knows what demon, he always took to the road again. Before he enters into our story, he had been twice to Jerusalem, once to the monastery on Athos, had wandered all over Siberia and much of Russia, had picked up shreds of lore and doctrine and liturgical language, and much knowledge of men and women and his power over those who believed in his holiness. He seemed to know that his healing powers would be useful at court, for police reports were to show that he had contact with "Doctor" Badmaev, from whom he learned something about hypnotism, for which he had an instinctive flair, and something about "Tibetan" drugs.

Rasputin came originally from a crossroads village in northeastern Siberia in the Province of Tobolsk, that Siberia which was the land of wandering and heresies, of Old Believers and schismatics of all sorts, of orgiastic sects like the *khlysty*, to which the police reports suggest he had belonged, and the *skoptsy*, zealots who castrated themselves to the glory of God.

He appeared in St. Petersburg in 1905, sponsored by the monk Iliodor, who then believed in him; by the Archimandrite Theophan, confessor of the empress; and by the devout bishop of Saratov, Hermogen. (All three of these men later turned against him and were ruined by his influence with the empress.) To the court itself he was brought by the two Montenegrin princesses, the Archduchess Militsa, who had already introduced Philippe to the tsaritsa, and the Archduchess Anastasia, whose husband, Grand Duke Nikolai Nikolaevich, had just had a dog cured by Rasputin.

The sovereigns saw a stocky, powerfully built peasant, a striking figure of a man, with a strong body odor, hair down to his shoulders, piercing steel-grey eyes that could narrow to steely points, under thick bushy eyebrows, a long, fleshy nose and a tangled beard and moustache which completely covered his ears, his thick lips, and the entire lower part of his face. He wore a cassock or robe resembling that of a monk, the high boots of a peasant, and perhaps, as others have described him, he may even have carried a pilgrim staff and a bag to hold food and money which the faithful might give him, a favorite icon, a few trinkets which he was wont to bless and bestow. Many have testified to the impressiveness of his face and figure and above all to the effect upon them of his hypnotic eyes.[3]

Rasputin's fame as a holy man and prophet preceded him to St. Petersburg. Born Gregory, son of Efim, without a surname (the lack of surnames was common among peasants), he had somehow acquired the surname Rasputin, that is to say, Gregory the Dissolute (though his daughter would maintain in her memoir that his name derived not from *rasputnyi*, "dissolute," but from *rasput'ye*, "crossroads," which would make him Gregory from the Crossroads.[4] Everyone else, however, accepted the first derivation, for he had led a wild and sinful youth, had several times to leave communities or monasteries because of scandals, and, by the time he reached the capital, was distinguished by a love of food and strong wine, of women, and of mystery and power. Surges of feasting, drunken revelry, and unfettered eroticism alternated in him with periods of genuine mystic devotion. Moreover, eroticism and salvation were inextricably mingled in the shapeless theological doctrine he preached and practiced. He was as ready to acknowledge that he was but human, and therefore weak and sinful, as he was to proclaim that he was holy and devout. Only those who had sinned greatly, he held, could repent deeply and win forgiveness for their (and all men's) sinful humanity and thus find the way to grace and salvation. To nobles and bureaucrats who accepted and believed in him, he could be familiar, even insolent, enjoying the impression he made upon them, enjoying his power over them, the power of a rude peasant still partly illiterate to humble the great and powerful. From the laying on of hands, the bestowing of a kiss, and other forms of blessing, he moved readily into sexual conquest of some of the more neurotic and hysterical of the ladies of the upper circles of St. Petersburg. He is known to have forced his attentions on the unwilling (simple rape) and to have assured the less unwilling that physical contact with his holy self could only purify.

Although the nature of the tsarevich's illness was supposed to be a jealously guarded secret, Rasputin already knew why he had been summoned. After speaking at length on the sufferings, hopes, and deep-lying moods of the Russian peasant, whose spokesman in the tsar's eyes he soon became, he told the tsaritsa what she wanted to know about God's presence and miraculous power. "Believe in the power of my prayers," he told her, "believe in my help, and your son will live."[5] Longing to believe with all her being and convinced that this simple muzhik was God's answer to her prayers and the sick nation's needs, Alexandra persuaded herself that her son's life was in his hands. It did not take him long to confirm his miraculous powers and to learn what advantage he could gain from entry into the royal household.

At the palace Rasputin was always a holy man, a shrewd muzhik and voice of the muzhiks, a man with the undoubted power to calm and soothe the sick boy, to comfort him in illness, to reduce his restlessness and fever, and in some measure—whether by hypnotism, suggestion, "Tibetan drugs"—to heal. To his secretary, Simanovitch, he explained that sometimes he gave drugs which he got from Badmaev, sometimes whatever came to hand, or he soothed the boy's brow, or pretended to use remedies such as an infusion of oak bark with which he wet a damp cloth to cover the prince's face during a nosebleed, or he mumbled incomprehensible words and made use of his powers of suggestion. He persuaded the royal pair that the boy would live as long as Rasputin himself were alive and able to help him (once even by telephone!) and that if he reached eighteen, the malady would go forever.[6] As one of the boy's nurses, Teglova, put it, "Call it what you will, he could really promise her the boy's life while he lived."[7] Once Alexandra became convinced of this, and her whole being conspired with him to convince her, she could not permit herself to doubt that he was a Man of God to whom it was given by the Savior to work miracles. For all his debauchery, cunning, and hocus-pocus, he does not seem to have doubted his religious vocation either.

Those who wished the monarchy well never ceased to oppose his influence at court, and Nicholas was the recipient of constant reports from his ablest ministers and from the police on Rasputin's scandalous conduct. But his influence grew, and despite perilous moments, all the scandal with which people assailed her own and the tsar's ears was to Alexandra only an evidence of the corrupt malevolence and unholiness, or downright disloyalty to God and tsar, of the talebearers themselves.

Nicholas was less fanatical and therefore less blind than his wife, but he too was deeply grateful for the healing power over the boy which Rasputin manifested. When scandal grew, or ministers were too insistent and circumstantial, Rasputin might be sent away from court for a while, but he was always recalled in some new emergency in the health of the heir, while Alexandra in the long run always contrived to get the offending minister or churchman or police official dismissed or sent into rustic exile.

Moreover, Nicholas felt need of "advisers" who were "disinterested" in politics and who would tell him what he wanted to hear: that he should be strong, that he should assert himself, that "a tsar's soul is in the hand of God," that his own weak and capricious will when it did assert itself was an expression of God's will. He felt need of the advice of this shrewd muzhik whose loyalty to the monarchy could not be doubted, for his own fate and power were linked to absolutism. (What constitutional government would have place for or tolerate such a figure?) The fact that disreputable people used Rasputin's influence for the pillage of the treasury, the advancement of the fortunes of incompetent and corrupt men, suggests that the "Man of God" did not have much understanding of politics or of Petersburg society. Yet he really gave evidence in time of crisis that he knew how the muzhiks of Russia felt and thought, and Nicholas, who, like his wife, expected that salvation would come from the muzhik, felt he was listening to the voice of peasant Russia. To the Palace Commandant Deyulin, who warned the tsar against Rasputin, Nicholas replied, "He is just a good, religious, simple-minded Russian. When in trouble or assailed by doubts, I like to talk with him, and invariably feel at peace with myself afterwards."[8]

Rasputin had a natural love for power. His access to the palace and his influence over the empress and her intimates gave him power in ever-greater measure. But he was not venal, and did not, as has so often been alleged, sell his influence. Rather he gave it freely to those who flattered him, those who fell in or professed to fall in with his notions of how the government should be conducted, those who served him, protected him in his scrapes, or were useful to his ambitions. He would insolently look over candidates for office and petitioners for favors, and tell the empress or her confidante Vyrubova what he thought of them, but he did not set a price on his favors nor ask for presents. When these were showered upon him, he accepted them as his due and as often as not passed them on to the poor. No doubt the more scoundrelly of his intimates did put a price on introducing suitors to him, but there is no evidence that this was with his knowledge. Under the cloak of his holiness and thaumaturgic power ever stranger and more dubious figures wormed themselves into government business, affairs of state, the entourage of the empress and ultimately that of the tsar.

One of Rasputin's first advisers in the ways of high society and the use of power over gentlefolk was his secretary and mentor, the Kievan jeweler, Aron Simanovitch, with whom he had taken up in the course of one of his early pilgrimages to the holy places of Kiev. "Simochka," he called this counsellor-servitor, giving him a ring inscribed "To the best of Jews." Simanovitch tried to keep him out of trouble, scolded him severely on occasion, instructed him in the labyrinth of Petersburg society, used his influence to entrench himself in the underworld of gambling dens, taverns, and cabarets, sought through him to modify the severity of the treatment of Jews in Russia. Sometimes through Simanovitch, sometimes through the light-minded, silly lady-in-waiting Vyrubova, who was the empress's confidante, all sorts of second-rate politicians, self-seekers, speculators, and intriguers got to Alexandra and through her to the tsar himself. Thus did this "Man of God" surround the monarchs with a thickening hedge of corruption and scandal.

Rasputin's influence had its ups and downs. At first he was careful about scandal. But, finding the high world of luxury and "breeding" at his feet, he could not refrain from taking advantage. Even his daughter, who writes only to defend him, admits that he "had mistresses" but she blames them for "tempting" him. In time scandal reached the royal palace when the governess of the princesses objected to his going into the girls' bedroom. Though Nicholas insisted that this should cease, the empress was merely infuriated by this scandalous attitude toward the saintly prophet: the governess was soon dismissed and from her the scandal spread outward and downward through society. When he seduced the tsarevich's nurse and she later made confession, the empress attributed it to hysterical fantasy. Having come out of these two scrapes with undiminished standing, Rasputin gradually abandoned all restraint.[9]

Rasputin's attempt to hypnotize the chairman of the Council of Ministers proved the last straw to the upright Stolypin. He had his Minister of Religion Lukyanov compile a dossier based on the reports of the police and, after handing the reports to the tsar, Stolypin banished Rasputin from St. Petersburg. From that moment, the empress conceived a hatred for the man whom I have repeatedly called the best adviser Nicholas ever had. She sent two of her ladies-in-waiting, Anna Vyrubova and Lili Dehn, to Rasputin's native village in Siberia to prepare a vindication of him. That same autumn Anna Vyrubova brought Rasputin with her to Kiev where the royal family was paying a state visit. As the procession passed the point where Rasputin was standing the tsaritsa in her carriage bowed her head to him and he answered with the sign of the cross. In the next coach rode the chairman of the Council of Ministers. Thereupon Rasputin cried to his companion, "Death rides behind him, Death rides toward him. . . ." That night, at a gala performance in the Opera House an assassin fired a shot, not at the tsar but at Stolypin, seated near him in the royal box.[10]

Stolypin was replaced by Kokovtsev, an upright adviser but less able and less strong than Stolypin. Lukyanov was replaced as Procurator of the Holy Synod by V. K. Sabler, a Rasputin creature, who remained as head of the church and Minister of Religion during the fateful years from 1911 to 1915.

Next, Theophan, who had been the empress's confessor and who, believing in Rasputin's saintliness, had vouched for him at court, tried to acquaint the empress with the scandals of the holy Gregory's life. Theophan was banished from the capital by being made Bishop of the Crimea. Metropolitan Antony bravely tried to warn the empress, but shortly after fell ill and died. The empress saw in his death the judgment of God. The monk Iliodor and Bishop Hermogen, who were also disillusioned former sponsors of Gregory Rasputin, summoned Rasputin to meet them at Hermogen's retreat in Tsaritsyn. The good bishop thundered the accusations he had gathered, always pausing to demand, "Is this true?" And Rasputin faltered, "It's true, it's true." The bishop struck him with a heavy cross, adjured him to abstain from touching women ever again and from returning to the royal palace, making him swear on a holy icon. But Rasputin hastened to give his own account of the affair to Vyrubova, who carried it to the empress. Hermogen and Iliodor were ordered without trial or hearing, by imperial fiat, to seclusion in remote monasteries. Hermogen obeyed, but Iliodor began a campaign against Rasputin which soon filled the press with scandalous tales. Mothers complained of the seduction of their daughters and women wrote their complaints. Iliodor was unfrocked and had to flee abroad. The tsar broke his pledge, solemnly given in 1905 against preliminary censure of the press, and ordered that no paper should print anything about Rasputin.

Rasputin by now had his appointees among the police and informers at every level of society and government and church. He would display his powers of prophecy by telling Vyrubova or the empress that he foresaw that a new attack was coming. Thus it was that Kokovtsev fell from grace, and when the leaders of the Duma took up the Rasputin case, Nicholas was persuaded, for the first time since the Duma had been created, to think of reducing it to a mere advisory body and to curb its powers of discussion and interpolation. One by one the upright and the courageous were alienated and exiled from the royal entourage, while the weak, the complacent, the servile, and the scoundrelly took their places. The mounting scandal kept Rasputin from the court and even caused him to return to his Siberian home, but there was always the telegraph. He would send his messages and recommendations to Vyrubova, who could be counted on to repeat them "like a phonograph record" to the empress, who in turn would repeat them as God's word to the tsar. And by long distance and absent treatment he still managed to perform his "miracles" for the boy or contrived to reappear in St. Petersburg with tidings that Alexei would recover.

In October 1912, the tsarevich slipped while getting into a boat, thus beginning a hemorrhage accompanied by agonizing pain. It was thought that the boy was dying, and Princess Irina of Prussia, who had lost three boys from hemophilia, came to comfort her anguished sister. But in answer to a wire from Vyrubova, Rasputin telegraphed: "The illness is not as dangerous as it seems. Don't let the doctors worry him." Though the crisis continued for a long time, the distraught mother was convinced that the boy began slowly to get better after the telegram arrived.

It was at this time, too, that the tremendous celebrations of the hundredth anniversary of the defeat of Napoleon (1812) and the three hundredth of the founding of the Romanov dynasty (1613) served to convince the tsaritsa and her husband that the people of Russia were delirious in their loyalty to the dynasty, the throne, and the sovereigns. More than ever did Nicholas listen to those who bade him remember that "the tsar's heart is in God's hand," and that listening to his inner voice, he need consult no institution and no minister. At the very moment when the Duma, which had begun in the turmoil of the 1905 revolution and a spirit of negative opposition, was beginning to learn how to do constructive parliamentary work; at the moment when Stolypin's reforms were laying the foundations for a settlement of the peasant problem and when Kokovtsev was succeeding in balancing the budget year after year and sustaining the credit of the government in the money markets of Europe; at a time when the zemstvos were making significant strides toward universal education and the Duma was undertaking a solid reorganization of army and navy and bureaucracy; and when an upright ministry was dismissing such questionable characters as the provocateurs, Azev and Malinovsky—in short, at a moment when down below, all Russia was moving toward more modern institutions closer to those of the West, at court the emperor, and still more the empress, dominated by this dissolute holy man straight out of Russia's legendary-superstitious peasant past, were reviving dreams appropriate to a medieval tsar. In this time of hesitation and uncertainty, when Old and New, each unsure of itself and too weak and uncertain to overcome the other, were fumbling in dubious battle, over Europe and over Russia broke the hurricane of universal war.

3

Gapon and Zubatov:
An Experiment in
"Police Socialism"

At the turn of the century four simultaneous efforts were started to inject some organization into inchoate Russian public life. The same years, 1901 to 1903, that witnessed Lenin's attempt to constitute an All-Russian Social Democratic party for the proletariat, witnessed the formation of a Social Revolutionary party to give leadership to the peasantry, a Constitutional Democratic party to organize the liberal and democratic intelligentsia, and an amazing series of experiments in police unionism and police "socialism." All these were so many minor eddies in a swiftly rising freshet—signs that the whole long-frozen political structure of Russia was about to thaw. But none of the new organizations was to prove equal to the task it had set itself: to channelize the rapidly rising flood.

In the bureaucracy there were striking differences of opinion on the attitude to be taken toward the nascent labor movement and the various embryonic political parties. To Plehve,[1] who as Minister of the Interior had charge of the secret police and public order, it seemed that the zemstvo liberals and Constitutional Democrats were the most dangerous, the Social Revolutionaries next, and the Social Democrats he put only in third place. His chief bugbear was the zemstvos, with their urge for local autonomy, their remonstrances and petitions reminiscent of the French Revolution's *cahiers de doléances*, their demand for a national council of zemstvo delegates or *zemskii sobor*, or national council, that might easily

This essay was published as part of *Three Who Made a Revolution* (New York: Dial Press, 1948). It is reprinted here by permission of *The Russian Review*, where it appeared in Spring 1948.

become the germ of a parliament, another Etats Généraux. He feared and detested them most because they represented socially the most exalted demand for constitutionalism, a species of treason to the autocracy amongst the landowners themselves.

Next in order came the manufacturers and financiers with their demands for subsidies, new tariff and taxation structures, a state budget, the transformation of the feudal-bureaucratic state in the image of modern capitalism and parliamentarism. These, and the moderate zemstvo elements were the more dangerous because they had their agent, Count Witte,[2] in the very Council of Ministers.

If the Social Revolutionaries came second in the order of Minister Plehve's attention, it was not by reason of their socialism nor their peasant committees, but because of their use of terror. Socialism never worried Plehve. With an inverted *narodnichestvo* common to many reactionaries in Russia, he looked on rural socialism as a kind of peasant communal village arrangement, not at all incompatible with the tasks of tax collecting, military levies, and absolutist dictatorship. The peasants he regarded as an unshakable rock of loyalty to the throne. Urban socialism he dismissed as a remote and impossible utopian dream, while Witte's projects for state ownership of railways and banks and the vodka traffic naturally troubled him not at all. The real problem was the owners of private industry whom Witte represented so ably at court.

Plehve pondered much over a report made by the conservative Governor of Moscow, General Trepov, in 1898: "In order to disarm the agitators—General Trepov had written—it is necessary to open and point out to the worker a legal solution of his difficulty, for we must bear in mind that the agitator will be followed by the youngest and boldest part of the crowd, while the average worker will prefer the less spectacular and quiet legal way. Thus split up, the crowd will lose its power."

The suggestion intrigued the Minister of the Interior. What were these restless workingmen, he asked himself, if not the same loyal peasants of yesterday, bewildered by the new industrialism, angered by the greed of the industrialists, led astray by revolutionary agitators from the intelligentsia. Why might the state not shepherd them and watch over them a bit more, weed out the hotheads, give the mass a chance to organize under the most dependable auspices, protect them by social legislation against the greedy and doubtfully loyal bourgeoisie, act as benevolent and impartial arbitrator in industrial disputes, avert strikes and disorders by friendly arbitration, bind them more closely to the paternal state and tsar? Would it not be a master stroke of statesmanship to set the workingmen against the factory owners instead of against the government? And as a by-product, might not even a little carefully directed labor disorder be a useful weapon on occasion to show whither Finance Minister Witte's industrialization and liberal flirtations were leading?

The real architect of police-regimented unions in a police-controlled paternal state was Sergei Vasilievich Zubatov, who now became chief lieutenant of General Trepov in Moscow. It was Zubatov and not Plehve or Trepov to whose name would be attached the honor of the great experiment in police unionism destined to go down in history as the *zubatovshchina*. As a gymnazia student he had entered the Narodnaya Volya,[3] enlisting with the police almost simultaneously as a secret agent. Thereafter he had risen rapidly in the service, being the sponsor of many progressive innovations: photography, fingerprinting, and a superior system of secret espionage on a scale hitherto unknown in Russia or in the world. "You must look upon your colleague, the secret agent," he once told the police, "as you would upon a woman with whom you are conducting a secret love intrigue: one rash step and you have dishonored her in the eyes of the world." Clearly a man of sentiment and imagination!

His biggest achievement so far had been the nationwide simultaneous raids that smashed the beginnings of the Social Democratic party in 1897, rendering nugatory the efforts of their First Congress at Minsk.[4] Now he had risen to the headship of the Moscow Okhrana or secret security police, his only superiors being General Trepov, in charge of all the police services of the Moscow Province, and Minister of the Interior Plehve. This, his most ambitious plan, was really the police counterpart of the urge for organization that was beginning to take possession of all classes in Russia. Against the zemstvo intellectuals, the students, the Social Democrats, and Social Revolutionaries, he would offer his experiment in police unionism and police "socialism." In May 1901, he founded in Moscow the Society for Mutual Aid for Workingmen in the Mechanical Industries. As an experienced secret agent, he tried to keep his guiding hand as unobtrusive as possible, but his less subtle superiors, Trepov and Plehve, insisted on tying up the society with all sorts of rigid and too obvious safeguards. The bylaws and financial expenditures had to be approved by General Trepov. The secret agents who were leaders of the union were supplemented by uniformed police openly present at each meeting.

But the Moscow workingmen, heirs to the ancient patriarchal tradition and hungering now for organization, were more trustful of the tsar and his officials than either Zubatov or the revolutionaries had believed possible. Assured that a paternal government was with them, they rushed into the strange union. Five days after it was formed, it was able to lead a procession of fifty thousand workers into the Kremlin for solemn prayer before the tomb of the Emancipator Tsar, Alexander II.

"Intellectuals" were barred from the organization, "hotheads" and "trouble-makers" among the workingmen were arrested and silently deported. Hence purists among the Social Democrats wanted to limit their activity to denunciation and exposure. The workers were too class-conscious, they contended, to continue to have anything to do with such a monstrosity once it was exposed to them. But the more realistic leaders knew that denunciation was not enough. "We must understand—Lenin wrote in *Iskra*—how to develop the struggle of the workers against every shameful intrigue and spy's trick. . . . This struggle will develop the political consciousness of all who take part in the police-gendarme-and-spy labor organization. . . . In the long run the legalization of the working class movement will be to our advantage and not to that of the Zubatovs . . ."

This freedom from sectarian aversion to working wherever work was needful was not limited to Lenin. At the Second Congress,[5] one of the resolutions passed unanimously during the exhausted closing hours of the last session was a decision that Social Democratic workingmen should join these unions where possible and try to defend and enlighten their members against the police. The startling successes even then being achieved by police unionism made any other attitude impossible.

The Moscow Society for Mutual Aid had begun, with Zubatov's encouragement, by discussing economic and cultural questions and formulating wage proposals. They chose as the first object of their attentions a "foreign exploiter"—a French factory owner. But he went crying to his ambassador, who in turn protested to Plehve concerning this quasi-governmental action against one of his nationals. The first demands had to be dropped.

Zubatov's next idea was to help the union draw up proposals for wages and working conditions, impartially for the whole of Moscow industry. As head of the Okhrana, he even went so far as to convoke a meeting of the manufacturers, berate them not a little, and insist upon concessions. With the first successes, the movement began to spread rapidly, from industry to industry, and then, on the wings of rumor and report, from town to town until particularly the newly industrialized factory centers of southern Russia were honeycombed with police unions and programs for police socialism.

While Zubatov supported labor legislation and repeatedly took the part of the workers against the employers, he simultaneously dispatched provocateurs into the revolutionary movement with an idea of "provoking you to acts of terror and then crushing you," as he once said to a labor prisoner in a moment of frankness. Chief of these agents was Yevno Azev, son of a poor Jewish tailor, who became a student spy, then, with Zubatov's aid, a Moscow engineer and one of the founders and the eventual leader of the terror section of the Social Revolutionary party. In that role, he was to take part in a plot which would cost his chief Minister Plehve his life! But his story is only tangential to the one we are following.[6]

In Odessa a Doctor Shaevich appeared as Zubatov's agent to start things moving. Colonel of Gendarmes Vasiliev, assisted by two Jewish woman agents, even formed a "Jewish Independent Labor party" in Kiev! A police-sponsored priest, George Gapon, offered himself as a leader of the working-class movement in St. Petersburg. Police socialism was booming all over Russia.

In the spring of 1903, the new industrial regions exploded in a series of little strikes that set each other off, merged with each other, began to grow into something too big for a police official to manipulate in comfort. In July, 1903, at the very moment when the Social Democrats in their London congress were adopting a resolution to send Socialist workingmen into the police unions, Doctor Shaevich lost control of the Odessa movement. A general strike started there and spread all over southern Russia and into the Caucasus, a dress rehearsal for the greater upheavals of 1905. Zubatov, Shaevich, and Vasilyev fell from grace and were banished to administrative exile in far northern Russia. Thus ended the first phase of the experiment in police unionism. But in the capital, Priest Gapon had not yet started his work, nor was he under the Moscow jurisdiction of the disgraced Zubatov. Minister Plehve did not interfere with the priest's plans.

Father George Gapon is one of the most interesting figures thrown up by the revolution, and one of the most peculiarly Russian. Son of a peasant of Ukrainian origin, at the time we meet him he was only thirty-two. He is described as intelligent, serious, meditative, energetic; he was undoubtedly handsome and an impressive orator. In his youth he had been given a clandestinely circulated manuscript tract of Tolstoy by one of his teachers, who was a Tolstoyan. The other main source of his inspiration seems to have been Zubatov and his police unions. As prison chaplain he showed his ability to handle men and won the confidence of his superiors for a project to substitute "spiritual supervision" for policing to guide the Petersburg workers, since they had proved more suspicious of the police than the workers of Moscow. His project for a Union of Russian Factory Workers with himself as leader received Plehve's approval shortly before the latter's death. The new union's aims included "the sober and rational passing of leisure time," religious and patriotic training, exclusion of drunkenness and gambling, the development of a "prudent view of the duties and rights of workers," and "self-activity for the legal improvement of the conditions of labor and life of the workers."

During the first half of 1904 the workers kept away from the new priest-led union. Gapon, torn between his Tolstoyan views, his moral and social ambitions and his police instructions, sought to increase the confidence of the masses in his organization by getting advice and support from more advanced workers. After a few secret confidences with such people, the society began to grow rapidly. Before the year was out it included practically all eligible workers engaged in the mechanical trades in St. Petersburg, together with a sizable sprinkling of police spies and a few men under the influence of Socialist ideas. More successfully than Zubatov he seemed to be deflecting the hostility of the members from the regime to the employers. Its great meetings sang "God Save the Tsar" with deep and undoubted fervor, for they thought of him as having overruled his wicked officials and sanctioned their legitimate hopes for organization.

In gauging the patriarchal backwardness of the Russian masses in the dawn years of the twentieth century, we must keep this picture clear in our minds. Nor was it only the unskilled workers, yesterday's peasants, who followed a priest and sang thus fervently, "God Save the Tsar." Actually, the main scene of our drama is the huge Putilov locomotive works and machine shops, the oldest and largest heavy industry factory in Moscow, containing the largest number of skilled metalworkers. Here Father Gapon had his greatest organization. Under his guidance, they formulated their moderate demands upon the enterprise. In December, the latter answered by firing the leading members of Gapon's committee. Thereupon, the entire force of the Putilov Locomotive Works walked out and urged Father Gapon to take them directly to the "Dear Father Tsar" that they might lay their troubles at his feet.

Priest Gapon was scarcely less naive than the men he had brought together and was influenced by the mass spirit quite as much as he influenced it. The movement was getting too big for its founder to control; its illusions were assuming independent life and taking control of him. At first he was hesitant at the audacious idea of going directly to the "Father of the Russian People." Then he sanctioned it, finally was carried away by it. He began to avoid his superiors, the officials of the police department and the Ministry of the Interior. Like his followers, he too now sought to go over their heads and seek direct contact with Tsar Nicholas. On January 21 (January 8, Old Style), the eve of the projected procession to the palace, he wrote the following confidential message to the tsar:

> Sire!
> Do not believe the Ministers. They are cheating Thee in regard to the real state of affairs. The people believe in Thee. They have made

up their minds to gather at the Winter Palace tomorrow, at 2 p.m., to lay their needs before Thee. If Thou wilt not stand before them, Thou wilt break that spiritual connection which unites Thee with them. . . .

Do not fear anything. Stand tomorrow before the people and accept our humblest petition. I, the representative of the working-men, and my comrades, guarantee the inviolability of Thy person.

(signed) Gapon

Next morning, according to the common estimate, more than 200,000 men, women, and children, workers and their families, gathered at many concentration points to converge in procession upon the Winter Palace. They were unarmed. In keeping with Gapon's guarantee, the few terror-ists, hotheads, or police agents who had brought arms were searched by his ushers and their weapons taken from them. Their intention was pa-cific, even reverential. Their women and children were there. It was Sunday. They marched with interlocked arms, some bore icons and pic-tures of the tsar. (This carrying of images of the ruler in procession is an ancient Russian custom that flourishes still today.) As they marched, they sang as only Russian multitudes can sing, and over and over again their song was "God Save the Tsar."

At their head marched Priest Gapon with a scroll. Its petition was a reflection of the medley in his mind and the variegated nature of his following:

Sire—We workingmen and inhabitants of Saint Petersburg . . . . our wives and our children and our helpless old parents come to Thee, Sire, to seek for truth and protection. We have become beggars; we have been oppressed; we are burdened by toil beyond our powers. . . . We are choked by despotism and irresponsibility, and we are breathless. . . . There has arrived for us that great moment when death is better than the continuation of intolerable tortures. We have left off working, and we have declared to our masters that we shall not begin to work until they comply with our demands. We ask but little . . . to diminish the working day to eight hours . . . minimum daily wage should be one ruble per day, to abolish overtime. . . .

The officials have brought the country to complete destruction, have involved it in a detestable war. . . . We workingmen have no voice in the expenditure of the enormous amounts raised from us in taxes. . . .

These things are before us, Sire, and they have brought us to the walls of Thy Palace. We are seeking here the last salvation. Do not refuse assistance to Thy people. Give their destiny into their own hands. Cast away from them the intolerable oppression of the officials. Destroy the wall between Thyself and Thy people, and let them rule the country together with Thyself. . . . Order immediately the convocation of a *zemskii sobor* . . . order that the elections to the Constituent Assembly be carried on under the condition of universal, equal, secret voting. This is the most capital of our requests . . . the principal and only plaster for our painful wounds. . . .

Order and take an oath to comply with these requests and Thou wilt make Russia happy and famous and Thou wilt impress Thy name in our hearts and the hearts of our posterity forever.

If Thou wilt not order and wilt not answer our prayer, we shall die here on this Square before Thy Palace. . . .

So the people, finding their voice through a priest who had picked up scraps of demands and slogans that were in the air, marched to the palace of their tsar to lay their troubles at his feet. But the tsar was not in his palace. He had left the city hastily, taking with him wife and daughters. In his stead he had left the officials: generals, police chiefs, and his uncle, the Grand Duke Vladimir.

Troops fully armed, guns loaded and not with blanks, descended upon the marchers, surrounded their separate detachments, fired at close range. Men, women, children fell. The crowds melted away. Crimson stains appeared on the white snow. How many fell, no one knows, for the wounded were treated in secret and the dead were withdrawn by their kin. The common labor estimate is 500 killed and 3,000 wounded. A public commission of the Bar Association set the figures at 150 and 200, respectively. In any case, enough blood was shed to baptize the day "Bloody Sunday" as it was called thenceforward.

An epoch had come to an end. It had been sufficient for the masses to get the fearful idea of acting on a cherished fairy tale for it to be exploded forever. That day millions of primitive minds took the leap from the Middle Ages to the Twentieth Century. In love and reverence their best had come to lay their troubles at the feet of the Dear Father Tsar. The bullets and the shed blood swept away all vestiges of love and credulity. Now they knew themselves fatherless and knew that they would have to solve their problems themselves. Now their minds were opened at last to the teachings of the Republican and Socialist party intellectuals. Constituent Assembly and Democratic Republic, General Strike and Armed Uprising, ceased to be phrases comprehensible only to the educated and the specialists in revolution. They took possession of millions and thereby became a material force for the transformation of Russia.

Father Gapon fled. With the aid of Social Revolutionaries he escaped abroad. From hiding, he dispatched one more note to his Tsar, this time without salutation or respectful capitals: "The innocent blood of workers, their wives and children, lies forever between thee, oh soul destroyer, and the Russian people. Moral connection between thee and them may never more be. . . . Let all the blood which has to be shed, hangman, fall upon thee and thy kindred!"

So ended the first experiments in "police-socialism" and a police-guided labor movement in Russia.

4

War Comes to Russia

Give us ten more years and we are safe.
S. I. Shidlovsky[1]

We need peace: a war during the coming
year, and especially in the name of a cause
the people would not understand, would
be fatal for Russia and for the dynasty.
Stolypin to Izvolsky in 1911[2]

. . . A general European war is mortally
dangerous both for Russia and Germany,
no matter who wins. . . . There must inevitably break out in the defeated country
a social revolution, which will spread to
the victor.
P. N. Durnovo to the tsar after the
Balkan alarms of 1913[3]

Let Papa not plan war, for with war will
come the end of Russia and of yourselves.
Telegram of Rasputin to Vyrubova on
learning of the mobilization[4]

St. Petersburg, stormy capital which a decade earlier had looked on
processions shouting "Down with the Tsar!," once more beheld workingmen marching from the workers' quarters to the Winter Palace. Ilyin-
Genevsky, revolutionary student home from Switzerland, saw men in
blue overalls marching with banners and roaring out a song. His heart
filled with immense joy: "It must be the Revolution!" Disillusion was
not long in coming, for now he could see portraits of the Tsar and hear
the words of the song. The voices were chanting: "Reign to confound
our enemies."

Even that unflinchingly internationalist and prosaic Théodor Dan
writes in more animated style than usual:

> The streets which but yesterday were filled with roving masses of
> strikers, today were dominated by "patriots." One demonstration
> followed the other to the Winter Palace and sank on its knees before

Reprinted with permission from *The Russian Review* (April 1963).

50

the Tsar standing on the balcony. . . . Nor did the bacchanal leave the working class untouched: not a few of those who the day before had been on strike, today marched in the ranks of the patriotic demonstrators. Even in the ranks of Social Democracy itself, confusion reigned.

In the Winter Palace, the president of the Duma was telling the French ambassador, "The Russian people has not experienced such a wave of patriotic emotion since 1812." Bernard Pares, looking out of the palace windows, saw "a vast multitude fall on their knees and sing 'God Save the Tsar' as it had never been sung before." Repeating word for word the oath which Alexander had taken before him in 1812, and which Stalin would take after him in 1941, Nicholas II swore to the populace that he would never cease from struggle until the last invader had been driven from Russia's holy soil. The British ambassador wrote in his memoirs: "Those wonderful early August days! Russia seemed to have been completely transformed."5

In the provincial capitals, too, strife was stilled. But foreign policy being more remote, the first reaction was bewilderment. General Mikhail Dmitrievich Bonch-Bruevich,6 remembering in his old age how war came to his regiment in Chernigov in the Ukraine in 1914, will serve as a paradigm for all provincial notables who have written memoirs of those days:

> Summer was at its peak. Tables somehow knocked together at the town fair were bursting under the weight of rosy apples, silver pears, flaming tomatoes, lilac-colored sweet onions, five-inch-thick pieces of salt pork that would melt in your mouth, fat-dripping, home-made sausages, all the things in which the flourishing Ukraine is so rich. A cloudless, blindingly blue sky hung over the dreaming town. Nothing, it seemed, could disturb the measured flow of peaceful provincial life. . . . The regimental ladies vied with each other in cooking up hams and jellies, putting up delicious salted cucumbers in casks; the gentlemen officers after unhurried accomplishment of their duties went to a meeting where on starched white cloths awaited sweating bottles of chilled vodka; the regiment was in camp, but the blinding whiteness of the placards, the shaped flowerbeds neatly trimmed by the soldiers, the carefully sanded paths, strengthened the feeling of undisturbedly peaceful life that dominated us all. Suddenly, at five in the afternoon on the 29th of July, the adjutant brought me a secret dispatch from Kiev . . . for the immediate putting of all units of the garrison on a *premobilization footing*. . . . Three days later came an order for general mobilization.

. . . But *with whom* were we to fight? No one knew. Only on the 2nd of August did it become known that Germany had declared war on Russia. And only somewhat later did there at last arrive to Chernigov the news that along with Germany, Austria-Hungary had also declared war on Russia, and we were told that the XXIst Army corps . . . was to proceed into action against the Austro-Hungarian Army.[7]

To the villages war came in still more unintelligible guise. Here was no press, no oratory, no talk of world affairs, no knowledge of what Austria-Hungary or Germany might be, nor of any world more distant than the nearest market town and the tsar in the Kremlin far away. What was Serbia or Belgium to the Russian villager? War came to him as a command from afar, incontestable and incomprehensible, breaking the seasonal round of his days, summoning him to give up horses and carts, sons, himself, for unexplained service in unknown regions of the world against an unknown foe.

> The capitals are rocked with thunder
> Of orators in wordy feuds
> But in the depths of Russia, yonder,
> Ever the age-old silence broods . . .

sang the poet Nekrasov. "At 100 versts from the big cities," Count Kokovtsev told a foreign correspondent, "all politics is stilled." Miliukov, seeking to sum up in his memoirs the reaction of the peasants to the war, found it in the formula, "*My–kalugskie,* [We are men of Kaluga] that is, to our Kaluga Wilhelm will not get." He felt that the "*age-old silence* hid within itself its unspent forces and waited—for its Pugachev from the Russian university."[8]

Fyodor Stepun[9] was in the tiny hamlet of Ivanovka, two versts from the village of Znamenka, both remote from the world, though they were in Moscow Province. One day the mail brought him a summons to appear in Znamenka "with his riding horse." How could he comprehend that this was the beginning of war?

He found Znamenka bursting with unwonted activity. In the village square, in front of the tavern, sat "a commission," a military officer, a clerk, a veterinarian, and, as equine experts, the two local horse dealers. The square was strewn with hay, overflowing with carts and horses, more carts coming from all directions, horses in front, horses on each side, horses tied to the rear, all trying to crowd into somnolent Znamenka. The commission was possessed by "bureaucratic exaltation." Without a word of explanation it was fixing prices, handing out receipts, requisitioning horses. Nobody spoke of Germany or Austria-Hungary or the defense of Russia, or of war.

The requisitioning turned the peaceful village into "a boiling kettle of human passion, gloom and anger." Above the commands, quarreling, and shouting rose "strong Russian curses." Few had faith in the fairness of the commission. They looked with contempt at "his Excellency," with mockery and distrust at the local experts, the veterinarian, the two horse traders. The poor were firmly convinced that the rich would not give up their horses: they would nail them up, rub tobacco into their eyes, buy their way out. "The Commission will take *yours* away at a fixed, low price, then that gypsy Malanichev [the local horse dealer was a "gypsy," i.e., a horse stealer] will bring you a new skinny nag at his own price, which he will take away again. You will feed him all summer with your own good oats, and in the Autumn he will see to it that he is paid again for a well-fed one."[10] Obviously, more widespread literacy and a government press and radio system—such as Stalin was able to count on in 1941—would have been of enormous advantage to an old-fashioned despotism about to engage in mass mobilization.

To Siberia, Kaiser Wilhelm and the lands of Europe were even more remote. Wladimir Woytinsky, out on the Siberian *taiga*, did not know the war was on until a month or so after it had begun, when he got to Yakutsk. Here is his account:

> A steamer arrived [at Nelkan on the Maya River] from the Lena, the last of the season. . . . The captain invited us to share his meals. . . . One day, he casually mentioned at the table that he had heard in Yakutsk that recruits were being conscripted, though he did not know why. . . . We did not learn about the beginning of war until we reached Yakutsk. Even now, after decades of research, historians have found it difficult to retrace the chain of events leading to the conflagration, but to people in the Siberian wilderness the events had a nightmarish quality. . . . In the middle of August, as our steamer passed villages along the way . . . landing places were crowded with men who had been called up. There was a spirit of sullen resignation among them and in the watching crowd. . . . The sudden shift from the solitude of the taiga to the turmoil of political events, rumors and passions was overwhelming.[11]

In this gulf between the garrulousness and enthusiasm of the capitals, the remote quiet of the provinces, and the age-old stillness of the village, between the literate "public" and the politically and alphabetically illiterate peasant mass, lay possibilities of misunderstanding, alienation, discord—a breach through which any "Pugachev from the University" or any rumormonger, might enter. The peasant was loyal enough to *his* Russia, obedient, enduring, strong, and courageous to serve as a stubborn wall of flesh against the invader. Still, as long as this *Wilhelm* did not get to Kaluga . . . or Yakutsk, the *Kalugskie* or *Yakutskie* would not know why they were fighting.

Thus the war began auspiciously for Russia. Deeply moved by the ordeal that had come upon his land, Nicholas summoned the Duma, which had so often given him trouble, for a one-day session to vote the war budget and to dramatize the unity of the *"public"*[12] with the tsar. In his Manifesto of August 2, Nicholas sounded this note of conciliation:

> At this hour of threatening danger, let domestic strife be forgotten. Let the union between the Tsar and His people be stronger than ever, and let Russia, rising like one man, repel the insolent assault of the enemy.

Rodzianko, answering on behalf of the Duma, told Russia's enemies:

> You thought we were divided by strife and hatred, and yet all the nationalities dwelling in boundless Russia were welded into a single family when danger threatened our common fatherland.

Miliukov, for the Constitutional Democrats (Kadets), was equally reassuring:

> In this struggle we are all as one; we present no conditions or demands; we simply throw into the scales of battle our firm determination to overcome the violator. . . . Whatever our attitude towards the internal policies of the Government may be, our first duty remains to preserve our country one and inseparable, and to maintain for it that position in the ranks of world powers which is being contested by our foes.

The spokesmen of the various nationalities, Lithuanians, Jews, Moslems, Baltic Germans and Volga German colonists,[13] all spoke in defense of the common Fatherland. Deputy Friedman, speaking for his Jewish constituents, was typical:

> We, the Jews, have lived and continue to live under exceptionally harsh legal conditions. Nevertheless, we have always felt ourselves to be citizens of Russia. . . . In this hour of trial we Russian Jews will stand as one man under the banners of Russia. . . . The Jewish people will do their duty to the last.

Yet faintly, a note was sounded which was a harbinger of storms to come. Miliukov expressed the hope that "in passing through the sore trials which confront us, the country may come nearer to its cherished aim [of freedom]." Kerensky, who spoke for the Trudoviki (Labor Group, a legal, moderate offshoot of the Social Revolutionary party) and who had spoken against the last military budget as pregnant with possible war, sounded a somewhat stronger note of discord:

> We are unshakably convinced that the great, irresistible power of the Russian democracy . . . will defend the native land and culture, created in the sweat and blood of generations! We believe that on the fields of battle . . . there will be born a single will to free the country from its internal shackles.

He hailed the efforts of the socialists of France, England, Belgium and Germany to avert war, protesting that "only we, the Russian democracy, were prevented" from openly joining that effort. "Citizens of Russia," he cried:

> Remember that you have no enemies among the laboring classes of the belligerent countries . . . remember that this frightful war would not have come had the great ideals of democracy, liberty, equality, and fraternity inspired the activity of Russia's rulers and the Governments of all other countries.
>
> Unfortunately, our Government, even at this dreadful hour, has no desire to forget internal strife. It denies amnesty to those who are fighting for the freedom and the happiness of our country . . . it does not seek reconciliation with the non-Russian nationalities, who have forgiven everything and are . . . fighting enthusiastically for our common fatherland. . . . Instead of ameliorating the condition of the laboring classes . . . it imposes upon these the main weight of war expenditures. . . .
>
> You, peasants and workers . . . gather all your forces, and then, having defended our country, set it free. . . .[14]

The stand taken by the Social Democratic deputies was not very dissimilar from that of Kerensky and the Trudoviki. Among the Social Democrats, as among the masses who had elected them, there was a yearning for Socialist unity. The Bolshevik Duma deputy, Roman Malinovsky, agent of the police and spokesman for Lenin, on the instructions of both his masters, had succeeded in splitting the reluctant fraction in two. But three months before war broke out, he had suddenly resigned his seat to avoid exposure as a police agent.[15] This left five Bolsheviks, all smallish men accustomed to have Lenin or Kamenev write their speeches for them, and seven Mensheviks, of whom the most articulate was Chkheidze. With Lenin far off in Austrian Galicia (Cracow) and his mouthpiece, Malinovsky, gone, instinctively the twelve Social Democratic deputies moved toward each other again. Since the two fractions felt that they had no differences in their internationalist feeling—after all Martov and Lenin had supported Rosa Luxemburg in her amendments to the Stuttgart Resolution—Bolsheviks and Mensheviks agreed on a joint declaration on the war.

According to the account written by the Bolshevik Duma deputy, Badayev, a first draft for this common statement was made by the Petersburg lawyer, N. D. Sokolov,[16] a nonparty attorney who defended clients from both groups and who, over the years, inclined now more to the Mensheviks, now more to the Bolsheviks. According to the Menshevik leader, Boris Ivanovich Nikolaevsky, who had been arrested in the prewar raids of the last days of July 1914, but was still in detention in Petrograd where he could follow the events closely, the declaration was of purely Menshevik origin. It was drawn up by the Menshevik leader, Peter Abramovich Garvy, who was not a Duma deputy but was one of the ablest Socialists in Petrograd at liberty at the moment. After he had drafted it, he went over it with Genrikh (Heinrich) Ehrlich, a leader of both the Bundists and the Menshevik organizations in Russia, and with Cherevdnin-Lipkin. When the declaration was already finished, the Menshevik deputy Khaustov was approached by the Bolsheviks with a proposal to draft a joint declaration. Khaustov replied: "Our statement is ready: if you would like to see it and make it a common declaration, we will be delighted." The Bolsheviks had no draft of their own. They read Garvy's statement and subscribed to it. In any case the declaration is Menshevik—Lenin would have said *Kautskyan*—in thought and tone. At the Duma session of August 8, the Menshevik deputy, Khaustov, read it as the stand of "the Social Democratic Fraction of the Duma."

Like Kerensky's statement, the Socialist declaration began with an attack on the horrors of war; praised the international socialist movement "with the German proletariat at its head" for its attempts to prevent it; protested that the Russian government, by its last-minute closing of journals and prohibition of meetings, had stopped the Russian proletariat from joining in the effort to avert war. Like Kerensky, too, the declaration rejected responsibility for the war, blaming it on "the greed" of the ruling classes of all belligerent countries. Where Kerensky spoke of the readiness of "the Russian democracy . . . to defend the native land and culture created in the sweat and blood of generations," the Socialist declaration read: "The proletariat, constant defender of the freedom and interests of the people, at every moment will fulfill its duty and will defend the cultural treasures of the people from all attacks, from wherever they may come—whether from abroad or from within the country."

In this defense of Russia's "cultural treasures," however, the socialists repudiated "the hypocritical call for unity" with a government which does not "carry out the conscious will of the people" and under which the people are without rights though they bear the heaviest burdens of war. In its outlook for the war's end, the Socialist declaration departed somewhat from Kerensky's statement, in the direction of a greater degree of pacifism and internationalism.

> We are deeply convinced that in the international solidarity of the proletariat of the entire world, humanity will find the means to the speediest possible ending of the war. And may the peace terms be dictated not by the diplomats of the predatory powers, but by the people themselves taking their fate into their own hands.
> . . . We express the deep conviction that this war will finally open the eyes of the popular masses of Europe as to the real source of violence and oppression from which they suffer, and that the present frightful conflagration will be the last such conflagration.[17]

When the vote was taken, the five Bolsheviks, the seven Mensheviks and Kerensky and the Trudoviks, wishing neither to vote for or against the credits, nor publicly to record themselves as abstaining, simply walked out of the chamber together. Their failure to participate in the voting enabled the newspapers to report that the Duma had voted unanimously "to stand up in defense of their country."[18] And in fact both the Trudoviks and the Social Democrats had pledged themselves "to defend the cultural treasures" [Kerensky said "the native land and culture"] from "all attacks from abroad." A year later, the Bolshevik deputies then being in prison, the Mensheviks repeated their walkout. This time the Trudoviki were not with them, and one of the Menshevik deputies, Mankov, decided to remain and vote for the credits. He was promptly expelled from the Menshevik fraction.

All that Lenin detested most was in that manifesto to which his followers had subscribed. As soon as he got out of his Austrian prison and was safely in neutral Switzerland, he would excoriate the declaration, without referring to his party's share in making it. Every idea in it was "Kautskyanism, the most dangerous position of all and that most calculated to deceive the masses." In it were all the main targets of his wrath: (1) the "priestly humanitarianism" which dwelt on the horrors of war in disregard of the fact that the socialists themselves needed war for their own aims; (2) the "priestly pacifism" which speculated on the hope of an early peace, instead of forseeing a prolonged war that could only be ended by its proper continuation, i.e., its transformation into a universal civil war; (3) the "treacherous and deceitful" idea that this war might be "the last conflagration," without any reference to the fact that more wars were certain as long as capitalism endured; (4) a "shameful" expression of a hope for "international solidarity," without any mention of the necessity of smashing the Second International and building a Third; (5) social-chauvinism, i.e., defensism covered with socialist phrases, in the pledge to defend Russia's cultural heritage from the inner and outer foe; (6) the propagation of the dangerous illusion that the peoples might dictate a just peace by their pressure, without a prior world revolution. In short, the declaration his followers had endorsed was pure Menshevism, pure Kautskyism, and Kautsky, as Lenin was to write to the first follower to whom he could send a letter after the war broke out, "is now *the most harmful of them all.*"

But here it was, and Lenin had to make the best of it until he should be able to whip his followers into line, or, as he had so often done before, get rid of those whom he could not convince and make a fresh selection. In the meanwhile, part of his stock-in-trade was to claim that all parties everywhere had committed treason to international socialism and the Stuttgart Resolution, *except* the Russian Bolsheviks in the Duma.

At this juncture came a lucky break. As often before, the police solved one of Lenin's internal problems for him. He sent the Bolshevik Duma deputies a copy of his own views on the war with a demand that they adopt his views as theirs. The core of his documents was a call for the defeat of Russia "as the lesser evil" (Thesis 6) and a call for the "transformation of the imperialist war into civil war" (Thesis 7). The deputies were shocked, as was Kamenev, Lenin's Central Committee representative in Russia. To them it seemed obvious that Lenin had no idea what it was like to live in a country at war and feel the pulse of its people. Dutifully, however, they called a conference of their five Duma deputies and five representatives from the local organizations, plus Kamenev for the Central Committee, to consider Lenin's views. Small though the conference was, at least two police agents in the party were privy to it. As if to make matters easier for the police, Deputy Muranov, in charge of the secret arrangements, was stupid enough to convene it at Ozerki, near Petrograd, in the northern war zone, already under martial law.[19] The police raided the meeting on the night of November 16–17 (November 3–4 Old Style), capturing not only all the participants and Lenin's *Theses*, but on the person of the not overly bright Muranov a complete list, uncoded, of the names and addresses of all the local Bolshevik leaders with whom, as Duma deputy, he was in touch.

Because it was a zone of martial law, it was easy for the police to override the parliamentary privilege of the deputies and avoid a public trial. They were tried on February 10–13, 1915. Kerensky, the noted labor lawyer and future rival of Lenin, took up their defense in court and intervened elsewhere on their behalf, even appealing to Foreign Minister Sazonov. He urged the adverse effect upon Russia's democratic allies of news that Duma deputies who had made an essentially patriotic declaration should be jailed for possessing a document drafted by Lenin. It was Lenin, he said, who should be tried *in absentia* to make his defeatist views more widely known. At their secret trial, the deputies expressly repudiated both the defeatist and the civil war points in Lenin's *Theses*. They pointed out that his document was in contradiction, as indeed it was, to "that declaration which in the name of both Social Democratic Fractions was read out in the Duma on August 8." Kamenev, for his part, declared that Lenin's views were rejected "both by the Social Democratic Deputies and by the Central Instances," i.e., the Central Committee whose spokesman he was. But the police charged all participants in the conference with the "dissemination" of Lenin's defeatist views and shipped them all off to Siberia.

Lenin was beside himself with fury at Kamenev. He wrote cautiously on March 29, 1915 that "they did not show sufficient firmness at the trial." But he pretended to believe that they had concealed their true convictions merely to trick the police. It was right to trick the police, "but to attempt to show solidarity with the social patriot, Mr. Yordansky,[20] as did Comrade Rosenfeld [Kamenev's real name], or to indicate disagreement with the Central Committee . . . this is impermissible from the standpoint of revolutionary Social Democracy." Yet, in the same article, Lenin praised his Duma deputies as having given an example of the use of parliamentarism for revolutionary purposes such as was unequaled in the entire history of socialism. In any case, Kamenev and the Bolshevik Duma deputies were silenced for the duration. Their joint statement with the Mensheviks on the day the Duma voted the war credits could henceforth be ignored, while Lenin could distinguish in his propaganda between the Bolshevik deputies, who had been arrested and sent to Siberia, and the Menshevik Duma deputies, whom the police left "untouched." For the rest of the war, the great wastes of Siberia would stand between the two fractions in the Duma and their yearning for unity,[21] while the real conduct and convictions of his Duma deputies and Russian Center could not trouble Lenin's defeatist propaganda.

5

Autocracy without an Autocrat

They say that he has a good heart. That wins a place in Paradise but not in history.
Alexander Herzen

This kingdom is without a head—
Like goodly buildings left without a roof.
Pericles, Act II, Scene 4

Kingdoms, like fish, begin to rot at the head.
Anonymous

Autocracy presupposes an Autocrat. In a time of social change and foreign challenge, he must be of firm will and strong purpose, with the energy to cope with all the problems which this type of government centralizes in his hands and the wit to choose able advisers and agents. One of the difficulties of monarchical legitimacy in general—much graver when the monarch is an absolute ruler—is that autocracy does not automatically engender autocrats. This is likely to be particularly true if the previous head of state was an autocrat also in his own household. History is full of accounts of witless, weakling, rebellious, or half-mad sons of powerful rulers, who, succeeding to the throne, undo their father's work, waste the substance of the kingdom, are subject to domination by unworthy favorites or regents, or are displaced by upstarts in a palace coup. If the basic forces which produced an autocracy in the first place remain in being, an interregnum or time of strife will be succeeded in the end by a new autocracy. But woe to the kingdom and its internal peace if the interregnum be a time of invasion by a powerful foreign foe or of rapid economic and social transformation.

Alexander III (1881–94) was narrow, stubborn, obstinate, vigorous, of fixed convictions and strong will, domineering in his household. His reign was peaceful. The revolutionary movement, having spent itself and its moral capital in its efforts to assassinate his father, was disorganized and helpless. Dissent was stilled, the monarch powerful, the people obedient, the treasury beginning at last to fill up. The firmness with which Alexander ruled surrounded him with an aura of majesty and power as old as tsarism, but which tended to dwindle and dissipate in the reigns of weak-willed and ambivalent tsars. In the nineteenth century there was a secular trend toward the diminution of this aura of power. Moreover, Alexander chose to follow unswervingly two disparate lines of policy which, now in retrospect, we can see to have been in inherent conflict with each other. He strove to transform Russia economically into a modern industrial country and to deny to the society thus awakening any voice in its destiny.

Few rulers of Russia either in the past or today, have been able to appreciate the wisdom of a policy that would combat revolution by generous reform. The policy is a hazardous one, unless the reformer is timely, magnanimous, farseeing, and knows how to win the assent of the articulate sectors of society. Even in his princeling years under the tutelage of Pobedonostsev, Alexander III had formed part of that faction at court which viewed with mistrust his father's reforms. With the shock of his father's murder, his reactionary stand was fixed for life. At the same moment, the popularity of the little band of revolutionaries melted away, while reverence for the tsar revived, so that he had no need of his father's dangerous, and to him distasteful, remedy.

The solid equestrian statue of Alexander III, which today still stands in the square before the old Nicholas Station in Leningrad, seems a fitting monument to the solidity with which he sat in the saddle and ruled over family and country. "The power I represent," it seems to say, "is granite, unshakable, and will last forever." Yet Alexander III was destined to be the last Autocrat. With his death the four-centuries-old autocracy really ended. The question which overshadowed the reign of his weakling son Nicholas was, what would now take autocracy's place?

Nicholas Alexandrovich was a man of reticent half-lights and shadows, by nature gentle, courteous, charming to those with whom he came into close contact, albeit often secretive and devious with them. By nurture he lacked will, was easily influenced, ignorant alike of the ways of men and affairs of state. In 1894 this twenty-six-year-old youth (still in every sense but the physical a youth) became Nicholas II, Tsar of All the Russias, inheriting the cares of a great empire which was hurtling forward into industrialism and stirring from the dreamless sleep in which his father had kept it.

He inherited, too, the ill-matched team of Pobedonostsev and Witte, political stasis and economic transformation. Pobedonostsev had been his father's chief tutor and spiritual guide in the maintenance of an unyielding regime; then he had confidently assumed the same functions with the son.[1] Witte was constructing the greatest railway in the world, the Trans-Siberian, a railway that would call into existence huge industries and cities, put hundreds of thousands of yesterday's peasants into workingmen's overalls, bring Russia's military power to Manchuria, Korea, and the shores of the Pacific. He inherited besides, although nobody had bothered to tell him of it, an agreement signed the year before his enthronement between the French General Staff and the Russian.[2]

He had been trained to be an obedient son, and would make a good husband and father, but he was not brought up to be the ruler of a great nation. In him had been planted the habit of obedience, not those of decision and command. He had been trained to stoic courage but not to initiative or audacity. Yet he had been indoctrinated with the belief that God was now putting upon his shoulders the burden of resolving everything, attending to everything, giving commands for everything, large and small, that might concern the Russian land and the inhabitants thereof.

Until his father's death, Nicholas had lived the quiet, invariant life of a high-born youth, free from care or the necessity to take thought, free to engage in all proper diversions, and, avoiding scandal, improper ones. He hunted, danced, skated, rode horseback, walked (all his life he was a swift and tireless walker with whom few could keep up), attended plays, ballets, operas, concerts, art exhibitions, parades, on at least two occasions lost as much as a hundred rubles at baccarat, and, at least once, drank so much that he had to be carried home. He danced with noble young ladies and cousins, sometimes to the point of exhaustion, took tea and meals now with one, now with another grand duchess aunt, wore various uniforms, witnessed field maneuvers, learned to sleep on a camp cot and in a tent. All these things, not excluding the gaming losses, the rare overindulgence in alcohol, and his brief affair with the prima ballerina, Kshesinskaya, were duly recorded in his diary. They were hardly enough to prepare a gentle, courteous, mild-mannered, obedient, intellectually smallish young man for the ardors of running single-handed the affairs of a great empire.

Nor was his formal education much. As befitted a scion of the royal house, he was not sent to school. Instead, he was lectured at by a succession of tutors, who were not allowed to ask questions to see how much their charge was getting from their talk. Old Pobedonostsev suspected that he was not getting much, but for him to ask the tsarevich questions was to infringe on royal etiquette.

When Nicholas's diary opens (he is then nearing twenty-two, having been born on May 6, 1868), he complacently observes that he has "finished his education once and for all." To be sure, two men from the General Staff continue to visit him once a week; their lectures on military science bore him, and he expresses the pleasure of a reluctant pupil let out of school when, later in the year, their talks cease.

It was traditional that the heir presumptive be initiated into affairs of state. However, his father thought him too childish to be entrusted with even minor responsibility. He was permitted to attend an occasional council meeting, but his diary shows that he was not interested in what was discussed.

When Witte, seeking royal sponsorship for his great railway building program, proposed that the then twenty-four-year-old heir should be made chairman of the Committee for the Construction of the Trans-Siberian, his father demurred: "But he is a mere boy, and his judgments are truly childish." That the old autocrat was not far wrong is suggested by the entries Nicholas made in his diary about his participation in state bodies. On February 18, 1892, he writes: "I received two French engineers who came concerning the building of the Trans-Siberian; they were both Senators." And on February 25: "For ten days now I have been a member of the Finance Committee, much honor but little pleasure. Before the meeting of the Committee of Ministers I received six members of this institution; I confess I did not even suspect it existed. We sat a long time, until 3:45, and because of that I was late and could not go to the exposition of the Academy."

The diary of Nicholas II is of the utmost importance to us, for it opens a window on his spirit. Enjoined to start it on January 1, 1890, he kept it faithfully all his life. Its fifty-one volumes, bound in leather, running from a hundred to over two hundred pages each, were among the papers that he was allowed to take with him when he was imprisoned.[3] In war, revolution, and prison, he did his best to keep up the entries, until within a few days of his death. Though the diary would be intolerably dull to read were it not a key to the spirit of the star-crossed ruler of a great land, he seemed to take a simple delight in keeping it. Poets assure us that the crowning sorrow is in adversity to remember happier things, but during his last year in prison, Nicholas writes: "Today is the anniversary of my dear Mamma and the twenty-third year of our marriage. . . . During morning tea I ran through my old 'Diaries'—it is an agreeable pastime."[4]

A meteorologist could learn more from Nicholas's diary than a historian. The average day's entry is only a half dozen lines, yet almost invariably one of them tells what time he got up, whether he slept well, whether the day was cold or warm, bright or dark, rainy or clear. A meteorologist could reconstruct Russia's weather from 1890 to the middle of 1918, when death ended the diary.

Meals are important, too: what time he took coffee, where and with which aunts or uncles and at what hour he had tea and dinner. Later, when as commander-in-chief at the Stavka, Nicholas is nominally running a great war, he is careful to record which officer-of-the-day, member of his suite, or "foreigner" (his word for members of the various Allied Military Missions delegated to the Stavka), he has had to tea or dinner.

As head of a behemoth state he becomes an industrious reader of all the papers and reports submitted to him. Night after night he "reads papers" until the early morning hours; though he read them without joy or enthusiasm, he was a conscientious worker and rarely went to bed until he had cleared his desk. He never read the great dailies which might have kept him informed as to the state of the nation, of public opinion and the world, absurdly limiting this side of his reading to a single reactionary and semiofficial paper, subsidized by him or his ministers to print what the government, or some wily courtier and meddler with a subsidy, wanted believed. Thus his misunderstandings of how the Russian people felt came back to him multiplied by their own dimmed echo in an unreadable and venial journal.

As the tsar's family grew, time permitting, he would read aloud each night to his wife and daughters. At the Stavka, lonely in his separation from his family, with long hours to spend alone, he read books, attended special movies, or found a member of his suite with whom to play dominoes, in each case reporting the fact in his letters to his wife. The high point of excitement, drawing exclamations of amazement from both royal spouses in their letters, came when, separately, they saw the serial cinema thriller, *The Mysterious Hand*. "We know at last," he writes, "who the *mysterious hand* is. Her cousin and fiancé, would you believe it? . . . tremendous excitement in the theater" (letter of December 7, 1916). And she writes back: "We also several times thought the bridegroom might be the mysterious hand—can imagine how excited all were" (December 8). Their absorption with this serial thriller is as good an index to their taste as are the ugly bibelots which still cover desk and tables and mantlepieces in the Winter Palace, now turned into a museum.

Their favorite novel, parts of which they could not reread without tears coming anew into their eyes and which is often mentioned in their letters to each other, is Florence Barclay's *Through a Postern Gate*, a saccharinely sentimental English novel whose hero is called "Little Boy Blue."[5] In the last year, when Nicholas and his family are under house arrest and confined under ever stricter prison regime, there is virtually nothing to record in his diary but the weather, what he is reading aloud to his wife and children, and what he is reading by himself. For the first time—perhaps because they were available in the mansion which served as prison—we get a list of books he is reading, which includes some

Russian besides English and French novels and detective stories. Now he reads Russian commentaries on the army and navy, the Christ trilogy of Merezhkovsky ("well written but produces a gloomy impression"), the works of Leskov, of Turgenev; and he finds most absorbing a multi-volume *Universal History* by Jaeger. In the circle of his family he continues to read the same meretricious, sentimental English and French novels and *romans policiers* which sustain the family circle to the end. But following the reading tastes of the royal couple has carried us ahead of our story. It is time for us to return to the diary of an earlier day to see how it reflects Nicholas's life as heir and as tsar in the first years after his coronation.

Cares of state have little space in these leather-bound notebooks, still less in the slender range of their emotional expression. Nicholas records the receiving of delegations or reports, but almost never records what the reports dealt with or what action they prompted. "Again Ministers and their reports," the diarist writes, perhaps impatiently, or perhaps merely matter-of-factly. If he goes hunting, however, he becomes remarkably precise and explicit, sets down the total bag (sometimes a veritable slaughter) and often his share in it. On January 3, 1892, he writes, "It is pleasant to shoot birds." On December 31, "We killed 667 with 1596 rifle shots. For my share I received 17 birds and 20 hares." The diarist has a simple love for the outdoors, records his walks, bicycle rides, hunts, reports sadly when the weather is too bad or cares of state too pressing for him to get out in the open. When he is too busy with a kingdom to go on frequent hunts, he does not forget to note that he shot some crows in the royal park, or went for a walk with his dog, Voron. One of the worst features of his last year in prison is that his walks are confined to the royal park of Tsarskoe Selo up to the sentry lines, and then, when he is taken to the Urals, to a small garden where he can only pace up and back, chop trees and saw wood. All these things, large and small, are told in short sentences, tied up into short paragraphs, virtually inarticulate as to thought and feeling, repeating the same trivia again and again on successive days in a style that resembles nothing so much as a language exercise book for beginners in a foreign tongue.

A year's end may get a few extra lines as he tries to take a backward glance over the gifts or blows its days have brought. Thus on the New Year's Eve that is about to usher in the year 1892, he writes:

> We spent the evening quietly at home and as usual we did not receive on the New Year. I cannot say that I regret that the year 1891 is over: it was positively fateful for all our family. The death of Aunt Olga, Uncle Nizi[6] and dear Alix, the sickness and long separation

from Georgi, and finally my incident in Otsu—all followed quickly one after the other. And the famine was added to our family misfortunes! Nothing to say [i.e., there's no question about it]! A difficult year! I pray God that the coming year 1892 should be like the earlier ones, those of the eighties. The only bright memory for me is the safe return home from Siberia and the glad reunion with the family in Fredensborg, and that was soon darkened by the terrible death of Alix!

The famine is mentioned as a pendant to family sorrows; the "incident in Otsu" is the near-assassination of Nicholas by a Japanese fanatic (of which more below). This imperturbability in the face of calamity and danger will characterize the diary throughout, as it always characterized its author. Some who approached him closely would consider this feature a lack of deep feeling, others saw in it irresoluteness masked by impenetrable reserve, others fatalism, yet others unassailable courage. But none would fail to note it.

As much to get him away from the ballerina, Kshesinskaya, whom he had met on maneuvers and with whom he had begun an affair, as to initiate him into affairs of state, Nicholas was sent, all unwilling, on a grand tour of Siberia, Japan, Indochina, Egypt, and Greece. This great journey with other princes and young grand dukes out for a good time[7] is reflected in the diary by the same banal and trivial entries on weather, heat, meals, minor pastimes, distances covered, times of anchoring and weighing anchor. In place of meals with aunts and uncles there are meals with khedives and princelings, in place of theater and ballet, Arabian "fantasies" and Egyptian dancers. One of the travel companions was Prince Ukhtomsky, who prided himself on being an Orientalist of sorts, an authority on Oriental art and religion, and a fanatical visionary of Russia's "mission" in Asia. The range of his expertise is suggested by one of the few mildly interesting entries about the journey:

> November 17. Saturday. At six we continued our voyage, and at noon for lunch we stopped at Luxor. We went to see the temple, then went on asses to the temple of Karnak. A striking massiveness. We rode to our consul where we took coffee. After dinner we went secretly to see the dances of the *almées*.[8] This time it was better; they undressed and did all kinds of steps with Ukhtomsky.

Insofar as the grand tour was meant to separate Nicholas from Kshesinskaya it was unnecessary, for the diary shows that at almost the same moment he fell in love with the German princess who was to become his wife. It was this love that made him reluctant to go on the journey.

Matilda Felixovna Kshesinskaya, daughter of a Polish ballet master and an excellent dancer, did not lose her connections with the court. She merely transferred her favors to Grand Duke Andrei Vladimirovich and later to Grand Duke Sergei Mikhailovich. Through the former she tried to control promotions in the world of theater and ballet; through the latter, who was in charge of the artillery, she managed to influence artillery contracts and artillery officer promotions. Though she retired from her position as prima ballerina in 1903, she continued to meddle in affairs of state for many years. Nicholas was not, as so many writers have suggested, the Maecenas who built her palace on the embankment near Peter-Paul Fortress, from which Lenin addressed the multitudes in 1917.[9]

The effect of the grand tour on the heir's political education was unfortunate. At Otsu, as we have noted, he narrowly escaped assassination thanks to the timely intervention of his cousin, Prince George of Greece, an incident which left him with an ingrained hatred of and contempt for the Japanese. From Ukhtomsky he learned that "there are no boundaries to Russia in Asia" and that "in the future Asiatic Russia will be simply synonymous with Asia." Thereafter, if we are to trust Witte's not always trustworthy memoirs, Nicholas referred to the Japanese, even in state papers, as *makaki* (monkeys).[10] He was the first tsar in Russia's history to have crossed Siberia (this part of the journey was made on horseback) and its vast extent made him dream that his unique contribution to Russia would lie in further expansion in Asia. This dream plus the "lessons" of Ukhtomsky and the near assassination at Otsu tended to make him vulnerable to the unsavory cabal of Bezobrazov, Alexeev, and Abaza, persuaded him to duplicity in his dealing with China, and promoted that unfortunate "little war" with Japan out of which came the Revolution of 1905 and the formation of the Petersburg General Strike Council or Soviet, which was so deeply remembered and so swiftly and automatically imitated in 1917.

Such then was the education of this heir to absolute and autocratic power. His journal shows that he had not learned to be interested in nor comprehend the business of state he was soon to take over. Old Pobedonostsev doubted that his pupil understood much of his solemn lectures on autocracy. According to the malicious Witte, the Procurator of the Holy Synod found his royal pupil "assiduous only in digging his finger in his nose."

Though he accepted much, he comprehended little of Pobedonostsev's doctrines. When he succeeded to the throne he at first saw nothing wrong in the congratulatory address of the Zemstvo of Tver (drafted by the liberal Rodichev), which expressed the not-improper "hope that the voice of the people and the expression of its wishes would be listened to . . . that the law would henceforward be respected and obeyed not only by the nation, but also by the representatives of the authority that rules it . . . and would stand above the changing views of the individual instruments of the supreme power."

His old tutor had to review sternly with him his dogmas: autocracy is a sacred trust; the only "voice of the people" is the voice of God expressed through the holy and beloved autocrat whom God has appointed; the law is the expression of the autocrat's will; the union of crown and people is unshakable; any shadow of representative government is a source of sickness in the kingdom. Only after the meaning of the congratulatory message—innocent enough in democratic lands but unacceptable to the last two tsars or to the present rulers of Russia—had been thus spelled out and critically clarified, did Pobedonostsev's royal pupil and sovereign summon up the wit to pronounce the message from Tver a "senseless dream," or the firmness to exclude its author from the reception and from the right to reside in St. Petersburg.[11]

The year 1894 seems like the preceding ones: uncles, aunts, cousins, playmates, dinners, teas, lunches, hunts, games, some reading, though the journal rarely says how it affected Nicholas. Less than a month before his accession to the throne, his father being critically ill, Nicholas records an epic battle with Prince George of Greece, fought with chest-nuts in the royal park. "We started in front of the house and ended up on the roof." A few days later, another battle, this time with pine cones. The tsar is dying, but the tsar-to-be is still a boy, pelting his cousin with pine cones.

Even with the cares of a giant kingdom on his head, the tone of the diary does not greatly change. Despite the meager notice of large events that sometimes breaks into its pages, the journal continues to have the air of the smallish thoughts and deeds of a gentle little private person who has somehow been thrust, like the protagonist of a Kafka novel, into the midst of affairs, the meanings of which escape him but which nonetheless crowd in on him until they bring about his doom.

> 20th October. Friday. My God, my God, what a day. The Lord has called to Him our adored, dear, warmly beloved Papa. One's head spins, one doesn't wish to believe it—so unbelievable is the terrible reality. . . . It was the death of a saint! Lord, help us in these difficult days! Poor dear Mama! The services were at 9:30 in the evening—in the same bedroom! I felt stunned. My dear Alix had a pain in her leg again!

Nicholas Alexandrovich, aged twenty-six, has become Tsar of All the Russias. Now one expects to learn something of how it feels to take an immense land with 150 million people under one's absolute and personal rule. But the diary, as before, remains the diary of a private man. Were it not for "beloved Alix," who begins to fill up more and more of its pages, and the occasional notice of a minister who insists on giving a report, it would still seem the diary of a boy, not the head of a household and a kingdom.

If we look to see how his public duties are seen by this private person, now the ruler of Russia, we find such entries as these:

> 11th November. Friday. In the morning walked in the garden. The darkness all day was terrible. After breakfast had reports from Witte and Krivoshein. Then received a second series of Governors General and Army Commanders. Lunch with Mama, Opapa,[12] and Georgi (Greek), for the others all left. Received the whole Senate in the ballroom. Walked and bicycled in the garden. Little to read [i.e., few reports], therefore spent the time marvellously with dear Alix until dinner. The two adjourning rooms are being furnished. After dinner we stayed with Mama until 10:30.

> 12th November. Saturday. Quite a tiring day: from 10 began the reports—Dehn, Count Vorontsov, Uncle Alexis and Chikachev. Then all the Atamans of the Cossack Troops presented themselves. Lunched with Mama, Opapa, and Aunt Alix. At 3 received in the Winter Palace a mass of deputies from all Russia, up to 460 all at once in the Nikolaevsky Hall. Returned with Xenia to Anichkov [Palace], walked in the garden when it was quite dark. My dear Alix sat with me before and after tea. At 7:45 went to Uncle Paul's for supper—Alix and her sisters were there, then Erni and Henry. We stayed until 10:30 and then returned to Anichkov, where my adorable Alix spent with me yet another little hour.

If we run on through the pages until the tsar has become thirty-eight and thirty-nine and watch how the great events of Bloody Sunday, 1905, or the promulgation and then the dissolution of the Duma are filtered through the screen of his preoccupation with weather, military deputations and parades, lunch and tea and dinner, this is what we find:

> 9th January [January 20, 1905, New Style, i.e., "Bloody Sunday"]. A difficult day! In Petersburg occurred serious disorders in consequence of the workingmen's desire to go to the Winter Palace. The army had to shoot in various parts of the city, there were many killed and wounded. Lord, how painful and difficult! Mama came to us straight from the city to lunch. Ate with everybody. Took a walk with Misha. Mama remained all night.

10th January. Monday. Today nothing special happened in the city. There were reports. Uncle Alex at breakfast. Received a deputation of Ural Cossacks who came with caviar. Walked. Took tea at Mama's. To unify the actions for stopping disorders in Petersburg decided to name Trepov Governor General of the Capital and Province. In the evening I met with him, Mirsky and Gesse. Dabich (orderly) dined with us.

6th August. Sunday. The weather is wonderful. Today was promulgated the constituting of a State Duma. At 12 on the Plaza in front of the palace took place a splendid parade of the Preobra-zhensky Regiment and First Battery of Mikhail Pavlovich. Gadon managed the parade very well. Named Obolensky commander of my company and Col. Svechin adjutant. Returned home at 3:15 and showed little Alexei [his baby son] to Gadon and some of the Preobrazhentsi. Read until 8. Rode with Misha (orderly) as a surprise to the Ulan stables, ate with the officers and spent some quite pleasant hours with the regimental family.

7th August. Sunday. [the epoch-making Duma already forgotten]. Got home at 4 a.m. Gadon accompanied me on horseback. Slept until 10. At 11 went to services. Breakfasted on the farm. We played tennis. After tea received report from Gadon. Andre (orderly) dined with us. Busy the whole evening. It began to rain.

In April 1906, the First Duma convened and began a fight to force Nicholas to name a cabinet responsible to it rather than to him.[13] Less than three months later, without preliminary notice to the Duma president, Nicholas posted a decree dissolving the First Duma. All Russia held its breath waiting to see if that would bring revolution, or reaction, or a new and different type of Duma, or another equally unmanageable one. Here is how Nicholas records the dissolution and the change of chairmen of the Ministers' Council, all his feelings being expressed in *a single exclamation point*:

7th July. Friday. A very busy morning. Went to the breakfast for the Siberian Army Corps, which took place on the Farm a half hour late. There was a storm and suffocating heat. We went walking together. I received Goremykin. I signed the ukaz on the dissolution of the Duma! We had supper at Olga and Petya's. Read all evening.

8th July. Saturday. A busy, tiring day, reminding me of the 17th of October last year [when he signed the Constitutional Manifesto and granted an amnesty]. In the morning there were reports. From 5 to

> 8:30 talked with Goremykin, who is leaving [this is the first time Goremykin learned that he had been dismissed], and with Stolypin, named in his place. Just the two of us ate on the balcony. In the evening, read.

Only the final tragic moment of his abdication in 1917—tragic for him and for Russia—gets a report as detailed as the dinners, hunts, and parades, wringing from him for once *an entire sentence* charged with feeling.

> 2nd March [O.S., 1917]. Thursday. In the morning Russky came and read his inordinately long telephone conversation with Rodzianko. According to his words, the situation in Petrograd is such that for the present a Duma Ministry would not be able to do anything because the Workingmen's Soviet as representative of the Social Democratic party is fighting it. My abdication is supposed to be necessary. Russky communicated this conversation to Headquarters and Alexeev to all the commanding generals. At 2 p.m. all the answers had arrived. The thing is that this must be done in order to save Russia and keep peace in the Army and at the Front. I consented. From Headquarters was sent a draft of a manifesto. In the evening Guchkov and Shulgin arrived, and I discussed the matter with them, and gave them the reworked and signed manifesto. At 1 o'clock at night I left Pskov with a heavy feeling about what I had just been through. All around, treason, cowardice and deceit.

Those last six words are the strongest expression of emotion in the diary. The next morning, with Russia driven before a storm, plunging ahead into an impenetrable mist, with a dual power in Petrograd and no power at all in the rest of the country, the ex-tsar's entry begins:

> 3rd March. Friday. Slept long and soundly. . . . Clear frosty weather. . . .

All who came in contact with Tsar Nicholas testify to his innate charm, good manners, graciousness to inferiors, and imperturbable calm. But none testified to his majesty, nor to any aura of power surrounding him. Even the best disposed, those who served and counseled and strove to honor him as befitted their notion of his office and their own duty, have left both witting and unwitting testimony to his weak will, his air of insignificance, his isolation from Russian society, the ease with which he was swayed from his purposes and conceptions by members of his "kitchen cabinet," his unfitness to discharge the multitudinous duties and wield the vast powers that inhered in his autocratic position.

The best Pobedonostsev could say for his royal pupil and subsequent sovereign was: "He has a naturally bright mind, is shrewd, quickly grasps the meaning of what he hears, but only understands the significance of some isolated fact, without connection with the rest, without appreciating the interrelation of all other pertinent facts, events, trends, occurrences. He sticks to his insignificant, petty point of view."[14]

One of the elder statesmen around him, A. A. Polovtsev, a member of his father's Imperial Council and a state secretary from 1883 to 1892, wrote in his diary: "The Emperor lacks real education or experience in affairs of state and most particularly any strength of character. Any one can persuade him to change his mind. The Emperor's uncle, Sergei, has the greatest influence on him, but Sergei is in every sense of the word a worthless individual. . . ."[15]

Vladimir I. Gurko (not to be confused with his brother, General Vasilii I. Gurko, who has also left memoirs) noted the "timidity" of the young tsar before his uncles and the ministers he inherited from his father. Gurko narrates episodes in which the emperor wanted to do something on his own initiative, appoint someone to a minor post or send out a personal representative to look into a situation, but let himself be intimidated and overruled by his elders.

> Repeated frustrations of this nature tended to make him stubborn, and in the last years of his reign his insistence upon petty matters, usually concerning individuals, assumed a pathological character. The sentence, *This is my wish!* was often on his lips. . . . As the years went by, the Tsar gradually became accustomed to his role as absolute ruler. But by nature he had no appreciation of the unlimited authority he possessed.[16]

The incongruity between the vastness of his powers and his sense of his own insignificance made Nicholas peculiarly vulnerable. When the Bolsheviks published his diaries and his correspondence with his wife, it became overpoweringly clear that it was the empress who had made up his mind for him on so many things, stiffened his will, instilled in him her ambitions, vanities, jealousies, fears, implanted her intense and narrow views on the nature and function of autocracy. It was she who had been jealous of the influence of his mother and uncles, she who had invested petty matters—in neurotic fashion—with large symbolic significance, thus increasing his natural inability to distinguish between trivia and things of consequence.

His gentle remonstrances often showed that he had a natural inclination to listen to any good counsel sincerely and disinterestedly given. But no sooner did he let Alexandra know such things than she redoubled her efforts, made him suspicious of the motives of his counselors and their advice, played on his doubts of himself, his distrust of those whose larger stature dwarfed him, and—trump cards in her hand—on his deep love for her, for "Baby" and for Russia.

The needs of autocracy with its heavy burdens, and the postulates of constitutional logic,[17] alike required that only large questions be settled by the monarch, with details left to the competence and care of the various ministers and civil servants. But Nicholas was constantly bewildering, upsetting, even alienating, the most devoted of them by reversing his approvals, bypassing his ministers, taking measures in direct contradiction to his own orders and ukazes.

In his father's time, everyone had stood in awe of the huge physical stature, massive dignity, assurance, power, and majesty of the emperor. But Nicholas never succeeded in making anyone feel such awe. He was more open to reasonable argument than his father, so much so, indeed, that the words of the latest comer would efface those of the preceding one to whom he might already have given his word; and the empress, the most devoted but one of the least wise of his advisers, too often had the proverbial woman's last word. He did not have the art of giving commands so that his ministers would feel a zeal to perform them, nor the wit to know when he had settled a matter, nor to recognize that two commands, often entrusted to different persons, might be in conflict. He was sincerely grateful to those who had the courage to tell him unpleasant things, yet, never liking to hear anything unpleasant, he might thereafter be cool toward the bearer of bad tidings. Almost never would he disagree openly. When he disapproved of an unwelcome counsel or an unwelcome counsellor, he would listen in silence, showing his disagreement and displeasure only by averting his gaze from the eyes of the speaker like a small boy being scolded, or by gazing out the window. The project against which a minister had argued so wisely he would continue to cherish, often carrying it out in devious ways through personal emissaries behind the back of the minister. The memoirs of those who worked with the tsar all testify to the fact that they constantly thought they had convinced him when they had not, that he never argued, never rebuked or showed anger, could not bear to say unpleasant things—beyond the one formula which might not have been unpleasant at all had it been reserved for matters of large scope: "This is my will."

On the other hand, he never formed a warm personal friendship with even the most loyal and devoted of his advisers. Indeed, as so many have recorded, the longer he worked with a minister, the less friendly was Nicholas's attitude toward him and the more eager he became to break with him. He was readily attracted to new views and new men, but soon wearied of persisting in any of the ideas or continuing with the new adviser. Nicholas remained in the shadow, seemingly without desires, without initiative, without resolve in large matters; yet the more initiative a minister showed, the more it seemed to the insecure Nicholas and his empress that the servant was usurping some of the power that the master somehow should be wielding. He could never, as Gurko has so well put it, distinguish clearly between "administration and determination of policy."[18] His quarrels with his ministers, or rather the silent misunderstandings, came precisely in the field of petty administration, personnel, and minor decision, matters which a wise autocrat would leave to his ministers and recognize as being in their field of competence and duty.

The only field in which he left a minister free to carry out practical and detailed tasks without petty bypassing and interference was finance. Here he recognized his incompetence and ignorance of matters large and especially small, hence Kokovtsev and Witte as Ministers of Finance seem to have enjoyed Nicholas's unswerving and unquestioning support, and Kokovtsev even some measure of affectionate gratitude. The same recognition of his own incapacity made him accord Stolypin complete support as Minister of the Interior in a time of storm. But the moment Witte, Stolypin, and Kokovtsev became, as each did in turn, chairman of the Council of Ministers, Nicholas's whole attitude changed and they began to lose favor in proportion to the initiative and energy they displayed. This explains why a servile and doddering old chairman like Goremykin, who showed no initiative, merely insisting that the ministers had no other function than to carry out the will of this will-less man, was called to head the Council of Ministers again and again, each time after a strong and able chairman had been ousted.

This relation of unconscious jealousy toward the able men that he himself placed at the head of various branches of administration explains the tendency of the emperor to have recourse to his "kitchen cabinet" and the suggestions of all sorts of irresponsible persons, not vested with any institutional power. To Nicholas it seemed that those who stood thus aside from the official administration of the state could not infringe upon his prerogatives; when he followed their advice he was convinced that he was directly exercising his own will. This explains the whole succession of shady characters from Bezobrazov and Meshchersky to Vyrubova and Rasputin, as well as Nicholas's increasing readiness to follow the counsels of the empress and the cabal with which she surrounded herself.

Though Nicholas felt it his duty to insist on the limitlessness of his power, power as such did not really attract him. When his father died he had been dreaming of becoming Commander of the Hussar Bodyguard Regiment, which was his favorite. His grief, his diary shows, was genuine when he had to give up this dream of the command of a cavalry regiment for the rule of an empire. There was nothing hypocritical about his viewing himself as a Job burdened with unwanted cares. His sorrow at his accession to power was a measure of both his sense of values and his fitness for his duties. Most at ease and happiest in the simple pleasures of cavalry barracks life, among officers of the guard he "breathed more freely." He enjoyed their gatherings, paid them surprise visits, treated them with hail-fellow-well-met cordiality, liked their free ways, their informality, their comradeship, their jests, the freedom from court etiquette that he could permit himself among them.

When power was "thrust" upon him, it was ordained by God, and will it or no, it was his sacred trust. His attitude toward his power, as Gurko has observed, was one of principle. He held that autocracy was the only form of government appropriate to Russia; that having become God's anointed ruler he could not evade or diminish his responsibility whatever his natural inclinations; and that he must keep the power intact as he had inherited it from his father and must hand it down intact in turn to his successor.

Yet in his heart he knew his own incapacity, and, as we have seen, turned first to his father's counsellor, Pobedonostsev; his father's empress, his mother; and his father's brothers, the grand dukes who were his uncles.

Count A. A. Bobrinsky, who served Nicholas long and faithfully and became in time his Minister of Agriculture (1916), wrote in the privacy of his diary this early note: "The Emperor remains a zero, a sphinx. His individuality is not shown in anything. It has been said that on more than one occasion he has interrupted the report of a minister by asking him to wait until he could consult his *matushka*!"

Matushka is of course Nicholas's mother, the dowager empress, Maria Fyodorovna, and Bobrinsky's remark refers to Nicholas's early rule, as does Polovtsev's remark that he was under the thumb of his Uncle Sergei. The history of Nicholas's twenty-odd-year reign may be written in terms of the gradual displacement of these more experienced counsellors by his wife, with a concomitant narrowing of the horizon and knowledge of affairs on which his decisions were based.

Maria Fyodorovna's long years at court had on the whole made her an able and disinterested adviser to her son, but as much cannot be said of all the grand dukes, his uncles and cousins and younger brothers. The institution of grand duke ("great prince," in Russian) was falling into decay. Under Nicholas's grandfather, princes of the royal blood still held important posts, including ministerial ones, and were trusted as the eyes and ears and executants of the tsar's will. They made despotism a family affair and thus made easier the exacting trade of master of everything. But under Nicholas's father, their role had declined, being increasingly limited to commanding posts in the army and navy. What with declining functions, a looseness in morals which excited the indignation of Nicholas's prudish empress, morganatic marriages which lowered the status of some of them, and quarreling and gossiping wives, the position of the grand dukes continued to decline under Nicholas. Moreover, there was no love lost between the empress and the grand dukes. It is probably her influence which explains the uncharacteristic letter of Nicholas II to his Uncle Vladimir, written on November 26, 1896, when he had been reigning only two years: "The whole fault lies in my stupid goodness. With the sole desire of avoiding quarrels which injure family relations, I give in again and again, until I finally appear to be a fool, without will-power or character."[19]

Yet he did not break the hold of his uncles upon him, still less that of his mother, until the birth of his son. In 1905 it was his uncles who persuaded him to be absent from the Winter Palace when Gapon marched at the head of his procession to petition the tsar. Uncle Sergei was then Governor General of Moscow (until Kallyaev that very year ended Sergei Alexandrovich's life with a well-aimed bomb). And then D. F. Trepov, Uncle Sergei's police chief and principal adviser, was made Governor General of St. Petersburg.[20]

At the other extreme of the grand ducal spectrum was Nicholas II's cousin, Grand Duke Nikolai Nikolaevich. Though it was he and his wife who first introduced Rasputin to court circles, Nikolai Nikolaevich represented all that was best in the tradition of useful service by princes of the royal blood. As commander-in-chief of the army in World War I, he compelled the admiration of Ludendorff and Hindenburg and aroused the envious fear of the tsaritsa that her husband was being displaced in the consciousness of the folk as the great war leader. In 1905 he had counseled Nicholas to yield to the demand for a Duma and a constitution. Though he would never disobey his sovereign, he came close to it when Nicholas II demanded that he put his growing popularity and undoubted administrative talents to use as "military dictator" at the most critical moment in 1905, to suppress the disorders. Nikolai Nikolaevich answered that if the distasteful task were thrust upon him, he would commit suicide in the presence of his sovereign, whereupon the tsar issued his Constitutional Manifesto of October 17, 1905. The tsaritsa never forgave the grand duke for "extorting" a constitution from her husband.[21] The second count in her indictment of Cousin Nikolai was that, having discovered the "man of God," Rasputin, he later turned from him and tried to warn the tsar that Rasputin was dissolute and his influence evil. She wrote Nikolasha off as "one who has abandoned a man of God." To make matters worse, Nikolai was deeply religious and his headquarters at the General Staff during the war were adorned with many icons, but when Rasputin offered to go to the staff to bless its work and hang yet another sacred icon, the grand duke wired in his bluff language, "Come and we'll hang!" Rasputin understood the grim jest and stayed away.

The Grand Duke Nicholas was a physical giant who completely dwarfed his insignificant-looking cousin, the tsar. He was more popular with the army, in the country, and among foreign diplomats and officers than his sovereign. Sir Bernard Pares, who interrupted his labors as a historian to act as a liaison officer during the war, writes of him: "He was a man, perhaps as we understand it, the only man in the imperial family."[22] The empress became convinced—quite unjustly—that Nikolai was planning to replace the reigning tsar as Nicholas III. Her letters to her husband contain continual incitements against "Nikolasha." She urges the emperor to visit the fronts, where his charm would offset the grand duke's popularity and give God's blessing to the army's efforts. She urges him to take the supreme command away from his cousin and exercise it himself. She writes venom about the grand duke's wife, a Montenegrin princess, who repays her in kind. In the end, just before the tsar fell, there were indeed those who dreamed of replacing Nicholas II by his son, with the grand duke as regent, but having examined all the correspondence and the memoirs of the principal figures who dreamed of this change, I cannot find any evidence that Nikolai Nikolaevich lent himself to the plan. He was a highly emotional and excitable man, who, according to Witte, "looked upon his sovereign as God."[23] Nikolai wrote his last letter to the tsar with obvious sincerity and affection, signing himself, *Nikolasha, your faithful subject who loves you with all his heart and with all his soul.*[24] The tsar continued to like his cousin and admire him as a "great soldier," seeking in vain to placate his wife with quietly favorable reports in response to her incitements. Her resentment and jealousy, however, ripened into implacable hatred when Nikolasha, just before the end, undertook the most ungrateful and difficult task of all, to warn his Sovereign that not only Rasputin, but the empress herself, was a source of bad advice and evil influence upon him, which she picked up from and transmitted to those who surrounded her.

The power behind the throne of Tsar Nicholas II was always a woman. During the first half of his reign it was his mother; during the second half, his wife. The watershed date is August 12, 1904, when a male heir was born, although the change began a little earlier and became more apparent and complete, and more unfortunate in nature, after it was discovered that the young heir suffered from hemophilia, and would have continual need of miracles to save him at every crisis from dangers with which no scientific expedients could cope.

As late as August 15, 1903, when Nicholas was dismissing Witte and appointing Pleske as Minister of Finance, he said: "I hear nothing but good of him. My mother likes him very much, too." But six months later, when he named Kokovtsev to take Pleske's place, it was of the young empress's approval that he spoke to the new appointee, bidding him present himself at once to the empress, who was waiting in an adjoining room. That she was even then beginning to think of herself as the co-ruler of Russia is suggested by her words to Kokovtsev: "I wished to see you and tell you that both the Tsar and I beg you always to be quite frank with us and to tell us the truth."[25]

In the last months of Nicholas's reign, Kokovtsev—and other loyal advisers of Nicholas—became convinced that the tsaritsa was actually listening in on the interviews between the tsar and his ministers, for they noted now a convenient curtain behind which she might hide, or a door left slightly ajar toward which the tsar would glance compulsively from time to time.[26]

Of those last days, Sir Bernard Pares writes:

> The main telephone in the palace was in the Empress' drawing room, where she sat at her writing-desk, staring at a portrait of Marie Antoinette which stood facing her. From this room had been constructed a plain wooden staircase which, passing through the walls, debouched onto a high platform at the back of her husband's audience room, concealed by a curtain, behind which she could lie on a couch and listen to the reports of his visitors.

Sir Bernard cites Ambassador Buchanan to the same effect, then adds this personal note: "These arrangements had been preserved when I visited these apartments in 1936 and 1937. That they were there at the time [1916 and early 1917] I have verified from Kerensky, who, as Minister of Justice of the Revolution, was almost the first to penetrate into the palace. He himself mounted this staircase."[27]

II
Lenin and Leninism

6

Lenin and
Inessa Armand

In 1924, immediately after Lenin died, the Central Committee of his party called upon all who had a shred of writing from his hand to deposit it in the party's archives. The holders hastened to comply. All his letters were ostensibly published in three substantial volumes, supplemented by items in a number of "Miscellany" (*Sbornik*) volumes. Not one letter to or from Inessa Armand appeared in that flood of Leniniana.

On February 27, 1939, Krupskaia died. Four months after her death, *Bolshevik* (No. 13, July 1939) published the first of two letters from Lenin to Inessa on the "woman question." The letters were not so much an expression of Lenin's views as a comment on Inessa Armand's. Planning in the course of her Bolshevik work with "working women" to write a brochure addressed to them, Inessa had dutifully submitted her outline to Lenin. Among her programmatic demands for woman's rights she included "free love." The Marx-Lenin Institute has not chosen to publish any of her letters to Lenin, although from a French Communist, Jean Fréville, who was permitted to consult her letters to Lenin when writing an authorized biography of Inessa, we know that the Institute has them.[1] Something of the nature of her plan, however, we can glean from Lenin's letter concerning it, in which he quotes hers. But first we must consider his letters to Inessa Armand as a whole.[2]

The first thing that strikes the Russian reader of Lenin's letters to Inessa is the use of the intimate pronoun *ty* in addressing her, in place of the usual polite second person pronoun *vy*. To the English-speaking reader it is hard to convey how unusual, and how intimate, it is for an

Reprinted with permission from the *Slavic Review* (March 1963).

educated Russian to address a woman as *ty*. Or for that matter to address another man thus, unless they were childhood intimates, companions from youth, members of the same family, or much closer to each other than adult friends and socialist comrades. In all the six-hundred-odd published letters of Lenin, except for his mother, his two sisters, and his wife, Inessa is the only woman to whom he ever wrote *ty*. Only two men ever received a letter with the intimate personal address. Both were comrades of his youth, one being Martov, for whom, as Krupskaia testifies in her *Memories of Lenin*, he felt a lifelong attachment.[3] Yet there is only one letter extant in which he wrote *ty* to Martov. After their first political disagreement, he never again addressed him except as *vy*.[4] The other was Krzhizhanovsky, who in the nineties lived near him as a fellow exile in distant Siberia along the Yenisei, for weeks on end sharing with him the same cabin. With Krzhizhanovsky, too, after the latter crossed him once in politics, though he afterward returned to unquestioning discipleship, Lenin never again used anything but *vy*.[5]

Neither Krassin, who made his bombs in 1905 and became his Commissar of Trade in 1918, nor Bogdanov, who was his chief lieutenant after the break with *Iskra*, nor Zinoviev, who held the same place from 1908 to 1917, nor Bukharin, whom he called the "darling of the party," nor Sverdlov nor Stalin, who each in turn became his chief organization man, ever received a letter that used the intimate pronoun. Sparing as most educated Russians are in the use of *ty* with each other, Lenin was even more so than most, always maintaining a subtle distance between himself and the closest and most useful of his disciples. Nor, to mention the women who served him longest and most faithfully and for whose work he was most grateful, did he ever write *ty* to Stasova, Ludmila Stal, Lilina Zinoviev, Alexandra Kollontai, or Angelica Balabanoff. Any of them would have been astonished had he done so.

In the letters to Inessa Armand, too, there is a sudden change from *ty* to *vy*, but not out of cooling friendship or disagreement. In his first published letter to Inessa Armand Lenin uses the intimate form, and he continues to do so until the day war is declared. Then, with wartime censors opening letters on every frontier, he drops the telltale *ty* for the more formal *vy*, for Lenin was conspirative even in this. Otherwise there is no change in tone.[6]

Inessa Armand was a dedicated, romantic heroine, who seemed to come out of the pages of Chernyshevsky's *What Is to Be Done?*—Lenin's favorite revolutionary novel, as it was Inessa's. Indeed, Chernyshevsky's novel was the chief instrument of the conversion of Inessa to socialism. The true story of her life has been obscured by the accounts of those who did not know her intimately and by an understandable reticence on the part of those who did. The sketch of her in the *Bol'shaia sovetskaia entsiklopediia* is meager, omits what is most important in her career, and is mistaken even as to the date of her birth and true name.

The encyclopedia gives her birth date as 1875, her name as Inessa Fedorovna (i.e., Inessa, daughter of Fedor), and her maiden name as Stephanie. Actually, she was born in Paris in 1879, of a French father and a Scottish mother, both music hall artists, and was christened Elizabeth d'Herbenville. The Inessa by which she came exclusively to be known was the name she assumed in Russia for party work. So much did she become known by it (though she sometimes used the pseudonym Blonina instead) that when she died, the obituary written by Krupskaia for *Pravda* was headed with the single word: "Inessa." The maiden name Stephanie given her in the encyclopedia is an obvious misunderstanding of her father's stage name, for in the French theater he was billed as Stéphen. The name Petrova or Petrovna, given by some sources, is the pseudonym she used when she appeared in Brussels on Lenin's behalf in July 1914, to defy the International Socialist Bureau, which was trying to unify the Russian Socialist movement. It was as Comrade Petrova that she delivered in French the speech Lenin had written for her; it was as Petrova that the police agent present reported on her. It was an appropriate name, for it is derived from *petra*, "rock," and signifies that she, as a good Leninist, was "rock hard" and would stand up against all the great men of the International, firm as a rock.

Her childhood was that of a daughter of people of the theater. Her father, Pécheux d'Herbenville, was a comedian and singer, known on the stage as Stéphen. Her mother sang in French and gave singing and piano lessons. As a child Inessa learned to speak both her native French and her mother's English tongue with equal fluency. The world of music and the stage were her home. When her father died and her mother could no longer support three fatherless children by teaching or music-hall work, the girl, Elizabeth, was taken to Russia by a French aunt and her English maternal grandmother, both of whom secured positions, as was the fashion of the day, tutoring in French and English respectively the children of a wealthy Russian industrialist of French descent, Evgenii Armand, a textile manufacturer in Pushkino, thirty miles from Moscow. Here the young girl grew up in a family with liberal views. She was accepted on an equal footing with the children of the Armand family.

At fourteen she too was provided with a tutor, who turned out to be a man of advanced, perhaps revolutionary, ideas. These she did not understand, but they excited her imagination. She mastered Russian, was introduced into the Orthodox church, and shared the interests that prevailed in educated circles in the closing years of nineteenth-century Russia. By now she spoke faultless German and Russian as well as French and English—polyglot talents that would make her invaluable to Lenin. Her aunt, who had been a teacher of singing and piano, taught her to be a virtuoso at the piano, another talent that Lenin was to prize. At eighteen she married Alexander Evgenevich Armand, the manufacturer's second son, slightly older than she. The couple moved to the nearby estate of the Armands at Eldigino, and later to Moscow. She lived with her husband for many quiet, apparently happy years, bearing him five children, three boys and two girls. But this substantial family, in the words of Krupskaia's memoir, "did not prevent her from going her own path all the same, and becoming a revolutionary Bolshevik."[7]

It was her husband's older brother, Boris Evgenevich, who by word and example first steered her course toward "advanced ideas." He took the side of the workingmen in his father's factory, tried to organize them, and was questioned by the police when they traced to him the ownership of a mimeograph machine on which his unsigned leaflets were being reproduced. It was most likely he who put into his sister-in-law's hands Chernyshevsky's novel, Chto delat'?, on whose utopian heroes and heroine, Vera Pavlovna, Inessa sought to model her own life.[8]

Like so many idealistic women of her generation, Inessa was not content with the sheltered career of wife and mother. Like her heroine, she too wanted to be "socially useful," to help the less fortunate members of her sex. She tried running the farm on her husband's estate, then teaching and doing works of charity. In time, the problem of prostitution became her obsession. She sought to redeem these unhappy women from their life of degradation, but was shocked to find them suspicious, unashamed, unwilling to be "redeemed." Since one of her sources of inspiration was Lev Tolstoy, she went to this fountainhead of wisdom for counsel. His answer ("Nothing will come of your work. It was so before Moses, it was so after Moses. So it was, so it will be")[9] turned her away from Tolstoyanism to a more exclusive dedication to Chernyshevsky. She would imitate Vera Pavlovna and her "uncommon" friends and tutors in their efforts to transform the structure of society. Thus she would put an end, she thought, to the hateful institution which had existed before Moses and which neither the Laws given to Moses nor the coming of Christ had been able to change. It was with "the woman problem in its relation to socialism" that she concerned herself for the rest of her life. She left husband and children, apparently without bitter scenes or rancor (just as Vera Pavlovna left Lopukhov). Later she sent for her two youngest to live with her abroad. But unlike her model, who was eager to earn her own way, Inessa continued to receive support from her husband all her life—until Lenin's seizure of power put an end to the fortune of the Armands in Russia.

In 1904 at the age of twenty-five, Inessa made her final break with her husband (they sometimes met as friends as occasion permitted thereafter) and went to Sweden to study feminism at the feet of Ellen Key. In Stockholm's Russian colony she got to know of Lenin's *Chto delat'?*, a title that reverberated in her spirit. In his organizational principles, his doctrine of the elite or vanguard, his hard line, she must have felt an echo of Rakhmetov, the "rigorist" of Chernyshevsky's novel. Thus before she met Lenin, she became his admirer and a Leninist.

An organizing mission for the Bolsheviks sent her back to Russia, where she landed almost immediately in prison, on January 6, 1905. The October Manifesto of the tsar, promising freedom and a constitution, contained an amnesty provision for politicals which released her. On April 9, 1907, she was arrested a second time for Bolshevik activities in the armed forces. Her husband furnished bail, but she landed in jail once more while awaiting trial, and from jail was deported by administrative order to Archangel Province in Russia's far north for a two-year period. She managed to flee abroad before her term was quite over.

Early in 1910 she went to Paris where she first got to know the Ulianovs. Lenin, Zinoviev, and Kamenev (then the *troika*) had just moved to Paris in December 1909. The leading Menshevik exiles were there too, and many Socialist Revolutionaries, so that Paris possessed a big Russian colony, in which Inessa soon assumed a leading position. She came with her two youngest children, a boy, André, and a girl, Ina. "She was a very ardent Bolshevik," writes Krupskaia, "and soon gathered our Paris crowd around her."

Those who knew her then remember her somewhat strange, nervous, slightly asymmetrical face, unruly, dark chestnut hair, great hypnotic eyes, and inextinguishable ardor of spirit. She had a wider culture than any other woman in Lenin's circle (at least until Kollontai became an adherent of his during the war), a deep love of music, above all of Beethoven, who became Lenin's favorite too. She played the piano like a virtuoso, was fluent in five languages, was enormously serious about bolshevism and work among women, and possessed personal charm and an intense love of life to which almost all who wrote of her testify.[10] When Lenin met her, she had just turned thirty.

In the course of his factional war with the Vperyodist Bolsheviks,[11] who had set up a party school in Gorky's home in Capri, Lenin rejected their invitation to teach, promoted (unwittingly aided by a police agent) a split in their student body, and opened a rival school in Longjumeau, near Paris. Inessa rented a large building there and set up lodgings and a dining room for the students. The Ulianovs dined there too. As a rare mark of Lenin's confidence, she was permitted to alternate with him in the course on political economy. The rest of the faculty were Zinoviev and Kamenev. No other Bolshevik woman had ever been so honored.

The Ulianovs generally held everyone at arm's length, with Krupskaia as self-appointed guardian to see that Lenin's work and privacy were not interfered with. But by 1911 it had become obvious to the little circle of Russian émigrés that Inessa had somehow breached the barrier: "He was often seen with her at a café on the Avenue d'Orléans. . . ." It struck even so unobservant a person as the French Socialist-Bolshevik, Charles Rappoport. Lenin, he wrote, "avec ses petits yeux mongols épiait toujours cette petite française. . . ."[12]

The Ulianovs now moved to 4, Rue Marie-Rose, and Inessa and her children to Number 2 of the same street. (The houses are still standing, in good condition, with a plaque outside Number 4 telling the passerby that Lenin once lived there.) "The house grew brighter when Inessa entered it," Krupskaia was to write six years after Inessa's death.[13]

In 1912 Lenin completed the final split in the Social Democratic party by designating his Bolshevik conference in Prague an official party congress and declaring Martov, Axelrod, Plekhanov, Trotsky, and their followers "outside the party" until they submitted to his "Congress." He moved to Krakow, in Austrian Poland, to be nearer St. Petersburg, where the legal daily *Pravda* now began to appear. To line up the underground inside Russia, he sent Inessa, who had also moved to Krakow, on a clandestine tour of Russia. There were so many police agents in his underground now that almost immediately she landed in prison once more. When she developed signs of tuberculosis in jail, her husband managed to get her out on bail after a year in prison. She immediately rejoined Lenin and his wife in Krakow and in Poronin in the Tatra Mountains.

> We were terribly glad . . . at her arrival. . . . In the autumn [of 1913] all of us became very close to Inessa. In her there was much joy of life and ardor. We had known Inessa in Paris, but there was a large colony there. In Krakow lived a small closely knit circle of comrades. Inessa rented a room in the same family with which Kamenev lived.[14]
>
> My mother became closely attached to Inessa. Inessa often went to talk with her, sit with her, have a smoke with her. It became cosier and gayer when Inessa came. Our entire life was filled with party concerns and affairs, more like a student commune than like

family life, and we were glad to have Inessa. . . . Something warm radiated from her talk.

Il'ich, Inessa, and I often went on walks together. Zinoviev and Kamenev dubbed us the "hikers" party. We walked in the meadows on the outskirts of the city. Meadow in Polish is *blon*, and Inessa from then on took the pseudonym of *Blonina*. Inessa was a good musician, urged us all to go to Beethoven concerts, and played very well many of Beethoven's pieces. Il'ich especially loved *Sonate Pathétique*, constantly begging her to play it.[15]

In 1921, when Lenin had taken power and Inessa was dead, one day he said to Gorky:

I know nothing that is greater than the *Appassionata*: I am ready to listen to it every day. It is amazing, more than human, music. I want to say gentle stupidities and stroke the heads of people who, living in this dirty hell, can create such beauty. But today you must not stroke the head of anyone—they will bite your hand. It is necessary to beat them over the head, beat without mercy, even though in our ideal we are against the use of force against people. Hm-hm, duty is hellishly hard![16]

It was this side of Lenin's nature—the side which he strove mightily, and on the whole successfully, to restrain—that Inessa ministered to. The gentleness she evoked in him (the desire to say gentle stupidities and stroke the heads of people) is reflected in his letters to her, despite the censorship to which they have been subjected, reflected even in letters arguing with her when she has disagreed and pressed her point hard.

Life in Krakow proved too cramping for Inessa's overflowing energies. She made a tour of the Bolshevik exile colonies, lecturing on the woman question, and then returned to her native Paris, where the main Bolshevik group abroad was settled.

At the beginning of January 1914, Lenin stopped over in Paris with Duma deputy (and police agent) Malinovsky, when they were on their way to address a Lettish Congress in Brussels. He returned to Paris alone, spending a month and a half in the French capital. To his mother he wrote on February 21: "I have just been in Paris, not a bad trip. Paris is not a good city to live in with modest means, and quite an exhausting one. But to be there a little while, to visit, to wander about a bit—there's not a better nor a gayer city. It refreshed me greatly."[17]

No other letter of Lenin's ever suggested a happier, more relaxed mood.

It was while Inessa was living in Paris and the Ulianovs were in Krakow, that Lenin's first letter to her was written. The published version has been censored and lacks salutation and closing and all personal touches. His last letter to her is dated in his works as "written between the 25th and the 31st of March, 1917," that is, after the February Revolution has begun and both Inessa and Lenin were getting ready to go to Russia. She was one of the eighteen Bolsheviks who accompanied him across Germany to Russia in the "sealed train" that enabled them to reach Petrograd on April 16/3, 1917.

During the war Lenin wrote more letters to Inessa Armand than to any other person, whether relative or disciple. As soon as he got out of prison in Austria and reached a safe haven in Berne, Switzerland, he wrote to Inessa, who because of her lung ailment was living in the Swiss Alps at Les Avants. Except for the first two sentences, Lenin writes this time as best he can in English. He tells Inessa of the need to gather materials on the war positions of all parties, then asks about her health, whether she eats better, whether she has books and newspapers, how the weather is in Les Avants, whether she is taking walks, and whether they can see each other soon. The letter must have been written after September 6. "Towards the middle of September," according to her official biographer, Inessa moved to Berne.[18] Thereafter there were no letters to Inessa for the rest of the autumn. A passage in Krupskaia's memoirs explains why:

> The memory of that autumn is interwoven in my mind with the autumnal scene in the forest in Berne. The autumn of that year was a glorious one. We lived in Berne on a small, neat, quiet street bordering on the Berne Forest. . . . Cater-corner across the road lived Inessa [the street was Distelweg]. . . . We would wander for hours along the forest roads covered with fallen yellow leaves. Generally the three of us went together on these walks, Vladimir Il'ich, Inessa, and I. . . . Sometimes we would sit for hours on the sunlit, wooded mountainside, while Il'ich jotted down outlines of his speeches and articles . . . I would study Italian . . . Inessa would sew a skirt and bask with delight in the autumnal sun. . . .[19]

As soon as Inessa left Berne, Lenin resumed writing to her. The twenty-four letters to her in the fourth edition of his works show that during the war years Lenin wrote more frequently and at greater length to her than to anyone else. In the brief period from November 20, 1916, to the outbreak of the February Revolution in 1917, he wrote fourteen letters to her, two brief notes to his younger sister, one to his older sister's husband, and four to other persons—in short, more to her than to all the rest put together. In his letters to Inessa, as always, preoccupation with politics is uppermost. But tone and depth reveal facets of his nature exhibited in no other letters, whether to members of his family or to other disciples. Most important to us are the letters examined by me elsewhere on Lenin's attitude toward war and national defense. Here we will look only at those which throw light on other aspects of Lenin's spirit.

Unlike the letters to other intimates of the Ulianovs, there are in the letters to Inessa no mention of Krupskaia, no regards from her, nor any personal note added by her. Only after Lenin has been writing to Inessa for three years does he once mention Krupskaia: "Nadia is ill: she caught bronchitis and has a fever. It seems she will have to toss about in bed for a while. Today I called a woman doctor."[20]

Several letters sound a rare note akin to self-pity and search for sympathy: how hard his life is, how unending and ungrateful his factional struggles, how dumb even the best Bolsheviks can be. Thus in the earliest letter from Krakow to Paris in December, 1913, he tells her that he is receiving protests from offended party cells because he does not work through them but picks his own men of confidence for confidential tasks:

> Clowns! They chase after words. Don't think how devilishly complicated and tricky life is, which *provides altogether new* forms. . . .
>
> People for the most part (99 per cent of the bourgeoisie, 98 per cent of the Liquidators, some 60 to 70 per cent of the Bolsheviks) are unable to *think*, only able to *learn words by heart*. They have learned by heart the word "underground." Good. They can repeat it. This they know by rote.
>
> But *how its forms* must be changed under new circumstances, how one must learn *anew* for this, and how to *think*, that we do not understand. . . .
>
> I am greatly interested in knowing whether you could explain this to the public. Write me in the greatest detail. . . . [21]

No doubt in this "dialectical" and "statistical" analysis of the class ability to think there is something intentionally comic, but the complaint is serious all the same, and flattering in its implication that Inessa is one who can not only think but perhaps write a pamphlet that will teach other Bolsheviks how to think.

The year 1916 was a bitter, quarrelsome year for Lenin. "Never, I think," wrote Krupskaia, "was Vladimir Il'ich in a more irreconcilable mood than during the last months of 1916 and the early months of 1917." "He had differences of opinion with Rosa Luxemburg, Radek, the Dutch, Bukharin, Piatakov . . . and Kollontai" and even with his sister Anna.[22] He wrote Inessa several letters full of abusive reproaches of comrades who were closest to him, and apparently she reproved him in reply.

But just at that point, Maxim Gorky, who at his request was trying to arrange the legal publication of Lenin's "Imperialism" in Petrograd, demanded that he omit some of the abusive epithets directed at Kautsky. This, Lenin wrote Inessa, was "ridiculous and offensive"; then he added: "There you are, that's my fate. One fighting campaign after another—against political stupidities, vileness, opportunism, etc. And this from 1893 on. And the hatred of the philistines because of it. Well, all the same, I would not change my fate for 'peace' with the philistines. . . ."[23]

This is one of the rare autobiographical reflections we have from his usually extrovert pen.

His big opportunity to use Inessa, as we have already noted, came when he sent her in his place to represent the Bolsheviks at the International Socialist Bureau Conference called in Brussels on July 16 and 17, 1914, to unify once more the Russian Socialist movement. He was sending her to meet and do battle with such large figures as Kautsky, Vandervelde, Huysmans, Luxemburg, Plekhanov, Trotsky, and Martov. He counted on her mastery of all the languages of the International, her literal devotion to him and his views, her steadfastness under fire. Apparently Zinoviev or some other close lieutenant found Lenin's confidence misplaced and thought Inessa too small for the task, so he wrote her:

> I am convinced that you are one of those who develops, grows stronger, becomes more energetic and bolder when alone in a responsible post. . . . I stubbornly disbelieve the pessimists who say that you—are hardly—nonsense and again nonsense! With a splendid tongue you will smash them all; you will not let Vandervelde interrupt you and yell. . . .[24]

> You must make the report. You will say that you demand it and that you *have* precise and practical *proposals*. What can be more practical and businesslike? We go our way, they theirs—and we'll see what happens. Either a general line is accepted or we say let's report to our congress, *we to the congress of our party*. (But in fact, it is clear, we will accept exactly nothing.)[25]

After a great deal more in this vein, Lenin breaks into English, as he delights to do in his letters to this master of five languages:

> *I've forgotten the money question. We will pay for letters, telegrams (please wire oftener) & railroad expenses, hotel expenses & so on. Mind it!*

If you succeed to receive the first rapport for 1 –2 hours, it is almost all.*

Then it remains to "kick back," to fish out their *contrepropositions** (on all 14 points) and to declare *we do not agree* (not one of their proposals will we accept . . .).[26]

In all the forty pages of instructions and *zametki privées*, although the time was nearly three weeks after the assassination of the Archduke at Sarajevo, Lenin has not one word to say about war, except his own war against all the other varieties of Russian socialism. Inessa, Krupskaia writes, was selected because it was necessary to have a firm person who could "resist a storm of indignation. . . . She carried out her task bravely." And the police agent's comment showed that she did so, to the "great disgust" of the ISB representatives and those from the other Russian factions, "as no one had expected the impudence of the Leninists to reach such proportions."

To follow up Lenin's and their advantage, the police instructed all their secret agents in the underground "steadfastly and persistently to defend the idea of the complete impossibility of any organization fusion whatsoever . . . especially a union of Bolsheviks and Mensheviks." Lenin, who was taking no chances either, determined not to attend the Emergency Session of the ISB on July 29, 1914, the day after Austria shelled Belgrade, for the sole purpose of trying to stop the war from spreading.

We turn now to three letters to Inessa, one written on June 5, 1914, and the other two in December 1916, which refer directly or indirectly to Inessa's preoccupation with the "woman question," her reading in this field, and her plan for a pamphlet.

The first deals with a novel by Vinenchenko, which Inessa had recommended to Lenin, then sent him to read. The novel was no doubt *Honesty with One's Self*, published in 1911 in the Fifth Yearly Almanac of *Zemlia*, St. Petersburg.[27]

I have read, *my dear friend*,[28] the new novel by Vinenchenko which you sent. What a nonsensical and stupid story!

To bring together as many "horrors" as possible of all kinds, to collect and unite both "vice" and "syphilis" and romantic villainy, with extortion of money for a secret (and the transformation of the blackmail victim into a mistress) and the trial of a doctor! All with hysterics, mental contortions, pretensions to a theory of "his own" on the organization of prostitutes. . . .

Coming singly, there are in life, of course, all the "horrors" which Vinenchenko depicts. But to join them all together. . . .

Once I had to spend the night with a sick comrade (Delirium tremens). And once I had to try to dissuade a comrade who was attempting suicide. In the end . . . he died a suicide. Both are memories à la Vinenchenko. But in each case these were small fragments of the lives of the two comrades. But this pretentious, arrant fool of a Vinenchenko . . . has made this a collection of nothing but horrors. . . . Brrr—dullness, nonsense, unpleasant to have spent time in reading it.[29]

A glance at the novel will convince the reader that Lenin was the better critic and that Inessa's interest was largely due to the author's "own theory on the organization of prostitutes."

Unfortunately, Inessa's letter outlining her plan for a pamphlet on the "woman's question" has not been published. But from Lenin's letters we can see that she had included among her list of "immediate demands" the "demand for free love." Pedantically, dogmatically, but with an effort to be tactful and gentle, Lenin sought to persuade her to strike it out. "This is really not a proletarian but a bourgeois demand," he writes in his first letter. "What *can* be understood by it?" Answering his own question, he enumerates ten possible interpretations:

(1) Freedom from material calculations in the matter of love?
(2) From material cares also? (3) From religious prejudices? (4) From prohibitions by papa, etc.? (5) From the prejudices of "society"?
(6) From a narrow environment (peasant or petit-bourgeois-intellectual)? (7) From the fetters of law, the courtroom, and the police? (8) From the serious in love? (9) From childbirth?
(10) Freedom of adultery?
Of course, you have in mind not Nos. 8–10 but Nos. 1–7. . . . But for numbers 1–7 you must select another term, for free love does not exactly express this thought. And the public will *inevitably* understand by "free love" Nos. 8–10, just for the reason that it is not a proletarian but a bourgeois demand. . . . It is not a matter of what you "want to understand" *subjectively* by it. It is a matter of the *objective logic* of class relations in matters of love.[30]

Something in Lenin's letter—perhaps his remark on "freedom of adultery"—must have hurt Inessa deeply. In reply to her protest, not available to us, he defends his "class analysis" of love:

Good, let us examine the question once more. . . .
You "object": [you say] "I don't understand how it is POSSIBLE to identify (!!??) free love" with No. 10. So it seems that it is *I* who do the "identifying" and you are getting ready to scold . . . *me*?
How? Why?

Bourgeois women understand by free love pts. 8–10—that is my thesis. Do you reject that? Then tell me what *bourgeois* ladies do understand by free love? . . . Don't literature and life *prove* that? You must *mark yourself off* clearly from them, *oppose* to theirs the proletarian point of view . . . . Otherwise *they* will seize upon the corresponding points of your pamphlet, interpret them in their own way, make of your pamphlet water for their mill, pervert your thoughts before the workers, "confuse" the workers (by sowing among them the fear that the ideas *you* bring may be *alien* to them). And in their hands are the powerful hosts of the press.

But, you, completely forgetting the objective and class point of view, pass over to an "attack" on *me*, as if it were *I* who "identify" free love with pts. 8–10. Strange, verily, verily, strange . . .

Lenin seems to sense that this pedantic self-exculpation does not touch the core of her hurt feelings, so he tries another approach:

"Even a temporary passion and love affair"—so you write—is "more poetical and clean" than "kisses without love" of vulgar, and worse than vulgar, spouses. [The words I have rendered with "vulgar and worse than vulgar" are *poshlyi* (vulgar) and *poshlenkii*, a pejorative diminutive of the same word.—B.W.] So you write. And so you are getting ready to write in your pamphlet. Splendid.

Is the contraposition logical? Kisses without love, of vulgar spouses, is *dirty*. I agree. To this must be counterposed—what? It would seem: kisses *with love*?

But you counterpose "temporary" (why temporary?) "passion" (why not love?). Logically it turns out as if kisses without love (temporary) are opposed to kisses without love (conjugal) . . . Strange. For a popular pamphlet, would it not be better to oppose to middle-class-intellectual-peasant vulgar and dirty marriage without love—proletarian, civil marriage with love (with the addition, IF YOU ABSOLUTELY INSIST, that a temporary affair-passion may also be dirty or clean) . . .

Truly I do not want to engage in a polemic with you at all. Gladly would I throw this letter away and postpone the matter until we can have a talk together.

But I did want your pamphlet to be a good one, so that from it *no one would be able* to rip out a phrase unpleasant for you. . . . I am sending you this letter only that you may perhaps re-examine your plan in more detail, as a result of letters, than on the occasion of a chat. A plan, you see, is a very important thing. . . . [31]

The pamphlet was never written!

Inessa continued to play an important part in Lenin's wartime activities. She served on the Bolshevik delegations to Zimmerwald and Kienthal. At the Berne Conference of Bolsheviks, she was one of a committee of three, the other two being Zinoviev and Lenin, which drafted the official resolution on war. (There is no doubt that the real author was Lenin.) She continued to lead the Bolshevik work among women. Despite her age—she was thirty-five in 1914—she represented bolshevism at the International Youth Conference. She became one of the founders and a foreign editor of the Petersburg legal Bolshevik journal, *The Woman Worker*, the other editors being Kollontai (who agreed with her on "free love"), Lilina Zinoviev, Krupskaia, Lydia Stal, and Lenin's sister Anna.

Inessa was on the "sealed train" that took Lenin and his wife, the Zinovievs, and other prominent Bolsheviks back to Russia. Thereafter Lenin's life in the maelstrom of revolution, and hers, scarcely less agitated and active, in woman's work, work among French Communists and sympathizers in Russia, activities as first chairman of the Economic Council of Moscow Province, editor of the Woman's Section of *Pravda* and *Bednota*, her struggle against the ubiquitous prostitution of the years of civil war and economic breakdown, her translation work at two congresses of the Comintern—the churning whirlpool of revolution left little time for these two to think of themselves or each other.

The descriptions of her dating from this period agree that she dressed plainly, carelessly, even neglectfully, in worn and shabby garments; that she was ill fed, often cold and hungry; that her face had begun to show the ravages of overwork and neglect of self. At last, her friends and comrades, frightened by the signs of physical breakdown, persuaded her to go to the Caucasus for a rest. There too was hunger, overcrowding, floods of refugees, civil war, breakdown, disease. She slept in freight cars, was carried from town to town, and nursed the sick on the train. At last she was struck down herself by typhus in the autumn of 1920, dying at the age of forty-one.

When Alexandra Kollontai, then serving as ambassador to Norway, died in 1952, Marcel Body, a French Communist who had been in Inessa's group in Moscow and then served as aide, intimate friend, and first secretary of Kollantai's embassy, wrote a memoir concerning the first woman ambassador in history. In the memoir he told how Kollontai had spoken to him of Lenin's deep love for Inessa Armand.[32] Krupskaia had known of it, she said, and in line both with the principles instilled in her by Chernyshevsky's "uncommon persons" in *Chto delat'?*, and the principles expressed in another favorite tale of Lenin's, "The Story of Kolosov," by Turgenev,[33] Krupskaia had bravely faced the thought that her husband would now leave her for Inessa. When he did not go, she offered to leave. More than once, she signified her intention of leaving, but each time Lenin said to her, "No, stay!" Dutifully, she stayed.[34]

After Body published this memoir, Angelica Balabanoff felt that she too might break the puritanical silence she had hitherto observed concerning Inessa in my many interviews with her on what she knew of Lenin.

> Lenin loved Inessa [Dr. Balabanoff told me]. There was nothing immoral in it, since Lenin told Krupskaia everything [again the same code]. He deeply loved music, and this Krupskaia could not give him. Inessa played beautifully—his beloved Beethoven and other pieces.

> He sent Inessa to the Youth Conference of the Zimmerwald Group—a little old, but she had a credential from the Bolsheviks and we had to accept it. He did not dare to come himself, sat downstairs in a little adjacent café drinking tea, getting reports from her, giving her instructions. I went down for tea and found him there. Did you come *na chai*, I asked, *ili na rezoliutsii?* (for tea, or for the resolution?) He laughed knowingly, but did not answer. [Inessa fought hard, but the resolution Lenin prepared for her was defeated 13–3][35]

> When Inessa died, he begged me to speak at her funeral. He was utterly broken by her death. She died miserably of typhus in the Caucasus. I did not want to speak because I did not feel close to her nor really know her well. Yet I did not want to refuse.

> Fortunately, at the last moment, Kollontai arrived, and delivered a moving address. I cast sidelong glances at Lenin. He was plunged in despair, his cap down over his eyes; small as he was, he seemed to shrink and grow smaller. He looked pitiful and broken in spirit. I never saw him look like that before. It was something more than the loss of a "good Bolshevik" or a good friend. He had lost some one very dear and very close to him and made no effort to conceal it.

> He had had a child by Inessa. She married the German Communist, Eberlein, who was purged by Stalin. What happened to Lenin's daughter then I do not know.[36]

This last belief of Dr. Balabanoff, which I heard also from Germans who had known Hugo Eberlein well, is nevertheless mistaken. When Inessa died, the Ulianovs adopted her daughter, Ina, and took her to live with them. It was at Lenin's home that Eberlein met Ina Armand, but she would have been too young to have been at a nubile age then if she had really been a daughter of Lenin and Inessa, whose personal acquaintance dates from 1910.[37] (Eberlein married for the second time in Moscow in 1921.)[38]

For the rest, Kollontai's account and Balabanoff's confirm each other. The account of Kollontai reads: "When her body was brought from the Caucasus and we accompanied her to the cemetery, Lenin was unrecognizable. He walked with closed eyes; at every moment we thought he would collapse." Always the romantic, Kollontai added: "He was not able to go on living after Inessa Armand. The death of Inessa hastened the development of the sickness which was to destroy him."

Be that as it may (he managed to continue active political life for two extremely full years, then died in the same way as his father, whom he so greatly resembled, at almost the same age), both accounts make it clear that Lenin deeply loved Inessa and that her death affected him profoundly. As Dr. Balabanoff put it, "It was something more than the loss of a 'good Bolshevik' or a good friend."

John Reed died in the same way that same autumn. One of the first native Americans to take part in the founding of the American Communist party, he had written *Ten Days That Shook the World*, which Lenin pronounced the best account of his seizure of power and the most useful, deserving of translation into all languages. Yet, when Kobetsky, then technical secretary of the Comintern, reported to Lenin that John Reed was dead, Lenin, always a great one for getting on with the work regardless of losses, answered:

> Comrade Kobetsky!
> 1. Your report (i.e., the report of the physician you sent me) and the note should be sent abroad.
> 2. Who is in charge of the Hotel Lux? Its remodeling for the Comintern? The management part?
>
> *Lenin* 18/X[39]

Both good comrades had "served the cause." Both were buried under the Kremlin Wall between the Nikolsky and Spassky gates. But what a world of difference in the emotion Lenin showed.

To Krupskaia fell the task of writing the obituary notice for the Woman's Section of *Pravda*, on October 3, 1920. She tried hard to summon up a sense of loss, but the obituary is formless and colorless. In time, however, this devoted woman learned to accept this aspect of her husband's life, like every other, as parts of a paradigm of perfection. In 1926, Krupskaia edited and wrote the opening article of a symposium brochure, *In Memory of Inessa Armand*. It is the warmest and most informative essay in the collection. When in 1930–32 she came to write her *Memories of Lenin*, the personality of Inessa shone through its pages, radiant and joyous, as Lenin saw her. Thus perhaps it was Krupskaia, even more than Inessa and Lenin, who deserved the appellation of "uncommon person" used alike by Chernyshevsky and Turgenev in their discussions of freedom in love. Whatever may have been their reason, it was no longer Krupskaia's personal sensitiveness that motivated the Marx-Lenin Institute in waiting for her death before publishing the letters of Lenin to Inessa Armand. But the officials of the Institute did not know Krupskaia's spirit well enough to be aware of the change.

Perhaps we should add a footnote on the subsequent lives of the family of Inessa Armand. Her husband, after the loss of his fortune, entered "agriculture," working in a kolkhoz until his death in 1943. Her oldest son, Alexander, fought in the Civil War, and in 1957 was reported to be working in the Thermotechnical Institute in Moscow. Fedor, her second son, was a military aviator, then engaged in the organization of athletics, until his death from tuberculosis in 1936. The youngest son, André, became an engineer and tank constructor. He died in battle in 1944.

The older daughter, Ina, lost her German Communist husband in the Stalin blood purges. In 1957 she was working in the Marx-Lenin Institute. The younger daughter, Varvara, is a "decorative artist." At least, such is the account given in the official French Communist biography of Inessa Armand. (All except the marriage to Eberlein and his subsequent purge, for unpersons did not then get into official biographies.)[40]

7

Krupskaia
Purges the People's
Libraries

What happened to us? How could we
have given in? What was the chief thing
that got us down? Fear? The idols of the
market place? The idols of the theatre?
All right, I'm a 'little man,' but what
about Nadezhda Konstantinovna Krupskaia? Didn't she understand, didn't she
realize what was happening? Why didn't
she raise her voice?
Alexander Solzhenitsyn, *Cancer Ward*

On 8 November 1923 Maxim Gorky wrote from Sorrento to his editorial
assistant, the poet Vladislav Khodasevich, then in England:

> For news that stuns the mind . . . in Russia Nadezhda Krupskaia
> and a certain M. Speranski have forbidden the reading of: Plato,
> Kant, Schopenhauer, Vl[adimir] Solovev, Taine, Ruskin, Nietzsche,
> L[ev] Tolstoi, Leskov . . . and many similar heretics. And it is further
> decreed: "The section on religion must contain only antireligious
> books." All this, supposedly . . . is printed in a booklet entitled *A
> Guide to the Removal of Anti-Artistic and Counter-revolutionary
> Literature from Libraries Serving the Mass Reader.* . . . I have
> written in "supposedly" above the line, since I still cannot make
> myself believe in this intellectual vampirism, and I will not believe it
> until I see the *Guide.*
>   My first impression was so strong that I started writing to
> Moscow to announce my repudiation of Russian citizenship. What
> else can I do if this atrocity turns out to be true?[1]

The letter is curious and complicated, showing Gorky's ability to stage
little dramas within his own spirit, for, while he was writing to Khodasevich that Krupskaia's circular "supposedly" existed, he had actually
had a copy in his hands two months earlier. Moreover, this was not
Krupskaia's first but her second sweeping order for the purging of the

Reprinted with permission from *Survey*, no. 72 (Summer 1969).

libraries intended for the popular masses, for her circular begins with this introduction:

> Already in 1920 the Political-Education Section of the People's Commissariat of Education sent instructions to the various local bodies on the re-examination of their catalogs in order to purge the public libraries of obsolescent literature.
>
> However, up to now [spring 1923], with rare exceptions, the Political Education Committees have completely neglected the task of re-examining and eliminating books from the libraries, and in some provinces it required the intervention of the GPU to get the task of removing books started.

The Krupskaia circular Gorky referred to was one of three sent out by her. The first of late 1920 I have not been able to secure, which is unfortunate since it was drawn up while Lenin was still in full possession of his powers and trying to check up on everything being done in the name of the proletarian dictatorship, and when Krupskaia, as was her wont, could consult him on any puzzling aspect of the purge of books.[2] But I do have a photostat of the second circular, sent out in the spring of 1923: an article by Krupskaia in *Pravda* of April 9, 1924, in which she attempts to answer the storm of criticism "abroad" (and surely not only abroad, for men like Lunacharski, her hierarchical superior as Commissar of Education, must have had their reservations and made them known to her[3]); and a photostat of the third circular signed by her and published in *Krasny Bibliotekar* (no. 1 of 1924).[4]

Krupskaia did not answer her critics until the following year, in her signed article on the "defects" of the Bureau of Political Education in *Pravda* (April 9, 1924). There had been two such alleged "defects" in the past year, she said. One was from the pen of her highly esteemed non-party assistant for library matters, A. A. Pokrovski, who had written: "Religion that is fully free from superstition concerning the intervention of higher powers in the affairs of our world, that puts no obstacles nor snares in the path of science, that recognizes in principle that the entire real world as cognizable, if 'not to the end' at least 'up to the infinite'—such a religion . . . is really not an enemy for us, and the struggle against it is not a task for our libraries." "In this," Krupskaia says, "A. A. Pokrovski is terribly mistaken. Such a religion is not less dangerous. . . . It does a better job of throwing dust into our eyes . . . which renders it still more dangerous." Here we get an echo of the view which Lenin had dictated to her in his famous letter to Gorky of mid-November 1913, where he expressed his preference for the gross priest "who seduces little

Всем Губ. и Уполитпросветам, Партко-мам, Облитам, Гублитам и Отделам ГПУ.

Инструкция о пересмотре книжного состава би-блиотек к изъятию контр-революционной и анти-художественной литературы.

Еще в 1920 году Политико-Просвети-тельным Отделом Наркомпроса разослана была на места инструкция о пересмотре каталогов к изъятию устаревшей литературы из общественных библиртек.

Однако, до сих пор доклады Полит-просветов, за редкими исключениями, со-вершенно не упоминали о работе по про-смотру и изъятию книг из библиотек, и в некоторых губерниях потребовалось вме-шательство ГПУ, чтобы работа по изъятию началась. Повидимому Политпросветы не-достаточно уяснили всей необходимости и важности указанной меры. Между тем она имеет безусловно громадное политическое

The first page of Krupskaia's "second circular"

Примерные списки книг к инструкции по изъятию устаревшей литературы из библиотек.

I. По отделу философии, психологии и этики.

а) Книги, подлежащие удалению из библиотек, обслуживающих массового читателя:

1. Аллан Кардек. Книга медиумов.
2. Битнер. Верить или не верить.
3. Волков. Френология.
4. Габбе. Как надо жить, чтобы счастливым быть (по Смайльсу)
5. Дебэ. Мир чудесного.
6. Друммонд. Высшее благо и др.
7. Жаколио. Спиритизм в Индии.
8. Кальмет. О явлении духов.
9. Кораблев. О нравственности (с приложением к практической жизни и рассмотрением революционных движений).

— 15 —

10. Ленорман. Истолкователь снов.
11. Мантегацца. Счастье, труд и др.
12. Меньшиков. Думы о счастье и др.
13. Смайльс. Долг, характер, самостоятельность и др.
14. Соколов. О долге. Солдатская беседа о долге повиновения властям.
15. Ф. Страхов. Дух и материя (против материализма).
16. Фламмарион. Люмен (о бессмертии души).
17. Штейнер. Мистика.

б) Книги по отделу философии, подлежащие удалению из небольших библиотек, но оставляемые в библиотеках крупных:

1. Грота.
2. Ланге. История материализма.
3. Лопатина.
4. Лосского.
5. Вл. Соловьева.
6. Челпанова — книги по философии и психологии.

Биографии и сочинения:

1. Декарта.
2. Канта.
3. Маха.
4. Платона.
5. Спенсера.
6. Шопенгауэра.

The first two pages of the attached list of books that were to be removed from Soviet libraries
Hoover Institution on War, Revolution and Peace, Stanford, California

girls" as easier to expose than the priest without a crude religion, and accuses Gorky with his "god-building" of "ideological copulation with a corpse."[5]

The other "defect" Krupskaia treated in more ambiguous fashion. The libraries for popular use, she said, contained many "unnecessary and harmful books." These included "moralizing talks, books about God of an arch-Black Hundred character [the use of *arkhi*—arch—to express a superlative was one of the peculiarities of Lenin's personal style], monarchist rubbish . . . patriotic literature of the period of the war, agitation and literature written on the current issues of the year 1917—in favor of a Constituent Assembly, etc. . . . literature containing explanations of decrees and laws that have long outlived their time." Yes, her circular had spoken of the need to remove this literature from the libraries serving the mass reader. "This is a simple protection of their interest."

> In the circular there was no "defect," yet a "defect" there was all the same. To the circular was affixed a thoroughly unfortunate list of books, a list compiled by the Commission for the Reexamination of Books, attached to the circular I had signed, without my knowledge. As soon as I saw this list I canceled it.
>
> Why was the list unfortunate? In the first place because it was beside the mark. In it, it was said that it was necessary to remove from the mass libraries Plato, Kant, Mach—in general, idealists. That idealist philosophers are harmful people is beyond question. But their presence in a library for peasants or the worker masses is not harmful at all, it is senseless: a man of the masses (*massovik*) will not read Kant. Hence the "list" actually did not alter matters in any way. Much worse was the fact that the list of books to be removed in the field of "religion" was extremely limited.

As I set down these words of Krupskaia, a woman possessing great power in the field of popular education, ideas crowded in upon my mind. I thought of Lomonosov, born in a little fishing village, son of a fisherman, who went to sea with his father to fish in northern waters, who early learned to read, reading everything he could lay his hands on, developed an encyclopedic mind, exhibited genius in science, philosophy, and other fields, becoming a literary and intellectual model for ensuing generations. I thought of Chekhov, whose grandfather was a serf, of Kluev, the poet, whose paternal ancestry leads to a tribal Eskimo tent of a Christianized Old Believer on the coast of the White Sea, the poet Klychkov, born to peasants in the village of Dubrovskaya in the Province of Tver, of Oreshin who sang of the Volga region in which he was born, of Esenin, born to peasants in the village of Konstantinovo, who became the greatest peasant poet of all until the very species was crushed by the harsh epithet, *kulak*. I thought of Shevchenko, a liberated serf who became the founder of Ukrainian literature and of a sense of Ukrainian nationhood. I thought, too, of Gray's *Elegy Written in a Country Churchyard* with its "village Hampdens," its "mute inglorious Miltons," and its generous thought that the lowliest and poorest hut in the humblest village may contain a genius if only access to "knowledge, rich with the spoils of time" is not denied to him. The *Elegy* reminded me of Lomonosov again, and of his lines:

Perhaps to our own Platos
Our Newtons swift of thought
Our Russian land may well give birth

In my mind arose the image of the throng of *raznochintsy*, who came from the lower depths and margins outside the recognized society of estates, sons of serfs, sons of poor priests, sons of wandering pilgrims, poor traders, and Old Believers, to lay impetuous hands upon the treasures hitherto the monopoly of an intelligentsia sprung from the nobility. I thought of the humble beginnings of the Russian theater in the performances of serfs to entertain their masters, and of M. S. Shchepkin, a serf until he was thirty-three, who became an actor in the Maly Theatre and one of the greatest actors in the history of the Russian stage. I thought of Sytin, a great publishing magnate who rose from poverty and sought to bring cheap books to the people, all of whose books for children were to be eliminated from the libraries by this self-same list where he is dismissed as "a publisher not deserving of trust." And I thought of his friend and collaborator, Maxim Gorky, who himself rose from the lower depths of vagrants and tramps, who formed his style on Old Church Slavonic and the Gospels, the vivid campfire talk of down and outers, and the folk tales of his illiterate grandmother, who became an omnivorous reader and a great writer, and then, in a compact with Lenin, made himself the custodian of Russian culture and the savior of the lives and dignity of starving and freezing intellectuals for whom Lenin's war communism had found no place. I thought, too, of a younger Krupskaia, devoutly religious until the age of twenty, eager teacher of reading circles for the illiterate until Lenin made fun of her zeal to bring letters and books to the people, and who doubtless venerated such philosophers as Plato, until Lenin taught her that "idealist philosophers are beyond question harmful people."[6]

Nor could I fail to think of my own personal fate, born into a poor family in a Brooklyn slum, none of whose members before me, neither mother nor father nor older brother and sister had had more than an elementary school education. Had it not been for Andrew Carnegie's generosity in endowing a public library in each of the slums in which we lived successively, and the broad criterion of the librarians who did not exclude Plato or Aristotle or Herbert Spencer or any of the other difficult writers I struggled with as a little boy who had no one to guide his reading, I should neither have developed any command of English style nor received a higher education at all. Fortunately, neither the people of my city who taxed themselves to maintain these free libraries, nor Andrew Carnegie whose bounty set them up, nor the branch librarians who selected the books, shared Krupskaia's feeling that it was "senseless" to make such works accessible to the children of the poor.   There were other "unfortunate" features in this list which Krupskaia so ambiguously criticized and canceled. One of its defects was that most of the authors to be purged from the shelves were listed only by their last names, without first names or patronymics, and without the title of their offending books. Since many of these family names belonged to more than one writer, what chaos such a list might cause among librarians anxious not to be behind in revolutionary zeal, playing safe by throwing out every work by a writer bearing the listed last name! Yet there were cases where actual titles of books were listed, as in the case of Lange's *History of Materialism*, and the proscribed list included the great Russian moral and religious philosopher, Solovev, the philosophers Lossky, Descartes, Spencer, Schopenhauer, Nietzsche, William James, a list that suggests that Lenin's simple division of philosophers into "idealistic" and "materialistic" does not exhaust the possible categories.

Also listed under one head or another were Taine, Maeterlinck, Nordau, Gessen (with the title *O neprikosvennosti lichnosti*—"On the Inviolability of the Person"); Lev Tolstoi, and Kropotkin. Only on these last two names did Krupskaia have anything to say, and once more what she said proved ambiguous. She wrote in her *Pravda* article:

> It was impermissible to prohibit some of the works of Tolstoi and Kropotkin. Of course the *Weltanschauung* of L. Tolstoi with his belief in God, belief in providence, etc. does not belong to those [views] that should be disseminated. Exclusive concern with one's self, concentration of all efforts on self-perfection, non-resistance to evil, the call not to combat it—all this is diametrically opposed to that to which the communists summon the masses. And these appeals of L. Tolstoi are especially harmful precisely because of his highly exceptional talent. However, the contemporary mass reader is already sufficiently imbued with a collective psychology, has fought too much, and for that reason the preachings of L. Tolstoi are

not dangerous, they will only stimulate thought. Nor are the anarchist tendencies of Kropotkin dangerous. Life teaches at every turn what a mighty force organization is. . . .

We must leave it to the reader to decide whether this is a repudiation or a left-handed justification of the inclusion of Tolstoi and Kropotkin on the ouster list, and whether libraries should be cleansed with especial zeal of books you do not like if they are written with talent by great artists.

However, since Krupskaia expressly "canceled" the list attached by her subordinates to her second circular, let us turn our attention to the third library purge circular, signed: Chairman of the Bureau of Political Education, N. Krupskaya; Chief of the Literary Censorship, P. Lebedev-Polyanski; Chairman of the Central Library Commission, M. Smushkova. It refers specifically to three supplementary "Model Lists of Books and Instructions for the Purge of Libraries." Both the circular and the three "model lists" were published in the "Official Section" of *Krasny Biblio-tekar* (no. 1, 1924, pp. 135–41), followed by two more supplements giving a model "Report Form for the Removal of Books in Accordance with the Instructions of the Central Library Commission for Submission to the Central Library Commission for Approval," and a "Form for a List of Books Marked for Removal, Sent for Approval to the Central Library Commission." The lists published in the three appendixes are not as ample as those attached to the second circular, for they are limited to 55 writers in the field of belles-lettres, 118 writers of tales for children, and 51 writers in the fields of history and historical fiction. But there is a footnote explaining that "Supplementary lists of books for the above and other sections will be printed in the following numbers of the journal." And this time the lists are more precisely drawn up, with the first initials of each author and the title or titles of his works to be removed. And, since the lists are referred to directly in the text of the circular, this time there is no doubt of their official character, or of Krupskaia's approval.

The circular itself has a tone of even greater urgency than the previous one. It is now almost four years, it said, since the first instructions went out in 1920 on purging the popular libraries, and still, with "rare exceptions," not a thing has been done except where the secret police have intervened. The local political education councils, aided by special ad hoc committees, must get busy at once with this all-important task if the popular libraries are to "free themselves from counter-revolutionary and harmful literature" and fulfill their "great political education task among the masses." Clearly, without such protective tutelage, the masses would be led astray.

Yet, along with this new tone of urgency, there is noticeable a new series of qualifications and warnings against too zealous misunderstandings. The circular warns that "books published by Soviet, Party, and communist publishing houses are in general not subject to removal." If there is doubt about their accessibility to the masses, "they should be sent to big or special purpose libraries." Books on philosophy, the history of philosophy, introductions to philosophy, philosophical monographs and the works of individual philosophers, it is taken for granted, should not be in libraries for the mass reader, but, "even where they are non-Marxist, they should not be removed from the larger libraries." The section on religious books repeats the sweeping language of the earlier circular, but then softens it to leave on the shelves the great basic classics of each creed.

In this one senses the influence of Lunacharski, who understood that the Old and New Testaments were themselves great literature, and that many passages in the classics of the literature of Russia would be unintelligible to those who did not know the Bible. The amended proscription reads: "The section on religion in libraries that are not large should contain only anti-religious and anti-ecclesiastical literature. It is permissible to leave [in such small libraries] only basic books of doctrine: the Gospels, the Bible, the Koran. . . ." This, too, is followed by an unconsciously funny warning against excessive and ill-informed zeal: "Books on the religious question are not subject to removal if they have been published by Soviet publishing institutions."

Books published for the people by institutions that existed under the tsar are to be removed, including those intended to spread literacy among the people, for they are all tainted by their origin. The same applies to books and pamphlets published by the other socialist parties against the Bolshevik stand on the war and the seizure of power in 1917. Also destined to disappear are legal reference works, collections of laws, and interpretations of laws no longer in force, whether they came from the tsar's legislation or that of the Provisional Government, or decrees issued by the Soviet before it became a Bolshevik transmission belt. Textbooks, too, should go if they tend to educate people in "the spirit of religiousness, monarchism, nationalist patriotism, militarism, respect for nobility and wealth." More interesting is the attempt to obliterate from the popular mind the memory of the earlier period of rule by Lenin, and the utopian promises and expectations of the first years in power. "In the section of the social sciences should be removed . . . obsolescent agitational and reference literature of the Soviet organs (1918, 1919, 1920) on those questions which at a given time the Soviet power has decided differently (the land question, the tax system, the question of free trade, the policy of food distribution, etc.)." Thus, so far as the popular masses were concerned, the whole period of war communism was to disappear without a trace into Orwell's "memory hole."

In orderly fashion the types of books to be purged were subdivided into six numbered, or rather lettered, classes, namely:

a. Philosophy, psychology, and ethics;
b. Religion;
c. Social sciences;
d. Natural sciences;
e. History of literature, history of geography;
f. Belles-lettres and children's books.

We have already considered some of these general instructions, but it is instructive to examine some of the other categories. In the natural sciences two types of works were to be removed: manuals that were published in the decades from the fifties through the seventies, and therefore are presumed to be obsolete; and "those mixing science with religious fictions and discourses on the wisdom of the Creator, and the immorality of Darwinism and materialism." To be sure some of the great classics were published during those decades, like Mendeleyev's *Principles of Chemistry* and Darwin's *Origin of Species*, and there is no warning against uncomprehending zeal in their possible removal. But if Krupskaia were reproached she might argue that they were not "manuals," or perhaps that these did not belong in the small libraries accessible to the masses anyhow.

The final category includes belles-lettres and children's books, and ends with a warning against excessive zeal that reads: "Classics of belles-lettres are not subject to removal."

This is followed by directions on how to set up an apparatus for the purging of libraries. "It should include representatives of the Department of Education, of the Communist Party, the communist youth, the trade unions, the local censorship, and where these do not exist, representatives of the GPU [secret police], and other interested organizations." Then come twelve instructions for the functioning of this purge committee and its subcommittees, with a deadline of October 1, 1924, for the completion of the entire task. The last two instructions are in bold type, and read:

> 11. Not more than two examples of each book removed as harmful and counter-revolutionary must be put in the central library. Such books must be kept in special locked cases and be given out exclusively for scientific and literary studies. For these books a special catalogue must be set up which is to be made available in necessary cases.

12. The remaining books indicated for removal from the libraries must be kept apart until confirmation by the Central Library Commission and not put into circulation until the approved list is received along with directions on how to proceed with the books that have been removed.

After completing my examination of this circular with its three appended lists and its two report forms, I turned hopefully to *Krasny Bibliotekar* for the promised supplementary lists in other fields, but they were not there! Had the criticism of others prevented the continuance of the lists? Or had some other means like direct mail or courier service replaced publication in the magazine? Although a deadline had been set for completing the purge of libraries by October 1, 1924, I had friends examine the subsequent issues of the journal not only for 1924 but also for 1925 and 1926. No such lists appeared, yet there was evidence that somehow such lists had reached the librarians and ad hoc purge committees, as will appear.[7]

What happened further is a matter of conjecture, but this much is sure: the removal of books continued and the purge of both popular and learned libraries grew in scope and intensity until, under Joseph Stalin, it became a veritable torrent sweeping all before it, clearing the way for new versions, and still newer versions of the past, the present, and the future.[8] The havoc created by Krupskaia's third circular and its continuations made itself felt in notes of alarm in *Krasny Bibliotekar*, in *Kommunisticheskoe Prosveshchenie*, and even in *Izvestia*, the official journal of the Soviet government.[9]

Thus *Krasny Bibliotekar* (no. 3, 1926) contained the following unsigned item:

> *The removal of books.* The library section of the Council of Political Education has completed its re-examination, undertaken in 1925, of the list of books removed from the libraries as obsolescent. The inspection showed that in some localities the approach to this work was incorrect, and in some libraries downright impermissible. Books were subjected to removal that should not have been removed from the libraries at all (in some places even the works of Marx, Engels, etc., were removed). As a result of this examination, the library section of the Council of Political Education has made up a list of books that *should not* be removed from libraries.

One wonders which of the two lists was longer and harder to compile.

Approximately a month later, Madame Smushkova, who had signed the last circular in her capacity as chairman of the Central Library Commission, wrote an article of almost 1,000 words "On the Problem of the Removal of Literature."[10] Here are some passages from her article:

> In the list of books subject to removal should go (1) all books which are removed in accordance with the instructions for removal of 1924; (2) and those which according to new instructions should be placed in central district libraries; (3) and also those books which are not being read in the rural libraries. . . .
>
> Practice in these removals has shown that the localities have gone about this without sufficient seriousness. The Central Bureau of Political Education has reviewed up to 2,000 pages of lists in which shocking errors have been found. If books had been immediately reduced to pulp according to these lists, our libraries would have been deprived of no small quantity of most valuable publications. In some places they even removed the works of *Marx* and *Lenin* (under his pseudonyms of Tulin and Ilin), not to speak of *Belinski, Herzen, Dobrolyubov, Pushkin, Tolstoi, Gogol* and so on and so on.
>
> All districts, without exception, committed some or other of these errors, with such mistakes, and such intentions, as do not even permit any classification into types. . . . Among the books removed we find publications of 1918 and 1919. Evidently it was reckoned that all works published before the NEP had become out of date, yet among these were books republished by the State Publishing House (GIZ) in later years. Non-Marxist works are removed, but alongside them the works of our Marxist economists are removed also. In some cases these errors are of a quite harmless character—books are removed that would scarcely find their readers in the given case of a not too large library of a district capital, for example the works of idealistic philosophers, a few books on the history of religion, and so on; no great harm will come of such removals. But what is most essential is what is done with this literature. If when they removed these books they would send them to the central library of the province, that would be one thing, but quite another if they sold them for waste paper. In that case they would be committing a serious error.
>
> But in the majority of cases the removals showed much grosser errors—they removed necessary, useful books. Thus in the Mtsensk District . . . were removed: Dikshtein, *Who Lives by What*; Bebel, *Christianity and Socialism*; Labriola, *The Situation of the Working Class in Italy*; Koropchevski, *The Men of Antiquity*; Konkol, *The Commune of 1871*. From the field of belles-lettres, they removed Dickens, Tolstoi, Hugo, Maupassant, the tales of Elpatevski,

Veresaev, Hauptmann, etc. Or in the Makarevski District . . . a special "banishment" was suffered by literature of the children's section and the section of belles-lettres. Thus from the children's section were removed Jules Verne, Mayne Reid, Cooper, Cervantes, *Don Quixote*, Kipling, *Captains Courageous*, Pakhomov, *The First Artist*.[11]

No less sweeping was the purge of the sections of science and geography. A whole series of materials for regional studies was removed. . . . In the Orlovski province they removed Baturin's *Outlines of the History of Russian Social Democracy*, Kerzhentsev's *How to Run a Meeting*, Gorky's *Song of the Stormy Petrel*.[12]

In some places they even removed Marx. Thus in the Buzulukski District was removed *Wage-labour and Capital*. In a number of places they removed the works of Lenin, Ryazanov, Trotsky, Kritsman [who wrote on planning], Lukin's *The Paris Commune*, etc. In some places the classics suffered particular persecution . . . Pushkin, *History of the Pugachev Uprising*, Aksakov, *Works*, Gogol, *Complete Collected Works*, Zhukovski, *Works*, Krylov, *Complete Collected Works*, Griboedov, *Woe from Wit*, Tolstoi, *Works*, Turgenev, Nekrasov, *Poems*, Nikitin, *Diary of a Seminarist*, Uspenski, *Works*, Shevchenko, *The Minstrel*, Shakespeare, Schiller, etc. . . . In the field of science they removed Wagner, *Tales about the Air*, the same author's *Volcanoes and Earthquakes*, Kostychev's *On the Life of Plants*, etc. (Incidentally, these books were published by the State Publishing House.)

Such examples could be cited endlessly. What does that signify? That the campaign for removing books was carried on lightmindedly to the highest degree, and everything was removed that seemed for any reason suspicious to any member of the commission. And this although the commissions were composed for the most part of very authoritative comrades. This confirms our conclusions that the commissions went about the removal with insufficient seriousness, at best sanctioning a list that someone had composed.

This campaign against the "lightmindedness" of the library cleansing commissions reached its climax when the official daily journal of the Soviet government, *Izvestia*, was enlisted for an ironical feuilleton, by G. Ryklin, with the resonant one-word title, "AMOK." The reader unfamiliar with this borrowed word from a foreign tongue was first given a solemn explanation. He learned that it was a sudden tropical ailment which occurred under a blazing sun, when the bamboo forests and even the missionaries were still, and all was "as still and boring as in the League of

Nations." Then suddenly some Malaysian would suffer a strange tropical seizure, be possessed by a violent uncontrollable frenzy to kill and, brandishing his dagger, run amok. "But with us, glory be to God, there are no tropics. Heat is not especially noticeable. On the contrary, we have really remarkable frosts. And not a single Malaysian. . . . Yet of people sick with the illness of running amok in our time we have enough. . . . And when we see one, our civic duty is to cry the warning, Amok! Amok!" At this point our feuilletonist settles down to his subject: officials running amok as they purge the libraries.

> In one library they catch a book of I. I. Stepanov-Skvortsov, *Essays on Religious Faiths*. The book is out. Motive, "ideological." Religion is the opium of the people, and there's no use embroidering on it. Amok!
> They grab *Fundamental Problems of Marxism* by Plekhanov, *Ethics and the Materialist Conception of History*, by Kautsky. Lock 'em up! "The resolution is short, but says a lot—mixed up in conciliationism."
> They discover *The Erfurt Programme*. Now that's just what they were looking for! Put it out of circulation! Why? "The author is not indicated on the cover, an anonymous work." Amok, comrades!
> After long effort the commission unearthed a book by Bebel, *Charles Fourier and his Teachings*. The inspector of the district education commission justified his order for the removal of this book with full clarity: "No teachings except those of the district education school are permitted on the territory of this district."
> Amok! Let each man watch out for himself!
> Then this same inspector arrested a book by Pokrovski.
> But enough is enough! And more than enough! Do you think it's fun to write about people who are going out of their minds? We are fulfilling a sad but a necessary obligation. We are sounding the alarm: "Amok! Look out, he's running! Block the road!"
> One last remark: there in the tropics, when a man is caught by the frenzy and runs amok, he runs without thinking about anything. But with us he thinks. He thinks that he is doing his task. He thinks that he is being useful. He thinks. . . .
> By special decree all such people should be forbidden to think. Without thoughts they will be a hundred times less dangerous. . . . With thoughts—amok!

With these three reproofs to the local librarians who were trying to carry out the instructions in Krupskaia's circulars, our story comes to a close, because the purging of libraries was taken over by far more power-ful and resolute hands than Krupskaia's: those of Joseph Stalin. There-after the purge of libraries, including the purge of books by communist authors who became unpersons and of party histories by communist historians that became unhistories, developed into a major operation, party histories, each for a moment true and official, succeeding each other as if they were being consumed by a giant chain smoker who lights the first volume of the new work with the last of the old.

When we hear the nostalgic cry for a "return to Leninist norms," when the officially inspired ancestor worship is soon to culminate in the cele-bration of the hundredth anniversary of Lenin's birth, we cannot help but think of that first circular of 1920 which librarians were so remiss or reluctant to enforce that it was "completely neglected with rare excep-tions" or was started only in those provinces where there was the direct "intervention of the GPU." This strange tree of unknowledge was planted by Krupskaia under Lenin, with his direction and advice. After his death, it was nurtured and tended by her in what she took to be Lenin's spirit. Stalin and his lieutenants have not let it die, but have tended it with zeal. It flourishes to this day in the very center of the Garden of Eden. The fruit is not forbidden, but, being mutable, it is alike hazardous to eat thereof, and hazardous to fail to eat. . . .

8

Soviet Party Histories from Lenin to Khrushchev

The Central Committee has recognized it as necessary to transform the work of the Institute of Marxism-Leninism in such fashion that the problems of the history of the Communist Party of the Soviet Union, of the international labor and communist movement, the theory of Marxism-Leninism, should occupy the leading role in its scientific-investigatory activity.

Voprosy istorii KPSS, no. 5 (1960): 3.

The history of the Communist Party of the Soviet Union—that is Marxism-Leninism in action.

Ibid., p. 49.

When Samuel Butler was planning an "Apology for the Devil," he made a plea for our attention by reminding us that "we have heard only one side; God has written all the books." As I look over the history of letters, I am moved to doubt that the Devil is without scribes. Indeed, the library of works inspired by him is probably the greater of the two. Be that as it may, there is either a special omnipotence in the ruler of a totalitarian state, or a greater freedom from ambivalence toward the Antagonist, which makes him come closer in his domain to an absolute monopoly of the publication of printed matter. In a well-organized totalitarian state it is almost literally true that you can "hear only one side." If the Leader be too busy to "write all the books" himself, or not too well versed in the art of writing, he is never too busy to prescribe how books should be written and what precise formulations they should contain. This is particularly true of party histories.

"Historians are dangerous people," Nikita Khrushchev explained to a French delegation in 1956. "They are capable of upsetting everything. They must be directed." Archives are perilous places, too, as Nikita Sergeevich learned from his Master—dangerous for the "archive rats"

This essay was read at the Conference on Soviet Historiography at the Institut Universitaire de Hautes Etudes Internationales, Geneva, July 18, 1961.

who rummage in them, dangerous for what may be fished up to reverse the supposedly irreversible flow down that drain which has come to be called the memory hole. "The laws of history are irreversible," wrote academician G. Alexandrov reassuringly in Stalin's last year.[1] But neither Stalin, nor his disciple at present in power, is disposed to take any chances. Hence the archives have been for a long period, as the most touchy still are, in the scholarly care of the secret police, fit symbol of the pen fastened down by ball and chain. Hence, too, the frequent reminders to historians that history must not be expounded in an objective spirit . . . [which would be] a departure from the Leninist principle of *partiinost* in science.[2]

Out of this flow the admonitions that "the sharp ideological struggle in the workers' movement is accompanied by no less ferocious battles in historiography";[3] the instructions for dealing with the future no less than the past ("It's a poor sort of memory that only works backwards," the Queen said to Alice in Wonderland); the proclamations that "historical science has been and remains an arena of sharp ideological struggle, has been and remains a class, party science," that "the struggle against bourgeois ideology has been and continues to be the foremost task of our historians,"[4] that "the historian of the party is not a dispassionate recorder of the events of the past but a scholar-fighter," and that "the science of the history of the party occupies an outstanding place in the ideological struggle of the Communist Party for the revolutionary transformation of society."[5]

From the same causes come the stern commands of the Central Committee, the Presidium, or the Leader, to the practitioners of the historian's craft; the steady hail of precise formulations which must be "verified" by history; the sudden changes in the editorial boards of the leading historical journals; and the emergence in due course of the single official history, besides which there shall be no other. It is the development of this sultry atmosphere in which historians must carry on their work, and the emergence amid storms and alarms of the single official history so suited to the totalitarian, single-party, dictatorial state, which will form the central theme here. In following these developments, we may hope to learn something of Soviet historiography in general, and even something of the "objective" (or perhaps I should say "bourgeois-objectivist") history of the Soviet Communist party.

Every Contender His Own Historian

Each of the leaders of the Communist party of the Soviet Union in turn, and each of the contenders for such leadership, has perforce been a historian of sorts. Given the strong dose of historicism which is ingrained in Marxist doctrine, Mensheviks as well as Bolsheviks, and a little less persistently, Populists, were ever wont to jab at each other with a historical pen. Plekhanov's writings are full of historical excursions. Such anti-Bolshevik Marxists as Potresov, Maslov, Ermanskii, Cherevanin, Balabanov, Akimov each tried a hand at giving his position historical sanction and plotting the way in which history has led right up to it. Of the Populist socialists, Mikhailovsky was most industrious in the older generation, and Chernov and Ivanov Razumnik among the later Social Revolutionaries.[6] Martov, Maslov, and Potresov tried to enlist all the Menshevik intellectuals with any pretension to historical knowledge in their ambitious five-volume *Obshchestvennoe dvizhenie v Rossii v nachale XX veka* (1909–14) (only four were completed and published). To Martov's pen, too, belongs the most objective of the various histories written by socialist activists of any school: his *History of the Russian Social Democracy*.[7]

Lenin as the Tireless Historiographer

But it was Lenin who set the example of rumpling up Clio every time he changed his tactics, every time he got into a fight within his own movement, or in the Russian revolutionary movement as a whole, every time he started another split, or celebrated the anniversary of one of these innumerable schisms in his life and that of his movement. Historicism, authoritarianism, pedantry, Marxist and historical learning or pseudo-learning, and Rechthaberei were all so strong in him, so charged with his passion for "theoretical" battle, that he never tired of enlisting for each ideological fray, faction squabble, or tactical maneuver, the entire panoply of the history of Marxism, the history of Russia, the history of its social movements, the history of his own faction and that of his opponents, and—not infrequently—the history of mankind.

To the Social Revolutionaries, when he was explaining to them that they could never be "socialists but merely revolutionary democrats," albeit "devoted and honest revolutionary democrats," and was graciously allowing that they had the right to a place in the Petersburg Soviet of 1905 since "we are at this moment making precisely a democratic revolution," he explained that with your "inconsistencies and vacillations we can easily get along, for history itself supports our views, at every step reality supports us."[8]

Lenin felt he could not give battle to populism without setting down his own propositions concerning that movement's history, and the past, present, and inevitable future of Russia. He analyzed the brighter pages of populism's history in such fashion that his movement became the "legitimate heir" of all that was admirable in it, leaving for latter-day populism only the dregs of "vulgar, philistine-bourgeois radicalism."[9] His stout volume *The Development of Capitalism in Russia*, his "What Are the 'Friends of the People?' . . ," and his "What Heritage Do We Reject?" are on varying levels typical of his use or abuse of history in his war against populism.

In the same fashion, his battles with the "Economists" prompted him to review the history of Marxism and social movements, while his war on the Kadets and Zemstvo Liberals called for similar excursions into the history of liberalism, socialism, and Russia. When *Iskra* fought the other socialist movements and journals, and again when the Iskrists themselves split and Lenin joined battle with the other five *Iskra* editors, one of his main weapons was a thumbnail history of Marxism and of Russian and non-Russian social movements. Just as he had sought to outflank populism by claiming all that was "good" in its heritage and identifying the residue with philistine-bourgeois radicalism, so now he claimed to be the heir of Marxism and of all that was good in *Iskra* tradition, while he sought to identify the other five *Iskra* editors with economism and with the Kadets. All this was done in the guise of historiography.

Nor did his technique vary essentially when his battle was with Bolshevik disciples who were deviating to Left or Right, or "conciliating" at moments when he wanted a split, or holding to yesterday's Lenin formulae and Lenin historiography against today's. The moment a fight began, he was ready with an ad hoc and ad hominem historical sketch of how his opponents got that way, of the various stages in their degeneration, of their "essential identity" with some movement he and they had previously denounced, and of the inevitable path of their further decline.

Materialism and Empiriocriticism contains its Leninist history of philosophical thought, marvelously constructed on the foundation of a gloss of a single irrelevant dictum of Engels, tailored to his own views and polemical needs. If Mach, Avenarius, Petzhold or Pearson, or even Bogdanov, could not recognize his own image in Lenin's pages, so much the worse for them.

State and Revolution professes to be both an intellectual and a textual history of Marxist thought on the two subjects in its title and the connection between them. *The Socialist Revolution and the Renegade Kautsky* is equipped with a history of the Second and Third Internationals, and of the German social democracy and the Russian, together with a history of Marxism, and a capsule history of Kautsky himself. *Imperialism* has imbedded in it an outline history of contemporary society, a history of recent economic development and a history of ideas concerning imperialism itself. And so it is with virtually all his works, large and small.

"Periodization" as a Leninist Device

One of the peculiarities of Soviet historiography is its obsession with "periodization." In part this is traceable to a vulgarization of Marx's famous 1859 listing of diverse, according to some Marxists successive, and according to others inevitable-progressive, stages in the history of society. With Marx the listing was ambivalently typological *and* "progressive" or "inevitable." But when pressed he was ready to declare that the listing of Ancient, Feudal, Capitalist, and Socialist was typology rather than inevitable succession and at most applicable to Western Europe at a certain stage of its development.

However, for Russian, or rather, Soviet historiography, every land has its unilateral path marked out for it: feudalism, capitalism, socialism, communism. For every society such periodization is obligatory. This is a marvelous device for assuring feudalism where there is no trace of it, and socialism where there is neither capitalist industry nor a working class.

But the real author of the habit of "periodization" in party history is Lenin. He is tireless in his use of it as a device for demonstrating the progressive rise and magnification of his own movement and the progressive decline of the opposing movements. His periodization is rarely twice the same, but its usefulness is invariant.

In his conclusion to *What Is to Be Done?* the history of the socialist movement in Russia is divided into three periods, one of "intra-uterine" existence without workers, a second of "birth" as a political party looking to the working class but separated from its spontaneous movement, a third of decline and confusion,[10] and a fourth triumphant age of true socialism fusing with the spontaneous movement of the working class and embodying itself in *Iskra*.

In a report prepared under Lenin's direction for the Amsterdam Congress of the International (1904), there are four historical periods: pre-*Iskra*; *Iskra* period; Second Congress with its split; post-Congress period with the triumphant development of bolshevism into the true movement. New variants appear in his "Introduction to the Collection, 'After Twelve Years'" (1907); "The Historical Meaning of Inner Party Struggles in Russia" (1910); "On Some Peculiarities in the Historical Development of Marxism in Russia" (1910); "The Ideological Struggle in the Worker Movement" (1914); and in his "result of the three-decade development of Social Democracy in Russia," as given in "Socialism and War," (1917). When Lenin begins to lecture Left Communists in other parties of the Communist International in his "Infantile Sickness of Left Communism," he gives a new periodization of "The Main Stages in the History of Bolshevism." All these periodizations may differ in periods (dating) and in summation (names and meanings assigned to the periods). In this sense the periodization is ad hoc and history as flexible as a rubber band. But they all have one single, repetitive, overall meaning, which may be summed up in the words of Lenin already cited in his "welcome" to the Social Revolutionaries in the 1905 soviet: "History supports our views, at every step reality supports us."

Soviet historians of the party have all made use of the methods, one or another of the periodizations, and the verbatim formulations of Lenin for their works. The formulae, cut off now from the living, nutrient medium of contemporaneity, are imbedded like fossils in every subsequent party history.

No one has yet compiled a *Sbornik* or collection of all Lenin's historical excursions, which would serve as a *Guide to the Perplexed* for party historiography. But there is evidence that work is being done to prepare such a treatise and compendium to be called "Lenin as Historian of the Party."[11] In the meanwhile, the following quotations from *Voprosy istorii KPSS* can give us some notion of the general conclusions and approach to this theme:

> 1. Together with the rise of the Marxist party of the working class arose its historiography.
> 2. There is scarcely a single work of Lenin in which is not illuminated from a Marxist standpoint the history of the revolutionary movement.
> 3. The science of the history of the party occupies an outstanding place in the ideological struggle of the Communist party for the revolutionary transformation of society. There exists a definite relationship between historical investigations and the political activity of the party, between historical problematics and the political tasks of the party.
> 4. The development of the science of party-history can be understood only in its general connection with the entire ideological work of the party, in connection with that struggle which the party waged at its various stages against the many-numbered enemies of Marxism.[12]

Early Party Historians

Though every polemical work of Lenin was thus equipped with an "offensive" history of the party and other historical weapons, Lenin himself was too busy to write a systematic textbook on party history. This task was left to faithful followers like Lyadov, whose *History of the Russian Social Democratic Labor Party*, published in 1906, was republished three times under the Soviet regime. But in 1909 Lyadov fell into sin, or deviation from Lenin, and never updated his history.[13]

After the Bolshevik seizure of power, everybody was too busy making history to write it. Lenin continued to clothe each polemic in the armor of history, his disciples echoing him as best they could. Minuscule works like Bubnov's "The Chief Moments in the Development of the Communist Party of Russia," no bigger than a single long-winded talk, were of little interest then and are of less interest now.[14]

But the year 1923 marked a watershed in party historiography, for in that year Zinoviev delivered six lectures on the "History of the Communist Party of Russia (Bolsheviks)" and Trotsky poured fat into a smoldering fire with his "Lessons of October, 1917." These two top leaders had turned their hand to historiography, not as a weapon of struggle against other parties but as a weapon of struggle for the succession in the Communist party itself. From 1923 until the end of the 1930s, when Joseph Stalin ordered and edited the *Short Course*, intraparty warfare was the main function of party history. The lesser lights who engaged in the perilous craft—Bubnov, Nevsky, Kardashov, Volosevich, Yaroslavsky, Popov, Kerzhentsev, and Knorin, which last did not write but edited a history written by a "Collective" of the "Red Professors' Institute of Party History"—all had to weigh every line not merely as a justification of the Bolsheviks against the world, but with still greater care, as a justification of the "true" Bolsheviks against the deviator Bolsheviks, who in due course would turn out to be anti-Bolshevik enemies within the party.[15]

The Crisis in Party History

For the next decade, party historiography was in a steadily deepening crisis. Histories succeeded each other at a faster and faster rate, as if they were being consumed by a more and more irritable gigantic chain smoker who lit the first page of each new work with the last page of the old. Histories, and a little later, historians, disappeared without a trace. Nevsky published the first part of a two-part history of the party in 1923, but there was no second part. The published part was scrapped, and in 1925 he started over again. Yaroslavsky did the same. Indeed, Yaroslavsky kept writing histories which kept disappearing in favor of new histories by the same Yaroslavsky, so that by now no bibliographer can decipher how many Yaroslavsky histories there really were and what happened to them.[16] In 1926 he gathered a team, or "kollektiv" of historians and issued a four-volume work (vol. 1, 1926; vols. 2–4, 1929–30). But the fourth volume was obsolete within a year of its appearance. In 1933 he issued a new two-volume work which had a longer life, being reissued various times until 1938, when it disappeared, and he nearly disappeared with it. At that time, Nevsky and Bubnov disappeared too, their histories having disappeared earlier.

The bewildering thing to the outsider is that each of these histories and cycles of histories had been entrusted to its respective authors by Joseph Stalin as weapons in his struggles with Trotsky, Zinoviev, Bukharin, and finally, with his own followers. Each had striven to belittle Stalin's opponents or annihilate them, and had striven to glorify his name. But the heroes of one work became the dubious weaklings of the next and the villains and traitors of the third; the persons of one work became unpersons in the next; the stature and single-handed achievements of Joseph Stalin became so much larger from one year to the next—that each earlier version had not merely to obsolesce but to disappear, lest, arising from oblivion, it might bear witness against its successor. When a man had written several successive histories, his memory of documents and earlier versions would itself become perilous.

In despair at the transitoriness of all these individual efforts of his faithful servitors to celebrate the power and glory of the party and its genius-leader, Stalin ordered a political lieutenant who was not even on speaking terms with Knorin, to assemble a *Kollektiv* of pliable Red Professors to write the definitive party history. Knorin was an Old Bolshevik of Lettish origin, who had joined Lenin's party around 1912, perhaps a little earlier. He had been in the Comintern as Stalin's overseer of the German Communist party at that fateful moment when Stalin compelled it to direct its main fire against the Socialists and the Weimar Republic while Hitler rose to power. This seemed to be a suitable qualification for acting as overseer over a group of the "Red Professors' Institute of Party History," with B. Ponamarev as "Group Leader" (Rukovoditel). Published in 1935, Knorin's history proved to be as mortal as its predecessors. In 1937, its editor was arrested, accused of a "Lettish nationalist deviation," horribly tortured, forced to confess that he had been a tsarist agent first, then an agent of the Gestapo. He was shot within a year of his "confession."[17]

This high mortality rate among Soviet party histories and party historians has compelled Western writers to have recourse to a kind of archaeological method, as if they were dealing with a long-buried institution in a long-buried civilization. They must dig through the mutually contradictory, successive layers of relative truth and calculated falsehood in an effort to determine which of the many layers represents the true Homeric Troy—with this difference: in this case there is no true Homeric Troy, for Lenin had already set the example of partisan distortion of history to present his positions as absolute truth and to misrepresent and obscure the positions of his opponents.

There is, however, a way of doing historical detection and reconstruction by tracing the successive versions (down to the unversions and the antiversions) of some tender or touchy point—for example, why the Bolsheviks played no significant role in the 1905 Soviet, or in the February Revolution of 1917; or what Trotsky's role was in the 1905 Soviet, in the 1917 October seizure of power, in the Red Army and the civil war. Whenever one finds a tender spot, and these works abound in them, one may probe with some hope of success for the cause of the tenderness.

What We Can Learn from Zinoviev's History

Or the historical detective may ask himself why a certain fact or a certain history had disappeared altogether. Thus we may well ask: Why is it that the most important party leader to engage himself in the direct writing of a party history (if we except Trotsky who did most of his historical writing after he was no longer in a position to make history and was outside the Soviet Union), namely Gregory Zinoviev, does not get into the canon at all of works which in their time represented "significant contributions but contained methodological and theoretical errors"?

Zinoviev's history, which unfortunately stops with February 1917, was the reprint of a series of six carefully prepared and interminably long lectures, which he delivered early in 1923 "on the eve of the 25-year jubilee of our party." In other words, they must have been delivered in January and February of 1923, when Lenin was already ill, but still able to dictate a few articles. His disciples were eyeing each other up and maneuvering for position, but the struggle for the succession had not yet flared up, nor were the disciples sure that the master might not recover enough strength to reprove them. Moreover Zinoviev was closer to the past and more intimately acquainted with it than any of the successor historians. Therefore we can learn many things from Zinoviev's history that we cannot find in any subsequent account.

The Bolsheviks, we can see from his history, were only beginning in 1923 to get used to the one-party system. Hence the first of these six lectures is taken up with the problem of what is a party and why the Bolshevik party is arrogating to itself a monopoly of power. Zinoviev grapples with various sociological definitions of a party; he tries to explain why a party is not a voluntary organization of like-minded individuals who agree upon a common program; he rejects this view for the one that defines a party as a fighting organization of a class. He is troubled by the existence of a number of parties of the working class, and the consequent implication that there may be "classes" and a "class struggle" inside the working class. He is troubled, too, by worker and peasant support for the SRs. We learn that the SRs claim to represent "in the first instance the working class, in the second the peasantry, and in the third, the toiling intelligentsia." This, he insists, cannot be so; the "true class party" can represent only one class. Thereby we are reminded that today the Soviet Communist party claims to represent and be made up of the selfsame three classes that the SRs were once claiming.

The lecture "What Is a Party?" is full of feeble rationalizations. There are "many parties of the working class" but "only one party of the *proletariat*." The bourgeoisie has many parties, liberal, conservative, etc., but they are really all "factions of one bourgeois party." Zinoviev realizes that this rule may also be applied to the many parties of the working class, making them really all factions of one party. His answer is that the other working-class parties must be reckoned as also "only factions of the bourgeois party."

We find names, and even currents of thought, that today are swallowed up by the memory hole. One learns that the Bund "in the darkest night of Tsarist reaction was the first to rise in struggle." One learns of the SRs that "as long as it was a matter of victory over tsarism, these revolutionists had elan, energy, enthusiasm and zeal . . . knew what they were fighting for . . . what they were sacrificing themselves for, and from their ranks came such great men as Gershuni." There is praise for Plekhanov in really moving language. We are told that from Martov's "instructive" *History of the Russian Social Democracy* we can learn much "despite its errors." We learn that Prince Obolensky was a member of the party at the beginning of the century and a contributor to *Iskra*. One will search in vain in all subsequent histories for such nuggets of information. But by using the "archaeological method" of ranging the various versions of an event side by side, and by probing for the "tender spots," one can learn something from even the worst of them.

The Long Life of the *Short Course*

Finally, after the blood purges had reedited the age of Lenin by turning all his close associates into traitors, save only one, the survivor determined to fix the past himself, as he fixed music, linguistics, genetics, philosophy, legal theory, economics, Marxism, Leninism, and all else besides—especially his own place in history.

Thus was born the first party history that lived long enough to grow up and circumnavigate the globe, "the book that," according to *Pravda*, "has sold more copies than any other in modern times, the work of a genius, 'The Short History of the Communist Party of the Soviet Union,' by Joseph Stalin."[18]

At this point, party history was "stabilized." No new history appeared for fifteen years. All works in the field, and in many other fields of political, economic, and philosophical writing, became glosses and exegeses derived in whole or part from the *Short Course*. There was even a secret Politburo decision that no one was to be permitted to remember anything new about Lenin or publish any memoir concerning him, while countless already published memoirs were burned or pulped.[19]

Stalin's *Short Course*, though virtually unreadable, could be memorized by the faithful, and indeed, as a life insurance policy, had to be. As Leonard Schapiro has written in his own not-so-official history of the Communist party of the Soviet Union, Stalin's book performed the function of insuring that no Communist "need ever be at a loss for the official answer to every problem. No one understood better than Stalin that the true object of propaganda is neither to convince nor even to persuade, but to produce a uniform pattern of public utterance in which the first trace of unorthodox thought immediately reveals itself as a jarring dissonance."[20]

Now the savings involved in having only a single version of the past seemed to make themselves felt. The dullest of all best-sellers became the greatest of all best-sellers—with the exception of the Bible. By 1953, fifteen years after its publication, it was still the definitive "work of genius" and had been printed in editions of more than fifty million copies in the Soviet Union, and in all the important languages of the empire and the world.

But fifteen years is a long time for eternal truths to endure. In March 1953 the author died. In July, some still duller writers calling themselves Agitprop issued 7,500 leaden words of "Theses on Fifty Years of the Communist Party of the Soviet Union." They were published in *Pravda* on July 26, 1953. Now the millions who had toiled to learn by heart every formulation in the dull and mendacious pages of the *Short Course*

realized with a pang of fear that their "insurance policy" had been can-
celled. For, in the "Theses," they perceived that Stalin, who for fifteen
years had been up in front at the right hand of Lenin—the two of
them alone remaking the world—was now no longer Vozhd (Leader), no
longer co-founder of the party, nor mastermind of the seizure of power,
nor creator of the Red Army, nor winner of the civil war.

Indeed, where was he? Lenin was mentioned eighty-three times in the
7,500 words, Stalin only four. Still worse, the "Theses" gave no clue as
to whom it was now necessary to cheer. In its 7,500 words there were
only three names: those of Lenin and Stalin aforesaid, and one mention
of Plekhanov. All safely dead! To the initiated, this was a sign that a new
time of uncertainty had begun and that no living name was mentioned
because no successor had yet emerged.[21]

The only thing that was certain in this new time of uncertainty was
that the *Short Course*, all fifty million copies of it, had to be scrapped,
and with it all the works of gloss and exegesis. The greatest book burning
or book pulping in history! The system of a single, unitary, official history
was not proving so economical after all.

The Historyless Party

From the summer of 1953 to the summer of 1959, the much-chronicled
Communist party was without any history, except the 7,500 words of
depersonalized, historyless history of the Department of Agitation and
Propaganda.

Before a new history could be published, Stalin's ghost had to be
wrestled with and its size at least tentatively determined. The dictatorship
had to beget its new dictator; infallible doctrine its infallible expounder;
authoritarianism its authority; a totally militarized society its supreme
commander. The "collective leadership," so unnatural to a dictatorial
society where there are no checks on the flow of power to the top, had to
be disposed of, one by one or in batches, until one should emerge as the
embodiment of the party, and the others disappear as "anti-party."

Further, where power is knowledge and power over everything equivalent to knowledge concerning everything, the emergent authority on all
things must have time to lay down the line on the problems, persons, and
events likely to find their way into history. Only then could a new official
history emerge. For the present to be projected into the past, the present
has constantly and authoritatively to be determined in all wayward and
moot things.

So it was that from July 26, 1953, to June 17, 1959, there was literally no history of the Communist party of the Soviet Union except the 7,500 words of the "Theses" of Agitprop. On June 17, 1959, a new manuscript was given to the press, with instructions to print a first edition of 750,000 copies. Thus was born the Gospel according to Khrushchev.

Not that he claims personal authorship. Khrushchev is free from that pathological greed of credit that made Stalin claim credit for everything. The new history was "prepared," like Knorin's history of 1935, by an "authors' collective"—eleven academicians, doctors, or masters of "the historical, economic, and philosophical sciences."

Where so many histories have perished so swiftly, it was pleasant to find that the *rukovoditel* or leader for the Knorin history, B. N. Ponamarev, has survived the death of his earlier work, and appears as *rukovoditel* once more. And I. I. Mintz, who has written so many legendary pages (*legend* is to be taken in its literal not its poetic sense) in histories of the civil war, is alive and present, too, though Stalin once denounced his work. Most of the other historians whose works were once official and translated into many tongues, are gone: Zinoviev, Volosevich, Nevsky, Bubnov, Popov, Yaroslavsky, Knorin. Party historiography is one of the more hazardous occupations, where natural death is not so natural, for only Yaroslavsky seems to have died without special assistance from party and state.

If Ponamarev is once more *rukovoditel*, there is no longer a general editor to replace Knorin. Rather, there are signs on many pages that Khrushchev and his Agitprop secretary, Suslov, took personal care of the political overseer's task. For what we now have is quite manifestly intended to be the official history for the age of Khrushchev.

The Gospel according to Khrushchev

In its day, it had seemed to me that Stalin's *Short Course* was the ne plus ultra of dullness. Surely, the history of Russia in the twentieth century has been a turbulent one: conspiracy, party strife, war, general strike and uprising in 1905, world war, fall of the tsar, seizure of power by the Bolsheviks, civil war and intervention, Kronstadt and NEP, liquidation of the private peasant as a class, purge of all Lenin's closest lieutenants by one of them, Stalin-Hitler Pact, World War II, forced communization of so many occupied countries, struggle for the succession, emergence of Khrushchev. What material for the historian! But if the *Short Course* seemed dull and devoid of actual personages, motives, and events, it at least had a kind of fascination by virtue of the malevolence, the pathological boasting, envy, and vengeance, the touch of the demonic on every page. Though in Khrushchev's history, as we shall now call it for short, whole pages are lifted from the *Short Course*, what was demonic in Stalin's history is only ruthless and formularized in the latest work.

The Khrushchev history calls itself a "concise account." "Concise" must be more extensive than "short," for it is over twice as long; nor is the additional flood of words altogether accounted for by the fact that an additional twenty years have had to be chronicled. Where formulas of boasting or denigration have not been copied verbatim (as Stalin's *Short Course* often copied passages verbatim from Knorin or Popov), the new book is likely to use many more words to recount an episode than the old. Yet its pages seem strangely empty—empty of men, empty of events. In the place of men, there are the Party, the government, the masses, and Lenin. In the place of events, there are theses and bureaucratic formulas.

No need to be surprised if the great Bolshevik holdups of 1905–07 are missing; no party historian has spoken of them. But where are the Moscow Trials which formed the closing section of the *Short Course* like the baleful hellfire which lights up the last scene of Mozart's *Don Juan*? All of Lenin's close associates save only one were tried, confessed, liquidated—surely a chapter in party history by almost any test. But not one word. Twice the party purges of the thirties, in which Nikita Khrushchev played a substantial role, are obscurely hinted at, obscurely justified, and as obscurely called in question. On page 463 we learn that the party was strengthened by purge but "mistakes were made in the unfounded expulsion of so-called passive elements." Yet, after the purges, "two-faced and enemy elements remained in the party" and Kirov's murder "showed that a party card may be used as the cover for abominable antisoviet acts." Twenty-one pages later we learn that "many honest Communists and non-party people underwent repressions, being guilty of nothing." But the villains now are Beria and Yezhov. Inexplicably, Yagoda, their predecessor as "flaming sword of the revolution," is missing, both as the first great purger and as trial victim and confessed traitor. Just as inexplicably, for time is slippery in this history without a fixed chronological framework, Beria, whom Stalin appointed to call off the fury of the Yezhov purges, here precedes Yezhov.[22]

It is the disappearance of such large events and so many persons which makes the pages of this thick history seem so interminable and so empty. A standard feature of earlier histories was a list of Central Committee members elected by each congress, a list of reporters at each congress, and many other such accounts of persons and their posts or their proposals or their deeds. Too bureaucratic to be exciting, yet it peopled the pages of the text. But with each successive history, the lists became shorter. More and more men were silently dropped into a special opening to the memory hole which bears the label *"and others."* Now many of those who still found a place in Stalin's *Short Course*, if only to be denounced, have been dissolved in the acid of oblivion.

Besides, Khrushchev has names to eliminate from honorific lists whom Stalin delighted to honor as extensions of himself. The indestructible-seeming Molotov has faded like the Cheshire cat, leaving behind him only an "anti-party" frown. Kaganovich, able and ruthless lieutenant of Stalin who saw to Khrushchev's advancement by taking him along as assistant on each of his promotions, has ended up the same way. The rotund Malenkov, once Stalin's chief of cadres, a party secretary, a member of the high military council that ran the Great Patriotic War, main reporter at the Nineteenth Congress, after Stalin's death both general secretary and premier—at least for nine days—has also ended up without a past, a bit of rubbish for the "anti-party" dustbin.[23] A historian cannot help but feel that each of these is entitled to more space, if not a better fate.

In such a bureaucratic history, a party congress is an epoch-making event. At the Nineteenth Congress, held when the aging Stalin was three months from death, Molotov made the opening address, Malenkov delivered the main political report, Beria the report on the nationalities problem, Saburov on the Fifth Five-Year Plan, Khrushchev, Bulganin, and Mikoyan on the revision of the party statutes, and Kaganovich on the revision of its program. Mysteriously now the Congress mentions reports but there are no reporters and no contents. Only N. S. Khrushchev remains as the sole reporter on the party statutes, from which statutes a seven-line quotation constitutes the only words immortal enough to get into the pages of history.

Even those whom Stalin execrated have suffered further diminution. Stalin still had need of Trotsky as the Antagonist in the drama of good and evil. He had to paint Trotsky as saboteur of each of Trotsky's own chief actions, since one of the aims of the *Short Course* was to replace in men's minds that unity in duality, Lenin-Trotsky, by a new unity in duality, Lenin-Stalin. Thus Trotsky's name was still bound to large events, if only by a minus sign.

Though Khrushchev's history copies some of these pages from the *Short Course*, Nikita Sergeevich does not have the same need of Trotsky to play anti-Christ to his Savior; hence the baleful glare that lengthened his shadow through the *Short Course* is subdued to the dingy light that is common to these pages. The October Revolution takes place without the chairman of the Petrograd Soviet and Military Revolutionary Committee, who directed the operations of the seizure of power and conceived its strategy. The civil war is fought and the Red Army built without him. The Kronstadt mutiny is gloriously crushed without either his or Tukhashevsky's intervention. Voroshilov has retroactively been appointed director of the attack on Kronstadt, while Marshal Tukhashevsky, who seemed on the way to rehabilitation until Zhukov fell, has disappeared from history again.

If the climax of Stalin's *Short Course* was the "Liquidation of the Remnants of the Bukharin-Trotsky Gang of Spies, Wreckers and Traitors to the Country," which is the actual title of the closing section of the last chapter, the new Khrushchev history has no climax. It just stops, because when it was issued the Twenty-first (Extraordinary) Congress was over and the Twenty-second had not yet been convened. It was obvious that it would not last the fifteen years of its predecessor, for history would keep adding to its bureaucratic sum, and had already subtracted several of the leaders designated by the Twenty-first Congress, like Belysev and Kirichenko.

Further evidence that the *Concise Account* is already obsolescing, and for really serious purposes unsatisfactory, is to be found in the plan for a new "many-volumed" history of the party (actually six volumes, the first of which by the end of 1960 was reported as having already gone to press, and the rest as being prepared "at high speed").[24] In that connection, both multiple archives and many of the earlier histories are being treated as "useful material." Most interesting is the partial rehabilitation of Stalin's *Short Course*, which Khrushchev had damned so thoroughly in his "secret speech." After listing the other histories which enter into the canon of those which in their time "contained a large amount of factual material . . . but [also] many methodological and theoretical errors," *Voprosy istorii KPSS* says editorially:

> From this [imprint of its time, and from these errors] the "Short Course of the History of the VKP (b)" was not free either, although it was also for its time a mighty stride forward in the development of party-history science. The fact that this book served for a long time as a peculiar standard for historical-party investigations significantly held back the further scientific working out of problems of the history of the party.

> Of course, this does not in any degree whatsoever justify the position of those historians who, incorrectly interpreting the decisions of the Twentieth Congress of the CPSU tried, under the flag of a struggle against the cult of personality and its consequences, to reexamine some of the fundamental propositions of theory and policy of the party laid down in the "Short Course. . . ." For this insignificant number of historians was characteristic a nihilistic attitude towards the entire party-historical literature of the end of the thirties and the years of the forties. They strongly called for a

return to the text books of the twenties and thirties which contain innumerable theoretical and political errors. . . . [25]

That Cult of Personality

Thus Khrushchev is still wrestling with the size of Stalin's ghost. In a historiography in which everything is "made to order" according to party needs, various sizes and patterns have been tried in an effort to determine Stalin's "place in history." To convince ourselves of that, we need only compare the Stalin of the secret speech at the Twentieth Congress with the Stalin of the 1959 history and of Khrushchev's subsequent utterances. Having reached the greatest diminution at the Twentieth Congress, Stalin's figure has been cautiously, but on the whole steadily enlarged ever since.

On the one hand, there was need to write Stalin smaller than in the *Short Course*, lest all his successors remain too dwarfed for any of them to succeed him. Moreover, his lieutenants not without cause, so feared each other, and the party so feared the inevitable struggle among them, that it was necessary to give assurance "that henceforth such occurrences should never again take place in the party and the country." This was promised by a resolution of the Twentieth Congress and is repeated in the new history. Insofar as it implies the rejection of the pathological extremes of Stalin's vengeful reign, it may be taken seriously.

On the other hand, Stalin's successor could not destroy the link which puts him in the line of apostolic succession. For what else but the apostolic succession from Lenin, who seized power, to Stalin, who usurped it by taking over and perfecting Lenin's machine, what other "legitimacy" and claim to rule over a great empire has the present First Secretary?

The inheritance includes many things for which the 1959 history gives Stalin great credit:

1. The annihilation of all rival parties, such as Mensheviks and Socialist Revolutionaries and Kadets. (Hence the history repeats the absurdities of the frameup trials of the Mensheviks, the Industrial party, the Toiling Peasant party.)

2. The annihilation of all anti-Stalinist Communist groups (Trotskyites, Zinovievites, Bukharinites, for whom there can be no rehabilitation).

3. Forced industrialization and the primacy of heavy industry over production for consumption.

4. The annihilation of the peasantry and the forced collectivization of agriculture.

5. The party penetration and control of all organizations and the

atomization of the individual. (This is a heritage from Lenin perfected by Stalin and is inseparable from totalitarianism.)

6. Stalin's conquests of the Baltic Republics, half of Poland, part of East Prussia, Finland and Rumania, and Tannu Tuva.

7. The "liberation" of the rest of Poland, of Hungary (two "liberations"), of East Germany *and* Berlin, of the Balkan lands including Yugoslavia, of China, North Korea and Vietnam.

8. The "struggle for peace" and the enlargement of the "peace camp" which permits, nay requires, the "liberation" of further parts of the non-Communist world but not the "reenslavement" of any part that has been liberated. (The book makes clear that "peaceful coexistence" is as old as Lenin and Stalin and not to be interpreted too differently from the way it was by them.)

This is a large balance sheet. In it Stalin's crimes against the Russian people, against the Russian peasantry, against allies and neighbors and occupied countries are all transformed into virtues listed on the credit side of the ledger. His crimes against other socialist and democratic parties and opposition Communists are listed as virtues, too, with only the reservation that he dealt too harshly with "good Communists" (which seems to mean Stalinists) when he liquidated them. Even then, when the vengeful guillotine is turned on loyal Stalinists, the history does not cry "Crime!" but mumbles "Error" or "harmful consequence of the cult of personality."

Its final verdict reads: "Under the leadership of the Communist Party and its Central Committee, in which J. V. Stalin played a leading role, the Soviet Union has achieved enormous, world-wide successes. J. V. Stalin did much that was beneficial to the Soviet Union, to the CPSU, and to the whole international workers movement."

Thus Khrushchev's tremendous indictment of Stalin's cruelty and paranoia in his secret speech dwindles into a bureaucratic formula for much praise and a little halting blame, now that Khrushchev himself is secure in the possession of his heritage.

What, then, is happening to the size of the "personality" of Nikita Sergeevich Khrushchev?

To get a perspective, we must bear in mind that this is not the final masterpiece of Khrushchev historiography but only a first attempt, analogous more to the early efforts of a Yaroslavsky than to Stalin's final chef d'oeuvre—the *Short Course.*

Moreover, Khrushchev has difficulties that Stalin did not have. It is not possible for a man who joined the party only after it had won power to picture himself as one of the party's co-founders. Hence the book's only living hero (the dead heroes being Lenin and Stalin) does not enter into its 745 pages until page 314, then modestly enough as one of a list of

Lenin's "comrades-in-arms and disciples hardened in the civil war . . . on whose backs lay the burden of liquidating the consequences of the war and constructing a socialist society." The list contains twenty-three names, in discreet alphabetical order, Stalinists all, and the impartial alphabet puts Khrushchev (in Russian it begins with an X) in the twentieth place and Stalin himself in the eighteenth.

Not until page 608, with the Nineteenth Congress, does Khrushchev begin seriously to employ the technique of self-enlargement learned from the master. Here, as we have seen, Molotov who delivered the opening address, Malenkov who delivered the main report, Beria, Kaganovich, and Saburov who reported too, all became unpersons, while Khrushchev holds the vast stage alone.

By the Twentieth Congress, Khrushchev had gotten such a hold of the party machine that he did in actual fact hold the stage alone and make all the reports. The proceedings left no doubt that the First Secretary was more equal than the others, who were permitted to share in but not equal his applause. The order of business was: opening address, Khrushchev; report of the Presidium and Central Committee (covering everything), Khrushchev; chairman of the committee to draw up a resolution on the report, Khrushchev; chairman of the new Bureau on Party Affairs of the Russian Republic, Khrushchev; secret report on the cult of personality, Khrushchev. Only Bulganin was permitted a subreport, a gloss on the First Secretary's remarks on the Sixth Five-Year Plan, and Bulganin has of course since disappeared from public view.

As for the Twenty-first Congress, which makes up the final chapter of this book, it had only one order of business: a report on the control figures for the Seven-Year Plan, by Nikita Sergeevich Khrushchev. Such is the fitting bureaucratic climax, or anticlimax, to the strange transformation of so many clashes of arms and deeds of blood into bureaucratic formulas.

In the closing chapter, Khrushchev is cited and his "ideas" as expressed in reports are summarized fourteen times in a scant twenty-six pages. Actually, this is a little higher score than the citations from Stalin in the closing chapter of the *Short Course*. Stalin's closing chapter ends with a quote from Stalin; Khrushchev's with a quote from Khrushchev. The First Secretary and once "best disciple of Joseph Stalin" has learned his trade.

In each case the closing chapter is followed by a brief coda called "Conclusion." In the *Short Course*, Stalin jostles Lenin here for first place. Whether it be good sense or greater need, in the conclusion to the new history Lenin and the party are given first place. Yet even here, Khrushchev is quoted four times. In the *Short Course*, the last words are a quote from Stalin. In the new history, Khrushchev bows out three pages before the end, while the last two sentences are eight words from Lenin on the party as "the intelligence, honor and conscience of our party" followed by twelve from Marx on Communism's promise: "From each according to his means, to each according to his needs."

Such is the nature of the party history in which the two new features, which were lacking in the *Short Course*, are the "liquidation of the harmful consequences of the cult of personality," and . . . the recording of the substantial beginnings of a new cult.

History Is Still Being Made

As this paper is being written, the Twenty-second Congress has been set for October 17, 1961. It will be the largest congress in the history of the party, a veritable monster mass meeting of the party officials and Soviet elite. As such it cannot discuss or resolve anything but it can and will be a huge sounding board. The order of business, already announced, shows that the only "political-theoretical" reports are to be respectively "The Report of the Central Committee of the CPSU—Reporter First Secretary of the CC of the CPSU, Comrade Khrushchev, N. S." and "The Draft of a Program of the CPSU—Reporter Comrade Khrushchev, N. S."[26] Thus it is clear that the man who monopolized the Twentieth and Twenty-first congresses will fill the stage of the Bolshoi Teatr at the Twenty-second also. This will obviously require a new chapter in the "Concise Account," for not at every congress does the Communist party adopt a new program. Indeed, it has adopted no new program since 1919 in Lenin's day, and Nikita Sergeevich, reporting on the draft of a program for the "Extended Development of Full Communism" is thus to pin upon himself the accolade of Marxist-Leninist theoretician, updater and continuer of Lenin.

Increasingly, "Nikita Sergeevich personally" has been receiving telltale messages and greetings, from party leaders, from scientific gatherings, from foreign parties and rulers, from outer space. On his sixty-fifth birthday (hitherto only round numbers such as sixty and seventy and the three-quarters of a century seventy-five have been fussed about, but Khrushchev is now a man in a hurry), the Presidium of the Central Committee of the CPSU set itself beneath him on the ladder of hierarchy by publishing these words: "Our dear Nikita Sergeevich, on your 65th birthday we warmly and heartily greet you—our elder comrade and friend, true disciple of Lenin and outstanding leader of the Communist Party, the Soviet State and the entire working class movement."[27]

Ulbricht, ever good on making an early leap upon a promising bandwagon, dedicated an eighteen-page article on Khrushchev's sixty-fifth birthday to the new "positive hero" of our era.[28] *Izvestia* found the report of Nikita Sergeevich to the Twenty-first Congress to be "a programmatic document for our party, the whole international working class and the Communist movement . . . one of the greatest works of Marxism-Leninism."[29]

Of the various learned societies which are beginning to send messages of admiration and appreciation to "Nikita Sergeevich personally," the most interesting to us is, of course, that of the historians. On October 20, 1960, the Section of Historical Sciences of the Academy of Sciences of the USSR convoked a general meeting of the section for the sole purpose of discussing "the results of the Eleventh International Congress of Historical Sciences in Stockholm." The report on this discussion in *Voprosy istorii* reaches its climactic end with these words so obviously relevant to the order of business:

> At the close of the General Meeting of the Section of historical sciences of the Academy, Academician N. M. Druzhinin read a letter addressed to the First Secretary of the Central Committee of the Communist Party of the Soviet Union, the Chairman of the Council of Ministers of the USSR, N. S. Khrushchev:
>
> Dear Nikita Sergeevich!
>
> The General Meeting of the Section etc. . . . warmly congratulates you, dear Nikita Sergeevich, on the great and important successes achieved by you at the Fifteenth Session of the General Assembly of the UN. [That was the session in which Khrushchev took his shoe off.] . . . You displayed such many-sided and fruitful activity in the interests of the happiness and progressive development of the whole of humanity.
>
> Your passionate and untiring struggle for peace . . . for general disarmament, for immediate liquidation of colonialism, has won for you the feeling of the deepest gratitude of all honest people. Your amazing capacity for clearly and simply explaining the high humanist principles of our advanced Marxist-Leninist ideology exercises the most powerful influence on the widest masses of people on our planet.
>
> We historians, specializing as we do in the study of the great events of the past, can easily distinguish in the contemporaneity of present events also those which have a transcendant historical significance.
>
> We do not doubt that your activity at the Fifteenth Session of the General Assembly of the UN will go down in the annals of history as a most valuable contribution to the cause of the struggle for peace,

as a bold and farsighted act worthy of the outstanding statesman of a Leninist type. Proud of the fact that at the head of the Soviet Government stands a man who so well understands the basic needs and demands of our epoch, we from the bottom of our hearts wish you good health and the continuance for long years of your inexhaustible energy in the pursuit of the goals of the fastest resolution of the gigantic historical tasks placed on the order of the day—the freeing of mankind from wars and the evils connected with them, and disarmament.

The resolution was unanimously adopted by all who attended the meeting.[30]

After the Section of Historical Sciences of the Academy has adopted this conclusion to their discussion of the "Results of the Stockholm International Congress of Historical Sciences," can there any longer be any doubt but that the "Concise History" issued in 1959 is already out of date, and that a drastic revision is needed, particularly of its closing sections? Small wonder that *Voprosy istorii KPSS* finds editorially in its number for September 1960, that the "History of the Communist Party of the Soviet Union," issued in 1959, though it "gives a Marxist-Leninist illumination of the basic stages of the historical road travelled by the CPSU up to our days, nevertheless is only a short textbook, in which, naturally the many sided activity of our party in its fullness and concreteness cannot be given."[31]

What we can look forward to now is a six-volume work with the sixth volume devoted to the age of Khrushchev, and, at the same time, a new version of the 1959 history, or a succession of versions, in each of which the "historians specializing in the study of the past" will also show how they "can easily distinguish in the contemporaneity of events those which have a transcendant historical significance." Can anyone doubt that what they are distinguishing now so clearly are the great deeds and thoughts, and the steadily expanding figure of Nikita Sergeevich Khrushchev? Today he is still called *Rukovoditel.* After he has displaced the program drafted by Lenin in 1919 and filled the vacuum left when "Marxism-Leninism-Stalinism" was cut shorter by amputation of its tail, will he not then achieve his ambition of being linked up directly with Lenin, and assume the title of Vozhd? And will not Clio, as usual, be called upon to justify and celebrate the event?

9

A Party of a New Type

He keeps chiseling—chiseling at the same spot—finally he chisels through. People become aware that a man has a high opinion of himself, that he gives orders—that's the main thing, he gives orders; consequently he's bound to be right, and one is compelled to obey him. All our schematics established themselves in just this way.
    Turgenev in *Smoke*

Wer einst den Blitz zu zünden hat muss lange—Wolke sein.
    Nietzsche

The age of total wars called for new leaders. Men of modest aims, transaction and compromise—the reasonable, knowing, sagely cynical moderate men who had played their parts in the concert of Europe according to the view that *politics is the art of the possible*—were not suited to the total mobilization of body and spirit and the waging of war "until final victory." Needed now were reckless spenders of lives and treasure, men of supernal energy, uninhibited demagogy, "charismatic" attributes.[1] The crisis that was to overwhelm Russia in the third year of the war was in great measure due to the refusal of an unimaginative and unimpressive tsar and a domineering and unloved tsarina to dismiss their aging retinue of routinary bureaucrats and favorites and put at the helm new men equal to the new tasks. In Austria-Hungary, too, an aging, moldering court paralyzed the war effort until the monarchy crumbled.[2]

But in most lands, those who had blundered into the war gave way to those who could wage it. The men who would dictate the treaties at Brest and Versailles seemed a different breed from those at the helm in 1914. Where an old leader was not replaced it was generally because he showed the ability, like the nation, to go through a transformation.

All institutions were transformed, from industry, which became in essence war industry, to finance, which worked not with calculated revenues and expenditures but with astronomical deficits; from the church of the Prince of Peace, which learned to bless the sword, to the social democracy, which replaced class struggle by civil peace and sacred union.

135

Whether their deaths were timely or not, gone forever was the world of Jean Jaurès and August Bebel.

In its way, history was kind to these two in letting them die before their day had quite ended. The others groped in the new darkness—grieved, shocked, robbed of certitudes, demoralized to their depths. They might wave flags or marshal self-justifying quotations, but something essential had gone out of their simple faith in class struggle, internationalism, peace, and socialism.

All but one! Lenin did not have to change his temper, nor his theories. Since the Russo-Japanese War and its aftermath of revolutionary unrest, he had held that war was the fruitful mother of revolution. Far from despairing, he was possessed by a new rage . . . and a new certainty. Rage at the great party of Marx, Engels, Bebel, and Kautsky, which he had expected to lead the international struggle in war as in peacetime. Certainty that the bourgeoisie, having begun this universal war, would never be able to end it. War was the begetter of revolution; world war would beget world revolution. Not "they," but the revolution would end it. That revolution with which he lived day and night, which possessed his waking hours, and of which in his sleep he dreamed—it would come in *his* time, out of *this* war.

"Great historical questions," he had written in 1905, "are settled only by force."[3] The thought had pleased him so much that on a number of occasions he repeated it. When the Balkan Wars came in 1912 and 1913, hope stirred in him that the war might spread, at least to Russia and Austria-Hungary. This would be a "very useful trick for the revolution in all of Eastern Europe," he wrote to Gorky, "but it is hardly likely that Franz Josef and Nikolasha will give us this pleasure."[4]

Not for him was the foreboding with which Marx and Engels had contemplated the prospect of universal war. Nor the dismay and disillusion which oppressed French and German socialists when they failed to prevent it. Now had come a time, Lenin wrote, "for heavy hob-nailed boots."[5] In these boots, he prepared to step from the Russian onto the world stage, to offer his analysis, outlook, tactics, ideas, his "rockhard, irreconcilable" temper, his personal leadership, as the only proper ones to the "newest age of wars and revolutions."

We must now take a closer look at this unique leader whose ideas and methods, whose moral code, whose attitude toward the civilization into which he was born, toward his native country, and toward war itself, have contributed so profoundly to the shaping of our age.[6]

Vladimir Ilyich Ulianov was forty-four and at the height of his powers. In a way peculiar to his self-confident, authoritative temperament and deeply Russian milieu, he had been "old" since his middle twenties. All memorialists agree to this, as do his own writings. A. N. Potresov, close colleague of Lenin's earliest political career and member of a *troika* with him from 1895 to 1903, falters when he tries to describe "the young Lenin," for "he was young only in his passport."[7] Even in that early time there was the bald dome with the thin fringe of dark-reddish hair, the sparse reddish moustache and beard, the "unyouthful hoarse voice" enunciating certitudes, judging people, selecting, admonishing, mocking, annihilating, binding to himself a little band of respectful followers, many of them older than he, who regarded him as the Russian folk regard a wise and revered elder. Before he was out of his twenties, they were calling him *Starik*—"The Old Man." "The Old Man is wise," they would chuckle exultantly, even when the wisdom lay in some not-too-scrupulous polemical thrust or maneuver. Lenin accepted the title *Starik* as if it were the most natural thing in the world for an authoritative young man to be thus addressed by his contemporaries and elders. Many of his early letters he begins, "*Starik* writing," or ends with the signature, *Starik*. Even to Gleb Krzhizhanovsky, intimate comrade-in-arms since 1895, who had lived near him in Siberian exile for seventeen months and one of the only two political persons whom Lenin addressed by the intimate second person singular *ty*, he nevertheless would open a letter with "*Starik* writing" and close with "*Ves' tvoj Starik*" (All yours, the Old Man).[8]

Furthermore, this youthful "patriarch" was addressed by the members of his circle—many of them older and longer in the movement than he— not by first name and patronymic (*Vladimir Ilyich* would have been the customary method of address), but by his patronymic alone (*Ilyich*). When his followers spoke among themselves about him, they called him Ilyich, too. His youth, and the supposed equality of comradeship in the socialist movement, made this form of address strange. No other Russian political leader was called so. Not even Plekhanov, older by a decade and a half and honored by all—Lenin included—as the "Master" and the "Father of Russian Marxism," was ever addressed or referred to as Valentinovich, in place of Georgij Valentinovich. In many a Russian village, there was a respected elder addressed thus by patronymic alone, as a mark of intimacy, respect and affection. In Lenin's case the element of intimacy was lacking, for who would dream of slapping *Ilyich* on the back or expect to be slapped on the back by him? Both the *Ilyich* and *Starik* were signs of his authoritative and charismatic predominance, a socialist leader of a different sort with followers of a different sort. Furthermore, both titles reveal, perhaps without their users being conscious of it, how deeply his group was saturated with habits inherited from the Orthodox Russian folk. Stranger still, and to the sensitive a little repugnant, even Krupskaia called him *Ilyich*, as if she were a worshipful disciple, not his wife.[9]

A second trait setting Lenin apart from his associates was his absorption with the mechanics and dynamics of organization. In a world where most intellectuals were in love with ideas, and accustomed—whether by temperament or the pressure of bitter circumstance—to a gap between dream and deed, Lenin was an *organization man*, indeed, *the* organization man, of whatever movements he planned or took part in. He was an enemy alike to the slippered sloth and to the dusk-to-dawn discussion of the Russian intellectuals, as well as to the "spontaneous" and "unreliable" flare-ups, subsidings, and conception of the Russian masses' own interests. All his life he was at work on a machine to harness the force of the waves and tides, to convert their fluctuating, unreckonable rise and fall into a single stream of energy. It was his aim, as he wrote, "to collect and concentrate all the drops and streamlets of popular excitement that are called forth by Russian conditions . . . into one single, gigantic flood." Tidily, yet passionately, he assumed the task of "choosing the people who are necessary and verifying the practical execution of decisions." In a world of intellectuals who lived by ideas, organization was his idea. "In its struggle for power, the proletariat has no other weapon but organization." "*Now* we have become an organized party, and that means the creation of power, the transformation of the authority of ideas into the authority of power, the subordination of the lower party organs to the higher ones." Amidst men dedicated to dreams, organization was his dream. "Give me an organization of revolutionaries," he cried, echoing Archimedes, "and I will turn Russia upside down."[10]

When, at the so-called Second Congress, which was called to form a party, delegate Popov spoke of the future Central Committee in liturgical language as a "Spirit, omnipresent and one," Lenin cried out from his seat, "Not Spirit, but *Fist*."[11] Before there was a party congress or a central committee, Lenin was already dreaming of this, his fist, which would hold all reins in its grasp, control all levers and springs of action. In 1902, a year before the congress, he wrote:

> The Committee should lead *all* aspects of the local movement and direct *all* local institutions, forces and resources of the party. . . . Discussion of all party questions, of course, will take place also in the district circles, but the *deciding* of all general questions of the local movement should be done only by the Committee. The independence of the district groups, it follows, would be permitted only in questions of the technique of transmitting and distributing. The composition of the district groups should be determined by the Committee, i.e., the Committee designates one or two of its members (or even those not members of the Committee) as delegates

to such and such a district, and entrusts these delegates with *setting up the district group*, all the members of which should be in their turn confirmed . . . in their positions by the Committee. The district group is a local branch of the Committee, receiving its powers only from the latter.[12]

Thus the Central Committee was to be the brain, the local organizations the limbs; the committee would decide, the locals execute; the committee would designate and confirm the local leaders in their posts, then the local leaders would in due course become delegates to a congress which would approve the Central Committee which had designated them. Such a Central Committee would be spirit and fist in one.

To his associates (as distinct from his admiring followers) there was something disconcerting in this zealotry of centralization. Yet their minds were on other aspects of the movement, its doctrine, its theory, its journalistic exposition. Organization was an unattractive concern. Not unwillingly, they handed over its practical burdens to this self-appointed, dedicated expert on organization. For their part, they dreamed of the day when Russia would know sufficient liberty so that the masses of workingmen might form their own organizations and democratically control and designate their central organs, which would then serve and obey rather than utilize and command the working class. But in the meanwhile Russia was police-ridden, and proper socialist organization was well nigh impossible. "Whether this revolutionary practice," Potresov was to write later, "which had not been so much experienced as thought up in the head of its future organizer, was really the practice which corresponded with the aims and methods of international social democracy, it was still difficult to judge." Later Lenin's associates "had to pay dearly for this misunderstanding."

The others might dream of the day when Russia would be free enough for the workingmen to organize freely and freely select their officials and determine their own program. Then the party, they thought, would become a simple instrument of the class, its creature and its servant, willing, expert, and dedicated to the task of helping the working class to achieve its own aims and its own freely decided goals. But Lenin did not see it that way. This was to him not Marxism, but a species of treason to Marxism. This was "bourgeois politics," as he wrote in one of his most uncompromising, and to his colleagues most incomprehensible, early utterances: "The task of the bourgeois politician is to 'assist the economic struggle of the proletariat.' The task of the socialist is to make the economic struggle assist the socialist movement and the victory of the revolutionary labor party."[13]

Could authoritarianism go further? To the question, do the workers exist for the party or does the party exist for the workers, Lenin had already found his sui generis, uncompromising answer.[14]

At first Lenin did not have the faintest idea that his concepts of organization and of the relation of the Central Committee to party and party to class were to set him apart from his fellow Marxists and embroil him in a lifelong war with them, which would end on opposite sides of a barricade.

He had always regarded Plekhanov as his teacher and one of the two greatest living Marxists (Kautsky being the other). Until 1903 he looked on the Marxists of his own generation as peers and partners. From 1895 to 1900 he formed a troika or "triple alliance," as he called it, with two close comrades, his future Menshevik opponents, Martov and Potresov. It was the first of a series of a dozen triumvirates which he was to set up in the course of a lifetime to give the cover of collective leadership to his strongly original ideas on organization and his de facto one-man leadership. But this first troika differed from all the subsequent troikas in one respect: despite Lenin's headstrong self-assurance and confidence in the correctness of the least of his ideas, there was about this first troika a sense of equal partnership which would be lacking in all the others.

While in exile in Siberia, where he was until early 1900, Lenin worked out in meticulous detail plans for a Marxist journal to be published abroad and smuggled into Russia. His "triple alliance" would associate with itself the prestige and wisdom of that older generation, led by Plekhanov, which had been living in foreign exile since the beginning of the eighties. That would give the new journal an editorial board of six —three "elders" to give prestige and theoretical wisdom, three "youngsters" to supply practical organization, editorial and clandestine distribution activity.

The elders, Plekhanov, Axelrod, and Vera Zasulich, living out their homesick lives isolated from Russia, were delighted with this energetic young man with a practical bent for organization. To be sure, there was a nasty moment when Plekhanov, taking it for granted that he would be the editor of the new journal, found that Lenin had come to the same conclusion about himself. Plekhanov was haughty, Lenin in a "rage" or "fury," a kind of overwhelming storm such as would well up in him from the depths of his being at intervals throughout his life.[15]

In a report to his faction, "How the Spark Was Nearly Extinguished,"[16] a document which takes up twenty-five pages in his *Collected Works* and is written in language more suited to a Russian novel than a political report, Lenin told how he had been "enamored" of Plekhanov, and "had courted him out of the great love I bore him. . . . Never, never in my life," he continued, "have I regarded any other man with such sincere respect and reverence . . . never stood before anyone with such humility, never been so brutally spurned. At times I thought I should burst into tears." But neither veneration or love, nor grief or humility suggested to him that Plekhanov, and not he, should be the editor. "My infatuation disappeared as if by magic . . . An enamored youth received from the object of his love a bitter lesson: to regard all persons without sentiment; to keep a stone in one's sling."

At that moment, the "youth" grew up. He never spoke of himself as a youth again. On the granite of his character, the lesson then engraved would last a lifetime. Three years later, when he was outvoted at a party congress on an organization, he would show that he could "regard without sentiment" not only the "elders" but the other two members of his triumvirate as well. In 1900, however, the "lovers' quarrel" was still patched up with a cold agreement to live together "without infatuation" —with Lenin having his way.

Iskra would be printed in Germany, where Lenin lived, not Switzerland, where Plekhanov made his home. Lenin's wife was to be its secretary, keep the confidential addresses, code, uncode, develop the invisible ink, handle correspondence with the underground, consult with Lenin, and, on his order, dispatch items of correspondence to the others. Lenin assumed the burden of rewriting correspondence from Russia into articles, the tasks of answering most of them, assigning themes to the other editors subject to their approval, nagging contributors, dummying, proofreading (usually with Martov's help), cutting, arguing with authors to get revisions. He wrote the exhortations and instructions to the agents in Russia, developed the apparatus for smuggling, dispatched escapees and exiles to become agents, selected people to come abroad, be briefed by him, and return again to Russia. His fellow editors were grateful that he took upon his single shoulders these ungrateful tasks. Thus, from the outset, Lenin was master of the *apparat* which he himself had conceived.

He was better than any of the other five at his self-chosen chores. Plekhanov had a wider-ranging mind and more learning in Marxist theory, Vera Zasulich more concern with the sufferings of the masses, Axelrod more respect for the autonomy and dignity of the workers' organizations; Martov was a better journalist, Potresov a better provider of funds— mostly from his own private inherited fortune. But Lenin was the systematic, doctrinaire thinker on organization questions and the fulfiller of his own doctrines.

Moreover, it was he who had conceived an especially large, indeed unique role for their journal. Plekhanov, Martov, or Potresov could have edited it, too, but it would have had another character. On the masthead was the old message of hope from the Decembrists to Pushkin: "Out of the spark (*Iskra*) shall come the flame." To Lenin this was more than a figure of speech. *Iskra* was to be "an enormous pair of bellows that would blow every spark of popular indignation into a flame." It was to be "not only the collective agitator but the collective organizer." It was to become the guardian of the purity of doctrine, the destroyer of rival revolutionary theories (heresies in Lenin's mind) and rival movements (enemies to him). It was to be "the scaffolding" of an all-Russian revolutionary party, the convoker of a unifying and homogenizing all-national congress, for the party that should issue from it must be not only unified but uniform, not only integrated but systematized, rigorously intolerant of variety, pluralism, multiformity, whether in ideology or structure.

Iskra's "network of agents" must become the vanguard and elite of the revolutionary movement. They must "devote to the revolution not only their spare evenings, but the whole of their lives." They must make revolution their profession and be professional in their revolutionary skills. No mere vendors or distributors of a clandestine journal, they must "introduce strict division of labor in the various forms of work," become "accustomed to fulfilling the detailed functions of the national (All-Russian) work . . . , test their strength in organization of various kinds of revolutionary activities . . . , form the skeleton of an organization . . . sufficiently large to embrace the whole country"; they must be sufficiently self-assertive, ubiquitous, and omnipotent to "utilize" every flare-up of discontent in "every layer" of society, whether zemstvo, or student, or peasant, or worker. The aim of the journal was "to gather a clandestine circle of leaders and to set in motion the greatest possible mass." Clearly this was not a group of newspaper distributors, but a party. More than a party, for a party might embrace all who agreed with it. The network of agents would be "the officers' cadres" of future armies, which it would lead in a storm attack against the citadel of tsarism. Their work for the paper "would serve as an exact measure of the extent to which . . . our military activities[17] had been firmly established. . . . This degree of military preparedness can be created only by the constant activity of a regular army. . . ." Not an ordinary army either, but an officer's corps, capable of expansion at any moment of unrest into the general staff of a multitudinous host. "The paper will bring forward not only the most competent propagandists but the most skillful organizers, and the most talented political leaders, who will be able at the right moment to issue the call for the decisive battle, and to lead that battle."[18]

While the other editors thought of themselves as agitators and propagandists, ideological guides and teachers, who told *Iskra* readers what to think and believe, only the rough-hewn, repetitive, audacious articles signed *Lenin* told them what to *do* and how high a value to set upon themselves and their routine-seeming work. In due course he elaborated all these articles into an epoch-making brochure called, after the celebrated utopian novel of Chernyshevsky, *Chto Delat'?* [What is to be done?].

Was ever a journal given so large a role in history? No wonder the *Iskra* agents in their narrow-horizoned, suffocating underground were attracted to this wise, old-young man. Here was a dream that gave one's smallest tasks enormous meaning. A dream that took one's breath away. Here was a commander one could trust, follow, worship. Even his amoralism seemed engagingly attractive when he wrote instructions on how to circumvent rival tendencies and journals, how to be sure that "our people" are elected as delegates to the coming congress, how to put "ours" into committees by taking advantage of police arrests of "theirs." With the representatives of other socialist groups, some older and better organized than the Iskrists, like the adherents of *Rabochee Delo* [the Workers' Cause] and of the Bund (the Jewish Workers' Union), he wrote: "Be wise as serpents and gentle as doves."[19]

By building an *apparat* for *Iskra* within the general revolutionary movement, Lenin was thus building a machine of personal loyalty to himself alone among the six *Iskra* editors. Though they did not yet know it, among the Iskrists there were already Leninists.

By 1903 the Iskrists had succeeded in establishing their ideological ascendancy—thanks chiefly to the prestige of the learned Plekhanov— and their organizational predominance—thanks chiefly to the detailed plans and directives of Lenin. They had managed to sidetrack or blow up all rival plans for a nationwide socialist congress. Now *Iskra* invited all local and national groups to send delegates to a congress it was calling. Out of respect for an abortive congress held in 1898, all of whose members had been arrested by the police, the convention called by *Iskra* was designated the "Second Congress." But its announced aim was to found a single, all-Russian, socialist party, on the basis, or so the *Iskra* editors intended, of *Iskra*'s program.

At the congress the Iskrists had a safe majority, all right. Lenin had seen to that. The Iskrist majority held together while they worsted rival tendencies. Then they themselves fell to quarreling over what seemed a trivial difference in the definition of a party member.[20] When Lenin was outvoted on this organization question, his fury knew no bounds. In one of his famous rages, he split the *Iskra* caucus, convoked a faction meeting of "true Iskrists," posting guards to keep out his fellow *Iskra* editors— except Plekhanov, who for the moment was siding with him. It was only two years since he had written to Martov that he would henceforth "regard all persons without sentiment and keep a stone in his sling." How well he had learned his lesson!

Could this be the unifying congress that was to give birth to a single, all-Russian party? Lenin was the first to realize that it had given birth to two parties instead of one; that the clash of temperaments concealed differences on organization, on relation of the party to the working class and to society, on the nature of the revolution itself—differences so profound that they could be resolved only by one faction's destroying the standing of the other. It took his five associates of yesterday, as it did the Russian underground, more than a decade before they realized it, too. During that decade, Lenin was often forced by party public opinion, including that of his own faction, to work together with those whom he thought of henceforth as ineluctable enemies, but no pretense at unity for tactical reasons ever caused him to give up his faction organization or alter his unique views one iota.

Though he had his slight majority for only a brief interval during the congress, his awareness of the power and propaganda impact of words caused him to arrogate to his faction the term *Bol'sheviki* (Majorityites), and to dub his opponents *Mensheviki* (Minorityites). Ineptly they accepted his label, coming to wear its stigma as a badge of pride. Actually, at the congress itself, the vote on which the Iskrists split into two factions, that on the "definition of a member," was 23 for Lenin against 28 for Martov, a clear majority for the "Minorityites." Only at the end of the congress, when a number of delegates had already left or withdrawn in protest, did Lenin manage to muster 19 votes on the personal issue[21] against 17, with three abstentions. Even then he did not have a majority of those present and recording their vote, while his 17 was a mere third of the original congress. Between 1903 and 1917 his opponents would most of the time have the majority of the organized behind them, but Lenin clung to the power-redolent name which gave his faction and his deeds prestige among the inexperienced.

When the congress adjourned, there were three central organs: the editorial board of *Iskra*, consisting now of Lenin and Plekhanov[22] (who for the next ten years was to waver between Bolsheviks and Mensheviks); a Central Committee, handpicked by Lenin, to function underground in Russia; and a Party Council, made up from the first two. Within a year Plekhanov broke with Lenin because of his merciless attitude toward the other old editors, and Lenin lost his post on the central organ. His Central Committee broke with him because of his "splitting tactics," thereby becoming in his eyes "worse than Mensheviks." The Party Council, of course, turned against him. Then the underground let him know that it wanted "unity."

Unshaken, he picked himself a new troika of men who had not even been at the congress, nor been elected to anything. And he managed to gather twenty-two random signatures for an endorsement of what he had done and contemplated, the twenty-two including his wife, his sister, and himself. But he called this scratchpile faction group by the large name, "Bureau of the Committees of the Majority." Like all future troikas and faction committees, it was an emanation of his own person, handpicked from those who were willing to agree to the letter with a position which in his strong-minded, self-confident solitude he alone had elaborated. To the secretary of this new handpicked "Bureau of the Committees of the Majority" he wrote: "For God's sake, don't trust the Mensheviks and the Central Committee [his own handpicked Central Committee of yesterday] and put through unconditionally, everywhere, and most decisively, split, split and split."[23]

But whatever the future might hold in store, in 1903, when the "unifying" Second Congress adjourned, it was Lenin and his wife who held in their hands all the threads which led to the underground agents and hence to the localities in Russia. As one of his opponents was to tell me years later: "Though Lenin was virtually isolated abroad where everyone had been able to follow the Congress fight closely, he had all the connections with Russia and we had none."[24]

Thus did Lenin in his first big test prove himself a master of the twin arts of organization and power—power for the Iskrists within the many-colored socialist and revolutionary movement, power for himself and his faction in the underground. In 1917, when power was lying loose in the streets, he would demonstrate his skill in using his machine to seize power in the state and hold on to it. So was his belief to be confirmed that it did not matter how many he lost in the course of building the party machine, so long as the machine remained effective and those he won accepted his organization conceptions and his leadership.

Marx had been vague on how the working class takes power, deliberately silent on what it would do with power once it had it. In Lenin, however, he had an innovative disciple who was theoretician, technician, and virtuoso of organization and power. His speciality was the how rather than the why or what. Conspiracy, centralized organization, military discipline, the ability to stir, manipulate, and coalesce the sources of discontent for one's own power purposes—a technique and indeed a technology for the art and science of taking power, of devising the instruments for seizing, holding, wielding, and maximizing power—what are these if not the levers of modern revolution? Here indeed was a revolutionist of a new type, determined to form what he himself would call "a party of a new type," to make, as it turned out, a revolution of a new type.

In 1903 his five associates of the *Iskra* editorial board contemplated the fury of his dictatorial centralism with uncomprehending wonder. In 1917, it would be the world's turn to stare and wonder.

For the three years from 1900 to 1903 the six editors of *Iskra* had been using a common vocabulary: *Marxism, orthodoxy, socialism, working class, party, central committee, member*. Plekhanov had written, and they had all approved, a common Program.[25] But at the congress their confident, self-chosen band of leaders had been rent in two over *the definition of a member*! It dawned on them then that every word they had been using in common was subject to directly opposite interpretations.

Factionalism has a logic of its own. It compelled five of the editors to ask for the first time how they could ever have permitted these strange organization doctrines to be uttered in their name by their specialist on questions of organization. And it led Lenin to invent for the other five a new heresy undreamed of by Marx: "Opportunism in the organization question." For this "deviation" he invented an entire new language of reprobation, derision, and condemnation: *khvostism* ("tailism," dragging at the tail instead of leading); "cringing before spontaneity"; "slavish kowtowing to the backwardness of the masses"; "dragging the Party backward"; glorifying unpreparedness and backwardness; "bourgeois trade unionism in the organization question," etc. etc. (All these expressions are culled from the rich new vocabulary of disparagement and abuse which Lenin introduced in his ground-breaking *What Is to Be Done?* Some of the terms are further analyzed below.)

It was "only" a question of organization (since they still kept the common program). Only a question of organization, but what a gulf it opened! Of course, both Lenin and his opponents appealed to Marxism, for both sides looked on Marxism as truth and science. But here as elsewhere, Marxism is ambiguous. Among these champions of orthodoxy and slayers of "revisionism," one text from the sacred canon could be made as probative as another. Alongside Marx's certitude concerning his own theoretical ideas, there was his insistence that ideas play only a minor role in history, as a reflection of more fundamental self-acting material forces. Though Marx fought ruthlessly for the supremacy of his own doctrine in the international, always he insisted that in the long run the working class itself would elaborate its own "consciousness" and organization, while "doctrinaire sects" would be outgrown or absorbed into mere servants of mass workingmen's parties. "The Emancipation of the working class must be conquered by the working class itself," wrote Marx as the first point in the "Statutes of the International Workingmen's Organization." And, even as he criticized the unity of Lassalleans and Marxians in Germany which had taken place without his advice, based on a program which seemed to him unsound, he nevertheless wrote: "Every step of a real movement is more important than a dozen programs."[26] By virtue of the very conditions of its life, he thought, the working class would develop its own revolutionary consciousness. From its increasing numbers and urban concentration, its mounting polarization at one pole of society, its ever-grander struggles and deeper experiences, its growing humiliation, degradation, despair, and indignation, it would generate its own mass working-class party, correct its own errors, coming at last to the point where "the conditions themselves would cry out: *Hic Rhodus! Hic salta!*" The "class *in* itself" would become a "class *for* itself," would elevate itself to the ruling class and revolutionize society.

If one goes from isolated texts to the overall context of Marx's thought, or if one takes the mighty German movement which Marx and Engels (and until August 1914, Lenin, too) regarded as the model, there can be no doubt that Marx assigned a decisive role to the spontaneous development, the self-organization, the *class* consciousness, the conditions of life and experiences of struggle of the working class. But in less than three years, from 1900 to 1903, Lenin put out quite a body of literature in the name of *Iskra* and "orthodox" Marxism which made it crystal clear that he did not share Marx's confidence in the working class.

The first peculiarity that strikes one in Lenin's doctrine is its extreme centralism, coupled with its extreme distrust of the rank and file of his party and the local organizations.

"What is bad," Lenin asked defiantly when he was in control of the central organ of the party, "What is bad about the complete dictatorship of the Central Organ?"[27]

Chided with suppressing party democracy, Lenin answered for himself and his band of professional revolutionaries: "They have no time to think of the toy forms of democracy . . . but they have a lively sense of their *responsibility* and they know by experience that to get rid of an undesirable member, an organization of real revolutionaries will stop at nothing."[28]

This is surely one of the most unresponsive answers in the whole of political literature. Lenin argues that under the conditions of police spying in Russia, party democracy is a "useless and harmful toy." But the context reveals that even in a free country the chief function of party "democracy" to him is to provide "the general control, in the literal sense of the term, that the party exercises over every member," a control which enables the party to decide whether to assign to a member one function or another, or to get rid of him altogether as unfit. It is his thought that in the context of illegality, democracy can be completely replaced by the mutual trust of socialists in each other, the absolute trust of all in the self-selected leading committee and in the ability of the latter to get rid of those who cannot be trusted.

Even more uncompromising is Lenin's championing of "bureaucratic centralism" as against the democratic autonomy of the primary or local organizations and their democratic control over the center. This *bureaucratic centralism* he considers appropriate to a socialist party in any country. The language of his celebration of "bureaucratism" is prickly and rough-hewn, but its meaning is startlingly clear: "Bureaucratism *versus* democratism, i.e., precisely centralism *versus* autonomy, such is the principle of revolutionary social democracy as against that of the opportunists. . . . The organization of revolutionary social democracy strives to go from the top downward, and defends the enlargement of the rights and plenary powers of the central body. . . ."[29]

It was impossible for this power-centered man to imagine that he would not be in control of the center. To Lunacharsky he said:

> If we have in the CC or in the Central Organ a majority, then we will demand the firmest discipline. We will insist on every sort of subordination of the Mensheviks to party unity . . .
>
> I asked Vladimir Ilyich:
>
> Well, and what if it should turn out after all that we are in a minority?
>
> Lenin smiled enigmatically and said:
>
> It depends on the circumstances. In any case we will not permit them to make of unity a rope around our necks. And under no circumstances will we let the Mensheviks drag us after them on such a rope.[30]

Not until Lenin had been bombarded by his opponents over half a decade for his rejection of party democracy did he finally seek to conceal somewhat his arch centralism and aversion to any democracy down below. Then he coined his celebrated term, *democratic centralism*! Even after he was in power and no longer could give as justification the tsar's police, in the third year of his rule he defined that self-contradictory term as "meaning only that representatives from the localities gather and choose a responsible organ. . . . The responsible organ must do the administering."

When Lenin's concept of democratic centralism was transplanted to the Communist International, its formulation read:

> The main principle of democratic centralism is that of the higher cell being elected by the lower cell, the absolute binding force of all

directives of a higher cell to a cell subordinate to it, and the existence of a commanding [*vlastnogo*, i.e., endowed with or clothed with power] party center [the authority of which] is unchallengeable for all its leaders in party life, from one congress to the next.[31]

Lenin's idea of what should be "centralized" and what "decentralized" would be comical were it not for its tragic implications for Russia and for communism. In his "Letter to a Comrade on Our Organizational Tasks," Lenin wrote:

> We have arrived at an extremely important principle of all party organization and party activity. In regard to ideological and practical *direction* the movement and the revolutionary struggle of the proletariat need the *greatest possible centralization*, but in regard to *keeping the center informed* about the movement and about the party as a whole, in regard to *responsibility* before the party, we need the *greatest possible decentralization*. The movement must be led by the smallest possible number of the most homogeneous groups of trained and experienced revolutionaries. But the largest possible number of the most varied and heterogeneous groups drawn from the most diverse layers of the proletariat (and of other classes) should take part in the movement. And in regard to each such group the center of the party must have always before it not only exact data on their activities, but also the fullest possible knowledge of their composition.[32]

If we add to this the rule which prescribes that the "committee should lead *all* aspects of the local movement . . . direct *all* local institutions, forces . . . decide all general questions" and leave "independence to the district groups only in the questions of the technique of distribution," then Lenin's conception of hierarchical centralism becomes terrifyingly clear. All power, all command, all decision should be with the center ("the district group receives its powers only from the latter") but the duty to carry out, obey, and report should be "decentralized" and accorded as a "privilege" to every local organization and individual member and even to party sympathizers.

Afraid that his readers might not get its full implications, Lenin, as was his wont, repeated it all again, with only slight variations and different underscorings:

> We must centralize the direction of the movement. We must also (and we must *for this reason*, for without the informing of the center its leadership is impossible) decentralize as much as possible the *responsibility before the party* of each individual member, of each participant in its work, of each circle which forms part of the party

or inclines to it. This decentralization is the necessary condition for revolutionary centralization and *its necessary corrective* . . . nothing else but the reverse side of *the division of labor.* . . . In order that the center may not only give advice, persuade, and argue (as has been done up to now), but may really direct the orchestra, it is essential to know exactly who is playing which fiddle and where; who, where, is learning to master which instrument or has mastered it; who, where and why, is playing out of tune (when the music begins to grate on the ear); and who, how and where should be transferred to correct the dissonance, and so on.[33]

From the outset Lenin's "center" was self-appointed. He began with himself, then gathered around him those who agreed with him. Again and again he removed players from his orchestra when *their* playing grated on *his* ears, gathering others more in harmony with his directing. Thus his "Leninist" center was self-perpetuating.

The same ideas reappear in the years of comparative open activity between 1907 and 1914, when *Zvezda* and *Pravda* were legal journals and the Bolsheviks could elect deputies to the Duma. The ideas continue during the six months of 1917 when Russia, in Lenin's words, was "the freest country in the world." And they continue when Lenin holds power in party and country. At first he sought to justify his centralism before its critics by pointing to the harsh conditions of a conspirative, underground movement, but in time it became clear that it sprang from the deepest necessities of Lenin's temperament, his confidence in himself and his pessimistic view of the dependability of his fellow men. He has been compared to a schoolmaster commanding his pupils (by Edmund Wilson) and to a general commanding an embattled army (in his own figures of speech on military discipline). Here, in any case, is "a revolutionary of a rare type: a revolutionary with a bureaucratic mind,"[34] for whom the complete centralization and control of all activities is—of all things—the road to a stateless utopia!

Hence Lenin's Archimedian cry for an organization of revolutionaries "to turn Russia upside down" did not cease when Russia was "turned upside down." Then as before Lenin repeated the cry for "organization, organization, organization." In power, as when fighting for power, he said: "Our fighting method is organization." But now he had something new to "fight" for. To the old dream of *centralized organization of the party*, which he did not for a moment abandon, he added the new dream of *total organization by the party*. Of what? Why, of Russia. Its industries and its agriculture, its feelings and its thoughts, its habits, even its dreams, total organization of slackness, of the waywardness of will, of deeds and desires. "We must organize everything," he said in the summer of 1918, "take everything into our hands."[35]

When, to the authoritarian trend inherent in an infallible doctrine, possessed and interpreted by an infallible interpreter who ruled an infallible party, from above, infallibly, Lenin added the further dream of an authoritarian organization doctrine and a party and state machine vested with exclusive and unique power and imbued with the determination to "organize everything, take everything into our hands"—totalitarianism was inescapable.

This ambition totally to organize everything was actually inherent in his doctrine and his spirit from the start. We have only to read attentively the outbursts against "spontaneity" and "elementalness" in the first "Leninist" pamphlet ("What Is to Be Done?") to see that the longing to give ordered and organized form to the spontaneously developing life of the masses was always at the heart of Lenin's thought. After he had taken power he would write in 1920, "Petit-bourgeois spontaneity is more terrible than all the Denikins, Kolchaks and Yudeniches put together."[36]

If it seems strange in a "democrat" to distrust the rank and file of the party and the local organizations, it seems stranger still in a socialist to express distrust of the very class whence "proletarian consciousness" was to issue and whose destiny it was to achieve socialism. But Lenin thought this distrust necessary and obvious. "Cut off from the influence of the Social Democracy," he wrote in his first signed article for *Iskra*, "the workingman's movement becomes petty and inevitably bourgeois."[37]

That dictum, only a single sentence in his first *Iskra* article, became the central thought of "What Is to Be Done?" There he spelled out his distrust, underscored it, repeated it tirelessly and monotonously.

An entire chapter is devoted to distinguishing between "The Spontaneity of the Masses and the Consciousness of the Social Democracy." The distinction between *spontaneity* and *consciousness* is worth pondering, for it brings us to the core of Lenin's spirit. The Russian word *stikhijnost'* means both spontaneity and elementalness. *Soznatel'nost'* is ordered and order-producing consciousness. Lenin opposed the two words to each other as one might light and darkness. The elemental and spontaneous were incorporated in the working class and the masses generally. It was the way they thought, felt, fought, when they had no guidance from "consciousness." Consciousness was the party. The party without leadership over the masses was mind without body. The masses without the leadership of the party was body without mind.

As his emphasis on centralism as against democracy had led him to invent the heresy of "opportunism in the organization question," so now his emphasis on consciousness as opposed to spontaneity led him to invent the heresy of *"slavish kowtowing before spontaneity."* The language is strange, the idea of the heresy stranger still. "Kowtowing" is the act of worship by which the devout in the Russian church prostrate themselves before a revered image. To call it "slavish" and "shameful" makes it clear that Lenin regards it as evil. But why? Because the working class, left to itself, without the tutelage of the party, will never in its life attain to so much as the conception of socialism! Socialism turns out not to be, as Marx believed, the quintessential thought of the proletariat, but a doctrine understood, possessed, and propagated by an intellectual elite. Hence to look to the working class to work out its own salvation, to seek only to serve the working-class movement rather than to take it in tow, is in Lenin's eyes to renounce revolution and socialism. Lenin describes this as dragging behind the working class instead of dragging it after you. This is the heresy of *khvostism.* Thus Lenin's distrust of "spontaneity" and his heresy of "tailism" are bound up with his distrust of the working class.[38]

In the introduction of *What Is to Be Done?* Lenin apologizes—for the first and last time—"for its numerous literary shortcomings." Actually, it has no "literary" form at all. It does not develop its ideas, it proclaims them, repeats them again and again, *hammers* them home. Repetition of his main points, not merely until they sink in, but until they "condition" the reader, hypnotize him, take possession of him, take on the air of indisputable truisms; this was, in speaking as in writing, a characteristic of Lenin's styleless *"style."*

He took a backward glance at the yesterday of the Russian working class. Their struggles had not made them socialists, nor could any amount of experience in struggle ever turn the working class into a socialist class or a consciously revolutionary one. For this there was needed a vanguard of professionals, professionals of theory, organization, and consciousness, professionals who made revolution their profession. There had not been, there was not,

> nor *could there be* social democratic consciousness in the workers. This can be brought to them only from the outside. The history of all lands testifies to the fact that alone by their own forces the working class is capable of working out only a trade union consciousness. . . . But the teachings of socialism have grown out of those philosophical, historical, economic theories which were worked out by the educated representatives of the possessing classes, the intelligentsia. By their social position, Marx and Engels, the founders of contemporary scientific socialism, belonged to the bourgeois intelligentsia, too. This is true for Russia also, where the theoretical doctrine of social democracy arose in complete independence from the spontaneous (elemental) growth of the workers' movement—

arose as the natural and inevitable result of the development of thought among the revolutionary intelligentsia.[39]

The workers have to be "pushed from the outside." There has never been, nor can there be, enough of this "pushing from the outside." Conversely, to "flatter the workers, to arouse in them" a sense of distrust toward all who bring them political knowledge and revolutionary experience from the outside" is to be a demagogue—a unique, Leninist definition of this term—"and a demagogue is the worst enemy of the working class."[40]

> Since there can be no talk of an independent ideology's being worked out by the workers themselves in the course of their movement, the *only choice is*: either bourgeois or socialist ideology. There is no middle term (for no "third" ideology has been worked out by mankind, and furthermore, in a society torn by class contradictions in general there can never be an outside of class or above class ideology). Hence *any* diminution of socialist ideology, any *departure* from it, signifies by that very fact a strengthening of bourgeois ideology. But the *spontaneous* development of the workers' movement leads precisely to its subordination to bourgeois ideology . . . for the spontaneous workers' movement is trade-unionism, etc., is *nur Gewerkschaftlerei* [the German term for trade unionism pure and simple], and trade unionism means precisely the ideological enslavement of the workers to the bourgeoisie.[41]

> Class political consciousness can be brought to the worker only from *the outside*, that is, from outside the sphere of relations between workers and bosses. The sphere from which alone it is possible to derive this knowledge is the sphere of the relation of *all* the classes and strata and the state and the government—the sphere of interrelations among *all* classes. Therefore, the question, what is to be done to bring to the workers political knowledge, cannot be answered . . . by "go to the workers." To bring to the *workers* political knowledge, the social democrats must *go into all classes of the population*, should send *in all directions* the detachments of its army.[42]

> We [what Lenin chooses to italicize is always of especial interest] must take upon ourselves the task of organizing such an all-sided political struggle under the direction of *our* party. . . . We must develop from the practical activists of the social democracy such political leaders as will be able to direct all the manifestations of this all-sided struggle, be able at the necessary moment "to dictate a

positive program of action" alike to rebellious students, and to dissatisfied zemstvo figures, and discontented religious sectaries, and indignant school teachers, and so on.[43]

Aided by historical hindsight, we can see that Lenin was driving at a party that was to direct not only the working class, but the entire populace, a party that would conceive as its duty to "dictate the positive program" of every class of society. That *dictate* was no empty figure of speech to Lenin became clear from the outset of his career. When he was still a member of the *Iskra* editorial board, he explained once in a memorandum to his colleagues that he proposed to show every kindness to the peasantry, "but not yield an inch" in our "maximum program." "If the peasants do not accept socialism" when the dictatorship comes, we shall say to them, "It's no use wasting words when you have got to use force." On the margin of this memorandum Vera Zasulich wrote: "Upon millions of people? Just you try!" When he and his party came to power, that is just what they did try.

It was to be neither a party "of" the entire populace nor "of" the working class. It was to be a carefully selected elite, offering itself as leader, director, guardian, *for* the working class and for all the discontented from religious sectaries to zemstvo councillors.

> The economic struggle against the bosses and the government does not in the least require—and therefore such a struggle can never give rise to—an all-Russian centralized organization, uniting in one general attack each and every manifestation of political opposition, protest and indignation, an organization consisting of revolutionaries by profession and led by the real political leaders of the entire people.[44]

Thus *stikhijnost'*, spontaneity, the natural liberty of men and classes to be themselves, was the enemy and opposite of consciousness. In Marx spontaneity and consciousness coincided, for though Marx had his own idea of consciousness, he thought that historical experience would be the connecting link to bring the proletariat to that "consciousness" in the course of its struggles. But for Lenin, spontaneity and consciousness were irreconcilable opposites. The party did not give expression to the consciousness of the class, but itself possessed that consciousness as its own infallible possession which it must inject into, impose upon the class. The party was the institutional organization of consciousness which needed the elemental or spontaneous movement, its rebelliousness and its numbers, to give it force, even as a General Staff needs an army. But it is the General Staff which possesses military science, does the planning of battles and campaigns, gives orders, decides on offensives and retreats, and—where General Staff and political party are one and the same—decides on objectives as well. The army is needed to provide numbers, muscle; the General Staff is the brains. What general worthy of his stripes would let his army determine its own tactics and actions? That way lay chaos. He must drill the army, give it experience under fire, keep it in a fighting mood, train it to obey automatically and completely, harden it by fire, supply officers for every detachment, discredit and eliminate the willful and insubordinate.

Obviously we have gone a long way from the original Marxist conception of a party of the working class, growing more and more inclusive as modern industry and experience develop, engendering more and more solidarity and consciousness in the course of its repeated struggles. To Lenin the crowd was but a rabble, its spontaneous thoughts and feelings mere false understanding, unless it could be turned into a disciplined, obedient force by officers who alone knew the aims and the art of war.

One question remained to be answered, and this Lenin did not altogether spell out. Yet, if we wander through the repetitive pages of his brochure, to this question Lenin gives answers again and again. *Who were these revolutionaries by profession?* From what class or classes would they be recruited? To what class would they belong?

If "consciousness" comes not from the working class but only from outside, if its bearers and formulators are "by their social position educated representatives of the possessing classes, the intelligentsia," then it is clear that the members of his elite band would come chiefly from those layers of society which had it in them to master this doctrine, namely the students and the intellectuals.[45] True, by becoming professional revolutionaries they were in a certain sense declassing themselves—but not thereby becoming members of the working class. Rather they would withdraw from their professions and economic functions, withdraw from the existing "classes" of society and from society itself, live in its interstices as masters of a profession new in history, the profession of revolutionary. They were not to be part of the present at all, but its challengers—bearers of the future, which they and they alone foreknew.

As a concession to the "working-class" element in Marxist theory, Lenin acknowledged that "the best of the workers" might also attain to this consciousness. Russia in due time would beget its own "Bebels," and, he hoped, many of them. But they too would have to leave the factory and the workbench, be extruded from their class, in short, declassed:

> The worker-revolutionary for full preparation for his job must also become a professional revolutionary. . . . A worker-agitator who shows any talent and is at all "promising" *should not* work in the factory eleven hours a day. We must see to it that he lives on party

support, that he should be able in time to go over to an underground status.[46]

Even when Lenin was in power and exercising the "proletarian" dictatorship, he repeated this judgment: "It is understood that the broad masses of the toilers includes very many people who . . . are not enlightened socialists and cannot be, because they have to work at hard labor in the factory and they neither have the time nor the possibility to become socialists."[47]

Among professional revolutionaries, whether declassed representatives of the propertied classes or declassed workers, "*all distinctions as between workers and intellectuals* must be obliterated."[48] This classless band of priest-guardians must "form a clandestine group of leaders, to set the largest possible masses in motion," become the leader and "dictate the program" to all the discontented of all classes, and lead them all in an all-Russian struggle against the existing order.

There was yet another sense in which Lenin held his organization of classless professional revolutionaries to be "the vanguard" of a particular class, the proletariat. When his opponents accused him of being nothing but a nineteenth-century revolutionary conspirator like those of the old *Narodnaia volia*, Lenin answered proudly:

> The very idea of a militant centralized organization, which declares
> determined war upon tsarism, you describe as *narodovolist*. . . .
> No revolutionary tendency that seriously thinks of fighting can
> dispense with such an organization . . . a powerful, strictly secret
> organization which concentrates in its hands all the threads of secret
> activities, an organization which must of necessity be centralized.[49]

Yes, in all these things he was a *narodovolets*, and "flattered" to be so described. Like them, too, he sought "to recruit *all* the discontented and hurl this organization into decisive battle . . . that was their great historic merit." Only two mistakes did the *narodovoltsy* make, and only in these did he differ from them. Their first mistake was not to realize that Russia would and must develop modern industry and modern capitalism, and with this a modern proletariat. Their second mistake, which followed from the first, was to believe that the main mass of discontented, the *main battering ram* to use against the gates of the fortress, was the peasantry. But the industrialization of Russia and the teachings of Marxism combined to show that the main mass force to be used as a battering ram, more concentrated, more organized by the barracks discipline of the factory, more accessible to the teachings and leadership of Lenin's elite— *that main* battering ram was the working class.

Herein lay the heart of Lenin's "Marxism." Namely, this made it essential that his elite, regardless of class origin, should proclaim itself the "vanguard of the working class." *This* made it so essential for the vanguard of society to claim recognition as the vanguard of the class which must in turn be recognized as the vanguard class in society. For this his vanguard must penetrate the working class, enter into its "essentially bourgeois" trade unions, indoctrinate it with the vanguard doctrine which was at the same time, whether the proletariat accepted or rejected it, the "proletarian" doctrine. For this it must seek to guide and control the workers' struggles, divert them from their "spontaneous" purposes to its conscious purpose, manipulate and utilize their number and penetrate their organizations for the aims of the vanguard elite, "dictate to them a positive program of action," force their organizations to transcend their natural aims and limitations, inject into the working class "from outside" the "consciousness" of the revolutionary mission assigned to it by its vanguard, by Marx, and by history.

Indeed, the workingmen and their organizations would be measured by this standard, a standard developed outside their movement and in opposition to its "spontaneous" aims, a standard impossible for the workingmen themselves to develop under any circumstances. For the workers, "consciousness" was neither more nor less than *acceptance of the leadership*, guardianship, guidance, program, and decisions of this elite band of professionals of revolution.

Thus Lenin's vanguard was the vanguard of the proletariat by definition. Its doctrine was the doctrine of the proletariat by definition. And its organization was the "highest form" of organization of the working class by definition.

He who regarded himself as the most orthodox of orthodox Marxists could rightly claim that the party he was to build was a party of a new type, which Marx and Engels would have been astonished to contemplate. It was not only new and unique; it was exclusive. For while there might be many parties with differing programs, even many rival parties all alike claiming to be socialist, there was room in any society for only *one* party to be *the* vanguard of the working class and then the vanguard of the "ruling class" and the vanguard of society.

There have been attempts to find "predecessors" and "influences" for Lenin's conception, in Babeuf and Blanqui, in Pestel, Nechaev, Tkachov, Chernyshevsky.[50] But when all of these, or the relevant fragments from their writings, are added together, they do not make Lenin's theory or practice. He is unique as its begetter, systematizer, developer, realizer in life, and—what gives it its great importance—the architect of its successful seizure of power.

Such a classless elite might well seize power, not as Marx had foretold, where the economy was most advanced and the working class most numerous, organized, cultured, and "conscious," but just as easily, nay more easily, where the economy was backward, the workers neither "mature" nor "conscious," and all political organization of all parties and classes rudimentary.

Once in power, it might continue to hold power in the name of the proletariat, since it was the vanguard of the proletariat by definition and self-proclamation. It might dictate to the rest of society in the proletariat's name, and dictate to the proletariat as well in the proletariat's name, for the vanguard knows best.

Moreover, this vanguard-elite theory would make it possible for restless intellectuals to seize power in the name of the proletariat in lands where the proletariat was in its infancy. In the name of this doctrine, Mao Tse-tung could seize power "for the proletariat" by means of peasant armies in an overwhelmingly agrarian land of rudimentary industry. Ho Chi Minh might do the same in a land where the only workers were plantation hands and craftsmen plying their ancient trades. All that was needed was opportunity and will plus the acceptance of the idea of the Leninist *apparat*.

Once in power, they could do as Lenin, and after him Stalin and Khrushchev: use the "proletarian power" to rule society as a whole, including the proletariat, for, as Lenin put it, "just because the revolution has begun, that does not mean that people have turned into saints." Far from it. One of the important duties of the "proletarian power" is "to resist the inevitable petit-bourgeois waverings of these proletarian masses." Indeed, one of its first tasks is to combat the demoralization which war and the party's own war against the Provisional Government had introduced into the masses. "Only by an extraordinarily difficult, prolonged, stubborn road can we overcome this demoralization and conquer those elements who are augmenting it by regarding the revolution as a means of getting rid of their old shackles by getting out of it as much as they can."[51] Surely, a proletarian party of a new type!

10

The Split in
the Socialist
Parties

Among the many differences between the first and the second Comintern congresses, those of participation and of the attitude toward the new international were the most conspicuous. There had been only a few delegates but no foreign delegations at the First Congress of the Communist International. Between that and the Second Congress there had been no cleavage within the socialist parties on the issue of joining the new International. At the Second Congress, however, there would be representative foreign delegations, and numerous rifts were to develop immediately afterwards in the various socialist parties.

As soon as it came into being, the Communist International launched an appeal for new members, and those on the far left in the socialist parties who had been won over to the communist idea began to examine their consciences. In the months following the birth of the International, votes were taken in many socialist parties, with widely varying results. In some instances a majority favored going along with Moscow, with only a minority opposed; in others the reverse was true. Either way, when the voting was over, the proponents and opponents of embracing the new International went on living together in the same parties. Soon, however, it became obvious that such a state of affairs could not last.

The European Socialist Parties after the Founding of the Comintern

Europe's first big socialist party to take a stand on the issue immediately after the founding of the Comintern was Italy's. Its executive committee, meeting in Milan on March 19, 1919, at the suggestion of Gennari, Serrati, and Bombacci, passed a resolution (by a vote of ten to three) concluding with the words: "The Party therefore resolves to resign from the [Socialist] International Bureau and affiliate with the new revolutionary Socialist International, founded on the principles of our Russian communist comrades. . . ."[1] After this decision the minority, which included men like Constantino Lazzari, party secretary from 1912 to 1919, remained in the party and continued to hold positions of responsibility. The majority, led by Serrati, never dreamed of taking disciplinary or punitive action against them.

The following month, at the special congress of the French Socialist party (SFIO) held in Paris from April 20 to 22, three motions were made calling for clarification of the party's position with regard to the old Socialist International and the new Communist International. One, made by Longuet expressing the "Centrist" point of view, got 894 votes. Another, by Mayèras representing the "Right," received 757. The third, by Loriot, who spoke for the far Left favorable to the Comintern, picked up only 270, and the motion to join that body was defeated. Even so, the far Left stayed in the party, and the majority took no action against them. That same month, April 1919, the Social-Democratic Labor party of Norway announced its readiness to join the Comintern, reaffirming this position at its conference on June 8. The vote taken concerning adoption and adaptation of the Soviet system in Norway showed clearly the numerical strength of the proponents and opponents of the Moscow line; 275 voted in favor, 63 against. Here again, the minority was not booted out of the party, nor did they themselves break with the party.

On June 14, by a vote of 186 to 22, the national conference of Sweden's Social-Democratic Left resolved to join the Comintern, and no attempt was made to evict the defeated minority from that party either, whose majority decision had been preceded in May by the similar resolution of the Social-Democratic Youth.

Two Left-Socialist parties that had broken with their official Social-Democratic parties did wind up in the Communist camp. At its congress on November 16 and 17, 1918, the Social-Democratic party of Holland changed its name to Communist party of Holland, imitating the Bolsheviks, who had made the same change at their own congress in March

1918. At their congress of May 25 to 27, 1919, the Bulgarian "narrow" Socialist party renamed itself the Communist party and joined the Comintern.

The Swiss Socialist party, at its congress in Basel in March 1919, resolving almost unanimously to break with the Second International, voted 318 to 147 to join the Communist International. But the decision had to be ratified in a partywide referendum organized by the membership at large, in which it was reversed: only 8,600 voted to go into the Comintern; 14,364 voted against. But again these two conflicting votes, with the party rank and file overruling their leaders, did not split the party.

The opposite occurred in the Socialist party of Greece, whose national council decided in May 1919 to sever ties with the Second International but voted against joining the Third International, while the party congress, convening in Athens on April 5, 1920, voted almost unanimously in favor of joining the Comintern.

At the congress of unification of the Socialist Workers' (Communist) party of Yugoslavia, held in Belgrade from April 20 to 23, 1919, and attended by Communists from different regions of the country, but also by Centrist Socialists from the old Serbian Social-Democratic party, the majority voted to break with the Second International and join the Third International.

The special congress of Germany's Independent Socialist party (USPD), held in Leipzig from November 30 to December 6, 1919, saw another clash of centrist socialists with socialists favoring the Comintern. The motion made, on behalf of the far Left, by Walter Stoecker calling for immediate affiliation with the Comintern was beaten 169 to 114; again the two factions did not split apart but continued to cohabit in the same party. At its congress in December 1919 Spain's Socialist party, by a vote of 14,000 to 12,500, vetoed immediate affiliation with the Communist International.

The significant fact that these divisions within Europe's Socialist parties were not deep enough to split them pointed to another truth, no less important, namely, that they did not betoken any predominance of pro-Comintern sentiment in Central and Western Europe, i.e., in those areas in which labor parties and trade-union movements were strongest. Except in the case of Italy, Europe's socialist parties—including those controlled by Centrists, e.g., the SFIO, USPD, and Austrian Socialist party—voted solidly against involvement with the Comintern. And of course those parties led by ex-"social-patriots" (as in Germany, Belgium, and England) showed no inclination whatever in that direction. Even when a Socialist party was not yet divided into these disputing factions, it was nevertheless cold to Comintern beckonings. On January 15, 1919, the twenty-five-member executive committee of the Czechoslovak Social-Democratic party passed the following resolution: "Our party has nothing in common and wants nothing to do with the tactics of the Russian bolsheviks and German Spartacists, which can only lead the nation and working class to ruin and spill the workers' blood in fratricidal battles. Anyone in favor of establishing an independent bolshevik party is an enemy of social democracy."[2]

One would have to wait another year, for the months after the Second World Congress, to see cleavages develop in Europe's big socialist parties.

Lenin—Prophet and Rift-Maker

Shortly after the Comintern's second congress Lenin saw his grand dream come true: the final break in Western Europe between reformist socialism and revolutionary socialism, hence repetition on the international stage of what had happened in Russia—the splitting of menshevism from bolshevism. The events ahead would confirm what Lenin had long foreseen. Again, to those around him, he was the infallible prophet, demiurge of history, which he kicked around and molded at will. That several years might have to lapse between a Lenin prediction and its faithful fulfillment did not matter, for it is a prophet's duty to foresee things before others think them possible. But, to his disciples, Lenin was no ordinary prophet, but a Marxist prophet, ergo a scientist, with a genius for foreknowing the unimaginable.

The first case in which his clairvoyance had disclosed horizons undreamed of by other Marxists, including even Bolsheviks, was when he succeeded in splitting Russia's Social Democrats in 1903. At first none of the leading Russian Social Democrats would follow him, and even among Bolsheviks there were misgivings about the savage fury of his attack, later characterized by Stalin as a "tornado in a teacup." But Lenin did not swerve. The split, consummated in fact in 1903, in 1912 became official and final. So while the process took only about ten years, it was not until after November 7, 1917, that its immense historical impact would be felt.

Another lag between a Lenin prediction and its subsequent fulfillment followed his proclamation in 1914 of the need to break with the Second International and create a third. It was then only a statement of principle, supported by no one and which he had no power to implement. Again it was November 7, 1917, at Petrograd that made possible translation of the word into the deed: founding of the Third International in March 1919.

But Lenin had predicted one more great event: the sundering of the Western Socialist parties. Ever since 1917 he had been calling upon Socialists to transcend the spirit of Zimmerwald and set up revolutionary Marxist parties distinct from "centrism" and "opportunism," even if this meant breaking up the existing parties. The big socialist parties paid little heed before the creation of the Comintern, and even for a year afterward. It was not until the second half of 1920 and beginning of 1921 that Lenin's idea started to become political reality, destined to help shape Europe's labor movement for decades to come.

The exact chronology of events or how long it might take for them to happen mattered little to the Great Prophet once he was firmly convinced that he had prophesied aright and that history would be his proof. In Russia, instead of waiting for economic conditions to ripen and fit the Marxist mold before triggering his revolution, he unleashed it forthwith, worrying about economics later. In the international communist movement, instead of biding his time until mass communist parties could be set up in the major Western countries, he simply conjured the Comintern into existence, pulling it, so to speak, out of an empty hat, so as to have a tool with which to hasten the creation of national communist parties. For Lenin, brute force was midwife to the communist revolution, the Comintern midwife to the communist parties.

Convinced that he was ahead of history, Lenin kept his eye peeled for it. When he saw it coming, he acted instantly, stepping on or brushing aside any around him who failed to see it too. In Russia, in April 1917, he was aware that his closest companions, assembled in party conference, had not yet perceived that it was possible to jump from a so-called bourgeois republican revolution straight to a proletarian socialist one. By October he sensed that the party, notwithstanding its vacillation and doubts, could successfully seize power. By March 1919 he believed the time had come to found the Comintern, regardless of what the Germans thought. By 1920 he saw that Europe's big socialist parties could be split.

Choosing the right moment was always the key factor in the execution of Lenin's grand schemes. Concerning November 7, 1917, at Petrograd, many Bolshevik leaders have since said and written that, had they not grabbed the power at that exact moment, they never would have been able to. Likewise, had Moscow not succeeded in splitting Western Europe's big socialist parties in late 1920 and early 1921, it never could have. Until then the right moment had not yet come, as evidenced by the lack of significant cleavages in 1919 and early 1920. After that, the right moment had passed. Actually, the rifts completed or begun in the months immediately following the second Comintern congress, which ended on August 7, 1920, proved very advantageous for the Communists, while those that came in 1921 were much less so, some even proving detrimental. In the first instance, the Comintern partisans could claim a majority of the membership of the workers' organization being split; in the second, they remained a minority. The congresses of the German USPD, French SFIO, and Left wing of the Social-Democratic party of Czechoslovakia, all held between the end of September and the end of December 1920, gave the victory to the Comintern supporters, while the congresses of the Italian Socialist party and French CGT in 1921 left them a vanquished minority. These ups and downs, generally favorable to the Comintern until the end of 1920, and unfavorable starting in 1921, were reflected within the parties themselves, depending on when exactly their "temperature" was taken. In the Spanish Socialist party, for example, at its second special congress on June 19, 1920, the faction in favor of the Third International won a majority (which it had not had at the first congress in December 1919), with 8,269 voting for, 5,016 against, and 1,615 abstentions. But by the time of the third congress, in April 1921, the number of Comintern supporters, as shown by the vote, had dropped to 6,025, the number of its opponents having jumped to 8,808.

These very different voting results during the second half of 1920 as compared with 1921 were in no way due to the aftermath of World War I, whose devastating effects and painful memories were surely more influential in 1919 and early 1920 than later in 1920, when these cleavages took shape. The difference cannot be explained by either the social or the economic conditions of the working class. There is no discernible correlation between a plight of the working class in 1920 that would have pushed it toward Moscow's revolutionary socialism and a betterment of its condition in 1921 that would have turned it away. The explanation is not to be found either in the mere fact of the Comintern's existence. Between the first and second world congresses that body never ceased calling for a clean break between communists and socialists and beating the drums for formation of communist parties in the different European countries, but with small effect.

The only factor that can account for the rifts that Moscow succeeded in producing during the second half of 1920 was Soviet Russia's political and military successes at that time. Communism's decisive victories in Russia and elsewhere came when its militants, armed to the teeth, seized power in Petrograd, or when its "red soldiers" were advancing. The second half of 1920 was marked by two spectacular triumphs of the Soviet Red Army. While thrashing the "Whites" in the civil war, it trounced the Polish Army and marched to the gates of Warsaw. But at the first months of 1921 any hope that it would resume its advance on Western Europe disappeared. Then came the "tactical retreat" represented by the NEP, which eclipsed the civil-war victories. A Soviet Russia marching unstoppably westward and building up its strength at home—and this was the outside world's impression during the latter half of 1920—could not help impressing many Socialist militants. This same Russia, forced to backtrack militarily and then retreat in major domestic and foreign policies, as it did in 1921, could not wield the same influence. The first communist groups had sprung into being in the afterglow of the Bolshevik victory of November 1917. The first mass communist parties in Europe were born on the heels of the Soviet gains in 1920. Since there were no more spectacular Soviet victories after that, there was also no further spectacular communist thrust in Europe. And, starting in the latter half of 1921, this turnabout accepted by Lenin for Soviet Russia would be extended to the Comintern.

But at the time of the Comintern's second congress, and immediately after, Lenin was still far from foreseeing his imminent "tactical retreat." He was still wholly on the offensive, both with his Red Army and Communist International. Having picked the moment at which to cleave Europe's big socialist parties, he also picked the cleaver with which the job was to be done. It was he who drew the line of demarcation within those parties, barring certain socialist leaders, despite their willingness to accept the Comintern framework. And it was the Comintern, actually Zinoviev, who under Lenin's watchful eye handpicked the Moscow emissaries sent to implement the rifts. Some were to play a public role and make speeches at congresses that would cause a big stir, e.g., Zinoviev at Malle, Clara Zetkin at Tours, Kabakchiev at Leghorn (backed up by Rakosi, the second delegate). While the former two had a certain international prestige and knew the language of the country, the third had neither political prestige nor any knowledge of Italian, which helped to produce the failure at Leghorn. But paralleling the activities of these delegates, who were the official Comintern spokesmen, were those of its secret emissaries, who worked within the three big parties for many weeks, even months, before the congresses at which the actual rifts occurred. This was the function of Radek in Germany, Zalewski and Degot in France, Degot and Liubarski ("Carlo") in Italy, whose job was to hammer into Moscow's supporters the rudiments of those two complementary tactics long used by the Bolsheviks in Russia and which were now to be introduced into the international stage: first penetrating a target organization and honeycombing it with one's own people, then splitting it. These were the field officers, dispatched to execute a maneuver planned by the Moscow General Staff, which is to say, by Lenin.

He alone had the authority to name his allies and enemies on the spot. He could slam the Comintern door in the face of any individual whose present or recent past attitude obviously qualified him for membership (men like Longuet and Serrati), as he could throw open that door to some other Socialist leader whose recent positions ought logically to have disqualified him (e.g., Cachin and Smeral). In 1920 Lenin supplemented this indulgence on the right with an indulgence on the Left. Despite the criticism that he was being too hard on "leftism," he was eager to retain in the Comintern not only the leaders of Left communism, like Bordiga, but even those on the far noncommunist Left, such as the supporters of revolutionary syndicalism and anarchosyndicalism. This double indulgence stemmed from a single major concern: to have within the Comintern those Western labor leaders who had the ear of the masses and were deemed "salvageable," notwithstanding their pasts, or assimilable despite their current politics.

Splitting the USPD at Halle

Of Europe's major countries, Germany was the first to have an important Communist party, and the first to see its "centrist" Socialist movement internally split. These two developments could not help strengthening the Kremlin conviction that Germany was the European country farthest advanced toward Communist revolution.

On their return to Germany, two members of its delegation won over to the Comintern cause, Stoecker and Däumig, began beating the propaganda drums in favor of joining, while two other delegates, Dittmann and Crispien, started agitating for the opposite. A Reichskonferenz aus den Vertretern der Parteibezirke (National Conference of District Party Representatives) was called for September 1 to 3, 1920, to hear the delegation's conflicting reports. According to USPD historian Eugen Prager: "Though no actual decisions were made at the conference, the words of Crispien and Dittmann made so deep an impression that one could safely assume that an overwhelming majority of the representatives would have voted against accepting the conditions. Stoecker and Däumig fell completely flat."[3]

But Moscow's partisans succeeded in turning the tide, partly owing to their own efforts but also because of direct personal intervention by three leading Comintern lights: Lenin, Radek, and Zinoviev. Thus, the battle joined on German soil between those for and against the USPD's joining the Comintern grew into a public fracas between Germany's Independent Socialists, who were opposed, and the Comintern bigwigs.

Lenin zeroed in on two articles by Dittmann, published at the time of the Reichskonferenz in the official organ of the USPD, which described the disappointment of German workers who had gone to help "build

Socialism" in Soviet Russia, and which had made a profound impression in USPD circles and on German public opinion as a whole, producing waves even in London and New York. On September 8, to a telegram on the subject sent him by a British journalist, Lenin made a typical reply. Without touching at all upon the articles' substance, he attacked their author personally, blackballing him in advance from Comintern membership, even before the USPD congress had had a chance to make up its mind:

> It is natural that Kautsky-ites of the Crispien and Dittmann stripe should be displeased with bolshevism. It would be a sad thing if people like that did like us. It is natural that such petit-bourgeois democrats—which is what Dittman is—should be exactly like our mensheviks, and in the decisive struggle between the proletariat and bourgeoisie be often on the side of the enemy. Dittmann is all steamed up about our having to shoot a few people, but it is natural in these cases that the revolutionary workers should shoot mensheviks, and that Dittmann might not particularly like it. It will be a dark day when the Communist International ever lets in any Dittmanns (of the German, French, or any other model).[4]

Not long after, on September 24, in a letter to the French and German workers, Lenin again took issue with Dittmann and Crispien, proclaiming that he had no choice but to break with them.

Karl Radek wrote a pamphlet, entitled "Die Masken sind gefallen" [The masks are off] against Dittmann, Crispien, and Hilferding, but, more important, he came to Germany secretly at the moment of the split. The public never knew this, but Radek himself confirmed it several years later in his autobiography: "In October 1920 I went to Germany secretly to help organize the congress, during which we were to bring about unification of the Left Independents and Spartacists."[5] That same month, October 12 to 17, the USPD congress did take place at Halle, and the German Communist party congress, expected to produce the unification, started on November 3, the actual congress of unification running from December 4 to 7, 1920, and Radek was in Germany the whole time. He was quite in his element there, because unifying the USPD Left with the German Communist party had been an obsession of Paul Levi's since 1919. Levi had established regular secret contacts with that Left (as came out at the USPD congress in Leipzig, held from November 30 to December 6, 1919). Radek, who was of the same mind, wrote in September 1919 while still interned in Germany: "With the USPD as a whole, so long as it is headed by people like Haase, Dittmann, and Hilferding, there can be no union or even alliance. . . . In any mass action a prime aim must be to reach an accord with the independent masses of workers, and for that we cannot bypass the Independent Leftist leaders."[6]

Zinoviev was picked to be the principal Comintern speaker at the Halle congress, which he was to attend in the company of Bukharin, who was replaced at the last moment, however, by Lozovski. But the Comintern president was not to be the only Russian speaker, for Iurii Martov, Menshevik leader and former friend of Lenin's, showed up too, having come all the way from Russia to contradict Zinoviev and plead with the USPD not to join the Comintern. Nothing better symbolized the triumph of bolshevism and bankruptcy of menshevism than the presence of those two personalities in Halle. While Martov stood head and shoulders over Zinoviev as a man, the latter was politically far stronger owing to the prestige of the Bolshevik revolution and to recent events in Russia, concerning which Däumig said at the Second World Congress that "The example of our Russian comrades . . . [who have shown] a clear and determined will to hold an entire people in their hands, that will travel through the channels of the International, will not fail to influence Germany. . . . Every kilometer which the Red Army puts behind it is a stimulus for the revolution, is a step toward revolution in Germany."[7] Zinoviev came to Halle on October 12. It was the first and last time that the president of the International had a chance to visit Europe in that capacity.

He did so under particularly favorable circumstances, Moscow's supporters being assured in advance of a majority at the congress, a fact which the Comintern president did not fail to learn of as soon as he set foot on German soil at Stettin: "The first question that we asked comrade Kurt Geyer was: 'Who are in the majority at the congress, we or they, the leftists or the rightists?' 'The majority are with us,' said comrade Geyer, 'and those supporting us are standing firm, like a reel.' "[8] Zinoviev's position was the stronger as he had the better role to play, that of demagogue and polemicist, at both of which he was a past master. On the congress program he gave free rein to his talent, delivering a four-and-a-half-hour speech, by his own account the longest he had ever given. It was a superb performance, as acknowledged even by Eugen Prager, USPD historian, who had little sympathy for the Comintern:

Zinoviev's report was undoubtedly a major oratorical feat. . . . He had complete mastery of the spirit of the German language, even if he did occasionally have to feel around for an expression, but that only gave his speech an appealing added flavor. He was characterized at that time as one of the greatest demagogues of the century. And that was certainly doing him no injustice. . . . His speech made an enormous impression on his followers. . . .[9]

The Zinoviev speech was more of an exercise in mob manipulation than in political analysis. He was more interested in stirring his audience up than in explaining to them the problems facing the labor movement in Germany and the world. For Zinoviev, Lenin's faithful mouthpiece, the issue was completely clear: "You must choose. Are you for menshevism or bolshevism? . . ."[10] The line laid down in that way hewed completely to the outlook prevailing at the Second Congress in the summer of 1920, an outlook that Lenin himself would start to revise only a few weeks after the Halle congress, having begun to believe it wrong. It consisted of a series of axioms, much in vogue in 1919 and 1920, the main one being that the situation in general was now ripe for Communist revolution, which had not yet occurred owing solely to the treachery of the Social-Democratic leaders and syndicalists:

> The situation is this. The working class is already strong enough to knock over the bourgeoisie by, say, tomorrow morning—if we all stand together and firmly support communism. If the workers are still slaves, the only reason is that we have not yet shaken off the accursed legacy of that foul ideology within our own ranks. . . . Every day that passes you can see how the so-called Trade-Union International is nothing but a weapon in the hands of the international bourgeoisie, indeed the sharpest and deadliest of their weapons and, one might add, the only serious weapon that they have left to use against us.[11]

With that viewpoint, Zinoviev saw everywhere the stirrings of revolution, despite the treachery of the Social-Democratic leaders and syndicalists: "Look at the situation as it really is! Have you not noticed that in Italy, for the past several weeks, we have a budding revolution, a budding proletarian revolution?! . . . Among British workers we are witnessing upheavals of world-historic import. . . . The Balkans, too, are dead ripe for proletarian revolution."[12] Having just returned from the Baku congress, Zinoviev naturally included the Orient in his cosmic panorama of imminent revolution: "The mullahs of China naturally aren't communists. . . . If you want world revolution, if you want to free the proletariat from the fetters of Capitalism, you must not think only of Europe, but must turn your eyes toward Asia too. . . . So we say to you . . . that a proletarian revolution without Asia would not be a world revolution. . . ."[13]

Addressing himself in conclusion to German Socialists ready to embrace communism, Zinoviev obviously sought to reassure them: "We do not ask you to start a new war or pull off the revolution tomorrow morning! What we do ask is that you get ready and systematically make propaganda not against communism, but for it. Not against the revolution, but for it. That is the only real condition. . . ."[14]

The most detailed reply from opponents of joining the Comintern came from Rudolph Hilferding, who set out to refute point by point everything that the president of the International had said. Stressing that Zinoviev had studiously avoided any mention whatever of many of the major problems (such as the true meaning of the twenty-one conditions for admission), he hammered, at both the beginning and the end of his speech, at the specifically Russian character of the Comintern, and at the fact that it was completely tied to Moscow:

> It is most characteristic how Zinoviev . . . equates world conditions with conditions in Russia, how he sees all party relationships in the Russian context. . . . I believe that we are entitled to say that the founders of the Communist Party of Germany [allusion to Karl Liebknecht, Rosa Luxemburg, and Leo Joguiches] would not sign the twenty-one conditions. Their true meaning is that the European labor movement, as well as that in the East, is to be . . . turned into a tool of the Moscow Executive Committee's power politics. And their Central Committee is nothing more or less than the Central Committee of the Russian Communist Party. Everything they tell us about representatives of other countries cannot for an instant close our eyes to the plain fact that these so-called representatives are actually under the thumb of the Russian communists. . . .[15]

Hilferding also refuted Zinoviev's optimistic predictions of early revolution in the Balkans and elsewhere:

> One should not make such prophecies; Zinoviev should not make them. . . . Tactics like that are little more than a game of change, an all-or-nothing gamble, on which no party can base its policies. . . . Why, in England and France the communist movement is completely without influence. As things are, even to dream of uniting the workers and bringing them into the revolutionary camp merely by organizational means, by founding new parties and writing bylaws, is quite utopian. . . . I fully understand how Russian comrades, vested with authority to govern in their country—and who thus have an effective, extraordinarily rigorous and far-reaching power —how these comrades might seriously overestimate the power situation even in countries in which the proletariat does technically have the power to govern, as in Italy. The course that this revolutionary development will follow cannot be decreed from without, but depends on economic and social power-relationships between and among the classes in the individual countries, and one must be dreaming to imagine that it can be hurried along by any solution or command concocted or issued from the outside. . . .[16]

Yet, despite all this criticism, Hilferding had no objection at all to joining the Third International. What he condemned was Moscow's desire to
split the USPD, and the way in which the Comintern was organized, with
a single party (Russia's) having already appointed itself master and all
the others its subordinates: ". . . we are being split from without over the
issue as to whether we should join the Third International, a thing we all
want to do."[17]

Hilferding was not deceived as to what Zinoviev and his followers
were really after at Halle. The split had been plotted in advance, the pro-
Bolshevik wing of the USPD, the leaders of the German Communist party
and the Comintern General Staff having closely collaborated in the execution of the plan, a prime element of which was selecting the exact line
of fissure that the split was to follow. The decision to join or not to join
the Comintern was not to depend on the opinions expressed by USPD
militants themselves, but on a line of demarcation pre-drawn by Moscow. The fact that the German Communist party was the most important
foreign party in the Comintern and was run by the headstrong veteran
leader, Paul Levi, was part of the reason that this demarcation line was
drawn only after consultation and agreement with German Communist
leaders, which constituted an exceptional privilege conceded by Moscow,
when one remembers that the decision to admit the two French "centrist"
Socialist leaders, Frossard and Cachin, had been made unilaterally by the
Soviet chiefs. This did not happen in the case of the USPD, as Paul Levi
was to note shortly before his break with Moscow: "When it comes to
splitting parties not organizationally bound to us, one can do as we
communists did and make the noose wider or narrower. In Germany, for
example, the Executive Committee drew the Comintern line so as to
satisfy the wish of us Germans to keep out the Ledebour people and
bring in everyone to the Left of Ledebour and Rosenfeld."[18]

When the congress voted on October 16, 1920, the Däumig-Stoecker
motion to join the Third International got 237 votes, and there were 156
votes against it. The split was thus consummated, and the left wing
remained in session without the right wing, in the presence of Zinoviev,
who welcomed the result and set the winners the following task: to bring
all the revolutionary elements together into a single Communist party.
The Left elected the new leaders of its own, since of the twelve on the
Central Committee only four had voted to join the Comintern. Their first
appeal, signed by the two new chairmen, Ernst Däumig and Adolph
Hoffmann, announced the vote of the ex-USPD membership as follows:
"Two hundred and thirty-seven delegates out of 395 decided in favor of
the Third International, whereas in the earlier poll 144,000 had voted
for, 91,000 against."[19] Returning to Petrograd in a euphoric state, Zinoviev provided even more glowing figures, asserting that: "It is obvious

that of the simple party members, the workers, at least nine-tenths support the (USPD) Left. The weeks and months to come will show whether
this is really so." As for the future communist party, to consist of this left
united with the Spartacists, Zinoviev foresaw a "workers' party that will
wind up with five to six hundred thousand members. . . ."[20]

With Radek secretly on the scene, steps were immediately taken to
effect the preplanned union. Published on October 30, 1920, was a joint
appeal signed by Zinoviev, the Central Committee of the German Communist party and the Central Committee of the (Left) USPD, and on November 3, in his report to the Comintern Executive Committee, Zinoviev
declared unification in Germany to be imminent. It was just at this time,
from November 1 to 3, that the German (Spartacist) Communist party
held its fifth and last congress in Berlin, attended by seventy delegates
representing the 78,715 members. The congress of unification was held
from December 4 to 7, and the new party took the name Vereinigte Kommunistische Partei Deutschlands (United Communist party of Germany)
or VKPD for short, with Paul Levi and Ernst Däumig as co-chairmen.

But the weeks and months ahead, hailed in advance by Zinoviev, were
to disappoint his expectations. By 1921 the majority of delegates who
attended the Halle congress were still unable to boast of having brought
in with them either a majority of the USPD voters or a majority of its
members. As for the voters, in the 1920–21 winter elections for deputies to seven state diets (*Landtage*), they gave more of their votes to the
Halle USPD minority (which, continuing under the USPD emblem, got
1,481,000) than they did to the United party comprised of the USPD Left
and the Spartacists, who received 1,440,000 (while the official Social-
Democratic party walked off with 5,309,000). On February 24, 1921,
the day after these elections, VKPD Chairman Paul Levi was forced to
conclude: "I have the feeling that as many ex-USPD voters switched to
the Socialists as to us."[21] As for the former USPD members, the VKPD report presented at their congress in August 1921 admitted: "It is probably
true, though, that many workers in the USPD who had originally voted
to join the Third International did not join the VKPD. . . ."[22]

Splitting the SFIO

During World War I, the labor movement in France had no equivalent
of the Spartacus League, nor was there any split in the official Social-
Democratic party—two political phenomena experienced by the Germans even before the November 7, 1917, coup at Petrograd. The splitting
that set in in Germany immediately after the war, evidenced by the existence of three different labor parties—the SPD, USPD, and KPD (Com-

munist party of Germany)—occurred in France only within the SFIO, the country's only labor party. But in the SFIO the process followed the USPD pattern, proceeding in three successive contradictory phases. In the first, during 1919 and early 1920, the party majority was against immediately or directly joining the Comintern. During the second, which spanned the latter half of 1920, the majority of delegates to its congress favored joining. In the third and final phase, during 1921 and 1922, the majority of the voters no longer sided with the Communists but with those who had remained Socialist.

The two factors largely responsible for producing the extreme Leftist trend among Socialists, opposition to the war and the Bolshevik victory at Petrograd, were influential in the French Socialist labor movement also, but later than in other countries. The reason was that the opposition to the war and support for the Third International proved strongest in defeated countries like Germany, Bulgaria, and Hungary; next strongest in countries in which some of the population believed themselves "cheated," despite being technically on the winning side (e.g., Italy and parts of Yugoslavia); then in countries that had remained neutral (like Sweden, Norway, Holland, Switzerland); and were least in evidence in victor countries such as France, Belgium, Czechoslovakia, England. The extreme Leftist trend was nonexistent in the SFIO when the war broke out in 1914, and was still very feeble immediately after the October 1917 revolution, and even when the war ended in 1918. At the SFIO congress in April 1919 only 14 percent of the voting delegates favored joining the Communist International, though some of the Socialist parties, like the Italian and Norwegian, were then voting almost unanimously to join, while others, like the Yugoslav party, had a heavy majority in favor. Ten months later, at the congress that opened in Strasbourg on February 25, 1920, the extreme Leftists, advocating joining the Comintern immediately, had only 34 percent of the votes, yet by the end of the year, at the congress in Tours, 75 percent voted to join it.

During World War I opposition on the far Left had never succeeded in becoming an important movement, until the October Revolution. Even after that, the Communists had to survive in power and consolidate their hold on Russia before the far Left abroad could pick up any significant new strength. If the Bolshevik seizure of power had turned into another Paris Commune, it could not have kindled any Communist movement in other countries. But Bolshevik power, firmly in the saddle with the end of foreign intervention, and having won the civil war and triumphed militarily in Poland, began to exert a fascination even upon people who, shortly before, were refusing absolutely to have any truck with Moscow, which they bombarded with bad names and criticism.

Suddenly this same regime in Russia, governed by the same men, was viewed in a different light by the same French Socialist militants. In 1918 Charles Rappoport, to be a member of the leadership (Comité Directeur) of the French Communist party after its creation at Tours, stigmatized Lenin and his bolshevism in these terms:

> By an act of force, Lenin has just overthrown not only the Constituent Assembly but also, and above all, his own doctrine, the international Socialist program. The Lenin-Trotsky Red Guard have just shot Karl Marx, whom they are always hailing as their patron saint against the militarist opportunists. It is a mad dash for the abyss! Blanquism with Tartar sauce! The suicide of the Revolution. One does not toy like that with the basic laws of a free country. . . .[23]

Marcel Cachin, who in 1920 would play a leading role in getting Socialists to join the Comintern and who from the outset until his death in 1958 would be a member of the Central Committee of the French Communist party, hurled some equally heavy charges at the Bolsheviks only six months later:

> We are not bolsheviks, and no more than Merrheim do we want to sign, as they did, a new treaty of Brest-Litovsk. Since Mirbach's execution, the bolsheviks have become so chummy with the German Government that the latter takes them openly under its wing. Revolutionaries everywhere are watching in bewilderment the bolshevik police doing Berlin's chores in hunting down and shooting Socialists who rid their country of the usurper.[24]

When in February 1920, at the Strasbourg congress, the motion of the Committee for Reconstruction of the International, inspired by Marx's grandson, Jean Longuet, carried with more than 49 percent of the votes (as against 34 percent for the pro-communists), the draft resolution bore the signatures of twenty-four leading lights on that committee. But by December some of the signatories had switched their support from reconstruction of the old International to joining the new, and wound up as leaders of the new Communist party: Amédée Dunois, Louis-Oscar Frossard, Henri Gourdeaux, Lucie Leiciague, Paul Louis, Daniel Renoult, Joseph Tommasi, Raoul Verfeuil. But the leader of the group, Jean Longuet, was missing. As in Germany, where the Bolshevik leaders had opened the Comintern gates to Walter Stoecker, who soon moved up to head the German Communist party and who in 1914 had been a "social patriot" and "social chauvinist," yet had closed them to Otto Rühle, who during the war was the first Social-Democratic deputy to follow Karl Liebknecht, so in France in 1920 the Bolshevik leaders let in Marcel Cachin, well-known "social chauvinist" during the war, but kept Jean Longuet out. This happened notwithstanding the praise given him as late as February 1920 by the official organ of the Communist International under the signature of V. Taratouta-Kemerer, who was in charge of problems of the movement in France and resided in the Kremlin itself, and who, writing about Jean Longuet and the editorial policy of the *Populaire*, emphasized that ". . . here in Russia we all recognize the valuable services that the *Populaire* rendered to the Soviet Republic with its editorial campaign. He . . . was the first to raise his voice in defense of Russia's workers and peasants then fighting for communism."[25]

For an entire year, from the end of 1919 until the end of 1920, the Longuet problem preoccupied Lenin, Trotsky, and Zinoviev; it was not solved until the congress at Tours. The case and Zinoviev's telegram, which settled it, provided the famous "pistol shot" episode. Even at the second Comintern congress one point was firmly established concerning the founding of the future French party: Frossard and Cachin were to be let in, the former as secretary, since his was the highest administrative rank in the SFIO, and the latter as director of *Humanité*, the party's top propaganda spot. To forge a mass Communist party in France, the Bolsheviks had to amalgamate two elements until then separate and often hostile: the Committee in Favor of Joining the Third International, and the ex-Reconstructionists, who wanted to resuscitate the old Second International and whose two spokesmen in Moscow were Frossard and Cachin. In Germany the goal had been to fuse the Spartacists and the left wing of the USPD in order to split that party; in France the fusion would be between the Committee for the Third International and the SFIO center, again for the purpose of producing a split. There was an important reason for letting in the ex-centrists. The leaders of the Committee for Joining the Third International had all been in jail since March 1920, waiting for a trial whose outcome threatened to put them out of circulation for who knows how long. The Bolshevik chieftains, aware of the true situation and knowing where the strength lay, could not expect to have a strong Communist party in France if the leaders of the Communist far Left were in prison and the Centrist leaders all blackballed. But a prerequisite to letting Frossard and Cachin into the Comintern of course was that they accept the invitation, i.e., that they consent to step inside when Moscow kindly opened the door. Two decisions taken by Moscow could make it hard for them to do this, or to bring any of their Paris friends in with them: the barring of Jean Longuet and the gist of the twenty-one conditions for Comintern admission. Thus the skillful and seemingly moderate tactic adopted toward the SFIO: it would not do to rush things with Cachin and Frossard still in Moscow, for too categorical a demand that the SFIO break with Longuet and jump lock, stock, and barrel, unconditionally, into the Comintern would have immediately alienated the centrist majority and their leaders. On the other hand, letting Longuet in and waiving the twenty-one admission requirements just for the French would have meant Lenin's abandoning two of his root ideas. Equally unthinkable. So Lenin decided on a third course. He would let the French swallow gradually, in small gentle doses, the bitter double pill: excommunication of Longuet and their submission to the twenty-one conditions.

Longuet symbolized for Lenin what Kautsky and Hilferding had in Germany. There was not therefore the slightest chance of Lenin's admitting him to the Comintern, though Longuet's thinking was much closer to Lenin's than that of many others who would be let in. On receiving a letter from Fernand Loriot and the Committee for the Third International at a time when ties with France (and Europe generally) were very tenuous, Lenin in his reply, dated October 28, 1919, named only one Socialist politician who had to be fought: "You of course still have a long fight ahead of you against French opportunism, a particularly subtle form of which is the mentality of Longuet."[26] At almost the same time Trotsky published an article attacking Longuet in the official organ of the Communist International (issue of November-December 1919), and in a letter to his friends in France he demanded that they dump him: "Putting an end to Longuet-ism is an urgent requirement for political health."[27] Despite these attacks, Longuet continued to seek to reach an accommodation with Moscow. He sent personally a letter to Lenin on the eve of the Strasbourg congress, along with the text of the draft resolution drawn up by the Committee for Reconstruction of the [Second] International. From February 8 to 14, 1920, Lenin wrote out his objections to the resolution, publishing an article on the subject in the March issue of the Comintern organ in which he was very harsh toward Longuet, his resolution and entire attitude: "With leaders like that [Longuet-ists] the proletariat will never be able to achieve its dictatorship."[28] On February 28 Lenin wrote Longuet a letter in answer to the one that the latter had sent him. A few days later, Longuet was again at the center of the dialogue between Moscow and Paris: "On March 9, 1920, the Administrative Commission appointed citizens Marcel Cachin and Jean Longuet to go to Russia on a mission of inquiry and negotiation."[29] But when the time came for them to leave, "citizen Longuet, who was busy and could not get away, was replaced by citizen Frossard."[30] In Moscow, despite his absence, Longuet was once more under discussion. On July 29, in a declaration signed by Frossard and Cachin, and read by the latter, it was stated: "We are convinced that if our friend Longuet were here, after some reflection he would have the same opinion as we."[31] Frossard, who supported Longuet's position, reported on his return:

> There never was or has been any Longuet policy. His policy is that of a group within the party who think and feel as he does. We accepted responsibility for it with him. We would have dishonored ourselves, had we for one moment even dreamed of abandoning the man with whom we had stood for so long in the interest of a common cause. . . . That was our attitude [in Moscow]. We were totally united, and finally wrang from Zinoviev an assurance that they would not insist on barring Longuet. . . ."[32]

Yet the seventh of Lenin's twenty-one "admission requirements" stipulated the opposite: "The Communist International cannot admit to membership avowed reformists like Turati, Kautsky, Hilferding, Longuet, MacDonald, Modigliani, and others of their stripe, nor allow them to be represented in it, lest the Third International become too much like the Second."[33]

Between Zinoviev's promise to Frossard and the attitude adopted by Lenin there was no possibility of compromise. In the months that followed the Second Congress it did seem that Zinoviev's promise was becoming the official Comintern line with regard to relations between Moscow and Longuet. In October 1920, at the Halle congress, the Comintern president had occasion to converse with a "Longuet-ist" delegation consisting of Longuet himself and Daniel Renoult. The chat between Zinoviev and Longuet was quite friendly, as Longuet later recalled at Tours: "In Halle I had a chance to talk with Zinoviev. . . . At the time he did not regard me as a social traitor."[34] At Tours also, the second participant in the conversation, Renoult, confirmed this in a remark to Longuet: "You remember how, in Halle, Zinoviev greeted you with brotherly courtesy."[35] At Halle, Longuet had publicly dissociated himself from the speech by Martov, a fact which Zinoviev himself was pleased to stress: "Longuet deemed it his duty to protest, directly from the speakers' platform, against the attacks on Soviet Russia made by Martov in his speech."[36] This amicable contact between the Comintern president and the Longuet delegation at Halle eventuated several days later in the signing, in Berlin, by Zinoviev and Renoult of a statement to the effect:

> The exception provided in article 20 [of the admission requirements] regarding the exclusion of "centrists" shall apply to Longuet, Paul Faure and the members of their group. If after the vote of the next congress they are still in the party and are willing to accept its decisions as well as the theses and conditions of the Communist

International, their admission under those conditions will then become final, subject to ratification by the Comintern's Executive Committee.[37]

Returning to Petrograd at the end of October 1920, Zinoviev went on to Moscow to attend the regular weekly meeting of the Bolshevik Polit-buro and Comintern Executive Committee, the latter to be held on No-vember 3. Fortified by his success at Halle, he did secure ratification of all that he had agreed to in Germany, including even the accord with the Longuet group. But he did not reckon with Lenin, who within twenty-four hours set forth his "objections to the untimeliness of his measure [admitting Longuet], giving his principal arguments for his decision [*not* to admit him]."[38] Lenin's proposal amounted actually to a veto, his opinion alone carrying more weight than the decision of the Comintern's entire Executive Committee. Longuet's fate was thus sealed, and the job of carrying out the decision against him was assigned, naturally, to Zinoviev—in line with Lenin's customary method of having a policy implemented by one who had disapproved it, but had to be bent to discipline.

The Lenin veto was not disclosed at the time. The first evidence of his intention did not come to light until 1963, in the fifth edition of his col-lected works, and even then without reproduction of the text. In 1920, nobody in France had any inkling of what was afoot, which is why Zin-oviev's telegram—countersigned by the Comintern Executive Commit-tee, headed by Lenin, Trotsky and Bukharin, and sent on December 24 —when learned of on December 28 by those attending the congress at Tours, caused a sensation. The ax had finally fallen on Longuet and his friends: "The draft revolution signed by Longuet and Paul Faure shows that Longuet and his group have no intention of being exceptions in the reformist camp. They have been and still are determined agents of bour-geois influence on the proletariat. . . . The Communist International can have nothing in common with the authors of such resolutions. . . ."[39] But the resolution, irrevocably damned by the Bolsheviks, proclaimed that "the first duty of party members is at all times and all places to go to the defense of the Soviet Republic," and it recommended that the party "apply for admission to the Communist International," though adding, "the party has the duty to say in all loyalty that a certain number of these conditions are, in its judgment, against the interest as well as tradi-tion of the French socialist movement and impossible to apply or in-advisable. It expressly takes exception to the conditions touching on its own internal setup."[40]

The Bolshevik tactic, which consisted in exploiting if not provoking conflicts in the enemy camp, had entirely succeeded in this case. The leader, Longuet, found himself cut off from his friends and supporters. Even Frossard did not stick to the protestations of solidarity with Longuet that he had uttered several weeks earlier. People supporting him only a short time before were now members of that same executive committee that had just barred his admission. As for the reason given for keeping him out, namely his reservations concerning the internal party setup called for in the decisions of the Second Congress, a number of those were shared by Frossard and his friends, who were let into the Comintern, and were held also by the Committee for Joining the Third International.

Regarding the requirements for admission to the Comintern, a misunderstanding between Moscow and Paris had arisen at the second congress. It stemmed from the fact that the congress, on July 26, in the Executive Committee's appeal to members of the French Socialist party, had stated only nine conditions for admission, whereas Zinoviev as the appointed main speaker on the subject, at the session of July 29, had laid down nineteen conditions, to which he then added a twentieth, stipulated by Lenin. The difference between the two sets of conditions was significant, for those beamed at the French sidestepped some important points—such as revolutionary agitation within the armed forces, activities among the farm population, the fight against the Amsterdam Trade-Union International, democratic centralism, periodic purges, the requirement that two-thirds of the new central committee be partisans of the Comintern, etc. The difference enabled Frossard to use a double line of argument. On the one hand, he could claim that the Comintern had laid down only nine conditions to the French Socialists, since the rest were unknown to them while they were in Moscow, which obviously was untrue, for, at the plenary session on July 29, Cachin read a statement on behalf of the French delegation in which he referred to the twenty conditions that Zinoviev had mentioned in his speech, and he consented to them. Frossard used this argument in the polemics preceding the congress at Tours, in his public dispute with his former centrist colleague, Mayèras, who was against going along with Moscow, and in his writings after the break (as well as in his memoirs). Yet at the time of his joining the Comintern, he raised another argument, expressing some reservations about conditions not included among the nine formally presented to the French, as in his speech at Tours, where he voiced misgivings about the Bolshevik position on the trade-union issue, on defending one's country, and on the expulsions that Moscow was demanding. Even the motion prepared by the Committee for the Third International written almost entirely by Boris Souvarine and published in the *Bulletin Communiste* on

November 4, 1920, set forth three reservations about the twenty-one conditions for admission: expulsion of the centrists, called for by article seven, the condition about penetrating the trade unions (point nine) and changing the party's name to Communist party (point seventeen).

These many reservations, expressed not only by Longuet and by Frossard, on the one hand, and by the Committee for the Third International on the other, were accompanied by another obstacle initially confronting the Comintern. While Moscow had sent to the congress at Halle its titular chief, Zinoviev, and its man responsible for Germany, Radek, it had no one of comparable stature in France to perform the same function at Tours. In Moscow, during the Second World Congress, Trotsky was still preoccupied with the civil war and the hostilities against Poland, and had not yet taken charge of Communist affairs in France. Those entrusted with them had no political authority remotely comparable to Trotsky's, Zinoviev's, or Radek's. They were Taratouta, member of the Russian delegation, Abramovich-Zalewski and Vanini, members of the French delegation, and Degot, Moscow's fourth emissary, who arrived in the capital only after the congress was over. Of the four, Abramovich-Zalewski was the only one to come to France on the eve of the congress at Tours, where he played the role of a great eminence. This prompted a Longuet supporter, André le Troquer, to protest to the congress from the rostrum: "I shall violate no secret, but I do find it annoying that our party is deliberating under conditions such as these. While I do wish to join the Third International, I am not willing to put up with the clandestine surveillance that is going on, surveillance even of this congress."[41]

In addition to this secret representative, whose presence gave birth to the term "the eye of Moscow," there was another one who was there openly, Clara Zetkin. Apart from the speech that she was to make at the congress, she got drawn into the typical double Bolshevik game, which here only Zalewski knew about and was actively playing: conspiracy with respect to the class enemy and honeycombing the target party with one's own people. The conspiracy was actually a staged show. On the morning of December 28, Clara Zetkin announced that she found it "impossible to take part in the congress and carry out the mandate entrusted to me by the Executive Committee of the Third International," yet that afternoon she appeared on the speaker's platform, made a speech ιo the congress, then immediately vanished, the lights in the room suddenly going out. This touch of showmanship was Zalewski's doing, and did not sit well with Clara Zetkin, as she wrote to Paul Levi a few days later: "The melodrama was not to my taste . . . but I had to go along with what our friends wanted."[42] The honeycombing of the party about to be formed, i.e., the separation of the Communists deemed reliable from those considered less so or not at all, also began in Tours while

Clara Zetkin was there. Since Frossard refused to have any truck with Zalewski, the latter being the moving spirit of the "reliable" Communist nucleus, the pro-Moscow faction, according to Clara Zetkin's letter, included the following: "I had two meetings with C——, Vaillant, Renoult, Renand, Rappoport, and A—— before attending the congress, and I regard those two meetings as having constituted the most important part of my work. . . ."[43]

As for the public debates at the congress, it was a case of the deaf debating the deaf. To begin with, since everything had been rigged in advance, everyone knew how the vote would go, and all the colorful speeches from the platform had little chance of influencing what the delegates were going to do. Then, too, there was no forthright confrontation on the problem that had actually split the SFIO, as there had been none in the USPD, i.e., on the twenty-one conditions for admission to the International, in other words, the "organizational" as opposed to the "ideological" aspect. Earlier, at Halle, Hilferding had noted that Zinoviev glossed this problem over, though its bearing on the Comintern's future was fundamental. At Tours the situation of those who advocated joining the International was the same. Some, like Frossard, themselves expressed reservations about the twenty-one conditions, while others, like Clara Zetkin and Marcel Cachin, avoided the subject, so that no serious analysis favorable to the twenty-one admission requirements was undertaken, though they were at the very heart of the criticisms raised in the speeches of Paul Faure, Jean Longuet, and Léon Blum.

Longuet, the best versed of the three in the affairs of the Socialist International up to 1919, including Russian socialism, subjected the Comintern to a withering critique similar to Hilferding's at Halle, emphasizing in particular that:

> The [second] congress of the Third International took place at a time when our Russian comrades were particularly elated by their victories over Poland. Convinced that the Red Army was irresistible, in that euphoric state, at that tragic moment, they begat an International which is not an International of the proletariat of all countries, but a specifically Russian one with Russian ideas and Russian discipline, and which cannot be adapted to other countries.[44]

Recalling Zinoviev's telegram, read to them the night before, Longuet exclaimed: "If you want us to stay in—and I am tied to the movement with every fiber of my being—the air must be breathable. Yesterday we received from Moscow an outrageous, provocative message. . . . The time has come to decide whether you are ready to submit to the lash. Myself, I am not."[45]

Léon Blum, spokesman for a group more to the Right than that of

Longuet and Faure, criticized both the organizing principle, as did Faure, and the Bolsheviks' ideas concerning the International itself, like Longuet. The future head of the SFIO put his finger on the three key features of the Communist International. First, though, he queried his colleagues on their ideology.

> You are in the presence of an aggregate, a doctrinal whole. This being so, the question that you face is: Do you or do you not accept this doctrinal package that has been formulated for you by the congress of the Communist International? And by "accept"—and on this I hope we all agree—I mean accept in one's mind, in one's heart and will. I mean accept with the resolve henceforward to adhere in thought and deed to this new doctrine.[46]

Blum then attacked the new idea that bolshevism was introducing into the international socialist movement: "But what we have here is not merely a revision or readaptation. I shall endeavor to show you—and it is at the very core of my demonstration—that this is a new Socialism, new in all its essentials: concept of organization, of the interrelationship of the political and economic systems, of revolution, and of dictatorship of the proletariat."[47] In conclusion, Blum turned to the bolshevization, i.e., russianization, of the Comintern:

> [This new Socialism] . . . rests, on the other hand, on a kind of vast factual error, which has consisted in attempting to generalize for the whole of international Socialism a handful of notions drawn from a particular local event, that of the revolution in Russia, and to set up as a necessary and universal rule for all Socialism the alleged experience post-distilled from the actual facts by those who gave life and reality to the revolution in Russia.[48]

This new International, according to Blum, was proposing to scrap numerous ideas dear to the SFIO, e.g., proportional representation for the different viewpoints within the Central Committee, freedom of discussion, etc., and impose other ideas foreign to the SFIO and typical of bolshevism, such as a centralized system requiring that every internal unit be subordinated to one hierarchically above it, secret agencies, purges, with ultimate supreme power in the hands not of the national party but exclusively those of the Comintern Executive Committee:

> In the final analysis, it is that Executive Committee that will have the ultimate power over you, that will have the right to bar groups and individuals, that will centralize all political action. It will have its own office in every country, an office reporting exclusively to it.

It will reserve unto itself the right to set up secret organizations to be imposed upon you. . . .[49]

But, as to be expected in a dialogue between the deaf, the unanswerable arguments were met with unanswering silence by the Comintern's supporters. In the absence of Loriot and Souvarine—the two real leaders of the movement favoring joining the Third International who perhaps could have taken up the challenge and given an effective reply—the main Communist speakers at the congress in Tours (Marcel Cachin in the name of the former centrists who had gone over to the Comintern, and Paul Vaillant-Couturier, spokesman for the Left) made no attempt at all to meet this critical objection. As for Frossard, in his many speeches and talks at the congress he expressed some doubts and disagreement with aspects of the Comintern line, as immediately after the speech by Clara Zetkin, when he spoke up against the exclusions being demanded by Moscow: "I speak here in the name of a united majority: no exclusions!"[50] In his last address at the congress, Frossard again voiced disagreement with Moscow's attack on Longuet: "Had I been able to yesterday, I would have said then what I am saying to you tonight, distinctly, clearly: I do not agree with Zinoviev. I do not regard you as handmaidens of the bourgeoisie."[51]

The final vote, to distinguish the supporters from the opponents, gave the former an overwhelming majority. The votes for the joint resolution of the Committee for the Third International and the Frossard-Cachin group numbered 3,208, and the votes for the resolution of the (Longuet-Faure) Committee for Reconstruction of the International numbered 1,022, the motion by the Committee of Socialist Resistance (Blum) having been withdrawn. The Pressemane motion received only 60 votes, while there were 397 abstentions coming from Léon Blum's friends.

Moscow's satisfaction, however, did not come up to the size of the vote. If the numerical outcome seemed to justify a feeling of triumph, the decisions taken at the congress had a different effect. So it was not surprising that the Executive Committee, meeting in Moscow after the affair in Tours and discussing the matter at length, confined itself to sending, on January 10, 1921, a message clearly indicating that it still regarded the problem of French membership as far from settled: "The Executive Committee of the Communist International warmly congratulates the French proletarians on their victory at Tours. . . . The Executive Committee of the Third International requests you to send a representative to it in order to settle, once and for all, the question of your affiliation."[52]

Thus, the French Communist party was no sooner born than its relationship with Moscow became a problem, one that would grow in importance as the years went by, becoming ultimately the Comintern's number one problem. From the beginning, a phenomenon started to emerge in France similar to the one experienced by the USPD in Germany, in that neither the members of, nor voters for, the old SFIO would be represented in the new Communist party in proportions equal to their relative strength at the time of the Tours congress. The Communist party never regained the nearly 75 percent of the former SFIO's voters that it had with it at the moment of the split in Tours. The municipal by-elections in April and July 1921, in the main centers of labor strength such as Paris, Marseilles, Lyon, and the Paris suburbs (Colombes), as well as the legislative elections in the Oise Department, showed everywhere the same pattern: Socialist candidates running ahead of the Communist candidates. Their percentage strengths at the congress of Tours were reversed by the voters in 1921, the SFIO capturing a majority going from 55 to 70 percent, leaving the Communists a minority. The same trend began to be reflected in the membership figures of the two parties, though another year or two would have to go by before the numerical ratio was reversed here also.

The Split in the Italian Socialist Party

Lenin's decision to slam the Comintern door on the leaders of centrist socialism dominated not only the second Comintern congress but the congresses of Halle and Tours as well. It had rougher sailing, however, in the case of the Italian Socialist party. Unlike the barred Germans and Frenchmen—Dittmann, Crispien, Longuet and their supporters unwilling to disown them—the head of both the Italian Socialist party and its centrist faction, Giacinto Serrati, had a seat in the presidium of the Second Congress alongside Lenin and Zinoviev. Yet only three months later, this same Serrati came under violent attack by Lenin and Zinoviev. In less than six months after the second congress, Moscow and Serrati had broken. The break, which took place at the congress of Leghorn in January 1921, was different in two ways from those that had preceded it at Halle and Tours. In Germany and France the split had occurred in socialist parties not previously belonging to the Communist International, whereas at Leghorn the eruption occurred in a party which as early as 1919, first in March through its directing committee, then in October at its congress of Bologna, had voted overwhelmingly to join. But unlike the congresses at Halle and Tours, where the majority voted to enter the Comintern, at Leghorn the majority voted to leave it. The consequences of what happened at Leghorn had more of an impact internationally. There were profound reverberations within the leadership of the German Communist party, which accelerated the crisis in that most important section of the Comintern.

Whereas the French Socialists in 1920 joined the Communist International in a state of ambiguity, the Italians had joined it in 1919 in a state of ignorance and frivolity. That it was an act of frivolity was confirmed by some of the Italian leaders, like G. E. Modigliani, who let fall some remarks to Longuet, reported shortly thereafter to the Executive Committee of the Comintern by Zinoviev himself: "Here is how, in a conversation with Longuet, he [Modigliani] urged the leader of the French 'independents' to join the Third International: 'Friend Longuet,' he said in effect, 'why don't we join the Third International? What does it commit us to, after all? Actually it involves nothing more than sending in, every couple of weeks or so, a pretty picture postcard.' "[53] These carefree words of Modigliani's enraged the Bolshevik leaders, who remembered all too well their own characterization of the Second International as a mere "P.O. Box." They could not tolerate such things being said about the Third. As to Italian ignorance of things Bolshevik, one need only note that the two cornerstones of the Lenin theoretical edifice, dictatorship of the proletariat and the system of soviets, received at best a whimsical interpretation at the hands of the Italian Socialists. Concerning the first, the delegate of the Swiss Socialist party, Graver, saw this well in October 1919. "At the congress in Bologna, on questioning the representatives of Italy's official party, he was constrained to observe that not one of the comrades whom he asked gave him a definition of dictatorship of the proletariat even resembling the definition given by the comrade whom he had asked just before."[54] As for the system of soviets, the party's national council, meeting in Florence in January 1920, had decided upon a makeup of the soviets which led to various interpretations within the party, starting with that of its secretary, Egidio Gennari, who wanted to abandon the idea of setting up a soviet system throughout Italy and concentrate instead on creating a model soviet in just one locality. The national council at its next meeting, in Milan in April 1920, reaffirmed "the need for soviets" and called upon the leadership to produce them. "So that the leaders will not flag in their accomplishment of this task, we are providing them a charter for the soviets, in which in a few dozen articles everything is spelled out. All we need now is for the soviets to be created. . . ."[55]

Their contacts with the Italian delegation at the second world congress only strengthened the conviction of Lenin and his colleagues that the men and affairs of the Italian Socialist party were in need of being straightened out. Apart from well-known reformists such as Ludovico d'Aragona, almost every one of the other delegates represented a different viewpoint within the party, including those who had finally come over to communism, men like Amadeo Bordiga, Niccola Bombacci, and Antonio Graziadei. But the most serious case was that of Serrati, who in his speeches (and sometimes with his votes) opposed many Comintern dicta, e.g., on that national and colonial question; on the agrarian issue (he was the only delegate to vote against the theses); on proposed immediate exclusion of Turati;[56] on the strict enforcement of the twenty-one admission conditions; on the need for British Communists to join the Labour party; and on the merits of the Comintern decision to admit the KAPD to the second congress. Now, all these Comintern decisions, theses, and directives were the work of Lenin himself. He was their father and mother. He had poured into them the ultimate quintessence of his inmost thoughts on tactics and organization. And here was this Serrati throwing them all overboard lock, stock, and barrel! It was around this time, one assumes, that Lenin started to deduce that there was no room in the Comintern for Serrati, whom he probably had in mind when, during a discussion in Moscow, he remarked: "We must simply tell our Italian comrades that the policy of the Communist International is the one being followed by the members of the Ordine Nuovo group, not that of the present majority of Socialist party leaders and their faction in parliament."[57]

The first public hint of the position that Moscow was preparing to take in the Italian question was an appeal addressed to the central committee of the Socialist party, all the party members and the entire revolutionary proletariat of Italy, an appeal drafted by Bukharin, edited and supplemented by Zinoviev, under Lenin's supervisory eye. On learning of it, the Italian delegation in Moscow discussed it with some heat and expressed their disapproval. Serrati in particular was dead against it. But the Comintern overrode the opposition and, while the Italian delegation was touring the Ukraine, the appeal, dated August 21, 1920, was published over the signatures of Zinoviev, Bukharin, and Lenin.

The appeal contained two central ideas. The first was that Italy was ripe for revolution:

> The working class in Italy is suffused with admirable unanimity. To a man, the Italian proletariat is for revolution. The Italian bourgeoisie cannot rely on its regular troops, for at the decisive moment they will join the insurrectionaries. The farm workers are for the revolution. Most of the peasants are for the revolution. . . . All the prime prerequisites for a grand victorious proletarian

revolution encompassing the whole people are now present in Italy.
. . . The Third International so concludes.[58]

The second thought was that a purge of the Italian party was becoming urgently necessary if the revolution were to be a success: "The very presence within your party of Modiglianis, Turatis and others of their stripe is a negation of any serious proletarian discipline. The enemy sits in your own house."[59]

When less than ten days later, on August 30, the workers at the Romeo plant in Turin, after finishing work that evening, refused to leave and stayed on to occupy the factory, and when, on the following day, some 280 metallurgical plants in Milan were seized by their workers, and when this movement spread to nearly all of Italy within a bare forty-eight hours, with "workers' committees" and "red guards" springing up all over the place, the news could be interpreted in Moscow in only one way: the imminent revolution in Italy foreseen by the Comintern was now beginning. Once again in the eyes of the Bolsheviks Lenin had proved right. When this development in Italy continued into September, the Comintern decided that the time had come to transform the takeover of factories into a revolutionary coup aimed at seizing power, and on September 22, in the name of the Executive Committee, Zinoviev addressed the Italian proletariat in these terms: "You cannot win merely by grabbing a few factories and mills. . . . Our conclusion is that you must broaden your takeover, make it general, indeed nationwide. In other words, you must expand the movement into a general uprising aimed at ousting the bourgeoisie, seizure of power by the working class, and establishment of a dictatorship of the proletariat."[60]

But by this time the movement was losing its steam, and four days later, on September 26, it petered out into a compromise, which did not, however, stop Lenin and Zinoviev from continuing to insist that Italy was in a state of revolution. On October 25, as he was about to leave Germany, Zinoviev sent another public letter to the Italian Communists, affirming: "All the necessary prerequisites for victory of a proletarian revolution exist in Italy. All that is needed is for the working class to be properly organized."[61] Yet, unable to ignore the fact that the first revolutionary wave had faded back out to sea, he drew the classic Bolshevik conclusion that its failure was due to treachery by the Italian "Mensheviks." Then, under the signature of the Comintern's Executive Committee, he wrote: "Supported by the reformists and trade-union bureaucracy, d'Aragona and his henchmen thwarted the workers' will. *The Italian capitalists were rescued by d'Aragona, Turati, Modigliani, Dugoni and other capitalist agents.*"[62] It was in the autumn of 1920 also that Serrati's fate was sealed, as confirmed by Longuet's report of a discussion that he had with Zinoviev at Halle that October:

> I was saying to Zinoviev: "But the Italian movement is headed by men whose thinking is closest to your own. They were raised, grew up in the very atmosphere of your movement, and Serrati, member of the Moscow Executive Committee, has told you that it is not possible to bring off a revolution in Italy at the moment." Zinoviev's reply was typical of a mentality which I leave to you to judge: "Then Serrati," he said, "is a traitor too."[63]

The conception held by the Bolshevik leaders, in the fall of 1920, of what was going on in Italy, while entirely consistent with their general outlook, was totally at variance with the facts. There was no treachery by Serrati that autumn, neither physical (since he did not get back to Italy until September 15, when the workers' flareup was dying down) nor political (his attitude being neither more nor less "defeatist" or "opportunist" than that of the local Communist leaders, who several months later were to found the Italian Communist party). The policy of these Communist leaders was far from one of promoting any immediate revolution, if reports from Italian and foreign Communist sources are to be believed. Angelo Tasca, a leader of the Turin group that had launched the Ordine Nuovo, recalled the reluctance of that city's Communist leaders to hazard any attempt at revolution: "Even in Turin, where there is, after all, a bold avant-garde, better armed than elsewhere, the communist leaders are refraining from any initiative in that direction, and are holding back the elements at the Fiat works who had their trucks all warmed up, ready to sally forth."[64] A leader of the Italian Communist Youth, Ignazio Silone, has described the attitude of one of the Communist party founders, a spokesman for that same Turin group, whose thinking was supposed to be closest to that of Moscow: "My most tenacious political recollection is of the appointment of Terracini, of the Turin Socialist delegation, along with Turati and others, to the committee that was to draft a law on the workers' control."[65] Anyway, there was nothing unusual about this state of affairs for Italy, as Serrati pointed out in his comments concerning one of the many manifestos of the Comintern Executive Committee addressed to the Italian Socialists and syndicalists: "It is quite true that representatives of the organizations have begun talks with the government, but this is something that everybody does, the reformists as well as the purest communists. Did not Bombacci negotiate with the government ministers during the railroad strike?"[66] From the speakers' platform at the Comintern's third world congress, Clara

Zetkin was to question publicly the official version of what was going on in Italy:

> Comrade Terracini has told us here that the party committee debated two days over the question as to whether they should or should not launch a revolution. Still, I cannot put all the blame on Serrati for the fact that they decided not to. Serrati wasn't even in Italy at the time. He was on his way home from Moscow. And I even think that we cannot blame only the Serrati-ites, since the maximalists were then in the majority on the committee.[67]

Once war had been declared on Serrati, Lenin had but a single goal: to win that war by isolating Serrati from his friends, as was being done in France with Longuet. Starting in October and November, an avalanche of manifestos, open letters, appeals, newspaper articles, etc., rained down upon the Italian Socialists from Moscow. They were signed either by the Executive Committee, by Zinoviev, or by Lenin personally, who on November 4 wrote an article on "The Struggle within the Italian Socialist Party," which was published on November 7 in *Pravda*, and reprinted the following month in *Communist International*. In it Lenin hit at two main points. The first was the revolution-ripeness of the crisis in Italy and the battle-readiness of the Italian proletariat: "Everyone sees and admits that the revolutionary crisis is becoming nationwide. By its actions the proletariat has shown itself capable of rising spontaneously and of uplifting the masses into a powerful revolutionary movement."[68] The second concerned immediate formation of a Communist party and exclusion of the centrist Socialist leaders:

> Today it is essential, utterly indispensable, for victory of the revolution in Italy that a wholly communist party, incapable of hesitation and weakness at the decisive moment, become the true avant-garde of the revolutionary proletariat. . . . Excluding [the reformist leaders] will not weaken but strengthen that party, for "leaders" of this type can only lose the revolution "in the bourgeois manner," even if they do remain loyal.[69]

Once the decision was taken, there remained only to implement it on the spot. Lenin knew better than anyone in the Comintern that the agit-prop was not enough unless supported by an efficient local organization doing the necessary factional groundwork. Since the Italian Communists knew nothing of this technique, one had to send them "teachers" from Moscow. Thus it was that two Russian militants were secretly in Italy during the months preceding the split.

The first was Vladimir Degot, who had spent time in Italy on a secret mission for the Comintern at the end of 1919 and in early 1920. On returning to Russia, he was received by Lenin, who questioned him at length on his work in Italy: "I talked a lot about Serrati," wrote Degot in his memoirs.[70] By the autumn of 1920 he was back in Italy, where he would spend the months preceding the Leghorn congress. The second "teacher" had arrived in Italy at the end of 1919. It was Liubarski, whose name remained unknown even to the Italian Communist leaders. They knew him only as "Comrade Carlo," though he wrote in the Italian Communist press under the pen name G. Niccolini. On arriving in Italy, where he had once lived as a political exile, he cooperated closely with Serrati. Together they launched the publication *Il Communismo—Revista della Terza Internationale*, to which Serrati lent his political authority, Niccolini contributing the moral support (and probably money) of the Comintern. In the course of 1920, even before the second Comintern congress, their cooperation stalled, and Niccolini made contact with the Ordine Nuovo in Turin. When open war was declared on Serrati, two emissaries from Moscow participated on the Communist side, if they did not actually run the show. Three weeks before the Leghorn congress, Serrati would learn, and publicly reveal, the role of these emissaries:

> The Executive Committee of the Communist International sends its own representatives to every country, individuals whom it selects from among Russian comrades whom its members know and trust. The Executive Committee alone judges whether these representatives possess the qualities needed for fulfillment of their appointed missions. And it is to the Executive Committee alone that these gray eminences send their private reports, reports whose contents may be totally unknown to those heading the parties in the countries in which these "informants" do their work. The information that they send is not subject to criticism or control. They report whatever they please, and that is that. And they don't tell you, let you know, give you any chance at all for discussion. And don't ask either what means the informant uses in the pursuit of his task. And, of course, please don't inquire whether such a state of affairs might not lead to corruption. . . . We had the naiveté to express these misgivings to Moscow and propose some practical remedies to preclude the dangers mentioned. The effort failed.[71]

The activities of "Comrade Carlo" in Italy were judged differently by different Communist leaders, depending on their respective viewpoints. On returning from Leghorn, Matyas Rakosi had only good to say about him to the German Communist party leaders: "A representative of the Communist International has also been in Italy for a year, and he is well-informed about everything that is going on in the Party."[72] But Paul Levi, when he returned from Leghorn, wrote from Berlin to the Executive Committee in Moscow:

> I would like also, in my evaluation of the group and person of Serrati, to mention the following. There is severe personal tension between Serrati and Comrade Carlo. It dates from the time when Comrade Serrati, as has happened to other comrades, got wind of some reports, while in Moscow, sent there by Comrade Carlo concerning Italy. Serrati claims that they completely violated the political and human trust that had existed between him and Comrade Carlo up to the time of the Serrati trip to Russia.[73]

In addition to these secret emissaries, in Leghorn as at Halle and Tours, there were publicly acknowledged Comintern delegates who were to speak at the congress. The original plan was for Moscow's first team, Zinoviev and Bukharin, to attend, but in the end they were unable to do so and were replaced by two delegates who were not even members of the Comintern Executive Committee—the Bulgarian, Christo Kabakchiev, and a Hungarian, Rakosi. The former had been a secret Comintern agent in Italy during the months preceding the Leghorn congress, before assuming his new role as an official speaker at the congress. His official biography states: "After the congress at Halle, he went to Italy, where on orders from the Executive Committee of the Communist International he helped prepare for the Socialist Party congress and helped unify the 'internationalist group' and Communist Left in their fight against the reformists."[74] While entrusting a Comintern mandate to these two militants who enjoyed no international authority and were completely unknown in the movement in Italy, Zinoviev refused to grant one to Paul Levi, who possessed all the qualities lacked by the other two, for he knew the country and could speak its language, did enjoy great prestige in the international Communist movement, and did belong to the Comintern Executive Committee elected at the Second World Congress. As the Italian congress drew near, Levi was asked by Clara Zetkin to go to Leghorn: "My dear Paul, please do arrange to come to Leghorn. Just your presence there is bound to have a good effect. The development of our Party has made a very great impression abroad."[75] But Zinoviev was not of that opinion, as Levi later reported to his own party's executive committee: "The Executive Committee, i.e., Comrade Zinoviev, refused to send me as a representative to Italy. . . ."[76] Nevertheless, Levi did go to Leghorn, accompanied by a second delegate from the German Communist party, Paul Böttcher, who belonged to the anti-Levi group, but it was Levi who spoke for his party's central committee.

The mission entrusted to Kabakchiev and Rakosi, and the position that Levi planned to defend, conflicted irreconcilably on one key point: the attitude to be adopted toward Serrati. The former had instructions from Moscow to pronounce excommunication upon the Italian leader, while Levi had come to Leghorn to try to prevent any break between Serrati and the Comintern. The Kabakchiev-Rakosi tandem worked busily against Serrati before and during the congress, without ever having any contact with him. In fact, Serrati was not even aware of their presence, though himself still theoretically a member of the Executive Committee that had sent them, the committee being a creation of the Second World Congress. This sufficiently telling fact about the methods that Moscow used against Serrati was reported by Levi in the memorandum that he sent on January 20 to the Executive Committee of the Comintern:

> Comrade Serrati appeared and said that he had reported my conversation with him to his comrades, and informed me that his comrades wanted to talk with me. He asked whether I were willing. I replied that I would be happy to, but asked whether they wished to have a representative of the Executive Committee present also, which I favored. Astonished, Comrade Serrati then inquired whether a representative of the Executive Committee were there. Taken aback by his question, I did not know whether I had jumped the gun in letting him know of the presence of an Executive Committee representative, so I replied evasively. Anyway, Serrati agreed, which I reported to Comrades Kabakchiev and Rakosi.[77]

Levi's position, approved by Radek, who had secretly been in Germany since October, and by the Central Committee of the KPD, was described in these terms by Levi himself:

> I left early Wednesday morning, having spent the night before, from eight until one in the morning, in a discussion with the Executive Committee representative, who was then in Berlin, and we went into the Italian matter in some detail. I read him the important passages from Comrade Zetkin's letter, which I had received that morning, and he agreed that we should work in that direction, namely to try to retain Serrati but definitely insist that he throw out the Turati crowd. . . . The Central Committee [of the KPD] was aware that this course might not run parallel in all respects to the Executive Committee line.[78]

Once at the congress, which started on January 15, Levi's efforts were of no avail against the strict orders that had been given the two Moscow delegates, as became obvious from his hour-and-a-half-long conversation with them and Serrati. The very next morning Kabakchiev mounted the rostrum and, in the name of the Executive Committee, read off a statement drawn up in collusion with Moscow (if not by Moscow), the main point of which was Serrati's excommunication. It was delivered in the form of a Russian-style indictment, i.e., an exposé constructed of long "theses," little suited to an Italian audience, a fact which Levi pointed out in his report to the Executive Committee:

> I feel I must say that the statement did not make a favorable impression, on structural grounds alone. It was twenty-six typed pages long, much too long to be read off at a congress, let alone an Italian congress, with any hope of its being at all effective. Another mistake was that the entire lengthy statement was devoted solely to an attack upon Serrati, which profoundly upset the assemblage, which after all did constitute a majority of the congress, where the Serrati supporters outnumbered the others at least three to one.[79]

This Russian-style pronouncement was greeted by the audience in the Italian style, which at the Third World Congress Zinoviev stigmatized as follows: "It [the Leghorn congress] was transformed literally into a circus. When Kabakchiev got up to speak, they shouted 'long live the Pope!' Someone released a dove, and there were unheard-of displays of chauvinism. Then everyone blamed Kabakchiev."[80]

Levi's apprehensions about a break between Serrati and Moscow were well-founded, as was his assessment of Serrati's superior strength at the congress, which he had pointed out on January 20 in his report to the Executive Committee, but at the election consecrating the split which took place the following day, the Communists got 58,753 votes against 14,695 for the revisionist Socialists (Turati), while an absolute majority, 98,023, went for Serrati and his group.

Moscow's decision was thus "translated into action," but with immediately detrimental effect. On January 10, 1921, in her letter to Paul Levi, sent ten days before the split and five days before the congress started, Clara Zetkin diagnosed Moscow's psychological error: "Our Moscow friends have done their best to kill off Serrati's love for the Party, to force him to the right instead of luring him to the left. They have not yet learned that while the fist is often a necessary instrument, striking people in the face has been out of fashion in the West since the Middle Ages. In the West, flies are caught with honey, not with vinegar."[81]

Her use of the term "our Moscow friends" raises the question as to who actually was responsible for the Leghorn split. The responsibility and initiative were certainly not Radek's, for he was in Berlin when suddenly notified of Moscow's decision, and had to do an abrupt about-face, abandoning the position that he had shared with Levi, as the latter later explained to the party leaders:

> On Sunday a telegram arrived from Moscow which the Executive Committee representative interpreted to mean that the Executive Committee's latest decision was: all-out war against Serrati. So their representative—and Comrade Däumig here was a witness—wanted a similar telegram sent to me so that I would know about the new policy. The telegram was sent off from here on Sunday, but because that was the day I left Leghorn, it didn't reach me.[82]

Even if the telegram had reached him in Leghorn, it is not certain that it would have made him change his stand, as Radek did. The two were thenceforward at odds on the Italian question.

The initiative behind Serrati's excommunication was not Zinoviev's either, nor did it originate with the Executive Committee, the entity statutorily empowered to author such decisions. It was Lenin's. Radek admitted this quite frankly to the Central Committee of the German Communist party at a closed meeting on January 28, 1921: "The Executive Committee was hesitant about sending the telegram. Zinoviev wanted to wait, but Lenin forced the decision through. . . ."[83] So Lenin's will had prevailed, just as it had shortly before in the case of Longuet, there too against the advice of Zinoviev, who would have been crushed in any contest with Lenin, for the vote would have been taken not by the Executive Committee of the Comintern, but by the Bolshevik party polit-bureau, as Paul Levi reported to the leaders of the German party: "I'm not at all sure that our Russian friends agree among themselves. According to reports that I have received, Zinoviev took a different stand but was voted down."[84]

In a message dated January 25, 1921, Lenin and the other Comintern leaders expressed their complete solidarity with the Italian Communists. Lenin in particular stuck to his guns in the matter of Serrati. When two months after Leghorn he received letters from Clara Zetkin and Paul Levi about the March action in Germany, in his reply of April 16 he accepted most of their objections concerning it, but added that they were wrong on the Italian question: "Regarding Serrati, I consider your tactic wrong."[85]

But events to come would soon prove that it was Lenin's tactic that was wrong, indeed triply wrong.

To begin with, he was wrong about the true strength and chances of the newly formed Italian Communist party. In their message of greeting of January 25 the Comintern's Bolshevik leaders said: "We are deeply convinced that the awakened workers of your country will join you in increasing numbers every day. . . . The future belongs to you and not to those who, in one way or another, want to make peace with the bourgeoisie through the reformists."[86] But the Bolshevik emissaries to the West, observing the Italian situation at first hand, were less optimistic. On January 28, only a week after the birth of the Italian Communist party, Radek frankly admitted to the German party's Central Committee: "I am convinced that the cleavage in Italy has greatly worsened the prospects for revolution there in the immediate future. Our having a communist party in Italy is an illusion. . . . We must expect that party to be weak for a long time to come."[87] Degot in his memoirs, recalling the climate in Italy on the eve of the Leghorn congress, had to concede:

> There were no reliable leaders to head up the future communist party. Bombacci, who enjoyed wide popularity, was a romantic, unstable, though devoted to the revolution. . . . Gennari unquestionably is a Marxist of great talent, but lacks initiative. Gramsci is a much deeper thinker than the others. He has a better understanding of the Russian Revolution, but no power of attraction for the masses, first because he is not much of a speaker, and second, because he is too young, too short, and hunchbacked, which makes the audience uncomfortable. Taken together, all this made it seem likely that, with leaders like these, the Italian Communist Party would be less influential than Serrati.[88]

Lenin made another mistake, both political and psychological, in dismissing as hypocrisy Serrati's many protestations of good faith and repeated insistence that he did want to stay in the Comintern. He was saying so before the congress to the KPD leaders, on October 28, 1920, during a visit to Berlin, at the very moment at which Moscow was launching its offensive against him. He said it, too, on the occasion of the split in Leghorn, as Levi reported in his memorandum to the Comintern Executive Committee: "Serrati told me again what he had already said in our first conversation, namely that he had no intention of going to Vienna to embrace the Second International, that he and his group were and would remain communists. If the Third International refused to accept them, then he would 'remain at the Third International's door, on bended knees, if need be,' but that he would have nothing to do with the Second International."[89] And immediately after Leghorn, on his return visit to Berlin, he repeated the same, as Curt Geyer, German representative on the Executive Committee, reported at the meeting of February 22,

1921: "Serrati came to Germany and approached the Central Committee. No official session was held with him. Some of the comrades on the Central Committee asked him what he was going to do now. He said he felt as though he were a member of the Third International. When someone remarked that that did not seem to be the case, however, he replied that, yes, they were still waiting in front of the church."[90]

These first two mistakes of Lenin's, concerning Italy's labor and Communist movements, were supplemented by a third, regarding Italy as a whole and the international labor movement in general. His predictions about the advance of proletarian revolution in Italy, urgently necessitating establishment of a Communist party, were scuttled by events as the months went by. Starting in the fall of 1920, the Comintern tactic in Italy was a carbon copy of that proclaimed by the German Communist party the previous March, at the time of the Kapp-Lüttwitz putsch. The difference was that then the Comintern had condemned the German party, while now in Italy it itself was urging this tactic. In both cases its diagnosis of the identity of the Communist movement's principle enemy was wrong. The Bolsheviks believed that the imminent death struggle was to be between Communist proletarian revolution and capitalist society (including the latter's arch-henchmen, the Social-Democrats), whereas the actual battle shaping up was between parliamentary democracy, which safeguarded the existence of all parties, including even the Communist (and which often did need the active support of Social-Democrats), and a Fascist dictatorship out to destroy all parties, starting with the Communists and finishing with the liberals and Catholics, after knocking off the Social-Democrats in between. At the time of the Kapp-Lüttwitz putsch the Communist party had not grasped this, but the consequences were not tragic, because the two other major workers' parties had grasped it and were able to thwart the putsch. But in Italy the two leading workers' parties, the Serrati Socialists and the Communists, did not see the real danger, and the Comintern contributed nothing toward helping them understand that, after 1921, the real enemy was not the parliament-oriented bourgeoisie but Mussolini and his movement. The Leghorn split weakened the Italian labor movement, making impossible any cooperation among the country's democratic forces (Catholics, liberals and Socialist reformists) to block Il Duce's victory. Serrati, still resolved to get into the Comintern, imitated the error. In October 1922, at the Socialist party congress, on the eve of his ultimate admission to the Comintern fold, he addressed himself to his party's reformist wing which was about to split off:

> You seek an alliance with Democracy, and you say that Socialism too is democratic. But Socialism is proletarian democracy, i.e., true

democracy, while the other is bourgeois democracy, a falsification of true democracy. . . . Let all who want to work for the revolution march with us, and those who want to prevent the revolution go with the bourgeoisie.[91]

A month later, in early November 1922, Serrati was again in Moscow to attend the fourth Comintern congress, while in Rome, instead of the heralded proletarian revolution, it was the Mussolini counterrevolution that had won the field. As Lenin and Serrati were making their peace in Moscow, Fascism was spreading its blanket over Italy. Thus did the far Left in 1922 help boost Mussolini to power, as it would Hitler ten years later.

Splitting the Czechoslovak Social-Democrats

There were only two countries in Europe of which the Comintern could boast that, after splitting the socialist parties and setting up a united communist party, the latter attained a membership numbering several hundred thousand: Germany and Czechoslovakia, two countries in which Social-Democratic parties, among Europe's first, had been established in the nineteenth century.

The cleavage process in Czechoslovakia occurred in the same stages as in two other countries, Germany and France, in which the Socialist majority, assembled in congress at the time of the break, had declared itself in favor of the Moscow position. In the beginning, in 1918 and 1919, the far Left was a very weak minority, especially as the proclaiming of the Czechoslovak State on October 25, 1918, and creation of the coalition government gave some of the power to the Social-Democrats. In June 1919 it was a Social-Democrat, Tusar, who became head of the coalition government (at the very moment at which the SFIO and USPD had just opted for the opposition). At the twelfth congress of the Czechoslovak Social-Democratic Workers' party, held from December 27 to 30, 1918, the far Left, a feeble minority, ran a candidate for the executive committee, A. Zapotocky, who got only 126 votes out of a total of 644. When in June 1919 the Czechoslovak government took part in the intervention against Soviet Hungary, the Left was still weak, as the party head Bohumil Jilek admitted to the Comintern's enlarged Executive Committee: "By June the bourgeoisie was already strong enough, with the help of the Social-Democrats, to launch an attack on the Hungarian Soviet Republic, and dealt it a mortal blow. The resistance of the Party's left wing to that attack was small."[92] At the Social-Democratic party's national conference, which opened on October 5, 1919, the far Left was present as an autonomous united faction, but its statement of principle in favor of communism was rejected by the majority 65 to 36, which indicated that, by the end of 1919, the far Left was gaining ground.

From then on, they asserted themselves as a "fractionist" organization within the Social-Democratic party, scheduling their first national conference for December 7, 1919. One of the decisions of that meeting proclaimed the need to sever relations with the Second International and join the Third. The next conference of the "Marxist Left" took place on March 7, 1920. Two months later its leader, Bohumil Smeral, in the absence of Alois Muna, who was in prison, betook himself to Moscow, where he talked with Lenin. Another delegation of the "Marxist Left" went to Russia to participate in the second world congress. It included the three militants Bratislav Hula, Antonin Zapotocky, and Milos Vanek, joined by Ivan Olbracht, who had been in Moscow since Smeral's arrival. Smeral did not attend the second congress.

When the delegation returned to Czechoslovakia, the campaign in favor of joining the Comintern and setting up a communist party gained vigor and popularity. When the thirteenth party congress was announced for September 26, advance pollings of the delegates showed a majority for communism and the Comintern. The official leadership decided to postpone the congress until December, but the partisans of the "Marxist Left" assembled on the original date, claiming the support of 321 of the total of 464 elected delegates, which represented 68 percent of the Social-Democratic party membership. The congress was held in Prague, and Smeral and Zapotocky were among the main speakers. It took no important step toward communism, however, nor did it vote to set up a Communist party or to join the Comintern. A few days later at Karlsbad, on October 3, at the congress of Czechoslovakia's German Social-Democratic party, the majority voted down the Communist Left's motion 295 to 144.

In December 1920 there were disturbances in Czechoslovakia, creating a situation similar to the one in Italy the previous September. On December 9, by government order, troops occupied the "house of the people," headquarters of the Social-Democratic party, seizing also the editorial offices and printing plant of its main newspaper, as well as its administrative offices. The Left responded by calling for a general strike, but the government proclaimed a state of siege, set up special tribunals, arrested about three thousand people, and the strike initiative collapsed, not from weariness or through compromise, as it had in Italy, but under the pressure of the police and army, who were assisted by the nationalist Sokol organization. On December 19, Zinoviev sent greetings to the Czechoslovak workers, phrased in the usual style, forecasting inevitable revolution and citing the great example of Russia: "The Communist International calls upon all Czechoslovak workers and soldiers to turn their bayonets against their oppressors. . . . To the workers of Czechoslovakia we say: courage, Comrades! After July, Russia had its October. You will have yours. . . ."[93]

In early 1921 the Communist Left in Czechoslovakia resumed its agitation for official establishment of a communist party outside the Social-Democratic party, but there were many reasons that the effort did not immediately succeed. One was the ethnic structure of the new state. In an ethnically heterogeneous country like Czechoslovakia, unifying the different groups favoring communism was more difficult than in ethnically homogeneous countries. From the outset the Communists had to contend with this ethnic factor, though refusing to admit it publicly. The three ethnic groups welded together to form the new Czechoslovak state acted separately and independently to set up their own Communist organizations. On January 16 and 17, 1921, 149 delegates of "the revolutionary class of Slovakia and Sub-Carpathian Russia" met first at Lubochna, then at Ružomberok. Among them were eighty-eight Slovaks, thirty-six Hungarians, fifteen Germans, six Ukranians, and four representatives of the Jewish movement *Poale Zion*. They accepted unanimously the twenty-one conditions for admission to the Comintern, with one exception. The vote on condition seventeen, requiring that the party's name be changed to Communist party, was postponed until the congress of unification and creation of a single revolutionary party for all Czechoslovakia.

After Slovakia, it was the turn of the Sudeten region, home of Czechoslovakia's Germans. Barred from the Sudeten Social-Democratic party at its Karlsbad congress in January 1921, the elements of the far Left, led by Karl Kreibich, met on March 12, 1921, at Liberec (Reichenberg), voted to accept the twenty-one conditions for admission, and proclaimed formation of a German section of the future Czechoslovak Communist party. Gyula Alpari, the Hungarian Communist leader who had fled to Czechoslovakia after the débâcle of the Hungarian Soviet Republic, and who was soon to hold an important job in the Comintern propaganda apparatus, attended the meeting, at which he played a significant role, as Kreibich has reported: "We always acted in agreement with Comrade Alpari. It was with him in particular that I worked out the stand that we would take at the party congress in Karlsbad [January 1921], and what I was to say concerning the report of the first speaker [at Liberec]."[94]

This left the main ethnic group, the Czechs, who had not yet established any Communist organization. That irritated Moscow, to judge from the criticisms leveled by Zinoviev at Bohumil Smeral, whom he charged with "vacillation" in his report of mid-March 1921 to the tenth Bolshevik party congress.[95] It was not until May 14 through 16, 1921, that the Left in Bohemia and Moravia finally got together in a municipal hall in Prague. The 569 delegates claimed to represent more than 350,000 members, not only Czechs but Slovaks and Hungarians also (representatives of the Communist Party's German Section were there as guests). Just before the congress started, the Comintern Executive Committee sent a letter calling urgently for immediate creation of a Communist party of Czechoslovakia:

> The Communist International sends its fraternal greetings to your party congress in the hope that it will become the founding congress of the Communist Party of Czechoslovakia. Two and one half years have passed since Czechoslovakia became an independent state. . . . We hope that the party congress will not only adopt the name of Communist Party, to set itself clearly apart from the Social-Democrats, soiled by their coalition with the bourgeoisie, but that it will also clearly and unmistakably declare its acceptance of the principles and tactics of the Communist International.[96]

The letter warned those attending the congress about the dangers of nationalist deviation and insisted upon the necessity for the Comintern to have a single, strongly centralized communist party within the framework of the Czechoslovak state.

The main speaker was Smeral, and two important resolutions were adopted unanimously. The first declared that the congress of the Left of Czechoslovakia's Social-Democratic movement favored joining the Third International unconditionally and changing its name from Social-Democratic Left to Communist party. The second laid down the procedure for establishing a Communist party for all of Czechoslovakia, stipulating:

> The Executive Committee is instructed to delegate from among its members comrades who, jointly with delegates of the Party's German section, shall comprise an action committee. It will be the duty and function of the action committee to complete preparations for unification of the regional parties, specifically: (1) to work out a joint set of organizational bylaws; (2) to draw up a program of action; (3) to lay the groundwork for a joint party congress.[97]

So instead of immediately setting up a single Communist party for the entire country, it was necessary to initiate a fusion process between two communist movements, a process involving successive phases and one that would take several months. Knowing that this would not please

Moscow, those attending the congress felt obliged to send the Comintern a letter of reassurance: "We can assure you, comrades, that the creation of a unified Communist Party of Czechoslovakia a section of the Third International has become, from this day, merely a problem of organizational procedure, a problem that will be solved in the immediate future."[98]

The Comintern's Third World Congress, to be held from June 22 to July 12, 1921, would not be able to boast of having a single Communist party for all of Czechoslovakia. This constituted an almost unique exception in the general panorama of the European Communist movement at that juncture. The Comintern subsequently sent one of its high-powered emissaries, "Comrade Carlo," who had proved his mettle in Italy, to implement its directives concerning immediate establishment of a Communist party. Quite probably he did play an important role, to judge from the report that B. Jilek, head of the Czechoslovak Communist party, made to the Comintern's enlarged Executive Committee (but which was not published in the Comintern press): "The committee of the six [whose task it was to unify the Czechoslovak communists] worked in close touch with the Executive Committee's representative, Comrade Carlo."[99]

The majority that the Communist Left had picked up by September 1920 started to melt away just as the Czechoslovak Communists were finally unified in the fall of 1921. The same decline of their influence was setting in as witnessed a few months earlier in Germany, then France. In June 1922, party spokesman B. Jilek, addressing the enlarged Executive Committee, confessed that "the party has fewer members now than it had at its birth." The statistics of that year confirm this. Its registered membership dropped from 350,000 in 1921 to 170,000 in 1922.

The Splitting of the Other Socialist Parties

Since the creation of communist parties throughout the world, the communist movement has become a permanent factor of political history. The communist parties themselves survived the demise of the Comintern in 1943. From the outset, especially in Western Europe, the numerical strength of the communist parties was in direct proportion to the support given them by the Socialists and syndicalists. The more the communist Left benefited from a split of the socialist and trade-union organizations, the more deeply the communist parties could take root in a country. Conversely, the less such a split propelled socialist and trade-union militants into the communist fold, the less the new communist party could thrive. Nowhere in Europe did it prove possible to set up a mass Communist party where the Socialists and trade-union organizations remained impervious to communism. Even when a Socialist party did rally to the Comintern, or split apart to facilitate the birth of a communist party, this was often only temporary and precarious. Thus, the two politically and numerically most important European socialist parties to join the Comintern in 1919, the Italian and Norwegian, did not stay in it long. The Italians broke away in January 1921, the Norwegians in 1923. In both cases only a minority of former Socialist party members lingered on in the Comintern. In Italy, that minority was moderately substantial, which enabled the communists to play a certain role in the country's political life. In Norway it was relatively much smaller. Of the 105,000 who in 1919 belonged to the old Labor party, which opted into the Comintern, only 15,000 were left after the break in 1923, which stripped the Norwegian communists of any political significance.

In three of Europe's most advanced countries—Germany, France, and Czechoslovakia—where at the moment of the split the wing favoring the Comintern got a majority of the votes at the socialist congresses, the Communist party did manage to achieve some temporary political importance, which started to dwindle after a few short months, and kept on dwindling through the years.

Almost everywhere else the split followed the same pattern. Socialist parties in Europe's unindustrialized regions favored joining the Comintern; those in the industrialized regions refused. The more industrially developed a country or region was, especially if it had a long-existing trade-union organization and well-established reformist socialist party, the less support it gave to the Comintern cause.

The strongest support for the Comintern came from a region that in 1914 was Europe's most backward from the standpoint of industrialization and in terms of entrenched trade-union and/or socialist-party strength: the Balkans. In Bulgaria the "broad" (reformist) Socialist party was stronger than the "narrow" (revolutionary) Socialist party prior to 1914, but after October 1917, and the founding of the Comintern, the latter became by far the stronger and thus a serious political factor in the country. In Rumania at its congress on May 9, 1921, the Socialist party accepted the twenty-one conditions for admission to the Comintern by a vote of 432 to 111, but the Communist party there never managed to become a mass party. Communism in Greece got off to roughly the same start. At the second congress of the Greek Socialist Labor party, held in Athens, on April 5, 1920, the vote went almost unanimously for joining the Comintern, but again the Communist party, born of a weak Socialist party, never got off the ground. In Yugoslavia, an ethnically heterogeneous country with a very mixed economy, when an effort was made in

1919 to unify the parties and affiliate with the Comintern, the socialists in the regions least developed industrially and trade-union-wise—Serbia, Bosnia, and Dalmatia—were unanimous for unification and joining. The Socialist party of Slovenia, on the other hand, the country's most industrialized region, whose party had existed since 1896, unanimously refused to join, as did the Social-Democratic party of Croatia and Slavonia, founded in 1894, the vote going 59 to 38 against. Equally characteristic was the fact that the first two general secretaries of the Yugoslav Communist party were Filip Filipovich, won over to Socialist ideas during his thirteen-year stay in Petrograd at the beginning of the century, and Sima Markovich, who advocated a Serbian version of revolutionary syndicalism. Typical, too, was the fact that in the legislative elections of 1920 the Communist party got its heaviest vote in Montenegro and Macedonia, which before 1914 had had neither Socialist party nor any trade-union movement.

At the two geographic ends of Europe, Finland and Spain, countries that still lacked much industry immediately after World War I, an important segment of the Socialist party rallied to the Comintern. In the case of Finland, the party had been founded in Soviet Russia in 1918 by exiled Socialists, e.g., Manner and Kuusinen, and could count on exerting a certain influence in the labor movement. The Spanish Socialist party, at its congress in April 1921, went back on its earlier decision to join the Comintern, the proposal this time being finally defeated by a small majority (8,808 to 6,025) so that the Communist party did have some influence in Socialist circles, but the majority of the hitherto registered membership of the Socialist party, more than 50,000, refused to switch to the Communist party.

Wherever Europe's socialist parties did not split, or wherever the cleavage was not deep, communist parties remained insignificant or nonexistent. The weakness of the communist parties was merely a reflection of the weakness of a country's socialist party and trade-union organizations.

In Sweden, apart from its official Social-Democratic party, there was the Left Socialist party, which supported the Comintern. In March 1921 it split over the twenty-one admission requirements. Afterwards the number of Comintern adherents dropped from 25,000 (in 1920) to 14,000. In Denmark, in 1921, the Social-Democratic party had 115,000 members, of which the communist party picked up only 1,200, the splinter groups of the far Left never succeeding in shaking the bastions of the official Social Democrats. England's big Labour party escaped the communist dissension altogether, and even the smaller Independent Labour party, at its congress of March 1921, refused to join the Comintern by a strong vote of 521 to 97. In 1921 the numerical strengths of the different

British labor parties were: the Labour party 4,417,000 registered members; Independent Labour party 35,000; Communist party 10,000. In Austria, too, the powerful Socialist party remained intact and united around its leaders, with 491,000 members, while the communists had 14,000. An equally solid disproportion prevailed in Belgium, where the Socialist party had 718,000 members, the Communist 1,100. In Holland in 1919 the Social-Democratic party had more than 42,000 members; the communists 500. In Switzerland, after the January 1921 referendum, which went against the Comintern by a vote of 25,475 to 8,777, the Socialist party had 54,000 members, the communists 6,000. Even in the United States, it was over the issue of joining the Comintern that the Socialist party split, the first time at the party congress in Chicago on August 30, 1919. The Left walked out and met separately the next day. The second time was when, at its congress in May 1920, the "centrist" motion calling for conditional affiliation with the Comintern got 1,339 votes, against 1,301 for unconditional affiliation. The chief result of all the bickering was that the Socialist party membership, up to 104,822 in 1919, dropped to 26,766 in 1920, taking a further plunge, to 11,019, in 1921. The Communists did not profit, their own membership declining from 15,000 in 1920 to 12,000 in 1921.

III

Stalin and Stalinism

11
Tito and Stalin

Ambiguities in the Marxist Attitude on the National Question

There is a certain ambiguity in the Marxian attitude toward the national question, which is the first matter which I propose to examine. If you read the Communist Manifesto, you will find on the one hand a declaration that the workers have no country to defend; next, that their aim is to establish themselves as the nation; next you will find an economic or market theory of nationalism and internationalism—that the idea of nationality grows up only when the nationwide market has developed, so that you would automatically expect a feeling of nationality to coincide with the size of a given national or nationwide market.

On the other hand, you also have a declaration concerning the rights of complete restoration of Poland as an independent nationality in the Communist Manifesto. Poland was geared at that time partly into the German market, partly into the Russian market, partly into the Austrian-Hungarian market. So it is quite obvious that Marx has abandoned his own economic interpretation of nationalism in favor of recognition that there is a kind of demiurge that has lived underground, something of the spirit of the Polish people which demands the restoration of Polish national independence. Thus even in the Communist Manifesto we find an ambiguity on the national question, which I take as the first background point in an approach to the question of Titoism.

Second, you will find in the relations between Lenin and Stalin a certain ambiguity on the national question. In 1920 Lenin was preparing a document (a series of propositions or theses) for the Communist International Congress: *On the National and Colonial Question*. He sent a copy of it to Stalin for his opinion (as he did to a number of other people) and Stalin wrote back a criticism, expressing a disagreement with Lenin's thesis. Now that criticism (and I call your attention to the early date—June 12, 1920)—that criticism is extremely interesting. Stalin writes:

> For nations which made up part of old Russia, our Soviet-type of federation may and must be accounted expedient as the road to unity. These nationalities either did not have a state of their own in the past or have long lost it, in view of which fact the Soviet centralized type of federation will graft itself onto them without any serious friction. But the same cannot be said of those nationalities which did not make up a part of old Russia—which existed as independent formations, developed their own states and which, if they become Soviet, will be obliged by force or circumstances to enter into one or another governmental relationship with Soviet Russia.
>
> For example, a future Soviet Germany, Soviet Poland, Soviet Hungary, Soviet Finland—[now this is 1920, and is a basic document which we might call Stalin's "Mein Kampf"]—these peoples, having had their own state, their own army, their own finances, will hardly agree—even though they become Soviet—to enter at once into a federal bond with Soviet Russia of the type of Bashkir or Ukrainian. For a federation of the Soviet type would be looked upon by them as a form of diminution of their state independence, as an attack upon it. I have no doubt, therefore, that for these nationalities the most acceptable form of rapprochement will be a Confederation [by which he means a kind of alliance or loose union of nominally independent states]. I say nothing of the backward nations; for example: Persia, Turkey—in relation to which or for which the Soviet type of federation, in general, would be still more unacceptable.

This criticism of Lenin's thesis (which, by the way, Lenin rejected) indicates that as early as June 12, 1920, Stalin already had a concept of a future Soviet Germany, a Soviet Finland, a Soviet Hungary. He recognized that they could not directly enter into the Soviet Union "Federation," and he proposed a transition form which today he calls "The System of People's Democracies." Thus the first approach of Stalin to what today we call "Titoism" can be found in this document. Now where can you find this document today? It is not in Stalin's *Collected Works*. He has excluded it from the canon of his *Collected Works* because it is too revealing. Nevertheless, you can find it in Lenin's *Collected Works*, in the Russian third edition, volume 25, page 624, as a footnote, in which Stalin's criticism written to Lenin is given in full. It is a document worthy of much more study than our leaders have so far given it.

The third point in Stalin's special views on the national question to which I wish to call your attention is a contempt on Stalin's part for the right of borderlands and neighbors to genuine independence. On October 10, 1920, he wrote:

> Central Russia, this fireplace of world revolution, cannot hold out long without the help of the borderlands rich in raw materials, fuel, food. . . . The separation of the borderlands would undermine the revolutionary might of Central Russia. . . . In the circumstances of the war to the death that is flaring up between proletarian Russia and the Imperialist Entente for the borderlands, there are possible only two outcomes:
>
> EITHER together with Russia . . .
> OR together with the Entente . . .
> There is no third possibility.

> The so-called independence of the so-called independent Georgia, Armenia, Poland, Finland, etc., is only a deceptive appearance covering up the full dependence of these governments (if you will excuse me for calling them governments) from this or that group of Imperialists.[1]

The fourth constituent element in the Stalinist attitude toward Titoism I find in his definition of an "internationalist." On August 1, 1927, he said: "A revolutionary is one who, without reservation, unconditionally, openly and honestly is ready to defend and protect the U.S.S.R., since the U.S.S.R. is the first proletarian revolutionary state in the world. An internationalist is he who unreservedly, without hesitation, without conditions, is ready to defend the U.S.S.R., because the U.S.S.R. is the base of the world revolutionary movement. And to defend, to advance this revolutionary movement is impossible without defending the U.S.S.R."

The last point of ambiguity in this Marxist-Leninist-Stalinist attitude towards the national question I offer in the form of a conversation between Bukharin and Armstrong, who wrote a book on Tito. Bukharin said to Armstrong: "National rivalry between Communist states is by definition 'an impossibility.' "

By definition it is impossible for the Soviet Union to be imperialist; by definition it is impossible for the United States not to be imperialist; by definition whatever the Soviet Union does is peaceful and by definition whatever the Soviet Union does is democratic. And so we are not surprised to find that national rivalry between Communist states is by definition "an impossibility." Just as capitalism cannot live without war, so war cannot live with communism.

Bukharin did not live long enough to learn better.

The Break between Stalin and Tito

We turn now to the open break between Tito and Stalin. This open break is as significant for our understanding of the Communist International, or the Cominform, as that famous unhealing fistula was for gastrointestinal observation. You remember there was a doctor who once tried to operate and heal a fistula in the stomach of a living man. He failed, so he finally put in a window, took advantage of that open porthole, and continued to examine the functioning of the stomach and the intestines through it. Thus modern gastrointestinal science developed. In the same sense, the break between Tito and Stalin opened a window into the deeply secret processes that go on inside the Cominform. In the early days of the Comintern there were public debates, rival proposals, and thus we could get some notion of what went on. But increasingly the Comintern became monolithic, and with it came unanimity and overwhelming blanket secrecy. Were it not for this break we would have very little notion indeed of how the Cominform functions.

How shall we interpret the break between Tito and Stalin? We can interpret it first in emotional terms and say that Stalinism underrates the everlasting determination of peoples to be themselves. The twentieth century's chief lesson thus far, I should say, is that national independence is one of the few things for which men are willing to fight and die.

Second, we can interpret it in historical terms—people with different experiences, different traditions, different cultures, inevitably have differing values. Even a world state would never be able to bleach out all the varied national colors from life.

Third, we can interpret it in terms of national interest and national traditions. The Yugoslavs have a tradition of resistance to outside tyrants —a tradition formed in the struggle against the Turks, strengthened in the struggle against Hitler, and now given fresh life and meaning in the struggle against Stalin.

Fourth, we can interpret it in terms of a special Balkan political tradition. Every Balkan Communist, every Balkan Socialist, every Balkan Democrat, every Balkan Liberal, has been brought up in the tradition of the need for a Federation of Balkan Republics. When we speak of "the Balkanization of Europe" we have in mind the same thing which has been the curse of life in the Balkans. The Balkan peninsula has been the playground of Great Powers—France, Austria-Hungary, Germany, Russia—and Balkan patriots have long felt that the only way their lands could cease to be a playground of the Great Powers was for them to federate and form a genuine federated power of their own. So it was almost automatic for Communists in Bulgaria, Yugoslavia, and Rumania —as it would have been automatic for Socialists or for Republicans and

Democrats, the moment they came to power in all those countries and felt a kinship with each other—it was automatic to propose a Balkan Federation. But, at that moment there was only one great power that was still to be kept out of the Balkans by a Balkan Federation: namely, the Soviet Union. And Stalin reacted angrily to the proposal of a powerful Balkan Federation which might have stood up against him.

Fifth, we can interpret the Tito break in terms of personal conflict, and this is the more instructive because Tito is a kind of "pocket" Stalin. Of all the disciples of Stalin, the one that learned most from him and was closest to him was Joseph Broz, known as Tito. Now Stalinism is a jealous "ism." It is a kind of ersatz religion in which Stalin has become the infallible, the omniscient, the omnipotent leader and father of the peoples. The *vozhd* is a jealous *vozhd* and beside him there is no other *vozhd*. He may have disciples—twelve, or twelve times twelve, or any number—but he may not have partners, associates, or second-string leaders. The disciple who challenges this becomes by definition a "Judas Iscariot."

Sixth, we might interpret Titoism in ideological terms. We might bear in mind that orthodoxies tend to breed heresies; dogmas, challenge; commands, disobedience. Then the heresies, in turn, will claim to be orthodoxies, even as so many heresies in the Christian churches appeal to "primitive Christianity." So Titoism has appealed to "primitive Leninism," against Stalin's modifications or "betrayals" of what Tito claims to be orthodox Leninism. It is within this closed circle that Titoism has developed, and only now—reluctantly, hesitatingly, dubiously—some of Tito's ideologues are beginning to question certain tenets of Leninism itself.

The Multiple Appeal of Titoism

Having made this multiple interpretation of the development of Titoism, I want to suggest something of the multiple appeal of Titoism. It appeals to national patriotism against treason to one's country; yes, and even to the class that a Communist professes to represent. Wherever you have to put the interests of the Soviet government above the interests of your own country, your own people, and against your own working class—then you are faced with the problem of treason. Reluctance to commit these forms of treason is one of the appeals that Titoism makes to the Communist in other countries.

Second, it appeals to "primitive Leninism" as a return to purity of doctrine and true egalitarian internationalism.

Third, it appeals to fellow travelers "out on a limb" and anxious to climb down without any loss of revolutionary posture. I refer to an O. John Rogge in this country or a Ziliakus in England. The cold war having created an intolerable situation for people out on that limb, the problem was how they could climb down, yet still appear faithful to some kind of revolutionary doctrine. Tito gave the answer, which I think helps to explain why a Ziliakus or a Rogge becomes so ardent a Titoist.

Fourth, Titoism has an appeal to its neighbors still needing a Balkan Federation to defend themselves—to Italy and to Greece.

Fifth, it is of especial interest to the Atlantic Pact nations, for it represents the crack in the armor, the breach in the walls. I have every sympathy for the plight of the Yugoslav people who are still under the heel of a totalitarian dictatorship; from their standpoint it would certainly be much better if Tito were a Democrat and not a totalitarian Communist dictator. But from the standpoint of our interest at the present phase of the cold war, I can't help thinking that Tito is more useful to us as a Communist than he would be as a Democrat.

Factors Which Made Titoism Possible

Now I turn to the genesis of the Tito break. The first aspect that we must consider is the special circumstances under which Titoist Yugoslavia was born. Like Poland, Yugoslavia resisted German invasion from the outset. There is this difference, however—Poland resisted both Hitler and Stalin while Titoist Yugoslavia resisted Hitler only when Stalin and Hitler broke.

Second, Yugoslavia is an ideal terrain for guerrilla warfare and although its main armies were easily smashed by the Wehrmacht, yet in the mountains of Yugoslavia guerrilla warfare was never abandoned.

Third, the Tito forces participated in the final liberation of Yugoslavia and functioned as a kind of junior ally to the Soviet Army.

Fourth, their mountains were never fully occupied by Hitler as their country was never occupied by Stalin. It was the only East European state to escape Red Army occupation, therefore theoretically self-liberated.

Fifth, geographically, Yugoslavia is farthest from Russia of the so-called People's Democracies. It has no contiguous border with the Soviet Union. It has direct contact with the non-Communist world—with Italy, with Greece and with the open sea along the shores of the Adriatic. These, then, are the special circumstances which made possible the rise of Titoism.

Differences Which Led to the Break

Now I should like to examine some of the differences—muted, but stubborn—that developed between Tito and Stalin long before either of them recognized that these differences were leading to a break. On March 5, 1942, Moscow sent a cable to Tito, criticizing him for being too pro-Soviet and too openly Communist in his conduct of the struggle inside Yugoslavia. I quote a few sentences from the Moscow cable:

> With some justification the followers of England and the Yugoslav government believe that the partisan movement is assuming a Communist character and that it intends to sovietize Yugoslavia. The basic and immediate task consists now in the unification of all anti-Hitler elements in order to crush the occupier and achieve national liberation. Is it really true that besides the Communists and their followers there are no other Yugoslav patriots with whom you could fight against the enemy?

Now this is an instruction—not to cease to plan for a Soviet Yugoslavia, but to slow up and dissimulate the tempo of progress in that direction. We thus find that Tito is more Communist and more openly pro-Soviet than Stalin wishes him to be at that moment. A similar instruction went to Mao and, as you know, Mao Tse-tung accepted the instruction and continued to collaborate with Chiang Kai-shek, but Tito stepped up his campaign against Mihailovich after receiving this cable. The Soviet Union continued to maintain a "hands-off" appearance until very late.

There was no Soviet mission in Yugoslavia until February 1944, although there was a military mission from Britain from May 1942 on. In 1944 a Yugoslav brigade, trained in Russia, came equipped with uniforms with royal Yugoslav emblems, and only after Tito protested were the emblems removed. In 1943, while Stalin was still uncertain whether Mihailovich or Tito would come out on top and still wished to avoid alarming the Western powers, he gave no direct help to Tito. Tito was puzzled, angered, and the only answer he could find was to step up his offensive and campaign of propaganda against Mihailovich. Only when the Americans and the British showed no unfavorable reaction and when all sorts of people in America and in Britain began to echo Tito's propaganda that Mihailovich was a Nazi collaborator—only then did Stalin conclude that his cautions and fears were exaggerated and only then did he begin openly to give help to Tito.

Another curious document of 1942 is a lecture from Stalin to Tito on "Internationalism" during World War II. I quote:

The defeat of the Fascist bandits and the liberation from the occupier is now the basic task and is above all other tasks. Take into consideration that the Soviet Union has treaty obligations with the Yugoslav king and government and that any open actions against these would create new difficulties in the common war efforts in the relations between the Soviet Union and England and America. Do not consider your struggle only from your own national viewpoint, but from the international point of view of the English-Soviet-American coalition. Strengthen your positions in the people's liberation struggle [you see Stalin is not averse to what Tito is trying to do] and at the same time show more elasticity and ability to maneuver.

On this Tito commented to his close crony, Mosa Pijade: "I did not give too many explanations to Grandpa. I merely asked for more weapons to carry out his instructions." And Grandpa, in turn, sent word that there were "technical difficulties" which prevented the sending of more weapons.

Next, it is well to remember that the party which Tito now leads is truly a Titoist party. A bit of biography will help. Tito was born Joseph Broz in 1892 in Hapsburg, Croatia. He was a war prisoner of the Russians in World War I. There he was indoctrinated by the Bolsheviks, joined the Red Army, and got his first military training in the civil war that followed in Russia after World War I. Sent back to Yugoslavia, he became secretary of the Metalworkers' Union of Zagreb. In 1928 he did a tour of duty of five years in jail, where he met Mosa Pijade, who was a fellow inmate, and their close friendship and collaboration began. When he got out of jail, he took a postgraduate course in the Lenin School in Moscow.

From the Lenin School he was sent to Paris to carry on some important Comintern duties in connection with the Spanish Civil War. In Paris he steeped his hands in the blood of "The Purges" when the Blood Purges were carried into Spain and served to demoralize the Republican side in the Spanish Civil War. By this participation in the purge, Tito rose from an obscure second-rank figure in the Yugoslav Communist party to the chief of that party. Those earlier leaders who had stood in his way and were his superiors largely disappeared in "The Purges."

In 1941 the Yugoslav party numbered 12,000 members. Less than 3,000 of them survived at the end of World War II, but by 1948 those 3,000 had swelled to 470,000—most of whom never knew any leader but Tito.

Now a glance at the Balkan Federation question: Dimitrov visited Tito at Bled in the summer of 1947. Their principal subject of conversation was the setting up of a Balkan Federation. Dimitrov for Bulgaria and Tito for Yugoslavia issued a joint communiqué about the immediate steps for the setting up of a Federation of Balkan People's Democratic Republics. Stalin reacted instantly with anger. Dimitrov was forced to retract and disclaim their joint initiative in articles which were published in *Pravda* and *Izvestia*. But Tito did not publish a disclaimer. This, therefore, is a key point in the break.

Nevertheless, in the autumn of 1947 (when the Cominform was established as a public body with the primary aim of fighting the Marshall Plan and a secondary aim of setting up a federation of satellites in the Balkans under Soviet domination, which would be just the opposite of a Balkan Federation such as Dimitrov and Tito had envisioned)—at that point Tito was still the shining example and his country the most advanced of all the People's Democracies that had been created during World War II. The Cominform headquarters were in Belgrade. Tito was regarded as the most outstanding of the Balkan leaders. Everyone admired him for his power, for his having attained that power independently, and for his general manifestation of independence. Yugoslavia was being used throughout the world by Communists and fellow travelers as the model Communist state of those that had been newly born. Only after the open fight between Stalin and Tito were headquarters of the Cominform switched from Belgrade to Bucharest.

Now let us examine the relations between Stalin and Tito during the critical period. Tito visited Moscow in April 1945. He came back with a twenty-year treaty of friendship and mutual aid, with a military mission to run his army, an economic mission to integrate his industry into the Soviet economic plan. And he learned, to his dismay, that that plan viewed Yugoslavia as a kind of second-class agricultural, raw-material, metal-producing land, subordinate in rank to Czechoslovakia, to Poland, and to Hungary (for Czechoslovakia, Poland, and Hungary were slated for a greater degree of industrialization). I do not have to tell you that Czechoslovakia, Poland, and Hungary possessed a greater degree of industrialization at the time when they were taken over by the Communists.

At that interview Tito was, moreover, urged into open battle with his own people. One way in which Stalin keeps puppets as puppets is to get them thus into open struggle with their own people. He was urged to go head-on into forced collectivization of Yugoslav agriculture. He recognized that his army was to be reduced to an auxiliary troop of the Soviet army and that the whole scheme reduced Yugoslavia to a subordinate part in a detailed blueprint from Moscow to all her satellites. He recognized, too, that far from "withering away," this form of state domination was destined to grow stronger and the Soviet empire would be ever more unified, and the Balkan portions of it ever more subjected and coordinated into the Soviet empire. He was faced with the dilemma that Yugoslavia was to remain as before—poor, backward, weak, dependent, and subject to the will of greater powers, in this case the Soviet Union.

He paid a second visit to Stalin in May and June 1946. Here they went into more detail on the same matters. He learned that the USSR was going to reorganize the Yugoslav army with modern tactics and modern equipment. There was to be no national manual of arms in this thoroughly national guerrilla army, but it was to take the Soviet manual of arms, just as, a little later, Hungary was ordered to teach its soldiers to take commands in Russian as well as in Hungarian. There was to be no national arms industry—generous equipment with weapons but if at any time they wore out or at any time Tito needed new munitions for them, he would have to come "hat in hand" to the Soviet Union once more. There was a Soviet mission to go to Yugoslavia and take virtual command of the Yugoslav army, just as the Yugoslavs were permitted to send a mission to Albania to take virtual command of the Albanian army.

The Soviet intelligence was to teach the Yugoslav intelligence how to operate and was to have such plenary powers that it could easily bypass the Yugoslav intelligence and act as an espionage system on Tito and his fellow Communists. The Soviet technicians were to get notably higher salaries, and, like the Soviet army officers, were to get plenary powers and be in key spots.

Tito Draws First

Tito left Moscow crestfallen and conferred with his Balkan confederates for closer cooperation to create counterpressure so that the Communists of the Balkans would be treated with more wisdom (as he thought) and more dignity than had thus far been the case. For the moment all the leaders of the other Balkan countries looked to Tito for leadership, not realizing how far things would go. There followed a period of maneuver. The Comintern, or Cominform, was ordering a sudden drastic turn to the "Left," in connection with the stepping up of its "cold war." In America, Browder was "ditched." In Czechoslovakia, Masaryk and Beneš were driven to their doom. Tito, as a good Stalinist, recognized the symptoms and made a sudden ultra-Left swing himself—went way to the "Left" of the orders which he expected would come from Moscow any day, and announced that he was determined to "liquidate immediately all remnants of Capitalism in trade and in industry and agriculture." This drastic turn to the Left is something for which Yugoslav economy and Yugoslav agriculture are still paying the penalty at present, as each day's news indicates.

Stalin was as smart as Tito, and when he saw Tito taking this Left turn on his own so that he could not be criticized as an "opportunist," he recognized that this meant "fight." And so the Politburo of the Communist party of the Soviet Union began secret consultations with selected members of other Central Committees concerning Tito's "errors" and Tito's "excessive independence." And the Cominform (which had been set up for the fight on the Marshall Plan) now sharpened its offensive instruments for a major war on Tito and Titoism.

In late 1947 the Cominform met in Belgrade—on September 27—and Tito was still a leader among the Cominform leaders. He criticized heads of other communist parties for their timidity. He was shown sympathy by Dimitrov, by Gomulka, by Gheorghiu-Dej of Rumania. Even Thorez and Togliatti, who were present, were hesitant and showed some admiration for the courage and the independence that Tito was showing. Zhdanov, representing the Soviet Union, was also friendly to Tito, but he was in the beginning of his eclipse in the Soviet Union and died in 1948. His people were rapidly removed from places of power.

At the beginning of March 1948, the vice premier of Yugoslavia, Kardelj, went to Moscow in a vain effort to persuade Moscow to send more machinery for the purpose of the industrialization of Yugoslavia. He came back empty-handed. On March 18, the Soviet government secretly withdrew all military advisers and instructors from Tito's army, charging that they were "surrounded by hostility." On March 19 they withdrew all civilian missions, charging "a lack of hospitality and a lack of confidence." On March 20, Tito demanded an explanation.

He wrote to Molotov, "We are amazed. We cannot understand. We are deeply hurt. Openly inform us what the trouble is."

On June 29, 1948, the unsuspecting world was startled by the publication of a Cominform blast against Tito entitled "Concerning the Situation in the Communist Party of Yugoslavia," and a Tito counterblast, defensive in character but nevertheless obviously a counterblast. The break was in the open. The period is an instructive one; it was the period when the Berlin crisis came to a head. Berlin was being blockaded by the Russians. We were debating whether we should smash the blockade by running armored trains, properly defended, through the blockade lines.

At that time the Soviet military men were considering a military plan in case open war should begin. That military plan involved something which was of great importance to Tito and helps to explain Stalin's attitude toward Tito's army. The plan was to smash westward, through

Germany in a frontal attack toward France and the Atlantic, but at the same time to outflank France by sending an army through the relatively less mountainous areas of Yugoslavia into Italy, following the valleys of the Po and the Adige and the Plains of Lombardy; then striking up into France through the most accessible of the passes, thus hitting our troops from the rear at the same time they were being hit from the front by the major forces of the Soviet army.

This makes clear why it was that Stalin conceived of Tito's army not as a guerrilla force to defend the mountains against invasion (for the only conceivable invader was the Soviet Union), but as an auxiliary troop to serve the Soviet army and to become a part of it in that outflanking movement in case war should actually break out. Stalin insisted upon equipping Tito's troops to be such an auxiliary force in a Soviet regular army, while Tito dreamed of maintaining his troops as essentially mountaineer guerrillas to defend the sovereignty and independence of Yugoslavia in case of any attack.

This same period was one in which International Red Aid (UNRRA) supplies had been completely used up and the Yugoslav Trade Delegation in Moscow was begging in vain for aid in the industrialization of the country to get its Five-Year Plan of Industrialization underway. It was directed instead to gear its minerals and ores into the more advanced industries of neighbor countries and of the Soviet Union.

Soviet Imperialism

This brings us to the notion of Kremlin imperialism, which Tito's break has made so clear. The subordination of the Yugoslav economy into the overall plans and profits of Soviet industry; the attempt by the Soviet Union to get proconsul's rights and extraterritorial status for its agents; its ambassador to be entitled to interfere in Yugoslav internal affairs; its agents to have the right to access to state secrets; its right to organize its own intelligence service to spy on the Yugoslav leaders, to be exempt from Yugoslav espionage and to recruit Yugoslav citizens as Soviet spies; its insistence that Soviet officers should get three or four times as much salary from Yugoslavia as the Yugoslav generals and to have overriding powers; its insistence on the rights of the Communist party of the Soviet Union to interfere in the affairs of the Communist party of Yugoslavia and of the Yugoslav state.

Now Soviet imperialism combines all the imperialisms that have ever been invented in the long history of man: from the most ancient direct pillage and plunder and kidnapping of populations and extermination of elites to leave peoples leaderless, and the sowing of waste lands for strategic purposes, to the early twentieth-century form of economic penetration, and then it has super-added its own forms of expansion of the total state through terror, concentration camps, deportations, police systems, and the like.

Let us examine for a moment what we might call "classic economic imperialism." The Soviet Union had set up (as Tito has now made clear by publishing the documents) mixed companies, *juspad* and *justa*—shipping and aviation. Theoretically, the stock is owned fifty-fifty by the Soviet government and the Yugoslav government, but the Soviet government paid in only 9.83 percent of its share during the period in which the Yugoslav government had paid in 76.25 percent of its share. The managing director in Yugoslavia was a Soviet appointee; his assistant was a Yugoslav who was, for all practical purposes, ignored. Soviet planes were allowed to fly into Yugoslavia, but Yugoslav planes were not allowed to fly into the Soviet Union. Yugoslavia paid 52 percent more for her freight shipment on the Danube than the Soviet Union did and 30 percent more (for reasons that are not clear to me) than any other satellite did. In other words, here was a system of direct economic exploitation thinly disguised as an equal partnership.

Similarly, to keep it in subjection, the army equipment of Yugoslavia was left without replacement parts. Yugoslavia sent metals (principally iron) to Czechoslovakia and asked in return for machinery in order to manufacture trucks. Czechoslovakia under Soviet orders sent not machinery to manufacture trucks, but trucks, meaning "you will never manufacture your own trucks." Yugoslavia found that all its molybdenum was being monopolized by the Soviet government. Its cost of production was fantastically high—500,000 dinars per ton according to the Yugoslav White Book; but the Soviet monopoly paid only the world price—instead of 500,000 dinars, 45,000 dinars—so that Yugoslavia lost 455,000 dinars on every ton that was delivered; the more it delivered, the more it lost.

Finally, in this relation of metropolis to colony there was an ill-concealed basic contempt. One example will suffice: In one of the notes of the Soviet government to the Yugoslav government, dated August 30, 1949, you will find this sentence: "The puppy is feeling so good that it barks at the elephant." Nevertheless, the puppy has so far checked the elephant. We must now examine how the puppy managed to hold the elephant at bay.

First, Stalin had unexamined illusions as to the absoluteness of his own power. Up until that time no one had been able to stand against him. Trotsky, Bukharin, Zinoviev—they all looked bigger to him than did little Tito, but at his breath they were blown over. He had only, he thought, to sound the trumpet and the walls of Tito's pocket Kremlin would collapse; he had only to hurl an anathema and Tito would vanish in a puff of smoke. Not only Bukharin, Trotsky, and Zinoviev proved vulnerable to his anathema, but he had no difficulty with Poland, Hungary, and Rumania. However, Tito had a power center of his own just out of reach. Moreover, he was the perfect disciple—a kind of pocket Stalin.

The Crack in the Kremlin Wall

In the chess game which now ensued both Tito and Stalin played by the same book. Tito was able to anticipate each move. Every time Stalin touched a piece, he envisaged the entire alteration of configuration of the game—for he was playing the same game. He was invited to Moscow to parley—he politely declined the invitation. He was invited to Bucharest to parley at the Second Cominform session—he stayed away. Attempts were made to assassinate him—he protected himself well, though not as cautiously as Stalin did.

But there is an invisible wall which helps to protect him. There is danger in assassinating him before he has been discredited, before he has gone through the process of acknowledging his errors, discrediting himself, spitting in his own face, crawling, apologizing, and doing all the other things that Cominform leaders have to learn to do at certain stages in their careers. Only then could he be safely exterminated, confessed, "purged," or assassinated. But to assassinate him before this has happened is to make a banner and a martyr of him. This, too, protects him. A coup d'etat was tried against him, but he comes from a land where people, as they say in Mexico, "learn to get up early"; that is, he drew first.

In April 1948, before the open break, he threw Hebrang and Zujovic in jail, recognizing that they were secretly organizing a Stalinist faction in his party. Hebrang is still in jail. When General Arso Jovanovic, who was trained in Moscow and returned to serve in his army, packed his bags one night and made for the frontier, Tito seemed to get the jump again and Jovanovic was shot trying to escape.

A "revolution" in Yugoslavia has been called for, and called for, and called for—but the calls fall on deaf ears. Tito, who had enormous opposition in his own country, undoubtedly has less opposition today than he had when Stalin attacked him, rather than more opposition. With his internal opposition, every knock from Stalin is a kind of boost. He was gradually moved over into the position of a national hero. Without ceasing to be a Communist he is also in the position of a national hero, defending Yugoslavia's independence against a great, bullying power. Therefore, Stalin's committees in exile have been branded as "puppets," "traitors," and Tito himself is a hero even with the people who resent his total state regime.

Charging Tito with ingratitude and lack of discipline has not proved effective, so Stalin has tried more complex ideological attacks. But an ideological attack permits an ideological defense. The Cominform has said that Yugoslavia has a police regime, terror, no party democracy, holds no party congresses. Tito answers, "You have a police regime; you have terror; you also, have no party democracy; you hold no party congresses."

So every article of the indictment has become a fortiori an article of the indictment of the Stalin regime itself, and this is the most distressing thing that has happened to Stalin since he came to power. Gradually Tito has stepped up his defensive until it has become an offensive, and he has done it with rare tactical skill. Today the Soviet regime is truly on the defensive against this tiny, ridiculous "puppy who is barking at the elephant"; on the defensive because from inside the Communist camp come the clear words of truth about Soviet imperialism and Soviet terror and Soviet ruthlessness which, when they come from non-Communists, have less effectiveness. This is the true crack in the Kremlin wall of infallibility. Therefore Stalin cannot tolerate it and refuses to tolerate it, but he tries expedient after expedient, move after move—and every time Tito, playing by the same book, having gone through the same hard school, and having a somewhat better moral case, outguesses Stalin and blocks each move on his part.

There are only two possible moves which might bring results. One of them is to drive all his neighbor states into an attack—an open war upon him. This is too dangerous. Danger No. 1: that the armies of the Balkan neighbor states are themselves infected with some admiration for this assertion of independence of a Balkan power; Danger No. 2: Tito has (on a Balkan scale) a mighty good army and may not be overthrown without the intervention of the Soviet Union; Danger No. 3 (and largest of all): during the period when Stalin wants neither total peace nor total war he cannot risk an open attack upon Tito, for out of a local war too easily can come a total war.

Now there is a certain logic to Tito's position which we in the democratic lands watch with the closest attention. He is engaged in a critique of Stalinism which has ended with a complete rejection of Stalinism. Nevertheless, the structure of his own state is still basically Stalinist in character; that is to say, he still has his political prisoners; he still has his forced collectivization; he still has his one-party state; he still has his secret police; he still has his terror—all the things he learned from Stalin. He has glossed them over a bit, undoubtedly softened them a bit as his relations with his own people become less tense; nevertheless, the structure is there. But the logic is one which compels him anxiously to reexamine that structure. I do not say to dismantle it—that is what we are watching with interest—but certainly he is constantly reexamining it.

The logic also of his position requires him to seek allies. He has been forced into calling off the war on Greece and in Greece. He has been forced into closer relations with Greece, Turkey, Italy, and Austria (which is all that is left of the possibilities of a Balkan Federation against Soviet aggression). He has been forced to apply for help from the free world, and we have given him help, and that too has its logic. We have not made conditions. We have had much debate as to whether we ought to make conditions and what conditions we ought to make, but the fact is that we have made no conditions. We are not endorsing his internal regime, but on the other hand neither are we making our critique of this internal regime a major criterion at present. The major criterion is that he represents a crack in the Cominform. He represents a Communist defiance of Communist aggressive imperialism that emanates from the Soviet Union, and he represents a struggle for independence of his country against the Soviet Empire. These things we are prepared to support to the extent that we are now supporting them because in the kind of world in which we live they are definitely assets, creating a better situation rather than a worse situation.

The full logic of his position is limited by his own dogmas and predispositions. I have recently spoken with Bebler, and I found that Bebler, Kardelj, and Pijade (who were the major theoreticians of Tito-slavia) are approaching very tenderly the question of reexamining Leninism. They are grave and bold in reexamining Stalinism. They are at the point now in their thinking where they are asking themselves, "Shall we also reexamine Leninism to see if in Lenin, too, there was some imperfection which gave rise to Stalinism?" And they are beginning to come to the conclusion that there was. How far that process will go, I do not venture to predict.

The final thought that I would like to leave with you is this: there is also logic to Stalin's position. Leninism was defined by a Russian Marxist once as "Marxisme à la tartare" (Marxism with tartar sauce). If that is true, we will have to find a much more drastic qualification for Stalinism. It is a kind of mountaineer blood-feud Marxism, geared to a total state and an aspiration to total rule of the world. But there within the Marxist-

Leninist-Stalinist camp Stalinism has suffered its first check. And I do not believe that Stalin is so dumb as not to learn from what has happened.

Just as the British after 1776 never lost another colony, so Stalin has determined after June 1948, never to permit another Tito and never to lose another Yugoslavia. But Britain's response was appropriate to the organic nature of the British regime. It was a slow, hesitant, blundering but incessant loosening of the bonds, until the British empire changed (and is still changing under our eyes) into the British Commonwealth of Nations.

We have watched India break the bonds and yet remain a part of the Commonwealth. I hope (and believe) that we will yet watch Egypt break the bonds and remain in organic relation to the Commonwealth. We have watched Ireland (where the situation was more tense certainly than in Egypt) break the bonds of colonialism and yet remain a part of the Commonwealth. So with Burma. In other words, the process continues and Britain has never lost another colony because according to its own inner nature it has gradually loosened the bonds.

Now according to the inner nature of the Stalin regime the direct opposite procedure is taken—to tighten the bonds. Given both the ruthless total state that the Soviet Union is and the kind of man Stalin is, he can think of nothing but to squeeze tighter; to coordinate the countries more rapidly into his machine; to hasten the conflict between rulers and ruled; to remove those who have any roots in their own country and put in their places puppets who are completely dependent upon him; to let loose a hail of blood purges, executions of faithful and devoted Communists like Laszlo Rajk, Traicho Kostov, Clementis, Gomulka, and like loyal collaborators such as Foreign Minister Jan Masaryk of Czechoslovakia. There has been a hail of accusations of Titoism, and one by one the men who have national roots in their own country, in their own Communist parties and in their own laboring classes—these men have been executed in advance of the possibility that they might some day commit the crime of considering the interests of their country as different from the interests of the Soviet empire.

However, there is also a danger in that method of solving the problem of Titoism. When you draw the bonds tighter and tighter you augment the potential discontent. Thus the Soviet empire appears to grow tighter and stronger with its more ruthless coordination of all of its parts, but at the same time that strategy introduces fresh elements of weakness into every one of the lands that Stalin dominates.

12

The Struggle for
the Soviet Succession

Joseph Stalin was dead six hours and ten minutes before the Kremlin flag
was lowered and the radio announced that the Dictator was no more.
In an age of split-second announcements of death, there is something
strange in this delay. No less strange were the official communiqués on
his last illness. "The best medical personnel has been called in to treat
Comrade Stalin. . . . The treatment is under the direction of the Minister of Health. . . . The treatment is under the continuous supervision of
the Central Committee and the Soviet Government. . . ." Nine doctors
watching each other; the Minister of Health watching the doctors; the
Central Committee and the Government watching the minister. And all
of this, by an inner compulsion, announced to the world. Who can fail to
sense that the laws of life and death are somehow different behind the
Kremlin walls?

Early on the morning of March 6, with all the morning papers missing
from the streets, the radio announced that the *vozhd* had died at 9:50 the
night before. The communiqué included a call to maintain "the steel-like
unity and monolithic unity of the ranks of the Party . . . to guard the
unity of the Party as the apple of the eye . . . to educate all Communists
and working people in high political vigilance, intolerance and firmness
in the struggle against internal and external enemies." This call was
repeated hourly all through the day.

Shortly before midnight the party chiefs, in continuous session since
their leader's death, announced that a joint session of the Central Committee, the Council of Ministers, and the Presidium of the Supreme Soviet

Reprinted with permission from *Foreign Affairs* (July 1953).

had come to the conclusion that "the most important task of the Party and the Government is to ensure uninterrupted and correct leadership of the entire life of the country which demands the greatest unity of leadership and the prevention of any kind of disorder and panic."[1] In view of the above, the communiqué continued, it was necessary to make at once a sweeping series of changes in the personnel and organizational structure of the leading party and government bodies. The changes completely undid all the personnel and structural arrangements made less than five months earlier by the Nineteenth Congress under the personal direction of the man who was not yet dead twenty-four hours.

The "call to steel-like unity and monolithic unity" and to increased "vigilance and intolerance in the struggle with internal and external enemies" continued to reappear in editorials and articles. It was repeated textually in Malenkov's funeral oration three days later. The warning against "disorder and panic" was paraphrased by Beria in his funeral oration and repeated verbatim in the leading *Pravda* editorial of March 11.

Disorder and panic! When Franklin Roosevelt died during his fourth term in office, could it occur to the vice-president who automatically succeeded him, or to the leaders of either political party, or to "the government," to warn against disorder and panic? When George VI of England or Gustav V of Sweden died while still in royal office, could such words creep into the communiqués or the funeral addresses of those who knew and loved them?

Not even in young states just being born in turmoil and conflict, not in Israel when its first president, Chaim Weizmann, died, not in Turkey when Kemal Pasha died, not in Pakistan when Liaquat Ali Khan died, not in India when her unique political-religious leader Mahatma Gandhi was assassinated, not in China when Sun Yat-sen breathed his last, could anyone think of pronouncing the ominous words "disorder and panic." Those strange words bring us close to the heart of the mystery of the nature of the total state, of the nature of the men who rule over it, of their relationship with each other, with the people they rule, and with the rest of the world.

One searches history in vain for a case of a peaceful and bloodless succession to a dictator who has climbed to power by force and based his rule upon force without troubling to restore the ruptured fabric of legitimacy. When Caesar was assassinated, the triumvirate that followed tore the Roman empire apart. The Directory that succeeded the terror of Robespierre was dislodged by Napoleon, who wrestled all his days with the problem of restoring legitimacy, only to end them on St. Helena. Hitler's *Tausendjähriges Reich* perished in a flaming bunker in Berlin and

Mussolini's Imperium Romanum did not outlast his hanging. There had been "disorder and panic" when Hitler and Mussolini died, for the lack of a procedure for the successsion to a dictator was reinforced by the invading armies closing in on the rubble of their cities. But the "disorder and panic" which Stalin's comrades speak of springs not from such external events but from their hearts and the essence of their system. A system that is based upon an unending war "on all existing conditions and institutions," an unending war upon their own people and upon all other peoples, cannot develop a legitimacy. The word "panic" escaping the lips of the rulers of the world's most powerful government betrays a fear that is ineradicably in their hearts: they fear the prostrate people over whom they rule, they fear the outside world which they plan to conquer, and they fear each other.

The Soviet government is not a government by soviets. The people have long ceased to elect or recall "deputies." The soviets have long ceased to elect their leaders or decide anything. Nor is the Soviet government a party government. Parties need each other as the sexes need each other, and party life ceases as soon as there is only one party and no opposition, just as sex life would cease if there were only one sex, i.e., no sex.

As the soviets have long ceased to decide anything or select their leaders and officials, so the party has long ceased to decide anything or select its leaders. What was once a party has become a "transmission belt" (the words are Stalin's) to convey and enforce the will of the leaders upon the masses. Both decision and personnel selection are from the top downward; a military-ideological-organizational apparatus, a pyramidal power structure culminating in what Max Weber has called a charismatic leader.

On the surface everything seems designed to last forever and to insure a simple, quiet, peaceful succession. Was ever such monopoly of power wielded by so perfectly organized a mechanism? Thirty-six years of continuity in government (is it not still called "Soviet"?). Thirty years of continuity of personal leadership in the person of the all-wise, all-powerful *vozhd*. Over a third of a century of uninterrupted happiness of the people, of nonexistence of opposition. More than two decades of unanimous decisions on everything. Not the unity of human beings, but the unity of a monolith. Where is there a crevice in which might sprout the seedcorn of doubt, much less of disorder and panic? The Leader controlled the Politburo so long that at the Nineteenth Congress (October 1952) he could abolish it altogether in favor of a diffuse body so large and scattered that it could not be called upon to make day-to-day decisions.[2] The Central Committee had long before been made into such a body.

The chain of command was so clear: the Leader controlling the Politburo, the Politburo controlling the Central Committee, the Central Committee controlling the party. And the party, in turn, controls an imposing apparatus of police, army, bureaucracy, press, radio, meeting halls, streets, schools, buildings, churches, factories, farms, unions, arts, sciences, everything. All the power levers seem to function so smoothly. What it had cost Lenin and his associates so much travail and struggle to build, and Stalin so much struggle and bloodshed to perfect into the all-embracing power apparatus of the total state, seems now so perfected, so smoothly functioning. A ready-made machine, the greatest power machine in all history. Yet the first words of the orphaned heirs on the death of the dictator are not human words of sorrow but ominous words about "disorder and panic" and "vigilance and uncompromising struggle against the inner and outer foe."

In all this mighty machine there is oppressive quiet, but no peace to insure a peaceful succession. There is a multitude of laws, but no legality to provide a legal and legitimate succession. The democratic revolution of March 1917 ruptured the legitimacy of tsarism, but it set to work at once to develop a new, democratic legitimacy, out of the state duma or parliament, out of the city dumas, the rural zemstvos and the soviets. It looked forward to convening a Constituent Assembly which would adopt a new democratic constitution and provide a fresh fabric of consensus, consent, acceptance, collective and democratic determination of policy, a multiparty system, a parliament, to secure the habits of willing consent which are the tissues of all normal governments and which make the death of a particular head of state a cause for grief but not an occasion of fear of disorder or panic. To use the terminology of the historian Ferrero, the provisional government set up by the first revolution of 1917 was a "pre-legitimate government," moving as quickly as the troubled times permitted from the ruptured legitimacy of the monarchy to democratic legitimacy. That is what it meant when it called itself "provisional."

But the Bolshevik party, in November 1917, overthrew this "pre-legitimate" Provisional Government by a violent coup d'etat, and then dispersed the Constituent Assembly which alone could have laid a foundation of democratic legitimacy. When they outlawed all other parties, including the working-class and peasant parties, they thereby drained the Soviets of all power as a "workers' parliament" or "workers' and peasants' parliament," and the party began to rule in the name of the soviets. Next Lenin outlawed all factions within the party, thereby draining it, too, of all political life. Always excessively centralist and hierarchical, it now became a transmission belt for the will of the Central Committee. When the "servant" of the Central Committee, its General Secretary, executed the majority of the members of the Central Committee which he was supposed to serve, that, too, ceased to be a decisive organ.

Even as Stalin purged all dissenters and all he had reason to suspect because they were injured or aggrieved or because they found it hard to sing the praise of his perfections, the whole machine of power and force and propaganda got into high gear to make this unpopular, colorless, and unloved man a synthetic charismatic leader. The Leader who possesses charisma ("divine" grace) acquires one by one the attributes of divinity: omniscience, omnicompetence, omnipotence. In him all power is concentrated. Whom he touches with his spirit partakes of his grace. Whom he denounces shrivels into nothingness. He decides everything: linguistics, genetics, the transformation of nature, the disposition of artillery on every front, the quota and technique of every factory. Others get power only by emanation and delegation, and even then must be prepared to give him the credit for all successes and take upon themselves the blame and punishment for all failures.

So at the death of the dictator, there are no parties to establish a legal succession by electoral contest. There is no Soviet constitutional provision for a successor to the post of self-appointed genius. There is no party which any longer decides anything, debates anything, selects anybody. There is not even a provision for a dictator, much less for a successor, in the constitution or in a party statute.

There is no moral code, either, to restrain the aspirants to the succession from framing each other up and killing each other off. Insofar as they follow the precedents bequeathed to them, and insofar as they follow the real inner laws of the total state, that is precisely what they will have to do. It is to themselves that they are speaking when they call to an awed populace for "steel-like unity and monolithic unity of party and of leadership." It is from their own hearts that the words escaped concerning "disorder and panic."

Why not, asks the reasonable man trying to project himself into the irrational atmosphere of totalitarian dynamics, why not then a collective leadership? A triumvirate? A heptarchy? A decemvirate? The Presidium, maybe? The Central Committee? The Council of Ministers? The Secretariat?

Even in Lenin's day, before the Central Committee and Politburo had been drained of all political life and power, it proved impossible to arrange a succession by purely peaceful means, or by means which, at least within the party purview, might be regarded as lawful and legitimate. Lenin got three solemn warnings from the Angel of Death in the form of three partial cerebral hemorrhages. Only after the second did this man, bursting with vitality and a will to power over the entire world, begin to believe in his heart that death was approaching. Then at last he tried to prepare a "legal" and "peaceful" succession. Recognizing that he had acquired enormous personal authority, that perhaps without willing it consciously, he had dwarfed the party and its leading bodies and become a personal dictator, Lenin began to fear that his lieutenants would tear each other to pieces if any one of them tried to become a Vladimir Ilyich the Second. With no clear understanding of the dynamics of the totalitarian process he had set in motion, he sought to reestablish the moribund authority of at least one "collegial" body, the Politburo. His testament proposed a collective leadership in which all his close lieutenants, working together, would replace him and together rule. For this purpose the testament was carefully constructed, with a warning of the "danger of a split in the Party," with an adverse judgment on each of his associates to keep him from thinking that he was big enough to rule alone, and a word of praise for each of them, to indicate that none should be eliminated.

Collective leadership is difficult at best, but without democracy it is impossible. Where there are no constitutional rules for collective procedure, where in all fields there is dictatorship, where force settles all things, where opposition is not part of the game of politics but something to be eliminated and crushed, the whole momentum of the state and the system drives relentlessly toward personal dictatorship. So it was with Lenin; so it was with Mussolini; so it was with Hitler; and so it was with Stalin.

Even before Lenin was dead, Stalin began "disloyally" to gather into his hands the reins of power. The dying dictator, speechless now from his third stroke, yet managed to add a codicil to his will: "Stalin is too rude, and this fault becomes insupportable in the office of General Secretary. Therefore, I propose to the comrades to find a way to remove Stalin from that position. . . ." But Lenin's will could not prevail against Stalin's will and the innate dynamics of the machine which Lenin himself had set in motion. Stalin did not even permit it to be published in the Soviet Union.

Precisely because Stalin did not possess Lenin's moral authority over his associates, he found it necessary to use more physical power. The cult of Lenin's person among his disciples was spontaneous, and personally distasteful to him. Lenin had frequently used his authority and prestige to get his own way in disputed matters, but he opposed the development of a cult of his person. The cult grew up only around his embalmed corpse, fostered above all by the very man who was undoing his Last Will. For Stalin could claim infallibility only by first developing the cult of infallibility around Lenin and then making himself into the "best disciple" and apostolic successor. Thus the last repositories of some kind of legality and legitimacy, the Party Congress, the Central Committee and the Politburo, were deprived of their right to say *yea* or *nay* to anything. Unanimity, monolithic conformity and synthetic infallibility prevailed.

Lenin had defeated his opponents inside the party by debate sometimes tempered with a touch of organizational maneuver and frame-up; but once they were worsted, he was careful to salvage the person and the dignity of the defeated opponent. But Stalin could not win by debate. His method was to enlarge the organizational maneuvers and frame-ups which were already a part of Lenin's techniques, to compel his opponents to besmirch themselves and to liquidate themselves morally by repeated "confessions." Then he killed them.

There is a fearful dynamic to totalitarianism that drives it to rupture the entire fabric of consent and consensus. From thence springs its fear that men will not believe and not obey. But once fear is present, it drives to the use of further terror. And terror exercised against one's people or associates begets greater fear.

The free political process needs opposition as the lungs need air. Once opposition is outlawed, there are no limits to terror and fear. The thermometer measuring opposition having been broken, the quicksilver of opposition is instinctively felt to be everywhere. Everywhere there is fear, therefore everywhere there must be terror. Terror cannot be used against other parties and public bodies without invading one's own party and its leading bodies; until even one's cronies, one's palace guards, and one's doctors are suspect. The more inert the body politic, the more suspect it is and the more cause there is to fear it.

Stalin exacted a cult of his person that was the more extravagant because all who knew him knew his personal limitations. He was keenly sensitive to his inferiority as a theoretician and a popular leader. He knew that the men around him were his equals, in some way his superiors. This drove him to kill off all of Lenin's associates, to kill off all his "successors," and to surround himself by only lesser men, courtiers, sycophants, faction lieutenants, executants of his will. He exacted a cult of his person even from those he was about to destroy, and from the entire nation even as he tormented it. If Lenin's prestige was unable to bind his closest associates, who loved and revered him, to carry out his will after he was dead, how much less likely is the enforced, repugnant, humiliating Stalin cult to bring his associates or his party to execute his will?

Besides, this time there seems to be no will. "In his unconscious," Freud has written, "no man believes in his own death." It is this which enables the soldier to hold on the shell-swept field where a third or two-thirds must die, yet cling to the conviction that "my number isn't up." In the case of a dictator who aspires to absolute rule over all things and all men there is an exceptionally strong will to disbelieve in ordinary mortal limitations, so far as he is concerned. Lenin got three warnings from the Angel of Death, but Stalin, though aging, was rugged, and interviews with foreigners held only a few weeks before his stroke testified to his apparent good health. The stroke came suddenly; he immediately lost consciousness; within three days he was dead.

Moreover, Joseph Jugashvili Stalin, as all who knew him can testify, was jealous, resentful, envious, capricious, and suspicious by nature. No one dared bid him prepare for death; none dared to try on the crown in his presence. As American presidents realize, it is unwise even in a democracy to announce too early in your term of office that you do not intend to run again. The very men of your own party begin to abandon you for the bandwagon of your anticipated successor, and power and leadership slip from your hands. But in a dictatorship, which tolerates only a single power center, it would be fatal to let anyone else openly try on the crown. A rival power center would begin to polarize, and the whole totalitarian regime would be called in question. His very benefactor and heir would become a danger to the dictator if he began this unnatural abdication or renunciation of part of his total power.

As soon as anyone around him began to shine, however faintly, by the light of his own deeds, Stalin was swift to remove him from the stage. Sometimes the removal by the law of fear-and-terror led to purge. At other times, it led to mere rustication, a shift to a minor provincial post, as in the cases of Marshals Timoshenko and Zhukov. Sometimes, rumors grew that some one man was the "heir apparent"; then, mysteriously, an assassin's bullet or a sudden illness, or if we are to believe Stalin's last frame-up, "poison-doctors" brought the heir to his end. When shall we really know how Kirov died, and how Zhdanov died?

Thus the nature of the total state and the personal psychology of the particular Leader combined in Stalin's case to make it ever harder for anyone to grow big enough or acquire the prestige to fill his shoes, or don the mantle of the apostolic succession. The cult of his person grew until it filled the horizon and overarched the sky. Those around him, many of them very capable in their own right, were systematically reduced to dwarfs around a giant. Each fresh extravagance exacted from them in this cult of the master-of-everything, each blasphemous phrase in the litany of worship of a living god, diminished further the stature of the men around him and made harder the process of building up a new charismatic leader after his death.

The only men who have a chance to try for the leadership are those who are in possession of the power levers which constitute the actual organs of government of the Soviet state. Molotov and Voroshilov, and to a lesser degree Kaganovich and Mikoyan, represent "Old Bolshevism." Insofar as any new *vozhd* may want to preserve an air of continuity with Lenin and the "Men of October," such "Old Bolsheviks" are useful as symbols. But they do not represent a real power lever. Stalin killed off virtually all the "Men of October" during the blood purges of 1934 to 1938. In 1947, on the thirtieth anniversary of the coup d'etat of November 7, 1917, only 438 Old Bolsheviks who had joined the party prior to the seizure of power were still alive and in good standing to sign a letter of thanks to Comrade Stalin for what he had done to the party. The most important of these is now Molotov. Lenin pronounced him an "incurable dumbbell" and "the best file-clerk in all Russia." He is obstinate as a mule. "Kamennii zad," Stone Behind, his own associates call him, and every diplomat who has tried to negotiate with him will agree. Unless he backs the wrong horse, he will undoubtedly be included in any entourage as a symbol of continuity, and someone like him or Voroshilov is likely to be vested with the title of Chairman of the Presidium of the Supreme Soviet or some other such honorary badge. But Stalin was boss before he had any state titles, and Molotov and Voroshilov could not be boss if a score of titles were showered upon them. For the "Men of October," of which they are the enfeebled, diminishing shadow, are no more.

The new men, from whom the new *vozhd* will emerge if the process is not interrupted before its completion, are the epigoni, the "sons," or perhaps the "grandsons." Lenin's Marxism was so different from that of Marx that one of his own admirers called it "Marxisme à la tartare." Stalin, killing off the Men of October, became the spokesman of the "sons"; his Leninism became as different from Lenin's as Lenin's Marxism was from Marx. The Malenkovs and Berias, and men still younger, who aspire to power, are men who never knew the great dreams and humane ideals of the nineteenth-century Russian intelligentsia, never knew the excitement, the fervor and the misery of the tsarist underground and exile, scarcely know except by hearsay the "heroic days" of the storming of the Winter Palace and the Kremlin. The world will watch with interest what these men, wholly formed and brought up not as underground revolutionaries but under the new regime of bureaucratic and totalitarian absolutism, will make of the heritage of Marxism and Leninism and Stalinism in the course of their struggle with each other.

The real power levers in this struggle are three: the party machine; the secret police; the armed forces. Potentially, other power groupings may be in process of formation: an esprit de corps among the state bureaucracy, for example, or among the industrialists and technicians. But these are only embryonic forces and not real power levers at present.

Who is in control of the party machine? While Stalin was alive, he controlled it. Whether he was General Secretary, or Premier, or simply *vozhd*, all power and all decision emanated downward from him and in his name. Because he had designated Malenkov in recent years as Secretary of the Party, or as first of a battery of three or five or ten secretaries (the number has fluctuated) it was assumed by the outside world, and by some in the Soviet Union, perhaps even by Malenkov himself, that he had his hand on the lever that moves that mighty machine. But often there is some central mechanism that is the key to the functioning of a machine, and, when that is removed, the levers no longer work. Stalin was such a central mechanism. All power concentrated in him, all cohesion. When he died, it soon became clear that no one was any longer in complete possession of the party machine.

For a few days, Malenkov acted as if he were, and the party seemed to act as if he were. On the day of Stalin's death, *Pravda* quoted some lifeless utterance of his in bold type in the lead editorial, as formerly it had quoted Stalin. It did the same on March 7, 8, and 9. On March 9, *Izvestia* printed a photo of Stalin with Malenkov and a little girl. On the tenth *Pravda* published a photograph, retouched by montage, showing Stalin, Mao Tse-tung, and Malenkov as a "big three," standing alone at the signing of the Sino-Soviet Treaty. Examination of the original photograph shows that Beria and Molotov were cut off in the "retouching," as well as Vyshinsky, who was actually signing the treaty, and many others. Sovfoto released a photograph of Malenkov with two of his three chins missing. Operation retouch had begun.

Greetings began to come from provincial congresses and gatherings to "the Chairman of the Council of Ministers of the USSR and Secretary of the Central Committee of the CPSU, G. M. Malenkov." The press began to use the phrase "headed by Comrade Malenkov." Then suddenly, the number of quotes diminished. The "fat type" gave way to ordinary print. Quotes from Molotov and Beria began to appear along with quotes from Malenkov.[3] On March 13–15, *Pravda* ceased to use a dual title for Malenkov. From then on, in place of stress on his person, there was stress on "the Central Committee, consisting of people taught by Comrade Stalin, into whose hands Stalin gave the great Lenin banner."

The Supreme Soviet which was called to meet on March 14 to "ratify" the changes made on the day of Stalin's death, was postponed for a day without explanation. When it met, the list of cabinet ministers presented to it differed from the list that had been broadcast on March 6. Again no explanation. Secretly, the "Central Committee of the Party" had met on

March 14 and come to significant decisions which were kept secret for a full week. The soviet met only for one hour, one of the shortest sessions on record. It applauded the reports of the changes made on the day of Stalin's death, as mysteriously changed again by the secret meeting of March 14, but it did not go through the formality of voting its approval on anything. Malenkov told the deputies: "The strength of the government will consist in its collective nature." Only on March 21, a full week later, was it announced that on March 14, Malenkov, "at his own request," had been removed as Secretary of the Party, and thereby deprived of the dual leading post which seemed to mark him for the succession.

Neither the editors of the regional and provincial press nor the Supreme Soviet had been informed of the decisions of the secret top party meeting of March 14. It is inconceivable that it was a full Central Committee meeting as stated, for that is so large (216 persons) that the news would have reached the editors and secretaries of the Constituent Republics. As late as March 21 and 22, provincial papers continued to carry greetings to Malenkov in place of the column headed "News of the Day," and references to his dual titles and his position as "head of the Party" or "the Government" or both. Then suddenly this ceased. Most papers skipped one full day without publication—in many cases not the usual off day—and a surprising number of them reappeared next day with the name of a new editor at the masthead. At this writing (with provincial papers available in the United States only through the first week in April), a few provinces are holding out for bold-type quotes and greetings to Malenkov, while in Georgia Beria's name has been advanced at Malenkov's expense and he is being given sweeping credit for things previously associated with the name of that other Georgian, Joseph Stalin. Thus the situation remains tense and unsettled, but the great "operation build-up" has clearly broken down, or been visibly reversed.

When Malenkov first reported to the Supreme Soviet on the changes being made in the "Stalinist" party and government, he presented them as having been "contemplated and approved" by Stalin. Actually, they reversed in significant ways things that Stalin had done at the Nineteenth Congress. The congress had abolished the Politburo in favor of a large and formless Presidium of twenty-five. Now the Presidium was reduced to ten, in most cases the old Politburo members. Never before has a deliberative body in the Soviet Union thus contained an even number of persons, because of the danger of a tie vote. This suggests a state of deadlock and of bargaining over a precarious equilibrium.

The Secretariat, raised by the Nineteenth Congress to ten Secretaries, was now reduced to five, with Malenkov as First Secretary. On March 14, when Malenkov lost his secretarial post, he was replaced by Khrushchev. A few weeks later, Ignatiev, who had been elevated to the place of a Party Secretary only on the death of Stalin, was peremptorily dismissed in connection with the "doctors' frame-up." Thus the Secretariat would now appear to be reduced from ten to four.

No less startling were the changes in Stalin's governmental arrangements. The inner cabinet of fourteen Deputy Premiers was reduced to five or six. Malenkov was made Premier, but he was surrounded by, and put under the obvious control of, members of the "Old Guard." To emphasize their importance, the party performed the miracle of appointing four "First Deputy Premiers" to work with him. Though all four are called "Firsts," their names had to be mentioned in some order; therefore Beria was named as first "First," Molotov second, Bulganin third, and Kaganovich fourth First Deputy Premier. In addition, one more member of Stalin's old guard, Mikoyan, was named a Deputy Premier, the only one with no "First" before his title.

The Ministry of the Interior and the Ministry of State Security were combined into one single body, and Lavrenti Beria, whom Stalin had "kicked upstairs," was restored to his old post as head of the combined secret police forces. The Ministry of War and the Ministry of the Navy were combined into one, and Bulganin was made minister, with two "First" deputies, Generals Zhukov and Vasilevsky. Thus the Army was brought back into the structure of carefully counterbalanced forces, and General Zhukov, whom Stalin had jealously exiled to a remote secondary post, reappeared as a kind of "representative" of the General Staff. Voroshilov, now aged seventy-two, was made Chairman of the Presidium of the Supreme Soviet. This might seem to be merely an honorary office, but in the delicate balance of forces, it too proved to have power implications, for on March 28, when Malenkov's recession had begun, it was Voroshilov, Chairman of the Presidium, rather than Malenkov, Premier and Chairman of the Council of Ministers, whose name was signed to the popularity-seeking decree on amnesty. If Stalin had chosen to issue an amnesty, he would never have let the chairman of a purely honorary body sign in place of him.

Lavrenti Beria seemed to be on his way out at the moment of Stalin's death. For more than a decade a favorite of Stalin's, he had first run Georgia as head of the Georgian police, and then risen to All-Union Security Chief. In 1946, after the post had been divided into two, a Minister of State Security and a Minister of the Interior, Beria was relieved of direct responsibility for either and elevated to Deputy Premier "to devote full time to his main work." People assumed that the main work was either atomic energy and atomic espionage, or overall supervision of both security forces. Beria's men were put in charge of both, as earlier his men had been put in charge of Georgia when he left for Moscow.

The first visible sign of Beria's decline was a large-scale purge of his appointees in his native Georgia during 1952. Mgeladze, an anti-Beria man, became first secretary of the Georgian party, and with the assistance of police chief Rukhadze "crushed in a Stalinist manner" many lesser leaders. Stalin, as was his fashion, forced Beria to discredit himself with his own followers by sanctioning these purges. At the Nineteenth Congress in October 1952, Stalin eliminated Beria's man, Abakumov, Minister of State Security of the USSR, from his party and government posts. And on January 13, 1953, the lightning struck again. After patient preparation by Stalin and Malenkov, it was announced that the top Kremlin doctors were "poisoners," and that the deaths of Shcherbakov and Zhdanov, which had occurred while Beria was still a power in the secret police, were brought on by the doctor-poisoners. All this had happened because the security forces were guilty of "lack of vigilance." Things began to look ominous for Beria.

As a cerebral hemorrhage saved Stalin when Lenin was about to remove him as General Secretary in 1923, so death intervened to save Beria on March 5, 1953. The very next day, the Ministries of State Security and the Interior were recombined into one, and Lavrenti Beria's hand closed firmly on the mighty power lever. Beria was one of the three speakers at Stalin's funeral. It was he who made the nomination of Malenkov as Premier. On March 21, Malenkov resigned the post of Secretary through which Stalin had paved his way to power. But Beria had two serious handicaps to overcome. The first of these was the unpopularity that has always clung to the head of the Secret Police. Beria's speeches began to include vows to protect the civil rights of the Soviet citizen and uphold the constitution. On March 28, a sweeping amnesty of petty offenders was proclaimed, and the penal code was ordered revised "within 60 days."

On April 3, the "doctors' plot" was declared a frame-up, the anti-Beria police leaders held responsible, and placed under arrest. In the name of undoing an injustice, a counterpurge thus got under way. On April 6, Semyon D. Ignatiev, whom Stalin and Malenkov had put into the post of Minister of State Security when Beria was losing his grip, and whom Malenkov had just made a Party Secretary, was accused of "political blindness and gullibility." On April 7, his ousting was announced.

Exactly one week later, on April 14, Beria struck back in Georgia. Secretary Mgeladze, Security Minister Rukhadze, and "their accomplices" were charged with having framed up innocent Georgian leaders, "trampled down the rights of Soviet citizens," extracted "false confessions by impermissible means" (torture), "cooked up charges of nonexistent nationalism," and shown themselves to be "enemies of the people." The accused were rehabilitated and restored to their posts. The same day, new police chiefs were appointed in virtually all the republics of the Soviet Union. All published names seemed to be Russian, regardless of the nationality involved, and many of them were known Beria men.

The other obstacle to Beria's rise to absolute power is a more insurmountable because more intangible one. Like Stalin, he is a Georgian. The once internationalistic Communist party has long been playing with the fire of Great Russian nationalism and chauvinism. Now, if a second Georgian from an obscure conquered province succeeds the first, the Great Russians will ask: "Are there no Russians left to rule over the Russian land?" It is impossible for a man laboring under the double handicap of police chief and Georgian immediately to lay open claim to the apostolic succession. More than any other of the aspirants, Beria needs for a time the protective shield of "collective leadership" and anonymous "collegial bodies"—to rule, in so far as he can, in the name of the party, the Central Committee, the Presidium, the cause of Lenin and Stalin. Thus his personal predicaments and the precarious equilibrium that marks the first phase of what will doubtless be a prolonged struggle combine to make an emphasis upon anonymity and collective leadership necessary for the present in a total state which cannot, in the long run, tolerate either collectivity or anonymity in its Leader.

The secret police has its tentacles everywhere, in every factory, in every kolkhoz, in every party organization. But the party, too, has its cells everywhere, even in the secret police. The Army is riddled with party agents and secret police agents and has been the most jealously watched power instrument of all. It was built by Trotsky, who died in exile with a pickaxe blow in the back of his head. It was mechanized by Tukhachevsky, who fell in the blood purges along with virtually the entire General Staff. Thereafter it bore a deep grudge against the secret police, which Stalin was apparently trying to mollify with his talk of "lack of vigilance of the Security organs" in the "doctors' plot against leading military figures." Generals Zhukov, Timoshenko, Vasilevsky, Konev, Sokolovsky, have been moved about by Stalin and Malenkov like musical chairs to prevent their popularity from growing too great, and watched over by a political "General, Marshal, and War Minister," Bulganin. Yet the Army has a strong esprit de corps, and if it can unite on a candidate it may well in a long struggle become the most powerful contender.

Moreover, in this totalitarian land, the Army is the only potentially democratic power instrument. The Russian and Soviet peoples cannot possibly identify themselves with the party machine that has enslaved and driven them and waged upon them an unending war of nerves. Still less with the secret police that has tortured, enslaved, purged. But the Army did serve them in defending their frontiers and homes against the invader. And the Army is a part of them and they of it, since all able-bodied males serve in it, and in it are better fed, clothed, and housed than at any other time in their lives. Finally, the Army is thought of as for defense rather than for a deeply feared aggressive war. The people trust the Army more than they do the party or the police, and around it they could most readily be rallied.

All three power levers, moreover, are not mechanical things, but living organisms with hundreds of thousands, even millions, of members. Such power levers can be used symbolically in maneuvering for position in a muted struggle. But they cannot be brought into actual play surreptitiously and behind the scenes. If the contenders do not manage to finish each other off, by some combination of subordination and purge, behind the scenes, then three great power machines, each embracing their millions of members and their families, may be brought into action in one or another combination.

Then whoever appeals to the party must appeal to some traditions, some program, something in the past and present and something proposed for the future. Whoever appeals to the Army likewise. And to the secret police the same. If the struggle is prolonged and enlarged, there are other reserves of power to be tapped: the moribund trade unions, the regions and nationalities, the local party members, the nascent esprit de corps of officials and technicians, the kolkhozes, the factories. In any case the struggle to replace the charismatic leader with another of the same type is inseparable from the total state. And, overt or covert, the struggle is bound to smolder for a long time.

If ever these power levers are to be used not merely as makeweights but brought into play as actual levers of power, then anything might happen. Then the empire, which cannot take orders from an upstart as easily as it could from Stalin, may regain its independent life. The Soviet peoples, so long in chains, may then recover their freedom, while the outside world, safe only when Russia is democratic once more, may regain its lost hope of a genuine, just, and enduring peace.

But the current "peace talk" must not be confused with such genuine peace. The men in the Kremlin are moving from weakness and the uncertainties of their internal struggle. As during the famine of the early twenties, they made their strategic retreats of the NEP and offered "concessions" to foreigners; as during the Anti-Comintern Axis they talked "Stalinist Constitution" plus "Popular Front"; as during the first onslaught of Hitler's invasion they "abolished" the Comintern; so once more they are moving from weakness and talking "peace." But during the NEP Lenin completed the political foundations of the total state. The Stalinist constitution was translated into life by the blood purges. The abolition of the Comintern was accompanied by the dispatch of its agents into the "liberated" countries to turn them into "People's Democracies." And once more, the very decrees of amnesty, and of justice to the doctors, contain menacing phrases about renewed "vigilance" and are accompanied by a fresh wave of purges, while the "peace talk" on Korea is given its real meaning in a fresh "limited global war" in Laos, and the setting up of a "Thai Autonomous Government" in Yunnan, China, with irredenta claims in Laos, Burma, and Thailand. The very *Pravda* of April 25 which printed President Eisenhower's appeal for peace declared that the Kremlin will not "halt the liberating movement of Asia's colonial and semi-colonial peoples" and that the forces driving into Laos are "the People's Liberating Army of Patet-Lao."

Still, totalitarianism's difficulty, whether writ large or small, is freedom's opportunity. The world, in this writer's judgment, except for the dangers which may spring from its own failures to understand what it is watching, is safer for the moment while a regime based on total force and total dictatorship goes through its convulsive struggles to solve the insoluble problem of a "legal" and "peaceful" succession in a system that knows neither law nor peace.

13

A New Look at the Soviet "New Look"

The men who have been ruling the Soviet Union since Stalin's death are *epigoni*, "sons," after-comers. They owe their power to an apostolic succession and style themselves disciples of Lenin and comrades-in-arms of Stalin. The structure and dynamics of their rule are dictated by the same philosophy, incorporated in the same single-party police state; it continues to be totalitarian in scope and aim, it is engaged in the same unending war on its own people, the same drive to reshape and control the globe. Still, they are new men, younger men, men with different formative backgrounds, and their regime has a new look.

Lenin's Marxism was so different from that of the West European, nineteenth-century Marx that one of Lenin's admirers dubbed it "marxisme à la tartare." Lenin's associates, Trotsky, Stalin, Zinoviev, Bukharin, ten to fifteen years younger than he, still belonged to the generation that had made the revolution. After a period of feigned subordination to a "collective leadership," Joseph Stalin established his claim to be "the best disciple of Comrade Lenin." He perfected Lenin's organization machine and monopoly of the organs of persuasion and force, suppressed some of Lenin's doctrines, dogmas, and hopes, retained and enlarged others, propounded some of his own. He killed off all of Lenin's close associates, surrounding himself with new and younger men, none of whom had been in Lenin's inner circle. Thus he became at one and the same time father image and voice of the epigoni: his Leninism became different from Lenin's even as the latter's Marxism had been different from that of Marx.

Reprinted with permission from *Foreign Affairs* (January 1955).

The Malenkovs and Khrushchevs, and men younger still, who now form the post-Stalinist "collective leadership," are the men Stalin gathered around him in his rise to personal dictatorship. They never knew the wide dreams and humane ideals of the nineteenth-century intelligentsia, the feverish disputation, hope, and wretchedness of the tsarist underground, prison and exile, nor the "heroic days" of the storming of the Winter Palace and the Kremlin. They were wholly formed in the Stalinist fight for a monopoly of power, and in the iron age of forced industrialization, forced collectivization, and blood purge. They were brought up not as underground revolutionaries but under the new regime of bureaucratic totalitarianism.[1]

They do not even look like the men who were Lenin's close associates. As one contemplates their pictures lined up on Lenin's, now Stalin's tomb, one cannot but be struck by the fact that they are all fleshy, solid, square, and squat—"fat boys," to borrow an old "Wobbly" term against labor bureaucrats. Harrison Salisbury has called our attention to a curious detail that none of them is over 5 foot 4 (Stalin's police record gives his height as 5 foot 3 and 3/4 inches)—as if they had been chosen not merely with regard to faction loyalty and party infighting and administrative capacity, but also that their height, spiritual and physical, should not dwarf the none-too-tall leader who had perforce to excel in all things. Actually Stalin managed to look taller than they on Lenin's tomb by having a little raised platform built under him.

There is, to be sure, a remnant of Old Bolsheviks among the new "collective leadership." But these older men, Molotov, Voroshilov, Kaganovich, and Mikoyan, owe their places, indeed their very survival, to the fact that they were cronies of Joseph Stalin. Second-string figures in Lenin's day, from the outset faction adherents of Stalin rather than Lenin, they came out of the crucible of the purges refashioned, so to speak, as "new men."

What is collective about this collective leadership and will it continue to be a collective? What can the world expect will be new in the work and ways and aims of these new men who have taken over Stalin's power? And what of continuity? It is these questions that constitute the real problem of the "new look."

In theory it is conceivable that a committee-government, a *Directoire*, a diumvirate, triumvirate, or decemvirate, can wield autocratic, dictatorial, and total power. But the whole course of Soviet history, and the whole dynamic of autocracy, dictatorship, and totalitarianism, are against it.

Lenin began by creating a party in which the Center selected the local committees, which in turn sent delegates to the conventions that confirmed the Center. He seized power by a minority conspiracy, drained democracy of authority by dispersing the Constituent Assembly, drained the soviets of authority by outlawing all other parties and deciding all things in the Communist Central Committee and its factions, drained the party of authority by forbidding factional controversy, the Central Committee by setting up the Politburo, and the Politburo by settling matters by telephone, direct wire, and personal conversation. Inside the Politburo he never altogether sloughed off the appearance of "collegial" power; at his death he left a will in which he sought in vain to preserve that one last redoubt of collectivity.

It took close to a decade before the "collective leadership," of which Stalin appeared but to be the faithful machine wheelhorse, was openly dissolved in favor of his personal power. With his death his lieutenants are faced with the problem that in a dictatorship there is no legitimacy and no legal succession. These men have been taught in a hard school to make many moves in their head before they touch one piece on the chessboard of power. The bloody list of their dead gives them every reason to combine forces against any man who moves too fast. That they would begin their orphaned rule with the proclamation of a "collective leadership" could have been predicted.

That first holding company included Beria who was nominated by Malenkov, and Malenkov who was nominated by Beria. Within a few weeks after Stalin's death, a newspaper buildup which seemed to portend Malenkov's rise to dominant power was put a stop to by some decision of his associates, and he was "relieved" of the post of Party Secretary "at his own request." That brought Khrushchev into a top ranking position as Party Secretary. Beria's undoing came from his too rapid moves to make the secret police independent of the party and through it to strengthen his control of certain "republican governments" and the party machine. This aroused the fears of so many of his associates that, suddenly, they combined against him and there was one "collective leader" less. At this writing, Malenkov would appear to be out in front. But the fact that he has dropped the key organization post in which he was so long Stalin's chief assistant—the post through which Stalin himself rose to power—and that this post is now in Khrushchev's hands, suggests a temporary system of "checks and balances" on each other by the men who together hold unchecked and absolute power.

As long as the power question is not settled and the pyramid of power is without an apex, these men will jealously watch each other and make promises of reforms to their subjects. They will continue Stalin's policy of avoiding either all-out war or all-out peace. They cannot tolerate all-out peace, since the very excuse for the existence of their perpetual state-of-emergency regime is "capitalist encirclement." Like Stalin, they have two reasons for avoiding all-out war. The first is doctrinal: their central belief teaches them that they are the wave of the future, that the capitalist order is in decay, that time is on their side. The other is a readiness to risk war at the periphery, limited engagements, "calculated risks," for in their activist theory History helps only those who help Her, but not to jeopardize their power center, the loss of which in all-out war might change the course of history.

To Stalin's hesitancies they add one more: as long as the power question is not settled, they dare not put live ammunition and overwhelming force in the hands of the army, lest "Bonapartism" settle the problem of power in its own fashion. Thus we would do well to remember that their present minuscule concessions in foreign relations come not only from their calculation that they may divide the free world, isolate America, and cut off her support from some sector of Europe or Asia, but no less from recognition of their own internal weakness. "Collective leadership . . . the Party and the Government . . . the wise Central Committee"—so far they have cast about in vain for an overwhelming power symbol that can paralyze dissent, command obedience and worship in union and empire, such as was commanded by the Stalin cult and Stalin's word and name. The struggle may be muted and concealed, it may be long or short, it may be compromised and blunted again and again, but the whole dynamics of dictatorship cries out for a dictator, autocracy for an autocrat, militarized command and militarized life for a supreme commander, infallible government for an infallible leader, an authoritarian setup for an authority, or totalitarian state for a *duce, führer, vozhd*.

The Stalin cult, whose high priests these men were, has made the problem of the succession more difficult. By attributing to Stalin all successes, and to themselves and their subordinates all failures, shortcomings, or unpleasant consequences, they enlarged his person until it filled the horizon, diminishing their own stature to the point of nullity.

In this swollen form, the Stalin myth was dead as soon as his body was cold. For what right did such dwarfed men have to be individual or collective dictators? Moreover, in the end they were irked by his arrogation to himself of credit for all they did, thought up, ghost-wrote for him, by the precariousness of their positions dependent entirely on the caprice of one man, by the need each day to kindle greater clouds of incense to his name. Their cold funeral addresses, concerned with programs and power, testified to the fact that he had exacted so much "posthumous tribute" while alive that there was no reserve to call on after his death. These historians of the pistol who had rewritten recent history so often and continuously in order to enlarge and glorify Stalin's works and name began immediately a fresh rewriting of history to cut him down to size— not to actual size, but to their own size, so that there could be some sense in their claim to individual or collective succession. Henceforth Lenin is the author of the great theories and the initiator of the great works, and Stalin is reduced to continuator, developer, and disciple. They, for their part, are co-disciples of Lenin and comrades-in-arms of Stalin, and, by virtue of membership in the same leading body, coauthors of all the theories, policies, and plans hitherto called Stalinist.

Many wrongly concluded that the process would not stop until Stalin's name had been extinguished and his policies abandoned. But his orphaned disciples had no intentions of doing one or the other. They cannot extinguish his name, for what other claim do they have to rule the Soviet land except association with Stalin and discipleship to Lenin in an unbroken apostolic succession? Nor do they wish to abandon his policies, for these are in fact their policies no less than his.

In Russia, the death of a despot has always awakened a lively expectation of change. The most unlikely princelings have been endowed with gentle attributes until their acts as tsars dispelled illusion. The greater the despotism, the greater the expectation of change. But only when the death of a despot coincided with some defeat to his system has the expectation as a rule been realized.

When Stalin died, the first reports of a nation all contracted in one brow of woe were soon replaced by more authentic reports of this general expectation of change. We now know that there was ill-concealed rejoicing, that men got drunk, that whole regiments celebrated in Germany, that, even in far-off Vorkuta, concentration-camp inmates turned their hopes into a strike for better conditions and were given concessions even as force was being used and ringleaders executed. Sweeping promises had to be made to the satellites; workingmen struck in East Germany and Czechoslovakia and stood up, unarmed, against Russian tanks. All this exerted powerful pressures upon men whose power position is unsettled and whose succession is based upon neither constitutional nor hereditary legitimacy.

Nor was the free world exempt from illusion. One of Britain's leading authorities on Soviet history rushed out a book to prove that Stalin by barbarous methods had so civilized and transformed Russia that further Stalinist barbarism was impossible. Another stoutly declared that since all thinking was colored by emotion he preferred "wishful rather than despairing thinking." American writers who had once assured us that the "realist and nationalist" Stalin had put an end to Trotsky's dream of world revolution, then that "the wise old realist" was curbing the hotheads of the Politburo, now declared that Stalin had been more than a little mad and that soberer and more realistic heads were taking over power.

Even the wise and wary Churchill, two months after Stalin's death, spoke of a "new regime" and what he hoped was "a change of attitude." He who had alerted America to the Iron Curtain and the need of united defense against aggression now permitted himself to dream that the last great act of his declining years might be a fresh four-power conference like those with Stalin and Roosevelt to settle unsettled things. On October 10 of this year [1954] he put it more soberly: "A year and a half ago, Stalin died, and ever since then I have nourished the hope that there is a new outlook in Russia, a new hope of peaceful coexistence with the Russian nation, and that it is our duty patiently and daringly to make sure whether there is such a chance or not."

In a land where secrecy and power are alike total, every smallest flutter of a leaf is likely to be magnified into the fall of forests. No longer badgered by his patron, Molotov proves a little gayer, makes fresh démarches, and tries altering his formulae without stopping to call up the Kremlin—but without yielding an iota of his essential, stubbornly held position; this is magnified into "concessions," a "new flexibility," evidence that there is real departmentalization and separation of powers. General Zhukov echoes Ambassador Bohlen's toast "to justice"; on the stubborn iteration is built an entire structure of fantasy: army independence, army paramountcy, open conflict between army and party. Khrushchev hangs back for a last word when his comrades are departing from a state banquet; this is reported as evidence that the Party Secretary is "an amiable chatter-box . . . garrulous . . . hail-fellow-well-met." Malenkov picks flowers for an English lady, clinks a lady's glass and toasts "the ladies," and the new Premier becomes a bashful fat boy, "full of old-fashioned grace and courtesy . . . a Little Lord Fauntleroy." Hence it becomes important to inquire how new these new men really are.

Khrushchev, the "amiable chatter-box" who now heads the party machine, began the really important part of his biography in 1929 with the great forced collectivization drive in the Ukraine and the mass liquidation of all who held back. Then in Moscow he took part in the *Yezhov-shchina*, without garrulousness contributing his share to the organization of the great blood purge. During the war he directed partisan warfare behind the German occupier's lines, visiting punishment on waverers and collaborators. He is credited with having strengthened Russia's support among the masses by acts calculated to increase the cruelty of the Germans, and with giving orders to assassinate the gentler puppet mayors and spare the crueler ones, as the best way of inflaming opposition to the occupiers.[2] After the war Khrushchev returned to the Ukraine as liquidator of small private landholdings, collectivizer, industrializer, Russifier, and avenger. This "chatter-box" worked quietly for a year and a half, then reported that "in the past 18 months more than 50 percent of all officials" had been removed from their posts. In 1950 he opened the war on the collective farm in favor of the development of "agro-cities." There were resistance, local criticisms by Aryutinyan in Armenia and Bagirov in Azerbaijan, partial retreat. But the number of collective farms was reduced from 250,000 in 1950 to 94,000 in 1953. And when Beria fell, Aryutinyan and Bagirov, Khrushchev's critics of 1950, fell too. At the Nineteenth Congress, Khrushchev delivered the report on the revision of the party statutes which represented a further tightening of totalitarian controls. Since Stalin's death, he has become First Secretary of the Party, and heads the new drives in agriculture.

As for Premier Malenkov, he began his career as Secretary of the Communist cell of the Moscow Higher Technical School, where he gathered around him the Saburovs, Pervukhins, and Malyshevs who switched like him from engineering to politics, becoming engineer-chekists, party commissars in technology and industry.[3] It is on the entrance of these engineer-chekist associates of Malenkov into the ruling circle that so many commentators have based the contention that party rule is now giving ground to the claims of the new technocracy. But these men are instruments of party penetration into and control of technology, just as Bulganin is not a military general who has gotten into the Politburo but an agent of the party and the police made Marshal and Minister of Defense to control the army.

In 1934 Malenkov became chief of the Department of Leading Party Organs, which had charge of placements, removals, dossiers. In the bloody years of the *Yezhovshchina*, he was the chief organizer of the purges in so far as they had a planned, centralized, and systematic party character. As Yezhov advanced, Malenkov was made his deputy in this department, supplying the dossiers and the indications as to chain reactions when any leading official fell. In December 1937, *Partiinoe Stroitel'stvo*, which Malenkov edited, carried the following lead editorial:

> Under the leadership of the Stalinist People's Commissar, Comrade Yezhov, the Soviet Intelligence Service has inflicted merciless and devastating blows on the Fascist bandits. The Soviet people love their intelligence service . . . it is their flesh and blood. . . . The faithful guardians of Socialism, the men of the NKVD under the leadership of their Stalinist People's Commissar, Comrade Yezhov, will continue in the future to root out the enemies of the people, the vile

Trotskyite-Bukharinite, bourgeois-nationalist, and other agents of Fascism. Let the spies and traitors tremble! The punitive hand of the Soviet people, and NKVD, will annihilate them! Our ardent Bolshevik greetings to the Stalinist Commissar of Internal Affairs, Nikolai Ivanovich Yezhov!

The troika that planned the purges under Joseph Stalin's personal direction was made up of Malenkov, keeper of the dossiers and supplier of leads, Vyshinsky, prosecutor and impresario of staged trials, and Yezhov, apprehender, inquisitor and executioner. When the fury had run its course, Yezhov was made expiatory goat, but Malenkov and Vyshinsky were promoted. The year Yezhov disappeared, Malenkov was made head of the new Administration of Party Cadres which "keeps a strict personal register of every party member and candidate" in some 2,500,000 dossiers on standing, public and private life, friends, talents, vulnerabilities, along with dossiers on perhaps 500,000 specialists in industry and agriculture. It is this key index which Malenkov has now surrendered, reluctantly I would imagine, to Party Secretary Khrushchev. In any case, Malenkov's connection with the *Yezhovshchina* should help us to keep our perspective on this "Little Lord Fauntleroy."

Thanks to our penchant for personalizing and the impact even on us of the Stalin cult, we are prone to forget that Stalin did not work out his policies alone. When the informed think of the Stalinist agricultural policy, they think of Khrushchev. When they think of the Stalinist line in literature and intellectual life, they think of Zhdanov, and, after his death, of Malenkov. In short, the Stalinist leadership was also a "collective leadership," with the difference that there was one top man who must always be credited, could never be blamed, and who had the sometimes arbitrary and capricious and always decisive last word.

Finding all about them the general expectation of change, faced with uncertainty as to their own authority and structure of succession, anxious to prevent "confusion and panic" (as the funeral ceremonies declared), the henchmen of the dead dictator were glad to take advantage of the credit opened to them on the theory that they were "new" men from whom a "change" could be expected. Yet one of their prime motives in cutting Stalin down to their size was to emphasize that all of them ("the Party and the Central Committee"), not Stalin alone, were the authors of the "great" policies and doctrines. They even denied, and we know that they did so rightly, that Stalin was the author of the *Short Course*, first published as the work of a collective and then arrogated to Stalin as his "Volume XVI." And we are compelled to admit that the liquidation of Beria and consorts was in the best "Stalinist" tradition.

The releasing of a few Soviet-born wives; gracious toasts at banquets; less surliness in conversation; repetition, as a rule in the self-same language, of the calculated utterances of Lenin and Stalin on "peaceful coexistence"—only on the background of Soviet truculence could this be taken as something significant. And then only if we permit ourselves to forget how many times this ebb and flow in the realization of an unchanging long-range aim has occurred before, either when internal weakness or too quick a build-up of resistance abroad, or the desire to cover an offensive with an umbrella of peace talk, has prompted Stalin to roar you gentle as any sucking dove.

This is not the place to go through the long history of "peaceful coexistence." We can trace various facets back to Lenin's declaration in October 1915 that if he got power he would propose an unacceptable peace and "prepare a revolutionary war"; to Trotsky's pronouncement two weeks after they took power ("We desire the speediest peace on the principles of honorable coexistence and cooperation of peoples; we desire the speediest overthrow of the rule of capital"); to Lenin's 1920 coexistence statement to a Hearst reporter followed the same year by a warning to the Moscow party cell leaders (kept secret till after his death) that "as long as capitalism and Socialism exist side by side we cannot live in peace"; to Litvinov's 1922 proposal of a "proportional reduction in arms" at a time when the Soviet Union was secretively arming with the aid of the Wehrmacht. The whole sequence of these utterances from the first down to Malenkov's amiable chat with Ambassador Bohlen and Congressman Wickersham while Migs were shooting down one of our planes boils down to this: divide and disarm your opponents while you work unceasingly for their destruction.

Nor is there anything these "new" men have so far done that would not accord with the last programmatic utterance on foreign policy by Joseph Stalin (in "Economic Problems of Socialism in the U.S.S.R.," 1952) in which he urged that through the "peace fight" they could undermine "bellicose governments," perhaps develop it into "a movement for the overthrow of capitalism," make more likely war between capitalist countries than between the non-Soviet and the Soviet worlds, and isolate the United States. ("To think that Germany, Britain, France, Italy and Japan . . . will not try to smash U.S. domination and force their way to independent development is to believe in miracles.")

The main foreign policy proposals were summed up this year by Marshal Bulganin in his speech delivered on November 7:

1. "A collective security system in Europe," i.e., Europe with Russia but without the United States.

2. German unification by "peaceful means," i.e., the continued dis-

arming of Germany and the holding of "elections" such as have been proposed in Korea, and practiced so resourcefully in the "peaceful unification" of all postwar satellite coalition governments.

3. Proportionate reduction of armaments, which would leave overwhelming superiority to the heavily armed Soviet Bloc; and "prohibition of weapons of mass extermination," which would eliminate the one weapon in which the free world has superiority, without the guarantees of a foolproof control and inspection.

The only thing one can find that is new in this third of a century of juggling with "peaceful coexistence" is that leading spokesmen of the free world are beginning to employ the term without sufficient attempt to analyze it and purify it of the corruption which infects it. Since for the free world peace is a matter of principle and for the Kremlin a calculated maneuver, surely our spokesmen should be able to express our desire for peace in some warmer and less tarnished language. It is up to us to remember that the Kremlin's tactical maneuvers can be most flexible because they are severely disciplined by an overall strategy and unshakeable objective of world conquest. But we can get lost in these tactical zigzags if our overall objective is lost sight of. I cannot believe that that objective is merely to survive while peace is steadily eroded and the more vulnerable parts of the free world picked off one by one. Our idea of peace is wrapped up with justice and with freedom, and is ultimately secure only to the extent that freedom can defend itself and that peoples everywhere gain control of their governmental policies. To take these corrupt words and artful maneuvers at face value is but to add to the confusion and moral disarming which is one of its objectives.

"Peaceful coexistence" has a long history now; in the words of Santayana, "those who will not learn from history are condemned to repeat it."

Of the new line in the arts and letters it is no longer necessary to speak. After the illusions nourished by Stalin's death and the first indecisions of the new men not yet sure of their power, a Second Congress of Soviet Writers is being called that promises to be more of a straitjacket than the First Congress held two decades ago. Furious attacks on Pomerantsev for saying the obvious thing that sincerity, honesty to the truth of his own vision, is the chief virtue of the artist have been followed by rebukes and expulsion for magazine editors, condemnation of critics, expulsion of Stalin-Prize writers from the fraternity of their craft, condemnation of all who thought there was a new "thaw." Such is the atmosphere in which is being prepared a Congress which will "systematically combat any deviations from the principle of Socialist Realism . . . any attempts to direct Soviet literature away from topical questions of the policy of the Party and Soviet State . . . any attempt to substitute a moral criterion unrelated to any specific society or time for the ideological, class-social judgments universally recognized in our literature . . . which can have no other interests but those of the people, the interest of the Soviet State."

In Stalin's last and most significant theoretical work, "The Economic Problems of Socialism in the U.S.S.R.," published late in 1952, he lays down the prerequisites for the transformation of the present "Socialist" Russia into "complete Communism." In this work is to be found literally the whole stock of formulae on which Malenkov, Khrushchev, and Company are now proceeding. Here is to be found the proposal rapidly to increase the satisfaction of consumer demand on the basis of "primacy in the production of means of production." Here is the outline of the drive to increase labor discipline on the basis of "the control over the amount of labor and the amount of consumption" until labor discipline is transformed into spontaneous self-discipline, from an "obligation into a prime necessity of life." Here, too, is the line on isolating America and promoting differences in the capitalist camp which we have already examined. The work is scrappy and fragmentary, but bears internal evidence of summing up in algebraic formulae all the trains of thought that were then actuating Stalin and his close associates.

In it Stalin distinguishes between two kinds of property in the present-day Soviet Union: "State, or publicly-owned production, and collective-farm production, which cannot be said to be publicly owned." The main task of the transition to communism which is now beginning is to "raise the level" of collective farm property to that of state or publicly owned property, and to create thus a "single and united" system. How "the formation of a single and united sector" is to be brought about "whether simply by the swallowing up of the collective-farm sector by the state sector . . . or by the setting up of a single national economic body," Stalin refuses to say. But he is emphatic that it can be done by the pressure of the "superstructure," the state, "upon the relations of production," that it can be done "without upheavals," that it represents a revolution from above, and that it must be undertaken gradually but without delay, that "it is of paramount importance for us," that in the process "the new" will not "simply destroy the old, but infiltrates into it, changes its nature and function without smashing its form." Until it is accomplished, the state has not as complete control of agriculture as of industry and is hampered in its precise planning and calculation. "It would be unpardonable not to see that these factors are already beginning to fetter the powerful development of our productive forces since they create obstacles to the full extension of government planning to the whole of the national economy, especially agriculture. . . . The task therefore is to eliminate these contradictions by gradually converting collective-farm property into public (state) property. . . ."

To this subject Stalin devotes more space and attention than to any other, and returns again and again. And in this, I think, we can find the theoretical foundation and the emotional force behind the latest Khrushchev-Malenkov drive for a revolution in agriculture. What was the drive to uproot the collective farms and combine them into agrogorods, begun in Stalin's lifetime, but an attempt to "raise collective-farm property to the level of public property . . . to infiltrate it, change its nature and function without smashing its form"? Does their opposition to what they thought only a personal project of Khrushchev explain why Beria fell into disfavor during Stalin's last days, and help explain why the agrogorod critics, Aryutunyan and Bagirov, fell with Beria? And what is the new plowing up of steppe, pasture, marginal and abandoned lands in Kazakhstan, Siberia, and other distant parts of the empire, with "volunteers" from the cities, but a new mass flank attack upon the recalcitrant collective farm?

Like any flanking movement, it has been presented with dissimulation as a fresh attempt to solve the problem of the shortage of grain and meat (cattle) created by the earlier revolution from above, the collectivization drive of the thirties. Like that drive it suffers from gigantism, recklessness, and lack of preparation. Like the earlier drive its shock troops come not from the farmers but from the cities. These young men and women may have no preparation for farming, but neither have they any loyalty to the collective and the private parcel or any memory of the days of individual farming. What is this mass displacement of young men and women and tractors and seeds to virgin or untilled lands but a gigantic step on the road that bypasses the kolkhoz and presents it with a rival in a new congeries of giant sovkhozes or state farms?

Of the 32 million acres of virgin soil to be brought under cultivation during 1954–55, 15.8 million acres are located in Kazakhstan. Without a word being said of it, the over 140,000 workers who have been "volunteered" into the new regions represent one more invasion in the long war against the Asiatic steppe, and its nomadic, cattle-raising, Turkic peoples. This war was not begun by the Bolsheviks but by the tsars. But the drive for forced collectivization of the early thirties hit hardest in individual-farming Ukraine and in cattle-raising Kazakhstan. In the latter, where the nomads follow the grass on the range, the wholesale slaughter of stock reached catastrophic proportions from which, as Khrushchev's reports show, Russia has not yet recovered in more than two decades. According to Khrushchev, the number of cattle in the Soviet Union in 1953 was below that of 1916 (last year of the tsars and in the midst of world war), and less than 1928 (before the collectivization drive began). But since 1928 there has been an enormous increase in population and in area so that the amount of meat, butter, milk, hides, as well as grain, per capita has frightfully diminished.

There is already a serious labor shortage on the old collective farms and a serious shortage of machines, but as in the earlier experiments in gigantism and revolution from above, everything is being thrown into the battle so that the old areas are being stripped of machines, and seed, and technicians, and hands, while the new lack drinking water, irrigation, housing, sanitation, food, tractors, and seed. Lands are being plowed up that are marginal. If the rains are good—this year they have been good— the lands will yield. When bad years come—and it is their semi-aridity that make them range rather than farm areas—they are likely to become dustbowls. There are deep inconsistencies in the promises of more meat on the one hand and the planned figures for increased cattle breeding on the other, and between both of these and the plowing up of the range. But as in the collectivization drive of the early thirties, Khrushchev and Malenkov in the best Stalinist tradition are counting that there is "no fortress that Bolshevik determination cannot conquer," that the "super-structure" (the state) can "without upheavals" force changes in "productive relations." While they are at it, they hope to solve the nationalities problem in the Turkic areas by mass Russification, and present the incompletely calculable and incompletely plannable kolkhoz sector with a completely controlled sector of new state farms.

To sum up. The "new men" who have succeeded to Stalin's power are not so new as they look to the uninquisitive eye, for they are Stalin's men. And a good look at the "new look" suggests that it is not so new either, for more than Stalin would admit or they dared to claim, while he was alive, they worked out the Stalinist policies with him. Now that he is dead they have been able to cut the losses of some of the minor errors with which his stubbornness or prestige had become involved, but all their major policies from "peaceful coexistence" to the sensational plowing up of the virgin lands are in accord with plans elaborated and drives initiated while Stalin was alive. They do but give "arithmetical values" to "algebraic formulae" already worked out in the decisions of the Nineteenth Congress and in Stalin's so-called testament, "Economic Problems of Socialism in the U.S.S.R." What the "new" men bring to their drives is the fresh vigor of younger men and a fresh flexibility in maneuver. But they are manifestly continuing the war on their own people—"the revolution from above"—and the war for the control of the world.

14

Stalin's Ghost at the Party Congress

When his Father Confessor asked Narvaez on his deathbed, "General, have you forgiven your enemies?" the General answered, "I have no enemies. I had them shot." So Joseph Stalin might have answered, too, had he believed in deathbed confession for himself, as he did for his victims. Yet one cannot have all one's enemies shot, for they grow by a chain reaction: each gap filled by tens and hundreds who knew, loved, believed in, or identified themselves with the executed. This was doubtless one of the reasons for the six hours and ten minutes of silence of Stalin's heirs before they announced his death.

What debates and deals went on in those terrifying six hours we can only conjecture. But the announcement, when it came, was not so much a lamentation as an anxious call to collective leadership, orderly succession, monolithic unity, the avoidance of *razbrod i panika*, "confusion and panic."

The earliest post-Stalin issue of the party's leading organ of theory, *Kommunist* (No. 4, March 9, 1953), declared that the party's greatest strength lay in "collective work, collective leadership and monolithic unity." And on April 16, *Pravda* invoked some of Stalin's own words to denounce leaders who "decide important questions individually, without consulting members of the bureaus." Thus, even before his corpse was cold, the orphaned sons of the Father of the Peoples began to wrestle with his ghost. But laying a ghost is not so simple, especially when the exorcists are his accomplices, and his heirs.

A party congress is supposed to be the "supreme body" of the Com-

Reprinted with permission from *Foreign Affairs* (July 1956)

munist party. It picks the executive, lays down the line, exacts responsibilities. But even in Lenin's day, the congress had been drained of its sovereign powers.

Though Lenin always kept up some consultation with others ("collective leadership"), he was possessed of a selfless egoism which enabled him at all times to identify his own views with the correct line and the truth. In the years of exile abroad, he personally selected a little group of followers, usually two, to form a troika. With them he laid down the line, edited the central organ, directed the groups abroad and the underground inside Russia. Whenever these triumvirs disagreed with him, he excommunicated them, or if need be seceded himself, to set up a new troika. Wherever two or three were gathered together with Lenin, there was bolshevism.

His devotion to centralism and his theory of an elite party both precluded any real devolution of power. A leadership of classless professional revolutionaries was to set up a guardianship over the working class, then take power in its name. Since anything done by his "vanguard" party in the name of the workers was, according to his theory, done by the workers themselves, it became all-important to him that no other party be permitted to call itself "proletarian." That explains the fury with which he branded every other Socialist party as "bourgeois" or "petit-bourgeois," as he did such factions in his own party as the Workers Opposition, which challenged his line and methods in the name of the working class itself.

Lenin's centralism led him to appoint the organizers who went to the localities; these returned in due course as delegates to a congress to confirm the Center which had appointed them. Where this would lead was foreseen as early as 1904 by the then-twenty-three-year-old Leon Trotsky: "The Organization of the Party will take the place of the Party itself; the Central Committee will take the place of the Organization; and finally, the Dictator will take the place of the Central Committee."

And so it came to pass . . . though when he joined fortunes with Lenin in 1917, Trotsky became himself an arch centralist. It is instructive to remember the order: *Party . . . Central Committee . . . Organization . . . Dictator.* Stalin, Malenkov, and Khrushchev each in turn has had his hands on the ultimate power lever—the Organization, or, as we would say, the party machine.

Once in power, Lenin drained the Central Committee of political life by settling important matters in the Politburo, or the Orgburo, or impromptu gatherings of whichever leaders happened to be at hand when a problem arose. At the Tenth Congress in 1921, he outlawed the Workers Opposition and other critical groups, pushed through a statute forbidding factions and the raising of platforms even during congress discussion and election periods, and had a secret decision adopted permitting the expulsion of Central Committee members elected by a congress, without recourse to a subsequent congress. Thereby the congress was drained of real political life and became a rubber stamp. When the new "collective leadership" proclaims that Lenin's greatest service "to Marxism and to mankind" was "the creation of a Party of a new type" (*Pravda*, April 22, 1956) and when they launch the slogan, "Back to Leninist norms of Party leadership," these are the type of party and the norms they have in mind.[1]

From the Eleventh Congress on, with Lenin's active approval of the first two purges, every party congress was prepared by a prior purge of dissidents, a procedure assuring a majority for the line and leadership of the Center. After Lenin's death, congresses became more and more infrequent. One was delayed until Trotsky had been beaten; another until Zinoviev and Kamenev had been crushed; yet another until Bukharin, Rykov, and Tomsky had had their strongholds taken from them.

Even after he had secured 100 percent unanimity, Stalin prepared each congress with a purge. Thus the Seventeenth (1934) was a unanimous celebration of his victory, at which he handpicked a "Stalinist Central Committee." Yet as the congress adjourned, the great purge was getting under way in which the "servant of the Central Committee," aided by a handful of natural deaths, was to eliminate all but 20 out of 124 Central Committee members and candidates. After the Eighteenth Congress in 1939 he did not trouble to hold a congress for thirteen years. The Nineteenth, often announced and always postponed, was held only in 1952, shortly before his death.

At Stalin's death, the "collective leadership" was headed by a troika: Malenkov, Beria, Molotov. An operation buildup began at once for Malenkov as "Head of the Party and the Government."

But nine days after Stalin's death, Malenkov was removed from control of the party machine "at his own request." And in February 1955 he confessed to errors ("my guilt and responsibility for the unsatisfactory state of affairs in agriculture") which could only have been committed by Khrushchev, and to "insufficient experience in local work . . . and in the direct guidance of individual branches of the national economy." At "his own request" he was relieved of the premiership, too, and made Minister of Electric Power Stations. This ended the succession claims of triumvir No. 1.

On June 26, 1953, Lavrenti Beria was arrested. He was "tried" according to "Socialist legality": without definite charges (at least four different official versions have been published); without being present or represented by attorney; before a Supreme Court which illegally included only one Supreme Court justice, the other "judges" being two generals, two trade union officials, a party official, a Deputy Minister of the Interior and the president of the Moscow City Court. Although he was not present, it was reported that he "confessed." Within twenty-four hours of the "trial" he was shot, made a retroactive imperialist agent, and then an unperson. Subscribers to the *Encyclopedia* received a letter instructing them to remove his picture and accompanying text and paste in their place an article on the Bering Sea. Thus ended triumvir No. 2.

In September 1955, Molotov confessed that he did not know socialism when he saw it. On June 1, 1956, "at his own request," he was relieved of the post of Foreign Minister. The third of the triumvirs was through.

When Malenkov "requested" his removal as General Secretary, Khrushchev became de facto the boss of the party machine. In due course he was named First Secretary and began reorganizing the powerful Secretariat by adding men of his own choosing.

The proverb "Knowledge is power" having been reversed by totalitarianism to read "Power is knowledge," Khrushchev now began to exhibit mastery of every field. He told architects how to design a building; constructors how to use concrete and prefabricated units; managers how to apply technology; urban youth where to invest their energy and enthusiasm; farmers where corn must, should, and would have to grow and why the range must be ploughed up; cotton growers why they should eat rice instead of potatoes; milkmaids how many times a day they should milk a cow; artists what are the proper proportions of sincerity and Party spirit in the arts. At the same time he became the authority on foreign affairs. With Bulganin, and often with Mikoyan or Shepilov, he went to Warsaw and Prague, China, Yugoslavia, Geneva, East Germany, India, Burma, and Afghanistan in his pre-Congress buildup. He has since been to England and has broadly hinted at his readiness to visit the United States. Thus during all this time Molotov was Foreign Minister in name only.

The humiliation of the troika and the execution of Beria were but the first stage of the purges that prepared the Twentieth Congress. In July 1955 the congress was announced and its date set for February 14, 1956, at which time it actually convened. A whirlwind of activity prepared its monolithic unanimity.

Simultaneously with the call, two new members were introduced into the Presidium: Suslov of the Central Committee Secretariat, and Kirichenko, First Secretary of the Communist party of the Ukraine. These were added not by the "sovereign" Congress, but six months before; both were known as Khrushchev men. At the same time, three new secretaries were added to Khrushchev's Secretariat: Aristov, Belyayev, and Shepilov, also Khrushchev men. Then or later, Shatalin, a Malenkov follower, disappeared from the roster of secretaries.

That same July began changes in party secretaries and other high officials in all republics, provinces, regions, and industrial centers. In a few cases, Khrushchev personally superintended the change; more often he sent Aristov, Chief of Cadres of the Central Committee Administrative Apparatus. These purges have been mere demotions and transfers without the shedding of blood, except among security police officials and in Georgia, where a continuous blood purge has been going on from that day to this. All the changes can be summed up in the general formula: key officials 100 percent faithful to the "collective leadership" have been replaced by others more than 100 percent faithful—that is, by Khrushchev's men. They in turn have been changing their subordinates so that the changeover has been filtering down and is still continuing. As late as February 1, Kruglov, Minister of the Interior, was replaced by the Khrushchev follower, Dudorov. This process was climaxed at the congress itself, where the Central Committee was "renovated" in similar fashion. Out of 255 members and alternates of the incoming Central Committee, 113, or more than 44 percent, are new. Of the 44 percent that disappeared in the process, Khrushchev had this to say: "Bolshevik criticism, without regard to persons . . . included a number of members of the Central Committee. A number . . . not having justified the high confidence placed in them by the Party were dropped from the Central Committee. Is it necessary to prove that the unity of the Party did not lose by that but only gained?"

No one thought it was necessary.

The congress left no doubt that the First Secretary was "more equal than the others." Opening Address, Khrushchev; Report (on everything), Khrushchev; Chairman of the Resolutions Committee, Khrushchev; Chairman of the newly created bureau for coordinating party affairs in the Russian Republic, Khrushchev; Closing Address, Khrushchev; secret report on Stalin's ghost, Khrushchev. The other addresses, even Bulganin's, were but glosses on *the* report made by Khrushchev. It took Joseph Stalin three or four congresses of "collective leadership" before he got to that point of complete domination of a congress.

There are reasons for this haste. Khrushchev is sixty-two, while Stalin got his hand on the main power lever when he was more than fifteen years younger. Moreover, the later it is repeated in history, the faster a process, once learned, can go. It took Stalin more than a decade of experimentation before he could engineer his first trial, confession, and execution such as was worked on Beria within less than a year after Stalin's demise. Nor is Khrushchev surrounded by a galaxy of stars such as surrounded Stalin. Finally, the new First Secretary had no "theoretical work" to his credit, his seven-hour report to the congress constituting his first claim to the role of interpreter and infallible repository of sacred doctrine.

One has only to compare Stalin's last congress with Khrushchev's first to become aware of the latter's sense of urgency. At the Nineteenth Congress, the Opening Address was by Molotov; the Report of the Central Committee, Malenkov; on the Nationality Question, Beria; on the Fifth Five-Year Plan, Saburov; on Party Statutes, Mikoyan, Khrushchev, and Bulganin; on Program, Kaganovich; on Political Education, Suslov; Closing Address, Voroshilov. Stalin signed the basic document, "Economic Problems of Socialism in the U.S.S.R." Published on the eve of the congress, it was glossed and celebrated by every speaker. Stalin spoke for ten minutes to the foreign delegations, laying down some general policy lines. The aging *vozhd*, secure in his patriarchal dominion over the dwarfed and terrorized sons, could allow far more semblance of "collective leadership" than could the parvenu leader on his anxious way up.

So long as a congress was supposed to lay down the line, both its function and the statutes made it an annual affair. As soon as it was reduced to a "monolith," it became a matter of convenience whether it was summoned or not. Stalin delayed his last congress for thirteen years; then the statutory term was made four years. But the post-Stalin leadership needed a congress to confirm it in office and to serve as a sounding board. They did not wait out the four years but held the Twentieth Congress three and one-half years after the Nineteenth. As a "sounding board" it must be pronounced the most successful of congresses.

Collective Leadership

Though Khrushchev had emerged as factotum and had openly played that role since the resignation of Malenkov, the slogan of "collective leadership" got all the headlines. Few seemed to remember that under the same slogan Lenin had run his personal dictatorship. Or that Stalin posed as plain wheelhorse of the "collective leadership" during four congresses, from 1923, when illness put Lenin out of action, to 1929, when the "cult of personality" began. Or that the new "collective leadership" with Khrushchev at its head had already announced at least thirty executions from Beria to Bagirov, whereas Stalin did not kill the first of his close comrades until he had held de facto power for a decade and sole power as *vozhd* for a half decade more. Stalin had made people so used to bloodshed that observers could not get over the fact that, though Beria be dead, Malenkov is still alive. Yet it was Stalin who entered the lists against bloodshed of comrades at the Fourteenth Congress: "The Party cannot be led without Rykov, without Kalinin, without Tomsky, without Molotov, without Bukharin. . . . We did not agree with Comrades Zinoviev and Kamenev [on the expulsion of Trotsky]. . . . The method of lopping off, the method of bloodletting . . . is dangerous and contagious. Today you lop off one limb; tomorrow another, the day after a third—and what is left of the Party?"

In the end Stalin was to verify the truth of his prophecy: bloodletting was to assume such vast, capricious, and paranoiac proportions that it is hard to believe that purges on such a scale will ever be repeated by his successors. Still that is no reason for forgetting Stalin's long "collective leadership" period; nor the speed with which the new leadership has "confessed" and executed Beria and twenty-nine others; nor the obvious fact that it was not Molotov or Mikoyan but Beria who was the main target of Stalin's charge of "lack of police vigilance" in the "doctors' plot." The present hue and cry about Beria is intended to cover up the fact that in this respect Khrushchev and Company have carried out Stalin's behest in a truly "Stalinist manner."

The New Men

Looked at closely, the new men turn out not to be so new. The Presidium of eleven contains seven of Stalin's old nine-man Politburo (all that are left now that Stalin and Beria are dead); plus two, Pervukhin and Saburov, added by Stalin at the Nineteenth Congress; plus two from Khrushchev's Secretariat, Suslov and Kirichenko, added not by a congress but six months before that "sovereign body" met. In short, the Presidium consists of Stalin's men plus Khrushchev's men.

The candidate members (alternates), however, with the exception of Shvernik, are new. Most important of these is Zhukov. His rise, like so many of the events publicized by the congress, did not begin there but immediately on Stalin's death. The first reshuffle found him returned from semi-rustication to a key post in the Defense Ministry. His programmatic speeches on military policy and on World War II, his place in *Pravda* pictures and high functions, his pointed toast "To Justice" made in the presence of Ambassador Bohlen, all told the observer that he had become part of the top leadership, even before the congress gave him the title of "first" Candidate Member. His rise would appear to be due to the lack of any other popular figure among Stalin's heirs; to the importance of the armed forces in international "diplomacy"; to the dependence of

Khrushchev and Company on the army when they seized and executed Beria. Marshal Zhukov has been a party member since 1920, but he is a professional field general in whose party loyalty there is undoubtedly some room for an army esprit de corps. He is regarded as a prime mover in the drive to rewrite the history of the war in a way which will downgrade Stalin and give the field generals their due, and in the drive to rehabilitate the five thousand officers who disappeared in the Tukhachevsky purge. When he spoke at the congress, he was one of the few prominent leaders who did not praise reporter Khrushchev or his report by name. The texture of his speech made it clear that one of his functions is to cover with the mantle of his popularity the new demands which the return to the Stalinist line of "priority of heavy industry" will make upon the people. Indeed, he gave a good working definition of that slogan when he declared: "The great achievements of heavy industry have made possible the rearming of our army, navy and air force with first-class military equipment."

In a regime based on absolute force, the army has become more important with the downgrading of the police. It is impossible to tell how many in the leading bodies are really *Chekists* (like Bulganin, for instance, who has been in the *Cheka* since 1918 and is an army Marshal only by virtue of being chief of the party's special section for watching and controlling the army); but the open practitioners of the profession have suffered diminution: three who were in the Central Committee were shot with Beria; three failed of reelection; and only three are on the new committee. These include Dudorov, not a professional policeman but Khrushchev's appointee as Minister of the Interior; Lunev, Deputy Minister and one of Beria's "judges"; and Serov, Chairman of the Committee of State Security. For the first time in party history there is no representative of the Security Forces on the Presidium. But Serov's name should reassure those who fear lack of "vigilance," for he acquired international renown when he took over the Baltic Republics and prepared lists of suspects, not by deeds, but—totalitarian fashion—by categories. His eleven suspect categories included Esperantists and philatelists. The man is thorough.

Khrushchev made sure that the need for strong security and "vigilance" would be understood. In his report to the congress he set down the limits to the "rehabilitation" of corpses:

> Our Party is more monolithic than ever . . . [its] unity has been
> built up over years and decades of struggle . . . with Trotskyites,
> Bukharinites, bourgeois nationalists, and others of the worst
> enemies of the people, champions of the restoration of capitalism. . . .

> Great attention has been and is being given by the Central Committee to the strengthening of socialist legality. . . . It is necessary to say that in connection with the revision and cancellation of a number of verdicts some comrades have begun to exhibit a certain lack of confidence towards the workers in the organs of State Security. This is wrong and harmful. . . . Our Chekists in their overwhelming majority are honest workers devoted to our cause, and we have confidence in these cadres. . . .

> Capitalist encirclement has sent in among us not a few spies and wreckers. It would be naïve to suppose that now the enemies will cease their efforts. . . . Therefore, we must in every way strengthen revolutionary vigilance . . . and the organs of State Security.

There is evidence of friction between the career generals and the political administration of the army, whose top figure is Bulganin. Brezhnev, added to the Presidium candidates as a Khrushchev man (his last job was as party overseer for ploughing up the range in Kazakhstan) is also a political general, and thus a counterweight to Zhukov. But there has been a clean sweep of political army officials from the Central Committee. This, too, suggests that, with the execution of Beria, Khrushchev and Bulganin became more dependent upon the army.

If Zhukov is no Khrushchev man, all the other new Presidium candidates are: Brezhnev (already identified); Furtseva, who accompanied Khrushchev to Peking and comes from his Moscow apparatus; Mukhitdinov, whom he designated as First Secretary in Uzbekistan for the drives to plough up the range and increase the cotton yield; Shepilov, from the Central Committee *Agitprop*, a secretary under Khrushchev since last July and now Foreign Minister.

For the first time there is no Georgian on the leading bodies. Historically, Georgia has furnished leaders to both wings of Russian socialism: Jordania, Tsereteli, Chkheidze, to Menshevism; Stalin, Yenukidze, Ordjonikidze, Beria, to bolshevism. The new boss of Georgia, Mzhavanadze, is a *Chekist* who served under Khrushchev in the Ukraine, a second-string figure. This downgrading of the proud Georgians was at the bottom of the recent Tiflis disorders. On the other hand, many Ukrainians from Khrushchev's old machine have been advanced to higher posts in Secretariat, Presidium, Central Committee, and army.

One aspect of the "new" leadership that has been little discussed is its age. Khrushchev is sixty-two. His associates, except Malenkov, Pervukhin, and Saburov, are in their sixties or seventies. The party, too, thanks to a restriction on new admissions, has been permitted to grow older. Its growth between the Nineteenth and Twentieth congresses has barely kept pace with the growth of the general population. And the congresses have "aged" faster than the party. At the Eighteenth Congress, 1.8 percent of the delegates were over fifty; at the Nineteenth, 15.3 percent; and at the Twentieth, 24 percent were over fifty years of age.[2] Though Stalin killed off almost the entire generation of Old Bolsheviks and of civil war veterans, so that these two categories form only 6 percent of the party, they have seven out of eleven members of the Presidium. Even if we assume that Khrushchev has won a secure hold on the top post, the problem of the succession is bound to arise again, and with it the problem of the aging party, the aged leadership, the rising generation knocking on the door.

The Stalinist Economic Line

Although more than nine-tenths of all discussion at the Congress was on economic questions, the newspapers had almost nothing to say on this.

When the heirs were newly orphaned and less sure of themselves, they flirted with the idea of a "rapid increase in consumer goods" on the foundation of the "priority of heavy industry." This slight turn, which came to be identified with the name of Malenkov, was abandoned about the time of Malenkov's fall. The subsequent reversal overcompensated for the brief "softening" so that the priority given to heavy industry for the power and military might of the state is now more "Stalinist" than in Stalin's day.

The same is true of agriculture. During the entire postwar period, Stalin's chief overseer for agriculture was none other than Khrushchev. In 1948 Khrushchev wrote: "We must bear in mind that the "little worm" of individual property still sits in the mind of the *kolkhoznik*. Now as in the past, the most important vestigial residue of capitalism in the consciousness of the *kolkhoz* peasantry is the tendency to private property. This tendency . . . is a great hindrance to the rapid restoration and accumulation of capital by the communal economy . . . [it is] directed against the correct balance between the interests of the state, the *kolkhoz* and the *kolkhoznik* peasant."

The purposes of the Khrushchev drive are to destroy the "little worm" represented by the private parcel, to uproot the kolkhozes built around ancient village nests of solidarity and to combine them into larger and larger units—so few and so large that each can be policed by its own Machine-Tractor Station, have a Communist as chairman and be infiltrated by a Communist cell. On January 1, 1950, there were 254,000 kolkhozes; by the Nineteenth Congress (October 1952), they had been reduced to 97,000; by the Twentieth, to 87,371. With this drive came the growth of Party units in the amalgamated kolkhozes so that now only 8.4 percent of them are without such units. Within the past year alone 30,000 urban Communists were sent to kolkhozes to be *"elected"* their chairmen.

When the hand of Stalin was removed, Khrushchev added a fresh agricultural revolution from above—in ploughing up the new lands, sending city Communists to till the new areas and setting up sovkhozes (state farms) instead of kolkhozes (collective farms). To this he added the drive for corn.

But it was when the Twentieth Congress had adjourned that Khrushchev delivered the keenest thrust of all. In 1933, Stalin had softened the new state serfdom by providing the small private parcel and promising: "We Bolsheviks will see to it that every one of our collective farmers soon has a cow [of his own]." But on March 10, 1956, the Central Committee published a new decree on the collective farm in which they declared their intention to increase the number of obligatory workdays on the collective and to reduce the private plot to "truly subsidiary importance," mere "gardens . . . to provide fresh vegetables, fruits, and berries . . . as an embellishment of the peasants' way of life." Agriculture remains the Achilles heel of the Soviet economy, and the new drives in agriculture will but serve to expose the vulnerable tendon.

The theory back of totalitarianism is: given a complete enough monopoly of all the levers of force and persuasion, and sufficient firmness, there is nothing which cannot be planned and controlled. Yet the surprise of the congress, in which everything was predetermined and "more monolithic than ever" (Khrushchev), was the inability to control the planned de-sanctification of Stalin.

For three and a half years, the heirs wrestled with the problem of reducing Stalin's size yet keeping his cruel "gains" in agriculture, industry, state power, and foreign conquest. Eighteen days after his death, his name disappeared altogether from *Pravda*; then it reappeared again; was writ smaller, then larger, then smaller; some of his victims were amnestied, Tito was wooed, some of the losses cut that were occasioned by the increasing rigidity and paranoia of his closing years. Yet the problem remained unsolved, and the spirit would not stay in its tomb. When the congress opened, it unexpectedly turned out that the most important delegate was Stalin's ghost.

For those who are attempting the operation are Stalin's men. Would any of them ever have become the rulers of a great nation except as his associates? Could the mediocre Molotov and Voroshilov have become symbols of "Old Bolshevism" if Stalin had not first killed Trotsky, Zinoviev, Bukharin, and the rest of Lenin's closest associates? Who raised

Malenkov to the Secretariat? Who made Khrushchev the boss of agriculture and purger of the Ukraine?

In some ways the operation was well prepared by men trained in Stalin's school. It was he who first taught them to cast responsibility for shared misdeeds upon a corpse, when he blamed first Yagoda, then Yezhov, for the "excesses" of the blood purges. Why should they not "use" Beria's corpse, or even Stalin's, in the same fashion?

But the trouble is that these men were Stalin's creatures and accomplices. Malenkov ran the card index and dossiers of the purges. Khrushchev carried them out in the Ukraine, where they raged with unexampled fury. Bulganin was the eyes and ears of Stalin in the army. Mikoyan, Kaganovich and Khrushchev worked together to purge Moscow and each took his turn in the two-decade holocaust in the Ukraine.

In the secret session, even as Khrushchev was speaking to an audience so accustomed to listen in obedient silence, a cry escaped someone's lips: "But why didn't you kill him?" And Khrushchev, bursting into tears, blurted out: "What could we do? There was a reign of terror." Even the *Daily Worker* editor, Allen Max, has permitted himself to ask in print: "Where were the present leaders during the period of which they speak? How about their own errors?" That they were terrified does not exclude the fact that they rose into the circle of the *vozhd* as active and willing accomplices, singing the glory of his name.

And what shall men think of a system in which not only a great people is terrified and tyrannized, but even the ruling party and the party bosses are terrified of the man they have raised to power, and powerless to restrain his fury?

Within a few weeks of Stalin's death, his heirs began a limited amnesty and "rehabilitation" of "enemies of the people" and "traitors." This operation, too, is difficult to control. Can it be limited to loyal Stalinists, while, as Khrushchev has decreed, it expressly excludes "Trotskyites, Bukharinites, bourgeois nationalists, and others of the worst enemies of the people?" Can it be limited to apologies to the corpses of Communists, without other corpses pushing their way into this strange dance of death— the millions of peasants of the forced collectivization and state-organized famine; the rightless lowest class of millions of workers in concentration camps; the extinguished nationalities?

And where shall be drawn the dividing line between the crimes of Stalin and the "great achievements"? Is it only "during his last few years" as was said at one point in the congress? Or "during the last 20 years" as was said at another? Or when Lenin lay dying, as Khrushchev admitted at another point? Or when all of Lenin's closest comrades, like Trotsky, Zinoviev, and Bukharin, were expelled by Stalin and the very lieutenants who are now his heirs? Was the conquest of the Baltic States and the Balkans one of Stalin's crimes or, as his heirs maintain, one of his great achievements? Shall the democrats who resisted be amnestied there? The corpses apologized to? The forced collectivization, still hated by every peasant and still resisted as every production figure testifies—was it one of the great achievements or one of Stalin's crimes? The attack on the rights of the Russian people as consumers, and on their standard of living ("the priority of heavy industry")—how shall it now be classified?

Nor is the confusion any less in the satellites. In every one of them Communists were framed as "Titoists" (apologies to the corpse!), as agents of foreign powers (apologies to some, but not to others). Social Democrats, Democrats, loyal patriots were jailed and executed (still "re-actionaries and enemies of the people," Khrushchev told Gaitskell and Eden). In every subjugated nation there are Stalin appointees at the helm, objects of a systematically fostered "cult of the personality"—like Mao in China and Rakosi in Hungary.

In Poland, the problem of "controlled exorcism" is even more unmanageable, for there Stalin outlawed the Polish Communist party in the thirties, killing its entire Central Committee. Then came the killing of Ehrlich and Alter and other Polish Socialists, Jewish and non-Jewish; the murders in the Katyn Forest; the betrayal of the Warsaw uprising to Hitler's army. The apologies, rehabilitations and amnesties in Poland already run into the tens of thousands. Where can a line be drawn short of setting this unhappy people free to nurse their unmerited wounds?

In short, the Twentieth Congress, "more monolithic than ever before," prepared by a purge like the others, its spokesman established well in advance, its Six-Year Plan completed and adopted earlier, the enlargement of its Presidium completed six months in advance, its roles allotted, its speeches prepared, its nearly 1,500 delegates dutifully cheering when the cue was given, asking no questions and voting *yes* on everything—has sprung its own great surprise. For three and a half years the heirs were wrestling with the problem of Stalin's ghost—alternately shrinking and enlarging it a little (the last enlargement being in December 1955). But at the congress the ghost eluded control; the sounding board displayed monstrous powers of amplification; "operation cutdown" burst out of the bonds of the plan.

Is it an insoluble operation for Stalin's heirs and accomplices, an operation which has developed a dynamics of its own? In any case, it must by now be obvious that they have opened a new Pandora's box. Dark, terrifying shapes continue to escape from it, and the heirs are having trouble getting the lid securely nailed down once more.

Out of the strange shapes, hovering over them all, emerges a gigantic question mark—addressed to totalitarianism as a system. If a Hitler, cruel and paranoiac, can take power over and terrorize a great people; if a Stalin, cruel and paranoiac, can take power over and terrorize another great people, and nothing be done about it until violence and death befall—is there not something paranoid about the system itself? Is there not something fatal about the concentration of absolute power, the power of life and death, the monopoly of all the means of persuasion and force in irresponsible hands? Is there not something about the arduous and superhuman trade of absolute dictatorship that unhinges the mind? Will not a totalitarianism of any kind tend to engender ever afresh the absolute dictator, corrupting him by the concentration of absolute power in his hands? Is not this the realization in life of what Lord Acton obscurely sensed when he wrote: *Absolute power corrupts Absolutely?*

15
The New Gospel according to Khrushchev

When Samuel Butler wanted to write an "Apology for the Devil" he bade us remember: "We have heard only one side; God has written all the books." It is doubtful that there are no servants of the Devil among scribes, but the absolute ruler of a totalitarian state is less ambivalent about the Antagonist and more attentive to his monopoly over books. In Russia one can indeed read only one side. If the man at the top is too busy to "write all the books," he is not too busy to prescribe how they shall be written. To a French delegation in 1956, Khrushchev said: "Historians are dangerous people. They are capable of upsetting everything. They must be directed."

Others may question History, puzzling over her dark answers. But where there is foreknowledge of History's duty and path, where there is an infallible doctrine expounded and applied by an infallible interpreter, what questions shall we ask? History is to obey the "science of society," not alter it or mock it by waywardness. History is to be fulfilled, not puzzled over; made, not learned. One does not ask her; one tells her. Marxism, says the new "History of the Communist Party of the Soviet Union," "enables us to know the present and foresee the future." If the present is so clear, the future foreknown, shall we permit ourselves to be puzzled by what is already past? To banish doubt, past events must be arranged to show that this or that mistake was never made by the Infallible Ones, or that it was made by the Antagonist, only to be uncovered

Reprinted with permission from *Foreign Affairs* (July 1960).

and overcome by the Infallible Ones. Or that what look to the blind like errors were really strokes of genius. In short, the past must be so written as to show that it was pregnant with the present and the future, certain with the future's certainties. Nor is this to be limited to Russia's past, for the new history proclaims "the inevitability of the repetition of the basic features of the Russian Revolution on an international scale."

To be sure, some of these liberties with the past may be taken by historians in any land, but it can be done thoroughly, systematically, persistently, and completely only where there is no free competition in the marketplace of ideas, where there is but one permissible version at any given moment. That is one of the manifest advantages of totalitarianism.

On the face of it, this monopoly of historiography seems to make everything very simple. Only one right and wrong, only one black and one white with no shades of gray, only one hero, assisted by his faithful band, only one villain, with his aides, abettors, accomplices, and paymasters, only one possible outcome. No conflicting testimony to consider. No archives to hunt for, decipher, weigh, puzzle over. That sort of thing, said Stalin ominously to the editors of one of his journals in 1931, that is for "archive rats."

Since there is only one permissible text to publish and to con by rote, this would also seem very economical. Yet the mortality among these official, single, and certain texts has proved frightfully high. Party histories have succeeded each other as if they were being consumed by a giant chain smoker who lights the first page of the new work with the last of the old. To mention only those that, having been in their moment official, were printed in huge editions and translated into many tongues, there was Zinoviev's *History* (1923); Yaroslavsky's various efforts at intervals between 1926 and 1937; Volosevich's (published in 1927, condemned by Stalin in 1931); Bubnov's (1931); Popov's (1930, at least sixteen editions before it was scrapped in 1935).

In despair at the transitoriness of all these individual efforts to celebrate the power and glory of the party and its leaders, Stalin ordered his lieutenant, W. Knorin, to assemble a "collective" of Red professors to write the definitive party history. Written by five of these with Ponamarev as their "group leader" (*rukovoditel*) and Knorin as political and editorial overseer, it appeared in 1935—and proved as mortal as its predecessors. Though all these histories except Zinoviev's were written by Stalinists to serve his purposes and celebrate his deeds while they execrated his rivals, each was short-lived because with every change of line and every change in the magnitude of the colossus, the past had to be retroactively altered once more.

Finally, after the blood purges had reedited the age of Lenin by turning all his close associates into traitors, save only one, the survivor determined to fix the past himself, as he fixed music, linguistics, genetics, philosophy, legal theory, economics, Marxism, Leninism, and all else besides—especially his own place in history.

Thus was born the first party history that lived long enough to grow up and circumnavigate the globe, "the book that," according to *Pravda*, "has sold more copies than any other in modern times, the work of a genius, *The Short History of the Communist Party of the Soviet Union*, by Joseph Stalin."[1]

At this point, party history was "stabilized." No new history appeared for fifteen years. All works in the field, and in many other fields of political, economic, and philosophical writing, became glosses and exegeses derived in whole or part from the *Short Course*. There was even a secret Politburo decision that no one was to be permitted to remember anything new about Lenin or publish any memoir concerning him, and countless already published memoirs were burned or pulped.[2]

Stalin's *Short Course*, though virtually unreadable, could be memorized by the faithful, and indeed, as a life insurance policy, had to be. As Leonard Schapiro has written in his own not-so-official history of the Communist party of the Soviet Union, Stalin's book performed the function of insuring that no Communist "need ever be at a loss for the official answer to every problem. No one understood better than Stalin that the true object of propaganda is neither to convince nor even to persuade, but to produce a uniform pattern of public utterance in which the first trace of unorthodox thought immediately reveals itself as a jarring dissonance."[3]

Now the savings involved in having only a single version of the past seemed to make themselves felt. The dullest of all best-sellers became the greatest of all best-sellers—with the exception of the Bible. By 1953, fifteen years after its publication, it was still the definitive "work of genius" and had been printed in editions of more than fifty million copies in the Soviet Union, and in all the important languages of the empire and the world.

But fifteen years is a long time for eternal truths to endure. In March 1953, the author died. In July, some still duller writers calling themselves Agitprop issued 7,500 leaden words of "Theses on Fifty Years of the Communist Party of the Soviet Union." They were published in *Pravda* on July 26, 1953. Now the millions who had toiled to learn by heart every formulation in the dull and mendacious pages of the *Short Course* realized with a pang of fear that their "insurance policy" had been canceled. For, in the "Theses," they perceived that Stalin, who for fifteen years had been up in front at the right hand of Lenin—the two of them alone remaking the world—was now no longer *vozhd*, no longer co-founder of the party, nor mastermind of the seizure of power, nor creator of the Red Army, nor winner of the civil war.

Indeed, where was he? Lenin was mentioned eighty-three times in the 7,500 words, Stalin only four. Still worse, the "Theses" gave no clue as to whom it was now necessary to cheer. In its 7,500 words there were only three names: those of Lenin and Stalin aforesaid, and one mention of Plekhanov. All safely dead. To the initiated, this was a sign that a new time of uncertainty had begun and that no living name was mentioned because no successor had yet emerged.[4]

The only thing that was certain in this new time of uncertainty was that the *Short Course*, all fifty million copies of it, had to be scrapped, and with it all the works of gloss and exegesis. The greatest book burning or book pulping in history! The system of a single, unitary, official history was not proving so economical after all.

From the summer of 1953 to the summer of 1959, the much chronicled Communist party was without any history, except the 7,500 words of depersonalized, historyless history of the Department of Agitation and Propaganda.

Before a new history could be published, Stalin's ghost had to be wrestled with and its size determined. The dictatorship had to beget its new dictator; infallible doctrine its infallible expounder; authoritarianism its authority; a totally militarized society its supreme commander. The "collective leadership," so unnatural to a dictatorial society where there are no checks on the flow of power to the top, had to be disposed of, one by one or in batches, until one should emerge as the embodiment of the party, and the others disappear as "anti-party."

Further, where power is knowledge and power over everything equivalent to knowledge concerning everything, the emergent authority on all things must have time to lay down the line on all problems, persons, and events likely to find their way into history. Only then could a new official history emerge. For the present to be projected into the past, the present has constantly and authoritatively to be determined in all wayward and moot things.

So it was that from July 26, 1953, to June 17, 1959, there was literally no history of the Communist party of the Soviet Union except the 7,500 words of the "Theses" of Agitprop. On June 17, 1959, a new manuscript was given to the press, with instructions to print a first edition of 750,000 copies. Thus was born the Gospel according to Khrushchev.

Not that he claims personal authorship. Khrushchev is free from that pathological greed of credit that made Stalin claim credit for everything. The new history was "prepared," like Knorin's history of 1935, by an "authors' collective"—eleven academicians, doctors or masters of "the historical, economic and philosophical sciences."

Where so many histories have perished so swiftly, it was pleasant to find that the *rukovoditel* or leader for the Knorin history, B. N. Ponamarev, has survived the death of his earlier work, and appears as *rukovoditel* once more. And I. I. Mintz, who has written so many legendary pages (legend is to be taken in its literal not its poetic sense) in histories of the civil war, is alive and present, too, though Stalin once denounced his work. Most of the other historians whose works were once official and translated into many tongues, are gone: Zinoviev, Volosevich, Bubnov, Popov, Yaroslavsky, Knorin. Historiography is one of the more hazardous occupations, where natural death is not so natural, for only Yaroslavsky seems to have died without special assistance from party and state.[5]

If Ponamarev is once more *rukovoditel*, there is no longer a general editor to replace Knorin. Rather, there are signs on many pages that Khrushchev and his Agitprop Secretary, Suslov, took personal care of the political overseer's task. For what we now have is quite manifestly intended to be the official history for the age of Khrushchev.

In its day, it had seemed to me that Stalin's *Short Course* was the ne plus ultra of dullness. Surely, the history of Russia in the twentieth century has been a turbulent one: conspiracy, party strife, general strike and uprising in 1905, world war, fall of the tsar, seizure of power by the Bolsheviks, civil war and intervention, Kronstadt and NEP, liquidation of the private peasant as a class, purge of all Lenin's closest lieutenants by one of them, Stalin-Hitler Pact, World War II, forced communization of so many occupied countries, struggle for the succession, emergence of Khrushchev. What material for the historian! But if the *Short Course* seemed dull and devoid of actual personages, motives and events, it at least had a kind of fascination by virtue of the malevolence, the pathological boasting, envy, and vengeance, the touch of the demonic on every page. Though in Khrushchev's History, as we shall now call it for short, whole pages are lifted from the *Short Course*, what was demonic in Stalin's history is only ruthless and formularized in the latest work.

The Khrushchev history calls itself a "concise account." "Concise" must be more extensive than "short," for it is over twice as long; nor is the additional flood of words altogether accounted for by the fact that an additional twenty years have had to be chronicled. Where formulas of boasting or denigration have not been copied verbatim, the new book is likely to use many more words to recount an episode than the old. Yet its pages seem strangely empty—empty of men, empty of events. In the place of men, there are the party, the government, the masses, and Lenin. In the place of events, there are theses and bureaucratic formulas.

No need to be surprised if the great Bolshevik holdups of 1905–7 are missing; no party historian has spoken of them. But where are the Moscow Trials which formed the closing section of the *Short Course* like the baleful hellfire which lights up the last scene of Mozart's *Don Juan*? All of Lenin's close associates save only one was tried, confessed, liquidated— surely a chapter in party history by almost any test. But not one word. Twice the party purges of the thirties, in which Nikita Khrushchev played a substantial role, are obscurely hinted at, obscurely justified, and as obscurely called in question. On page 463 we learn that the party was strengthened by purge but "mistakes were made in the unfounded expulsion of so-called passive elements." Yet, after the purges, "two-faced and enemy elements remained in the party" and Kirov's murder "showed that a party card may be used as the cover for abominable antisoviet acts." Twenty-one pages later we learn that "many honest Communists and non-party people underwent repressions, being guilty of nothing." But the villains now are Beria and Yezhov. Inexplicably, Yagoda, their predecessor as "flaming sword of the revolution," is missing, both as the first great purger and as the trial victim and confessed traitor. Just as inexplicably, for time is slippery in this history without a fixed chronological framework, Beria, whom Stalin appointed to call off the fury of the Yezhov purges, here precedes Yezhov.[6]

It is the disappearance of such large events and so many persons which makes the pages of this thick history seem so interminable and so empty. A standard feature of earlier histories was a list of Central Committee members elected by each congress, a list of reporters at each congress, and many other such accounts of persons and their posts or their proposals or their deeds. Too bureaucratic to be exciting, yet it peopled the pages of the text. But with each successive history, the lists became shorter. More and more men were silently dropped into a special opening to the Memory Hole which bears the label "and others." Now many of those who still found a place in Stalin's *Short Course*, if only to be denounced, have been dissolved in oblivion.

Besides, Khrushchev has names to eliminate from honorific lists whom Stalin delighted to honor as extensions of himself. The indestructible-seeming Molotov has faded like the Cheshire cat leaving behind him only an "anti-party" frown. Kaganovich, able and ruthless lieutenant of Stalin who saw to Khrushchev's advancement by taking him along as assistant on each of his promotions, has ended up the same way. The rotund Malenkov, once Stalin's chief of cadres, a party secretary, a member of the high military council that ran the Great Patriotic War, main reporter at the Nineteenth Congress, after Stalin's death both General Secretary and Premier—at least for nine days—has also ended up without a past, a bit of rubbish for the "anti-party" dustbin. A historian cannot help but feel that each of these is entitled to more space, if not a better fate.

In such a bureaucratic history, a party congress is an epoch-making event. At the Nineteenth Congress, held when the aging Stalin was three months from death, Molotov made the opening address, Malenkov delivered the main political report, Beria the report on the nationalities problem, Saburov on the Fifth Five-Year Plan, Khrushchev, Bulganin, and Mikoyan on the revision of the party statutes, and Kaganovich on the revision of its program. Mysteriously now the congress discusses reports but there are no reporters and no contents. Only N. S. Khrushchev remains as the sole reporter on the party statutes, from which statutes a seven-line quotation constitutes the only words immortal enough to get into the pages of history.

Even those that Stalin execrated have suffered further diminution. He still had need of Trotsky as the Antagonist in the drama of good and evil. And he had to paint Trotsky as saboteur of each of Trotsky's chief actions, since one of the aims of the *Short Course* was to replace in men's minds that unity in duality, Lenin-Trotsky, by a new unity in duality, Lenin-Stalin. Thus Trotsky's name was still bound to large events, if only by a minus sign.

Though Khrushchev's history copies some of these pages from the *Short Course*, Nikita Sergeevich does not have the same need of Trotsky to play Antichrist to his Savior; hence the baleful glare that lengthened his shadow through the *Short Course* is subdued to the dingy light that is common to these pages. The October Revolution takes place without the Chairman of the Petrograd Soviet and Military Revolutionary Committee, who directed the operations of the seizure of power and conceived its strategy. The civil war is fought and the Red army built without him. The Kronstadt mutiny is gloriously crushed without either his or Tukhashevsky's intervention. Voroshilov has retroactively been appointed director of the attack on Kronstadt, while Marshal Tukhashevsky, who seemed on the way to rehabilitation until Zhukov fell, has simply disappeared from history.

If the climax of Stalin's *Short Course* was the "Liquidation of the Remnants of the Bukharin-Trotsky Gang of Spies, Wreckers and Traitors to the Country" with which its last chapter closes, the new history has no climax. It just stops, because the Twenty-first Congress is over and the Twenty-second has not yet been convened, nor the Paris Summit Conference been held. It is less likely to last its fifteen years because history will keep adding to its bureaucratic sum, and has already subtracted two of the leaders designated by the Twenty-first Congress (Belyaev and Kirichenko).

The indictment of the "anti-party group" is stern and ruthless, indeed inexorable, but it has the formularistic and bureaucratic flavor with which the readers of newspaper accounts are familiar. The charges that Khrushchev first leveled against Malenkov, Molotov, and Kaganovich are repeated unchanged. Shepilov is still fixed forever as "inclining to them," and Bulganin is still a year late in being "factually" in their camp, while Zhukov, as the cult of a new personality in the Soviet Union grows, is still charged with encouraging "the cult of the personality of himself."

We cannot close our examination of the Khrushchev history without some consideration of this "cult of the personality," the coining of which formula seems to have been the biggest event in party history since the publication and scrapping of the *Short Course*. Around this formula was fought the struggle with Stalin's ghost to determine afresh his place in history. And the extent to which the formula shall be a self-denying ordinance for Stalin's successor determines the content and color of the closing chapters of the new history.

[*Mr. Wolfe used the following paragraphs in an address to the Conference on Soviet Historiography in Geneva in 1961, which is reprinted as chapter 8 in this book.*]

On the one hand, there was need to write Stalin smaller than in the *Short Course*, lest all his successors remain too dwarfed for any of them to succeed him. Moreover, his lieutenants, not without cause, so feared each other, and the party so feared the inevitable struggle among them, that it was necessary to give assurance "that henceforth such occurrences should never again take place in the party and the country." This was promised by a resolution of the Twentieth Congress and is repeated in the new history. Insofar as it implies the rejection of the pathological extremes of Stalin's vengeful reign, it may be taken seriously.

On the other hand, Stalin's successor could not destroy the link which puts him in the line of apostolic succession. For what else but the apostolic succession from Lenin, who seized power, to Stalin, who usurped it by taking over and perfecting Lenin's machine, what other "legitimacy" and claim to rule over a great empire has the present First Secretary?

The inheritance includes many things for which this history gives Stalin great credit:

1. The annihilation of all rival parties, such as Mensheviks and Socialist Revolutionaries and Kadets. (Hence the history repeats the absurdities of the frameup trials of the Mensheviks, the Industrial party, the Toiling Peasant party.)

2. The annihilation of all anti-Stalinist Communist groups (Trotskyites, Zinovievites, Bukharinites, for whom there can be no rehabilitation).

3. Forced industrialization and the primacy of heavy industry over production for consumption.

4. The annihilation of the peasantry and the forced collectivization of agriculture.

5. The party penetration and control of all organizations and the atomization of the individual. (This is a heritage from Lenin perfected by Stalin and is inseparable from totalitarianism.)

6. Stalin's conquests of the Baltic Republics, half of Poland, part of East Prussia, Finland and Rumania, and Tannu Tuva.

7. The "liberation" of the rest of Poland, of Hungary (two "liberations"), of East Germany *and* Berlin, of the Balkan lands including Yugoslavia, of China, North Korea and Vietnam.

8. The "struggle for peace" and the enlargement of the "peace camp" which permits of, nay requires, the "liberation" of further parts of the non-Communist world but not the "reënslavement" of any part that has been liberated. (The book makes clear that "peaceful coexistence" is as old as Lenin and Stalin and not to be interpreted any differently than it was by them.)

This is a large balance sheet. In it Stalin's crimes against the Russian people, against the Russian peasantry, against allies and neighbors and occupied countries, are all transformed into virtues listed on the credit side of the ledger. His crimes against other socialist and democratic parties and opposition Communists are listed as virtues, too, with only the reservation that he dealt too harshly with "good Communists" (which seems to mean Stalinists) when he liquidated them. Even then, when the vengeful guillotine is turned on loyal Stalinists, the history does not cry "Crime!" but mumbles "Error" or "harmful consequence of the cult of the personality."

The final verdict reads: "Under the leadership of the Communist Party and its Central Committee, in which J. V. Stalin played a leading role, the Soviet Union has achieved enormous, world-wide successes. J. V. Stalin did much that was beneficial to the Soviet Union, to the C.P.S.U., and to the whole international workers movement."

Thus Khrushchev's tremendous indictment of Stalin's cruelty and paranoia in his secret speech dwindles into a bureaucratic formula for much praise and a little halting blame, now that Khrushchev is secure in the possession of his heritage.

What, then, is happening to the size of the "personality" of Nikita Sergeevich Khrushchev?

To get a perspective, we must bear in mind that this is not the final masterpiece of Khrushchev historiography but only a first attempt, analogous rather to the early efforts of a Yaroslavsky than to the final chef d'oeuvre—the *Short Course*. Moreover, Khrushchev has difficulties that Stalin did not have. It is not possible for a man who joined the party only after it had won power to picture himself as one of the party's cofounders. Hence the book's only living hero (the dead heroes being Lenin and Stalin) does not enter into its 745 pages until page 314, then modestly enough as one of an alphabetical list of Lenin's "comrades-in-arms and disciples hardened in the civil war . . . on whose backs lay the burden of liquidating the consequences of the war and constructing a socialist society." The list contains twenty-three names, in discreet alphabetical order, Stalinists all, and the impartial alphabet put Khrushchev (in Russian it begins with an X) in the twentieth place and Stalin himself in the eighteenth.

Not until page 608, with the Nineteenth Congress, does Khrushchev begin seriously to employ the technique of self-enlargement learned from the master. Here, as we have seen, Molotov who delivered the opening address, Malenkov who delivered the main report, Beria, Kaganovich, and Saburov who reported too, all become unpersons, while Khrushchev holds the vast stage alone.

By the Twentieth Congress, Khrushchev had gotten such a hold of the party machine that he did in actual fact hold the stage alone and make all the reports. The proceedings left no doubt that the First Secretary was more equal than the others, who were permitted to share in but not equal his applause. The order of business was: opening address, Khrushchev; report of the Presidium and Central Committee (covering everything), Khrushchev; chairman of the committee to draw up a resolution on the report, Khrushchev; chairman of the new Bureau on Party Affairs of the Russian Republic, Khrushchev; secret report on the cult of personality, Khrushchev. Only Bulganin was permitted a subreport, a gloss on the First Secretary's remarks on the Sixth Five-Year Plan.

As for the Twenty-first Congress, which makes up the final chapter of this book, it had only one order of business: a report on the control figures for the Seven-Year Plan, by Nikita Sergeevich Khrushchev. Such is the fitting bureaucratic climax, or anticlimax, to the strange transformation of so many clashes of arms and deeds of blood into bureaucratic formulas.

In the closing chapter, Khrushchev is cited and his "ideas" as expressed in reports are summarized fourteen times in a scant twenty-six pages. Actually, this is a little higher score than the citations from Stalin in the closing chapter of the *Short Course*. Stalin's closing chapter ends with a quote from Stalin; Khrushchev's with a quote from Khrushchev. The First Secretary and once "best disciple of Joseph Stalin" has learned his trade.

In each case the closing chapter is followed by a brief coda called "Conclusion." In the *Short Course*, Stalin jostles Lenin here for first place. Whether it be good sense or greater need, in the conclusion to the new history Lenin and the party are given first place. Yet even here, Khrushchev is quoted four times. In the *Short Course*, the last words are a quote from Stalin. In the new history, Khrushchev bows out three pages before the end, while the last two sentences are eight words from Lenin on the party as "the intelligence, honor and conscience of our party" followed by twelve from Marx on communism's promise: "From each according to his means, to each according to his needs."

Such is the nature of the party history in which the two new features, which were lacking in the *Short Course*, are the "liquidation of the harmful consequences of the cult of personality," and . . . the recording of the substantial beginnings of a new cult.

IV
Totalitarianism: The Longer View

16
The Durability
of Soviet Despotism:
Forty Years of
Revolution

At every turn the historian encounters the unpredictable: contingency; historical accident; biological accident intruding itself into history, as when the death of a history-making person brings a change of direction; changes of mood; emergence of new situations; sudden leaps that seem to turn an accretion of little events into a big one; the complicated interaction of multiple determinants on every event; the unintended consequences of intended actions.

Still, history is not *so* open that any event is just as likely as any other. As in the flux of things we note continuing structures, as in biology we note heredity as well as variation and mutation, so in history there is an interrelation between continuity and change.

Though all lands go through a history, and all orders and institutions are subject to continuous modification and ultimate transformation, there are some social orders or systems that are more markedly dynamic, more open, more mutable, even self-transforming, while others exhibit marked staying powers, their main outlines continuing to be discernibly the same through the most varied vicissitudes.

It may be difficult to determine except in retrospect just when a system may be said to change in ways so fundamental as to signify its transformation; still, it is possible and necessary to distinguish between self-

Reprinted from *Commentary* (August 1957), by permission; all rights reserved.

conserving and self-transforming systems, between relatively open and relatively closed societies, and between changes so clearly of a secondary order that they may be designated within-system changes, and those so clearly fundamental that they involve changes in the system or basic societal structure. That this distinction may in practice be hard to make, that there may be gradations and borderline cases and sudden surprises, does not relieve us of this obligation. Merely to reiterate endlessly that all things change, without attempting to make such distinctions, is to stand helpless before history-in-the-making, helpless to evaluate and helpless to react.

If we look at the Roman empire, say from the time of Julius Caesar to the time of Julian the Apostate, or perhaps from Augustus to Romulus Augustulus, we can perceive that for three or four centuries, despite its many vicissitudes and changes, it continued in a meaningful and determinable sense to be the Roman empire. In similar fashion we can easily select a good half millennium of continuity in the Byzantine empire. Or if we take one of the most dynamic regions, Western Europe, in one of its more dynamic periods, we can note that monarchical absolutism had a continuity of several centuries. This is the more interesting because monarchical absolutism, though it was one of the more stable and monopolistically exclusive power systems of the modern Western world, was a *multicentered system* in which the monarch was checked and limited by his need of support from groups, corporations, and interests that were organized independently of the central power: the castled, armed, and propertied nobility; the church with its spiritual authority; the burghers of the wealthy, fortified towns.

It is the presence of these independent centers of corporate organization that makes Western monarchical absolutism an exception among the centralized, long-lasting power systems. It was these limiting forces that managed to exact the charters and constitutions, the right to determine size and length of service of armed levies, size and purpose of monetary contributions, thus ultimately transforming the absolute monarchy into the limited, constitutional monarchy of modern times. And it is from our own Western history, with its exceptional evolution, that we derive many of our unconscious preconceptions as to the inevitability, sweep, and comparative ease of change. To correct our one-sided view it is necessary to compare the characteristics of multicentered Western absolutism with other, more "complete" and "perfected" forms of single-centered power and despotism.[1]

In the *samoderzhavie* of Muscovy we find a more truly single-centered power structure, stronger, more completely centralized, more monopolistic, more despotic, more unyielding in its rigid institutional framework than was the absolutism of Western Europe. The tsar early managed to subvert the independent boyars and substitute for them a state-service nobility. The crown possessed enormous crown lands and state serfs. Bondage, both to the state and to the state-service nobility, was instituted by the central power and adjusted to the purposes of the recruiting sergeant and the tax gatherer. When the Emancipation came, in the nineteenth century, it was a state-decreed "revolution from above" (Alexander's own words for it), and carried with it state supervision and the decreeing of collective responsibility to the village *mir*.

To this universal state-service and state-bondage, we must add the features of Caesaro-papism: signifying a tsar and a state-dominated church. And the administrative-military nature of the Russian towns checked the rise of an independent burgher class.

Industrialization, too, was undertaken at the initiative of the state. From Peter I to Nicholas II, there were two centuries of state-ordained and -fostered industrialization; the state-owned and -managed basic industry—mining, metallurgy, munitions, railroad construction and operation—and some commercial monopolies, all crowned with a huge state banking and credit system.

The rudiments of a more multicentered life were just beginning to develop in this powerful, single-center society when World War I added to the managerial state's concerns the total mobilization of men, money, materials, transport, and industry.

The "model" country in this new form of state enterprise was wartime Germany. The system of total management by the state for total war has been variously, but not very intelligibly, termed "state capitalism" and "state socialism." In any case, Lenin was quick to welcome this development as the "final transition form." In it, as in the heritage from the tsarist managerial autocratic state itself, he found much to build on in making his own transition to the new totalitarianism.

From Ivan the Terrible on, for a period of four centuries, "the state had been stronger than society" and had been ruled from a single center as a military, bureaucratic, managerial state. Amidst the most varied vicissitudes, including a time of troubles, wars, conquests, invasions, peasant insurrections, palace revolutions and revolutions from above, the powerful framework endured. Weakenings of the power structure, even breaches in it, were followed by a swift "restoration" of its basic outlines. When the strains of a world war finally caused its collapse, there came a brief interlude of loosening of the bonds. Then Lenin, even as he revolutionized, likewise "restored" much of the four-century-old heritage. Indeed, it was this "socialist restoration of autocracy" which Plekhanov had warned against, as early as the 1880s, as a danger inherent in the longed-for Russian revolution. He admonished the impatient Populists that unless all the bonds were first loosened and a free "Western" or "bourgeois-democratic" order were allowed to develop and mature, the seizure of power by would-be socialists could not but lead to a restoration of Oriental, autocratic despotism on a pseudosocialist foundation with a pseudosocialist "ruling caste." Things would be even worse, he warned Lenin in 1907, if this new "Inca ruling caste of Sons of the Sun" should make the fatal mistake of nationalizing the land, thus tightening even more the chains that bound the peasant to the autocratic state.

The term "Oriental despotism" applied to Russia in the course of this controversy among Russian socialists serves to remind us that there are yet more durable social formations with even greater built-in staying powers than those we have so far noted. These reckon their continuity not in centuries alone but even in millennia. As a Chinese historian once observed to me: "Your Renaissance was a fascinating period. We had seven of them." If we substitute restoration for renaissance, both in the sense of restoration of vigor and restoration of basic structure, he was right. For though China suffered upheavals, invasions, conquests, falls of dynasties, rebellions, interregnums, and times of trouble, a Chinese villager or a Chinese official of the nineteenth century, if transported to the China of two thousand or more years ago, would have found himself in a familiar institutional and ideological environment.

With the exception of Western monarchical absolutism, what all these enduring social structures had in common was a single power center, a managerial state, a lack of independent social orders and forms of property, an absence of checks on the flow of power to the center and the top, and an overwhelmingly powerful, self-perpetuating institutional framework.

Modern totalitarianism, I believe, is one of these comparatively closed and conservative societies, with a powerful and self-perpetuating institutional framework calculated to assimilate the changes which it intends and those which are forced upon it, in such fashion that—barring explosion from within or battering down from without—they tend to remain *within-system* changes in an enduring system.

At first glance the word conservative may seem out of place in speaking of a society that is organized revolution. And indeed there is a striking difference between Communist totalitarianism and all previous systems of absolute, despotic, undivided (and, in that sense, total) power. For whereas despotism, autocracy, and absolutism were bent on preserving the status quo, Communist totalitarianism is dedicated to "the future." This powerful institutional structure which tolerates no rival centers of organization has a vested interest in keeping things in flux. The omnipotence of state and ideology is maintained by carrying on a permanent revolution. Like Alexander's, it is a revolution from above. But unlike Alexander's, its aim is nothing less than to keep a society atomized and to create, as rapidly and as completely as the recalcitrant human material and the refractory surrounding world will permit, a new man, a new society, and a new world.

Like the earlier systems referred to, it possesses a state that is stronger than society. Like them it represents a system of total, in the sense of undivided, power. Like them it lacks any organized and institutionalized checks on the flow of power to the top. Like them, it possesses a state-centered, state-dominated, state-managed, and, for the first time, a completely state-owned economy.

But if the other societies are distinguished by the high specific gravity of state ownership, state control, and state managerial function within the total activity of society, under Communist totalitarianism state ownership and state managerialism aspire to be total in a new sense. In the other cases, we have been contemplating total power in the sense of undivided power: power without significant rival centers of organization. But now, to the concept of *undivided power*, we must add that of *all-embracing power*.

No longer does the state limit itself to being "stronger than society." It now strives to be *coextensive* with society. Whereas the earlier power systems recognized certain limitations on their capacity to run everything, leaving room, for example, for pocket-handkerchief farms and the self-feeding of the *corvée* population, for private arts and crafts unconnected with the managerial concerns of the state, for certain types of private trade, and even finding room for village communal democracy under the watchful eye of the state overseer—what Wittfogel has aptly called "beggars' democracy"—the new totalitarianism strives to atomize society completely, to coordinate the dispersed villages into its centralized power system, to eliminate even the small private parcel of the *kolkhoznik*, already reduced from a "pocket handkerchief" to a mere swatch.

For the first time a total-power system in the earlier sense of undivided and unchallenged power aspires to be totalist or totalitarian in the further sense of converting the state-stronger-than-society into the state-coextensive-with-society.

We cannot deduce much from a comparison with other modern totalitarianisms. For historical and physical reasons Italian fascism was more totalist in aspiration than in realization. And, though nazism and Stalinist communism suggestively moved toward each other, nazism did not last long enough to complete its evolution. But it did live long enough to dispose of certain illusions concerning the supposed incompatibility of totalitarianism with certain aspects of modern life.

Thus it is widely held that the monopoly of total power and the attempt to embrace the totality of social life and activity are incompatible with the complexity of modern industry and advanced technology. But Germany adopted totalitarianism when it was the foremost country of Europe in industry and technology.

Indeed, it is precisely modern technology, with its all-embracing means of communication, its high-speed transmission of commands and reports and armed forces to any point in a country, its mass-communication and mass-conditioning techniques and the like, which for the first time makes it possible for total (undivided) power to aspire to be totalist (all-embracing) power. That is what Herzen foreboded when he wrote: "Some day Jinghis Khan will return with the telegraph." If total power tends to arise wherever the state is stronger than society, totalitarian power can aspire to prevail over a great area and in great depth only where the state is both stronger than society and in possession of all the resources of modern technology.

Closely akin to the illusion of the incompatibility of totalitarianism with modern technology is the view that totalitarianism is "in the long run" incompatible with universal literacy, with advanced technological training, and with widespread higher or secondary-school education. Once more it is Germany that serves to remind us that one of the most highly literate and technologically trained peoples in the history of man adopted totalitarianism. Nay more, modern totalitarianism *requires* that everybody be able to read so that all can be made to read the same thing at the same moment. Not the ability to read, but the ability to choose between alternative types of reading, is a potential—and only a potential—liberating influence.

When Stalin died in 1953, bolshevism was fifty years old. Its distinctive views on organization, centralization, and the guardianship or dictatorship of a vanguard or elite date from Lenin's programmatic writings of 1902 (*Where to Begin*; *What Is to Be Done?*). His separate party machine, which he controlled with an authoritarian hand, dates from the Bolshevik-Menshevik split of 1903 in the Russian Social Democratic party.

During these fifty years bolshevism had had only two authoritative leaders, each of whom set the stamp of his personality upon it. Lenin, as we have suggested, inherited much from tsarist autocracy, yet his totalitarianism is different in principle from the old Muscovite despotism. He regarded himself as an orthodox Marxist, building upon and enlarging some aspects of Marx's conceptions while ignoring, altering, or misrepresenting others. His Marxism was so different from Marx's that a not unfriendly commentator, Charles Rappoport, called it "Marxisme à la tartare." Stalin's Leninism, in turn, differed enough from Lenin's that we might term it "Marxisme à la mode caucasienne." Yet there is discernibly more continuity between Stalin and Lenin than between Lenin and Marx. The changes Stalin introduced involved the continuation and enlargement of certain elements in Lenin's methods and conceptions, along with the alteration of others. He inherited and used, now in Leninist, now in his own "Stalinist" fashion, an institutional framework involving a party machine, a state machine, a doctrine of infallibility, an ideology, and the determination to extend the totalization of power, to transform the Russian into the "New Communist Man," and win the world for communism.

With Stalin's death, once more there are new leaders or a new leader. It is impossible to believe that this new personal imprint will not make alterations in Stalinism as Stalin did in Leninism.

But it seems to me useful, after four years of unsystematic talk about changes, that we should remind ourselves that the "new men" are not so new, that they have inherited a going concern, and that actually we are confronting changes within a single-centered, closed, highly centralized society run by a power that is both undivided and all-embracing. And we should remind ourselves, too, that such societies as I have classed it with have tended to exhibit built-in staying powers and a perdurability despite changes like the death of a despot, an oligarchical interregnum, or a struggle for succession.

These "new men" are, of course, Stalin's men. They would not now have any claim to power over a great nation were it not that they managed to be the surviving close lieutenants at the moment of Stalin's death. It is my impression that they are smallish men. There is a principle of selection in personal despotisms which surrounds the despot with courtiers, sycophants, executants, and rules out original and challenging minds. This almost guarantees a crisis of succession where there is no system of legitimacy, until a new dictator emerges. Moreover, the heirs are no longer young (Khrushchev is sixty-three), so that a fresh crisis of succession may well supervene before the present muted and restricted crisis is over.

I would not write these "smallish men" too small, however, for when you have a sixth of the earth, 200 million population, and a total state economy and a great empire to practice on, you learn other trades besides that of courtier or faction lieutenant. Even so, not one of them at present exhibits the originality and the high charge of energy and intellect that characterized Lenin, or the grosser but no less original demonic force of Stalin.

Whenever a despot dies, there is a universal expectation of change. The new men have had to take account of it, and have taken advantage of it to introduce changes which the old tyrant made seem desirable even to his lieutenants: they have taken advantage of the expectation of change to rationalize elements of a system which has no organized, independent forces which might change it from below, and to make limited concessions while they are consolidating their power. But the institutional framework they have inherited is one they intend to maintain.

Some parts of this power machine are now more than a half century old, others date from 1917, others from the consolidation of the Stalinist regime in industry, agriculture, politics, and culture in the thirties. But even these last have been established for more than two decades.

What the epigoni have inherited is no small heritage: a completely atomized society;[2] a monolithic, monopolistic party; a single-party state; a regime of absolute force supplemented by persuasion or by continuous psychological warfare upon its people; a managerial bureaucracy accustomed to execute orders (with a little elbow room for regularized evasion); a centrally managed, totally state-owned and state-regulated economy including farms, factories, banks, transport and communications, and all trade domestic and foreign; an established dogmatic priority for the branches of industry which underlie the power of the state; a bare subsistence economy for the bulk of the producers; a completely statized and "collectivized" agriculture which, though it has never solved the problem of productivity, threatens to reduce even the small parcel to a mere "garden adornment"; a powerful, if one-sided, forced tempo industry centralized even beyond the point of rationality from the standpoint of totalitarianism itself; the techniques and momentum of a succession of Five-Year Plans of which the present is the sixth; a completely managed and controlled culture (except for the most secret recesses of the spirit which even modern technology cannot reach); a monopoly of all the means of expression and communication; a state-owned system of "criticism"; an infallible doctrine stemming from infallible authorities, interpreted and applied by an infallible party led by an infallible leader or a clique of infallible leaders, in any case by an infallible "summit"; a method of advance by zigzags toward basically unchanging goals; a system of promotion, demotion, correction of error, modification of strategy and tactics and elimination of difference by fiat from the summit, implemented by purges of varying scope and intensity; a commitment to continuing revolution from above until the Soviet subject has been remade according to the blueprint of the men in the Kremlin and until communism has won the world.

It is in this heritage that these men were formed. In this they believe. It is the weight and power and internal dynamics of this heritage
that in part inhibit, in part shape such changes as these men undertake,
and enter as a powerful influence into the changes which they make
involuntarily.

It would require a separate study to attempt an inquiry into what
is fundamental to totalitarianism, so that a change in it would represent a "change in the system," and what is of a more superficial order, so
that a change may readily be recognized as a "within-system" change.[3]
Here we shall have to limit ourselves to a glance at a few post-Stalin
political developments. The first change that obtrudes itself is "collective
leadership."

The party statutes do not provide for an authoritative leader, a dictator
or *vozhd*. Just as this, the most centralized great power, still professes to
be federal, a mere union of autonomous republics, so the party statutes
have always proclaimed party democracy and collective leadership.

It was not hard to predict that Stalin's orphaned heirs would proclaim
a collective leadership at the moment of his death, even as they began the
maneuvers that led to the emergence of a still narrower ruling group
(triumvirate, duumvirate) and a muted struggle for the succession. Stalin,
too, for a half decade found it necessary to proclaim a collective leadership and pose as its faithful wheelhorse, and took a full decade before he
killed his first rivals.

Stalin's successors had the same reasons as he for proclaiming the
collective leadership of the Politburo, and some additional ones as well.
The harrowing and demoralizing experiences of the thirties, the signs of
the beginnings of a new mass purge (in the "poison doctors' case") a few
months before Stalin's death, the terror that gripped even his closest
collaborators, and their justified fears of each other—all combined to
make necessary the proclamation of a "collective leadership."

There is nothing inherently incompatible with total, undivided power,
nor with totalitarian, all-embracing power, in the rule of an oligarchy, or
in an interregnum between dictators or despots. What is noteworthy here
is the swiftness with which the first triumvirate (Malenkov, Molotov,
Beria) were demoted, compelled to confess unfitness, and, in the case of
Beria, killed. It took Stalin ten years to shed the blood of potential rivals
or aspirants to power; Beria disappeared in a few months. In less than
two years the skeptical were obliged to recognize that Khrushchev was
"more equal than the others" and was making all the important programmatic declarations.[4] Those who follow the Soviet press can perceive that
Khrushchev is already the *Khozyain* (Boss), though not yet the *vozhd*
(Führer, Duce, Charismatic Leader).

This is not to say that Khrushchev must necessarily emerge as the undisputed and authoritative leader in the sense that either Stalin or Lenin was. Combinations and counter-forces in the oligarchy and limitations in his own capacity may check or slow or, in view of his age, even nullify the manifest trend. But triumvirates, duumvirates, directories are notoriously transitional in the succession to a despot where there is no legitimacy in providing a successor, and no checks against the flow of power to the top. Moreover, the whole dynamics of dictatorship calls for a personal dictator, authoritarianism for an authority, infallible doctrine for an infallible interpreter, totally militarized life for a supreme commander, and centralized, undivided, all-embracing, and "messianic" power for a "charismatic" symbol and tenant of authority. Unless the "collective leadership" should broaden instead of narrowing as it already has, unless power should flood down into the basic units of the party (which was not the case even in Lenin's day), and then leak out into self-organizing corporate bodies independent of the state, restoring some initiative to society as against the state—in short, unless the whole trend of totalitarianism is not merely slowed (as may be expected during an interregnum) but actually reversed, there is good reason to regard a "directory" or a "duumvirate" as transitory.

Both purge and terror were instituted by Lenin and "perfected" and "over-perfected" by Stalin. Leaving on one side the purely personal element (paranoia and relish for vengeance), both purge in the party and terror in society as a whole serve many of the "rational" purposes of the totalitarian regime: the establishment of the infallibility of the party, of its summit, and its doctrine; the maintenance of the party in a "state of grace" (zeal, doctrinal purity, fanatical devotion, discipline, subordination, total mobilization); the atomization of society as a whole; the breaking up of all nonstate conformations and centers of solidarity; the turnover in the elite, demotion of deadwood and promotion of new forces; the supplying of scapegoats for every error and for signaling a change of line; the maintenance of the priority of heavy industry, of forced savings for capital investment, of unquestioned command and relative efficiency in production, of "collectivization" in agriculture, of control in culture, and a number of similar objectives of the totalist state.

All of these institutions have been so well established that to a large extent they are now taken for granted. Stalin himself promised in 1939 that there would never again be a mass purge. Except in the case of the army and the Jewish writers, the purge became physically more moderate, until, with increasing marks of paranoia, Stalin gave every sign of opening another era of mass purge a few months before his death. The first thing the heirs did as they gathered around the corpse was to call off the purge, both because it had no "rational" purpose and because it had threatened to involve most of them.

But it would be a mistake to believe that the "moderated" purge can be dispensed with. In the preparation of the Twentieth Congress the heirs showed how well they had mastered the "Leninist norms," according to which every congress since the Tenth had been prepared for by a prior purge of the party organization. All the regional secretaries and leading committees were "renewed," 37 percent of those who attended the Nineteenth Congress disappeared from public view, 44 percent of the Central Committee failed to be elected as delegates or to be reelected to the new committee. All we can say is that the purge today resembles those of Stalin's "benign" periods or of Lenin's day. Yet the liquidation of Beria and at least twenty-five of his friends shows that the techniques of the blood purge have not been forgotten. That the party ranks breathe easier and are glad of the self-denying ordinance of the leaders in the struggle for position we do not doubt. But there is no evidence that the party ranks ordered this change, or could do so, or would venture to try.

The terror in society as a whole has also diminished. No longer are there such bloody tasks as forced collectivization to carry through. Habitual obedience, the amnesties and concessions of an interregnum, the shortage of manpower for industry, agriculture, and the army because of continued expansion, and the deficit of wartime births that should now have been reaching the labor age—these and many other things account for the fact that artists and writers, workmen and peasants and managers, do not at this moment feel that public reproof (which they are very quick indeed to heed) must necessarily be followed by incarceration in the concentration camp. In a time of manpower shortages, the fact that the concentration camp is the most wasteful and least productive way of exploiting manpower is especially felt. The camps are gentler now, yet they are there. Their size is shrinking, yet no one dares to propose their abolition or even to take public notice of them. Even as this paper is being prepared, at least one new class of young people, the rebellious student youth, is being moved in increasing numbers into the camps.

The police has been downgraded and, in a regime so in need of naked force, the army has been upgraded, i.e., given more internal political functions. The public prosecutors have been given more control of trials and pretrial inquisitions—like making the fox the guardian of the chicken coop. There are some other minor legal reforms. Above all there has been much fuss made about the promise to codify and regularize the laws.

This new code was begun in Stalin's last months. It was promised "within sixty days" by Lavrenti Beria when his star seemed in the ascendant. It has not been promulgated yet, four years after Stalin's and almost four years after Beria's death. Sight unseen, we can predict that the new code will not touch the foundations of the totalist state: it will not alter the subservience of courts and laws and prosecutors and judges and police to the will and purposes of the oligarchy or the single leader. It is necessary to remember that any total power, and *a fortiori* any totalist power, may obey its own laws whenever it suits it to do so without giving those laws power over itself or making them into limitations upon its powers. A power center that is both legislator and administrator and judge and enforcer and even self-pronounced infallible "critic" of its own acts, may declare any activity it pleases a crime. In the Soviet Union, even loyalty to the underlying principles on which the state itself was founded has been declared a degrading crime and punished with incredible cruelty. How easily this totalist state may set aside its laws and negate its most solemn and "binding" promises is evidenced anew—after the proclamation of "socialist legality"—by the sudden repudiation by the "workers' state" of the state debt owed to the workers themselves, without so much as the possibility of anybody making a murmur. The owners of the repudiated bonds, in which they had invested their now wiped out compulsory savings, were even obliged to hold meetings and pass resolutions in which to express their delight at being expropriated.

The longer such a regime endures the more it has need of regularization of the duties and expectations of its subjects, even as it keeps up undiminished its powers of sudden reversal and unpredictable and unlimited intervention. The only guarantee against a totally powerful state is the existence of nonstate organizations capable of effective control of or effective pressure on the governmental power. Otherwise, to attempt to check, or limit, or even question is to invite the fury of exemplary punishment.

"Betwixt subject and subject [Locke wrote of the defenders of despotism], they will grant, there must be measures, laws and judgments for their mutual peace and security. But as for the ruler, he ought to be absolute, and is above all such circumstances; because he has the power to do more hurt and wrong, it is right when he does it. To ask how you may be guarded from harm or injury on that side . . . is the voice of faction and rebellion. . . . The very question can scarcely be borne. They are ready to tell you it deserves death only to ask after safety. . . ."

It is well for us to remember that the most despotic rulers have on occasion handed down elaborate law codes. The famous and in many ways justly admired Roman Code was compiled and proclaimed only after the emperor himself had become a god, no longer subject to question or limitation, only to worship. Though laws must multiply and be regularized so that the subjects may know what is expected of them and what they can count on in their relations with each other wherever the central power is unaffected, the lack of independent courts, of independent power groups or corporate bodies, of an independent press and public opinion, deprives these laws of any binding force upon the rulers. In Communist totalitarianism, the place of imperial divinity is taken by the infallibility of doctrine, the dogmatic untouchability of the dictatorship, the infallibility of the masters of the infallible doctrine, and by such spiritual demiurges as "revolutionary consciousness," "historical necessity," and "the interests of the revolution and of the people." Those who *know* where History is going surely have the right and duty to see to it that she goes there.

"The scientific concept, dictatorship," Lenin reminds us with beautiful simplicity, "means neither more nor less than unlimited power, resting directly on force, not limited by anything, not restricted by any laws or any absolute rules. Nothing else but that."

And to Commissar of Justice Kursky, when he was elaborating the first legal code, Lenin wrote:

> [My] draft is rough . . . but the basic thought, I hope, is clear: openly to set forth the proposition straightforward in principle and straightforward politically (and not merely in the narrow juridical sense) which motivates the *essence* and *justification* of terror, its necessity, its limits.
>
> "The court should not eliminate the terror: to promise that would be either to deceive oneself or to deceive others, but should give it a foundation and a legalization in principle, clearly, without falsification and without embellishment. It is necessary to formulate it as broadly as possible, for only a revolutionary consciousness of justice and a revolutionary conscience will put conditions upon its application in practice, on a more or a less broad scale."

In these regards the new men do not have to "return to Leninist norms," for they have never been abandoned for a moment.

If we can hope for, even perhaps count on, the diminution of the apocalyptic element in the ideology of a going, long-lasting society, we must remind ourselves that Leninism was peculiar in that its central "ideas" were always ideas about organization, and they have been strengthened rather than weakened in the course of time.

Bolshevism was born in an organizational feud about the definition of a party member, and who should control a paper (*Iskra*) which should act both as guardian of the doctrine and organizational core of the party. "Give me an organization," Lenin wrote at the outset of his career as a Leninist, "and I will turn Russia upside down." The organization he wanted, he explained, must be one in which "bureaucratism" prevailed against "democratism," "centralism" against "autonomy," which "strives to go from the top downward, and defends the enlargement of

the rights and plenary powers of the central body against the parts."
When at the 1903 Congress an exalter of the Central Committee urged
that it should become the "omnipresent and one," the all-pervasive,
all-informing and all-uniting "spirit," Lenin cried out from his seat:
"*Ne dukh, a kulak!*" ("Not spirit, but fist!"). The idea of the rule of
the elite, the idea of a vanguard party, the idea of the hatefulness of all
other classes and the untrustworthiness of the working class, the idea
that the working class too required a dictator or overseer to compel
it to its mission—it is amazing to note that these "ideas" about organization form the very core of Leninism as a special ideology. Far from
"eroding" or growing "weak" and merely "decorative," it is just precisely
these structural principles which have grown and expanded, and become
systematized.

Resentments, discontent, longing for a less oppressive regime and an
easier lot exist under despotisms, autocracies, total-power states, and
totalist states, even as in other social orders. Indeed, whenever hope or
expectation stirs they are apt to become endemic and intense. The problem of "state-craft" in a despotism is that of preventing the discontent
and longing from assuming *organized* form. Since the totalist state pene-
trates all social organizations and uses them as transmission belts (destroying whatever organization it cannot assimilate to its purposes and
structure), it is particularly adapted to keeping discontent fragmented
and unorganized.

By 1936, Lenin's central idea of an elite, single-centered dictatorship had gotten into the "most democratic constitution in the world" as
Article 126, which proclaimed the party to be "the vanguard of the
working people and the leading core of all organizations both social and
state." And last summer, when Khrushchev and the rest were summing
up the discussion over Stalin, they declared in *Pravda*: "As for our country, the Communist Party has been and will be the *only master* of the
minds, the *thoughts*, the *only spokesman, leader and organizer* of the
people" (my italics).

It is foolhardy to believe that they did not mean it, self-deluding to
persuade ourselves that the forces pressing for concessions within the
country are likely to find the road open to separate and effective corporate organization, which is the condition precedent to the development of
a limited, multicentered state and a society which is stronger than it.

Even before Stalin died, we got evidence that the spirit of man is
wayward and not as easily subjected as his body—the mass desertions at
the war's end; the escape of millions who "voted with their feet" against
totalitarianism; the two out of three "Chinese volunteers" in the Korean
prison camps who preferred exile under precarious and humiliating "dis-

placed person" conditions to return to their native scenes and homes. Since Stalin's death there have been East Berlin and Pilsen, Poznan and Vorkuta, Warsaw and Budapest, to prove that men will sometimes stand up unarmed to tanks and cannon and machine guns. They have proved too that the armies of the conquered lands have never been the pliant instruments of the Kremlin that fainthearted men thought they were.

We have seen that forty years of *Gleichschaltung*, corruption, and terror have not rooted out of the artist the ineradicable notion that sincerity to his creative vision is more to be desired than *partiinost* and *ideinost*. We have seen that the youth—although the fainthearted had thought they would be turned off the conveyer-belt as "little monsters"— are born young still, and therefore plastic, receptive, questioning, capable of illusion and disillusion, of "youthful idealism" and doubt and rebellion. Now the expulsions among the university youth are for the first time providing a pariah elite as a possible leadership to future undergrounds which may form under even this most efficiently regimented of societies.

I have never for a moment ceased to cast about for grounds of hope: that weaker heirs might make less efficient use of the terrible engines of total power; that a struggle or series of struggles for the succession might compel a contender to go outside the inner circles and summon social forces in the lower ranks of the party or outside of it into some sort of independent existence; that the army, disgraced as no other in all history by the charge that it gave birth to traitors by the thousands in its general staff, might develop sufficient independence from the party to make it a rival power center or an organized pressure body; that intellectuals, technicians, students might somehow break through the barriers that hinder the conversion of discontent into an organized, independent force.

But if I put the emphasis on the nature of the Soviet institutional framework and its built-in staying powers, it is by way of bending the stick in order to straighten it out. For the Western world has found it hard (or so it has seemed to me) to gaze straight and steadily at the head of Medusa, even if only in the reflecting shield of theoretical analysis. Brought up in a world of flux and openness, we find it hard to believe in the durability of despotic systems. Our hopes and longings are apt to betray us again and again into a readiness to be deceived by others or to deceive ourselves. And the "journalistic" nature of our culture has made us too ready to inflate the new because that alone is "news," while we neglect to put it into its tiresomely "repetitious" historical and institutional setting.

From the NEP to Socialism in One Country; from the Popular Front and Collective Security to the Grand Alliance and One World; from

Peaceful Coexistence to the Geneva Spirit—the occupational hazard of the Western intellectual has been not to read too little but to read too much into planned changes, involuntary changes, and even into mere tactical maneuvers and verbal asseverations.

Each has been hailed in turn as the softening of the war of the totalist state on its own people and the world, as the long awaited "inevitable change" or "fundamental transformation"; "the sobering that comes from the responsibilities of power"; the "response to the pressure of the recognition of reality"; the growing modification of totalist power by "a rationalist technocracy"; the sobering "effect of privilege upon a new privileged class"; the "rise of a limited and traditionalist despotism"; a "feeling of responsibility to Russia as against World Revolution"; the "quiet digestion period of a sated beast of prey" no longer on the prowl; the "diffusion of authority which could lead to a constitutional despotism"; the "mellowing process that sooner or later overtakes all militant movements"; the second thoughts on the struggle for the world which have come at long last "from a recognition of the universal and mutual destructiveness of nuclear war"; the "inevitable work of erosion upon the totalitarian edifice." (Each of these expressions is quoted from some highly respected authority on Soviet affairs in the Anglo-Saxon world.)

Because of the nature of our mental climate and our longings, because too of the injection of "revolutionary methods" into diplomacy in a polarized and antagonistic world, the danger does not lie in a failure on our part to watch for change, nor in a failure to "test"—though generally without sufficient skepticism—the meaning of each verbal declaration. No, "the main danger," as the Communists would say, has not lain in insensitivity to hope, but in too ready self-deception.

When Hitler's attack on Russia threw Stalin into our camp during World War II, I wrote an article entitled "Stalin at the Peace Table," which contended that there would be no peace table and general settlement as after other wars, and that the peace would be settled piecemeal by the strategic acts of the war, so that, if the war were not planned accordingly, there would be no decent peace. The illusions of the Grand Alliance were such that this view could not get a hearing.

This is not surprising in the case of a Cassandra who is merely a cloistered writer on totalitarianism and Soviet affairs. But Winston Churchill, participating in the directing councils of the Grand Alliance, tried to get an agreement on a strategy for the joint occupation and liberation of the Balkans and Eastern Europe, and even he could not prevail against the overpowering Grand Alliance illusions of wartime Britain and America. As a result, where the Soviet army was in sole occupation, there are conquered countries. Where there was joint occupation, there is a divided

Germany and a divided Korea. Where the Soviet army was not admitted, there is a Japan free to criticize its occupier and remake its own destiny. Thus our trying to understand and estimate Soviet totalitarianism is not mere exercise in sociological abstraction or historical generalization. For literally every judgment about the nature of totalitarianism and the scope of the changes in it is fraught with significance for the fate of millions of men.

17

Reflections on
the Future of
the Soviet System

In Mexico City there is a *pulquería* or *cantina* with the intriguing name, *Memorias del Porvenir*—Memories of the Future. Not having access to *pulque* at the moment, I have no such memories on which to draw. Moreover, if there is one thing that has impressed itself upon me most forcefully in a quarter century of striving to write, with the aid of archeological methods, the history of a living society, it is precisely this:

> More than the historian likes to admit, at every turn he finds
> the unexpected and the unpredictable: contingency, historical
> accident, biological accident intruding into history, as when the
> death of a history-making personage brings a change in direction;
> sudden changes of mood and flare-ups of mass-madness followed by
> mass-passivity; emergence of totally new and unanticipated situa-
> tions; leaps that seem to turn disparate series of ambiguous
> little events into a definite large one; the unintended consequence
> of intended actions. . . . [1]

A similar caveat appeared in a paper prepared by me for St. Antony's College, Oxford, ten years ago[2] and applies to the present article as well.

The Oxford paper examined the view, widely held ten years ago and again being urged today, that "the attempt to embrace the totality of

This essay is a condensed version of the author's chapter in *The U.S.S.R. after Fifty Years: Promise and Reality*, edited by Samuel Hendel and Randolph Braham (New York: Alfred A. Knopf, 1967). It is reprinted here by permission of *The Russian Review*, where it appeared in April 1967.

298

social life and social activity is somehow incompatible with the complexity of modern industry, advanced technology and a literate working population." I reminded my hearers that Germany adopted totalitarianism when it was the foremost country of Europe in industry, technology, literacy, and higher education. Indeed (I said) it is precisely modern technology with its all-embracing means of communication, its high-speed transmission of reports from the localities and of commands from the center and armed forces to any part of a great country, its mass-communication and mass-conditioning techniques that for the first time makes it possible for despotic (undivided) power to aspire to be the totalist (all-embracing) power. That is what Herzen foreboded when he wrote: "Some day Jinghis Khan will return with the telegraph."

And, so far as universal literacy is involved: Once more it is Germany that serves to remind us that "modern totalitarianism requires that everybody be able to read so that all can be made to read the same thing at the same moment. Not the ability to read, but the ability to choose between alternative kinds of reading is a potential—but only a potential—liberating influence."

"There is a principle of selection in personal despotism (I wrote in my Oxford paper) which surrounds the despot with courtiers, sycophants, executants and rules out challenging and original minds . . . I would not write these 'smallish men' too small, however, for when you have a sixth of the earth, a population of over 200,000,000, a total state economy, and a great empire to practice on, you learn other trades besides that of courtier or faction lieutenant. Even so, not one of Stalin's lieutenants exhibits the originality and the high charge of energy and intellect that characterizes Lenin, or the grosser, but no less original, demonic force of Stalin."

With a longer time span and a third exemplar to contemplate, I should like to amplify this "law of diminishing dictators." Like other generalizations which prolong the past by extrapolation towards the future, this "law" should be formulated with the anticipation of possible surprises, such as the appearance of a new dictator, who, after attaining power, may display a demonic dynamism or a complacent benevolence hitherto unknown. It is essential to note that although Stalin has been written smaller now and the leaders have made public if faltering pledges not to restore "Stalinism," no institutional safeguards have been set up to make a new capricious or cruel or even a paranoid dictatorship impossible. Beyond a doubt, however, Stalin was smaller than Lenin, Khrushchev than Stalin, while Brezhnev and the men in the present, I think transitory, "collective leadership" seem smaller still.

With the diminution in the size of the dictators there goes a diminution in content and dynamic charge in the ideology in the name of which they claim the right to rule over a great nation. A Marx or Lenin in any case is not born every day. Though circumstances may permit a wielder of power to grow with his exercise of power, the appearance of a great man is a genetic accident, not as Engels and Plekhanov would make it, a law of history. Circumstances do not set their impress upon men so much as great men set their impress upon their age and circumstances. Undoubtedly, Marx was greater than Engels in his passions, and the sweep of his more lawless, less systematic, and more demon-possessed intellect.

Though Lenin liked to think of himself as the successor to both Marx and Engels, in actuality he represents an amalgam of the voluntarist and inevitablist aspects of Marxism with the extremist revolutionary and organizational traditions of Russian populism, on which explosive mixture he set the stamp of his own unique personality. His Marxism was so different from Marx's that an amused but not unfriendly observer, Charles Rappoport, called it "Marxisme à la tartare"—Marxism with tartar sauce. Stalin's Leninism, in turn, differed enough from that of Lenin that we might term it "Leninisme à la mode caucasienne"—Leninism marinated in a sauce of mountaineer blood-vengeance.

As for Nikita Khrushchev with his proverbs and clichés, his random remedies, his bumptious outbursts of temper and bossy humor, his shoe off at the United Nations, his "state of all the people," "butter on the bread of communism," "we will bury you" and "I have seen the slaves of capitalism and they live well,"—though he belongs in the succession of diminishing dictators, we cannot really find a place for him in the series of ideological titans. Brezhnev, who at this writing would seem to have his uncertain hand on the power lever of the party machine, appears to be no more than an insignificant transition figure in a new interregnum and a succession crisis that has not yet come to a head.

In view of the tendency inherent in "the law of diminishing dictators," and the accumulation over five decades of countervailing interest groupings and pressures for relaxation inside Russia, and in view also of the, in the main successful, if vacillating and hence not always complete, "containment" by outside resistance and outside countervailing power, it is not surprising to find seedcorns of doubt and signs of erosion in the fanatical, crusading ideology. Facts, too, are stubborn things and contribute to the work of erosion.

Yet it is well to remember that this process of erosion began not with Stalin or Khrushchev but with Lenin himself, at least as early as two years after he seized power.

His first "eroding" discovery was made even earlier, namely, his discovery that the "peasants had voted with their feet" against the continuing of the war and its transformation into civil war and world revolution. The result was his surrender of much of the Russian empire at Brest-Litovsk merely to hold on to power until the world revolution should spread to the West. (Actually he got most of the land back not because of world revolution but because of the victory of the Allies over the Central Powers.)

For two years he saw world revolution everywhere. His ideology was an encapsulating compulsive monologue with himself in which he persuaded himself and his followers that capitalism was finished; that World War I was the "final crisis"; that the seizure of power in Russia was only the first act in a worldwide or at least Europe-wide revolution; that the Second International and the mass unions were dead and discredited beyond revival. The masses needed but to be summoned to battle, "International Menshevism" isolated and destroyed by the purge-net of the Twenty-one Conditions, built to admit minnows and exclude whales, and Soviets would spring up in every land in a worldwide international dictatorship.

"The Soviet form has conquered not only in backward Russia (Lenin told the First Congress of the Comintern) but also in the most developed country in Europe, Germany, and in the oldest capitalist land, England." Genuinely imprisoned in the envelope of his ideological misunderstandings, he misread the German *Betriebsraete* and the British Shop Steward movement, too, fancying the latter's strikes to be revolutionary, and seeming to anticipate a march on Westminster Palace with rifles and cold arms to disperse the ancient Parliament and set up rule by the Shop Steward Councils. On March 12, he told a credulous Petrograd Soviet that "at present soviets are being established in America." The only correlate I could find in the real world was the setting up of a General Strike Committee during the Seattle General Strike to run the municipal services of food delivery and garbage collection "by Order of the General Strike Committee."

Thus the first "erosion of ideology," or as it is sometimes called, "relativization of absolute ideas," began a half century ago, in the mind of Lenin himself, when he recognized "the delay of the revolution in the West," the revival of the mass unions and parties, the need of "united front" tactics and "infiltration of mass organizations," and of a New Economic Policy in Russia. With the first erosion, arose the first erosion illusions. It is sobering to think how the world might have been saved the cold war and Eastern Europe decades of subjection, if we had not nourished so many illusions concerning the "death" of Lenin's and

Stalin's ideology, and had so planned the acts of World War II that our soldiers would have been at the war's end in positions which could have guaranteed a decent peace in Prague, Berlin, Bucharest, and Belgrade. And no less sobering to remember that this work of erosion has been going on now for half a century, yet totalitarianism *as a structure* still endures. We must ask once more, as I did ten years ago, what is it that still endures, and for the foreseeable future, seems likely to continue to endure, in this institutional system?

Lenin's brief period of "absolute expectations" was over within two years of his seizure of power. They were illusions promoted by the ease with which he had conquered power ("as easy as lifting up a feather") and the certitude that that seizure was but the first act of a drama whose second act would begin almost immediately in another part of the forest: namely, Germany. Once these "infantile leftist" illusions were over, he returned to the durable core of his earlier Leninism, his doctrine of total and totally centralized organization.

Marx had been vague on how the working class takes power, though he stressed that it was to be through a party embracing the entire class. The few other remarks he made when pressed by Duehring or Lasalle were taken literally by Lenin and Stalin; even now their successors, though aware of the mischief some of these precepts are occasioning, seem unable to shake off their spell.

From the dogma of labor-time receipts instead of money, and from centralized distribution of every slice of bread and pen nib, Lenin soon recovered. On the abolition of the market, Lenin beat a partial retreat with the NEP ("seriously and for a long time"). In this respect it is well to remember that there has been not erosion but reinforcement in the form of central command planning of everything and abolition of the NEP. At most, in these fifty years, there has been an ebb and flow with more flow than ebb. On the doctrine of the withering away of the state there has also been the reverse of erosion. "The State of All the People" is only an enlargement of the State's claims to speak for everybody, claims first staked out for the party's dictatorship by Lenin himself in 1902, when he wrote: "The Social Democrats must go *into all classes of the population* . . . to dictate a positive program of action alike to rebellious students, to dissatisfied Zemstvo figures, discontented religious sectarians, and indignant school teachers, and so on."[3]

In Lenin Marx had an innovating disciple who was a theoretician, a technician, a militant defender, propounder and virtuoso of organization and total power. Conspirative secrecy, centralized organization, command performance, military discipline, detailed instructions, the ability to mobilize, manipulate, and organize discontent and hatred—a technique, indeed an elaborate technology and pedantic systemization of the art and science of seizing power, extending power by frontal attack or by zigzag and by feeling out the weak spots in the adversary, a technique and technology for holding power, utilizing power, regularizing and bureaucratizing power, extending power in width and depth even unto the affairs of the spirit—what are these if not levers of modern totalitarian revolution and totalitarian rule?

The first peculiarity that strikes one in Lenin's organizational doctrine is his centralism, and his extreme distrust not only of whole classes (the intelligentsia, the petty bourgeoisie, the peasantry, and the working class itself), but even of the rank and file of his own party, and his own local organization. "Bureaucratism versus autonomy, such is the principle of revolutionary social democracy as against the opportunists" (he wrote at the outset of his career as a Leninist). "The organization of revolutionary social democracy strives to go from the top downward, and defends the enlargement of the rights and plenary powers of the Central Body."

In the third year of his rule with his power secure and the Civil War at an end, far from permitting the principle of centralism to "erode," he reinforced it by plugging up the last vents of public discussion. It was then that he abolished the very basis of such party democracy as had existed in the early years before he could complete the act of *Gleichschaltung* by prohibiting party groupings, platforms for proposal of changes, gatherings of like-minded communists to discuss their views, with expulsion provided for any violation. Having already drained the Constituent Assembly and the Soviets of political power, he now did the same with the trade unions and his own party.

In power Lenin was fulfilling the dream of his early "Letter to a Comrade on Our Organizational Tasks" which had so impressed Stalin:

> We have arrived at an extremely important principle of all party organization and activity. In regard to ideological and practical *direction*, the movement and the revolutionary struggle of the proletariat need the *greatest* possible *centralization*, but in regard to *keeping the center informed* . . . in regard to *responsibility* before the party, we need the greatest possible *decentralization*. The movement must be led by the smallest possible number. . . . But the largest possible number of the most varied and heterogeneous groups drawn from diverse layers of the proletariat (and other classes) should take part in the movement. . . . *Now* we become an organized party and that means the creation of power, the transformation of the authority of ideas into the authority of power, the subordination of the lower party organs to the higher ones.

Here, as early as 1902, is Lenin's whole schema: the dictatorship of the party over all classes of society, the transmission belt system of implementing that dictatorship, the rule of the many and most diverse groups by the fewest and most homogeneous, the transformation of the authority of ideas into the authority of power in all the manifold activities which were to concern the party—and which activities were not?

Lenin's Archimedean cry for an organization of revolutionaries to turn Russia upside down did not cease when he had indeed turned Russia upside down. As before he continued to call for "organization, organization, organization." To his old dream of centralized organization of the party, he added the new dream made possible by power: the dream of total organization of life by the party in accordance with its, i.e., his, blueprint for society and man.

Now he would remake the spirit of Russia, its industries, its agriculture, its interchange of goods, its foreign trade. He would remake the Oblomovs, the Lopakhins, the Ranevskayas, the Stroganovs, the Morozovs, and even the Ivan Ivanoviches, all according to his blueprint of the New Soviet Man. He would remake Russia's emotions, her thoughts, her feelings, her habits, even her dreams, eliminating by total organization all slackness, all waywardness of will, all indifference to or tolerance of other ways. "We must organize everything," he said in the summer of 1918, "take everything into our hands." To the authoritarianism inherent in an infallible doctrine, possessed and interpreted by an infallible interpreter who rules an infallible party infallibly from above, Lenin added the further dream of "organizing everything, taking everything in our hands."

Thus the most obvious trait setting Lenin apart from his associates in the Russian intelligentsia and the revolutionary movement was his absorption with the mechanics and dynamics of organization and power. In a world where most intellectuals were in love with ideas, and accustomed—whether by temperament or the pressure of circumstances—to a distinction, even a yearning gap, between the dream and the deed, Lenin was an organization man—indeed, the organization man of whatever movements he took part in. When he broke with his colleagues on *Iskra* it was on the question of organization. Amidst men dedicated to dreams, organization was his dream. But such an ideology, the ideology of complete control of society by the party, and complete centralization of power within the party, does not erode as easily as do other ideas such as egalitarianism, or international socialism, or permanent revolution or "complete communism."

In other words, totalitarianism has an ideology that is the ideology of a structure. What is growing thin, shallow, passionless, and lacking in conviction is the ideology of the structure's purpose. Every effort is made to diminish or check this process of "erosion" by the enforcement of *partiinost*, by the exclusion of the foreign press, radio and television, by the deliberate suppression of articles of criticism or challenge, by a continuing war on freedom in the arts, and, where they impinge on matters of power, in the sciences, by the outlandish denunciation of "archive rats" (Stalin), "historians" (they are "dangerous people" —Khrushchev), "bourgeois objectivity," "bourgeois falsification," and "vulgar Factology."

There seem to be no good reasons why those who enjoy the prerogatives of absolute power should give it up merely because they have become somewhat vaguer as to why they are exercising it. What I wrote in my 1957 paper is still valid: "If in general it is dangerous to relax the screw ever so slightly or to measure out homeopathic doses of freedom, there is an additional specific danger that big announcements and big promises may seem to mean more than they intend. Illusion, to paraphrase Marx, once it takes possession of great masses of men, becomes itself a material force."

One has only to look at the trouble caused by "destalinization" both in Russia and in its satellites, and the consequent awkward efforts at partial "restalinization," to convince one's self that to play with freedom is to play with fire.

One of the key powers of a totalitarian regime is the absolute monopoly of all means of communication. The rulers own and control the newspapers which should criticize their misdeeds. They control the critics; they decide who is to be criticized for what, who made the scapegoat, who lauded to the skies. They control the printing plants, the publishing houses, the libraries, the bookstores, the reviews, the reviewers, the size of editions, what shall be published and what remain unpublished; they control the telephone set, the radio, television, the loudspeaker on the public square. They control procurators and lawyers, police and mass meetings, the staging of mob scenes, the packing of the courtroom with unconditional adherents, the exclusion of friends and relatives of the accused.

In a totalitarian land, the rulers can dictate the editorials which misrepresent the accused and their deeds, can intimidate the judges, dictate the verdict before the trial, deny meeting halls to the accused, pack the courtroom with secret police dressed as workingmen, peasants, and intellectuals to drown the words of defense and to clamor for punishment. The victorious clique or single leader can put words of guilt and confession into the mouth of the accused.

Will the Russian people ever know what Bukharin really urged as a program for them? Or what Malenkov, Molotov, and Kaganovich actually proposed, or what it was that made them "anti-party"? If we know what Sinyavsky wrote, it was because of his heinous crime of getting published abroad—an honor for the writers of other nations— and because some courageous friend, at the risk of his own freedom, smuggled his courtroom defense out of the country. Inside Russia the ordinary mortal has not heard nor read his speech of defense, nor the work which he succeeded in getting published in other lands when it was self-evident that he could not publish it in his native tongue for his own people in his own country. Is there any plight more terrible than to be charged with infamous imaginary crimes in the name of a voiceless people who are not even permitted to hear one's answer to the charges that they did not really make?

There is no sign of erosion of this monopoly of the means of communication. Authors, emboldened by the lapsing of the death penalty for unpublished and unpublishable writings, recite unpublished poems, pass tiny handwritten or mimeographed editions around, but this they did even under Stalin and under Lenin, though under Stalin the punishment in all things was more awful when the dictator's sickly suspicion or resentment was aroused. Even the bit of freedom thus assumed by authors in their corporate solidarity arouses the fury of the party potentates, though many of our commentators like to speak about the scant freedom taken, without noticing the crackdowns which follow.

No lover of freedom can take comfort in the brutal treatment of Russia's great poet Pasternak; in the critical pearls concerning him that issued from the mouth of the youth overseer and secret police chief, Semichastny; in the unfeeling rantings of Sholokhov against defenseless colleagues at a party congress; in the trials of Sinyavsky and Yuri Daniel and their condemnation to long terms of hard penal labor for the crime of practicing their profession; in the incarceration of Tarsis and the mathematician-poet, Yesenin-Volpin, and the promising young poet-translator, Brodsky, in a madhouse; in Tarsis' subsequent deprivation of citizenship by tyrants who rule the land in which he was born; in the sentencing of the gentle poet Brodsky to shovelling manure in a forced labor camp in the Arctic Circle, a barbarous sentence which only an internal barbarian who hates culture and poetry could have thought appropriate for the crime of wanting to be a poet. (One looks in vain for an analogue in the treatment of men of letters under the tsars; the only analogy one can think of is that of the Nazi leader Baldur von Schirach proclaiming, "When I hear the word *Culture*, I cock my revolver.")

I am deeply shocked when callous colleagues write that once Russia too has modern industry, poetry and literary freedom will take care of themselves (the "convergence theory"). Indeed, heavy industry can get along very well without freedom for poets, who do more for industry when they shovel manure.

It is dispiriting to find the publication of *One Day in the Life of Ivan Denisovich* printed and critically praised one day at the whim of a Boss whose only knowledge of literature is the knowledge which comes from power over everything which is ipso facto expert knowledge of everything. And then to find the same work condemned at the Twenty-third Congress at the whim of another Boss whose power over everything enables him to know with equal authority that the work is bad.

It is a cheerless task to read the speeches delivered in that great "deliberative body," the "supreme authority of the Party," the Twenty-third Congress. It is still worse than preceding congresses, for it was not even used as a sounding board to propagate a new line. For all the "deliberations" that took place in this august body, its almost five thousand "delegates" and its two thousand honored guests might have been replaced by so many phonograph records, for each speaker took the floor only if assigned to do so, and developed the point assigned to him to develop, in the language prescribed for him by previous decision of the higher body which decided everything in advance before it convoked the congress. It would be deadly dull were it not so frightening.

We must take note of the fact that the tolerant and courageous editor of *Novy Mir*, Alexander Tvardovsky, was not even on the roster of delegates or invited guests (he was a delegate to the Twenty-first and Twenty-second congresses, where his knowing voice contributed something valuable to the omnipotent party's discussion of literature, but this time his voice was silenced, his wisdom suppressed, and the incoming Central Committee no longer lists his name as a Candidate-Member so that his voice will not be heard in their meetings either).

This time, in place of Khrushchev, the man who knows all about art and literature is Brezhnev, for as before, power over everything gives knowledge of everything:

> Unfortunately [Brezhnev told the Congress] such practitioners of the arts are to be found who, instead of helping the people, choose to specialize in denigrating our regime and slandering our heroic people. Of course these are only isolated cases, by no means expressing the feelings and thoughts of our creative intelligentsia .... These renegades scoff at what is most holy to every Soviet man—the interest of the socialist homeland. It goes without saying that the Soviet people [i.e., the police] cannot ignore the shameful activities of such people. It treats them as they deserve.

This is not merely a reaffirmation of the sentences meted out to Sinyav-sky, Daniel, Brodsky, Tarsis and Yesenin-Volpin, but a warning to those Soviet writers who would like to support them or follow their example. If this be "erosion" or "convergence" then some of my colleagues have found new meanings for old words, or have developed a new indifference to freedom and to the differences between regimes.

There are styles in theories as in clothes. Just now it is the fashion to talk of the "convergence" of the Soviet Union and the United States. As near as I can follow it, this theory seems to assert that as soon as two countries develop heavy industry and can land rockets on the moon, (some would insist that there must also be an abundance of managers and of consumer goods), the two systems will converge, developing similar institutions, similar traditions, similar ways of life, in short, become fundamentally like each other.

One examines the history of mankind in vain for confirmation of such simplification. The abstracting mind talks, for example, of "feudalism," but the historian turns to Medieval England, France, Germany, Russia, Poland and finds the most diverse traditions, institutions, freedoms, forms of natural obligation or lack of it, in the various latifundial lands, finds too the most diverse forms of bondage, or localism, of sovereign power and rebelliousness, of the reign of law and of arbitrariness, and so on through the entire warp and woof of life.

So too, the historian watches the rapid industrialization of Germany and England and the United States during the later nineteenth century, and in the last few decades from 1880 to 1914 of Russia as well, but he cannot find that their institutions or their traditions became nugatory. Germany remained an empire with an autocratic emperor, *Junkertum* militarism and Prussian plural voting, while the Britons counted that their navy would prevent them from ever being "slaves," that a small volunteer army was all they needed, while they continued to extend their charter of liberties, their reign of law, their supremacy of parliament, and the steady reduction of the powers of their sovereign until he became little more than a cherished symbol. In matters of history, traditions, attitudes and institutions of a country, its philosophy, its intellectual priorities, its freedom, we must hold with Aristotle that "Differentiation is the beginning of wisdom." To note resemblances in some economic or institutional feature is barely the beginning of studying a great nation. To stop there is to abstract from all the rest, from the things that give color, flavor and distinction to each nation. One has only begun the task of studying a people and its history when one begins to note the *differentiae*, the qualities that distinguish members of a generalized abstract class from each other.

Joseph Stalin once charged the writer with being "an American exceptionalist." The more I considered this curious charge, the more convinced I became that I was guiltier than the indictment suggested, for suddenly I realized that I was an "exceptionalist" not only for America but for all the lands on earth. I came to the realization that every country moves towards its own future in terms of its own past, its own institutions and traditions, and that even when they borrow some features from each other, they transform them according to their unique differences. To abstract from these differences, as Marx and Lenin did, and at that moment Stalin was trying to persuade me to do, is to miss the essence of each country's life and history. In that moment of challenge to the "terrible simplifiers" and their abstractions, I think a historian was born.

Latterly a new generation of such simplifiers has appeared. They employ—unwittingly, no doubt—a grossly vulgarized Marxist concept to the effect that "economics determine politics" and the entire spiritual "superstructure." This vulgarized Marxist abstraction would have made Marx himself wince and repeat his famous line, "I, myself, am not a Marxist." It is terribly easy to forget that technology is neutral as regards freedom, that it may be used either to liberate or to enslave, to inform or to brainwash. "Some day," Herzen wrote in fear and trembling, "Jinghis Khan will return with the telegraph." "Hurrah!" cry our convergence theorists, "Then men will cease to be Jinghis Khan."

Are we to believe that when every man can read, it will no longer matter whether he lives under a system which gives him freedom to choose what he will read or under a system which gives him no choice but prescribes that he shall be reading the same slogan at the same moment in the same officially prescribed books and the same controlled press in every corner of his land?

Are we to believe that because there are mass-circulation journals, a television set in every home, and perhaps a loudspeaker in every square and public place, that it no longer matters whether there are many parties or one, rival candidates to choose from or no choice at all, a chance to rebuke, tame, turn out one's rulers, or no such chance? Is the presence of heavy industry, and perhaps some day of abundant consumer goods, supposed to make us forget that the central problem of politics is not *Who rules over us?* but, *How do we choose our rulers?* and still more, *How do we tame them? How do we escape from their continual supervision?* and *How do we keep some ultimate control over them in our hands?*

Are we to assume that because mass-circulation journals can make a great sensation out of every court case, it therefore makes no difference whether judges can stop a newspaper from discussing a case while it is under adjudication, as judges can in England, or whether judges are compelled to obey slogans bombarding them in the controlled press and come to the verdict shouted at them in advance in the name of a voiceless people, as was the case in the Sinyavsky trial?

Are we to assume that when in all great lands there is modern industry it will no longer matter whether a single-party state owns all organizations and operates them as transmission belts, or a whole complex of nonstate organizations exists under the control of their members who use them to exert pressure on officials, parties, and the state? Can it be that once there is modern industry and an abundance of consumer goods (the latter still a mere iterated and reiterated promise in the Soviet Union), then it will no longer matter whether there is a more or less open and pluralistic society or a more or less closed, monolithic command society with centralized control of everything including what to read, what to think, feel, do, hope, hate, love and dream about?

Fifty years have passed since Lenin seized power and established his dictatorship which has proved by a half century of continuity and contained change to be the most durable institutional regime, or, if you wish the most durable "party" regime, in the modern world. Yet one of its striking peculiarities is that in the course of a half century it has not succeeded in establishing a legitimate mode of succession.

Broadly speaking there are three kinds of legitimacy: the hieratic, the monarchical and the democratic. In the first case a leader is chosen by a religiously recognized procedure and invested with religious-magisterial authority. In the second, legitimacy depends upon blood relationship. Where it prevails, when a monarch dies it is clear through blood relationship who his successor shall be. "The King is dead, Long live the King" is a formula which makes it possible even for a minor child under a guardian regent to be invested with royal power. In the third case, the normal procedure for choice of a successor is a popular election. But there are also rules for determining a democratic succession in the case of sudden death. Thus one cannot imagine Harry Truman or Lyndon Johnson appealing for "the avoidance of confusion and panic" as the frightened lieutenants of Joseph Stalin did in a broadcast to their subjects after six hours and ten minutes of silence concerning his death.

The Russian democratic Provisional Government of 1917 represents an intermediate stage in the establishment of a new legitimacy after the old monarchical legitimacy had broken down or been terminated by revolution. The chief characteristic of the Provisional Government from its standpoint was that it had the political grace to call itself *Provisional*. By this act, it proclaimed itself as *pre-legitimate*, a government which openly considered itself to be provisional and recognized as its primary task in the sphere of politics the convocation of a constituent or constitution-making assembly to be freely and democratically elected, which would write a new constitution for the Russian land, thus establishing a new procedure for democratic legitimacy.

Lenin rightly recognized that he must at all costs prevent the creation of that new legitimacy. That is why he set so precise a date for the seizing of power: "History will not forgive a delay by the revolutionaries who can win today . . . but risk losing everything tomorrow."

Even then he did not take too seriously the ideological program of the revolution on a "mere" Russian scale. "The seizure of power is the point of the uprising; its political aim will clarify itself after the seizure. . . . Any delay in the offensive is like unto death."

Lenin opened that article, written on the eve of the seizure of power, with almost the same words with which he closed it: "I write these lines on the evening of the 24th, the situation is impossibly critical. The clearest thing of all is this, that now, really and truly it is clear that any delay in an uprising is like unto death."[4]

Once Lenin had power in his hands, he laid his plans to prevent the establishment of a new democratic legitimacy: "We say to the people that their interests are higher than the interests of a democratic institution. It is not necessary to go back to the old prejudices which subordinate the interests of the people to formal democracy."[5]

With the forestalling of the Constituent Assembly by his seizure of power, and the rupture of democratic legitimacy by the dispersal by force of the only authorized representatives of the Russian people, Lenin bade farewell to legitimacy and established a permanent dictatorship.

Now there was neither hereditary monarchical legitimacy nor democratic legitimacy nor any thought of pre-legitimacy. In a half century the dictatorial regime has not once submitted its actions or its personnel to the approval of the Russian people in a free election, nor has it the intention to do so in the future.

What then was the basis of Lenin's claim to rule over a great nation? Simply this: we have made a revolution in one nation with the intent to use it as a springboard for world revolution. We Communists have seized power over this nation because we possess an infallible doctrine which lets us know what history wants a country to do or to be. We are the sole possessors and only true interpreters of a "scientific" and infallible doctrine which enables us to work out a blueprint for the remaking of Russia and the remaking of man. It is this which justifies the dictatorship which we have set up over our own people, and aim to extend to all the lands on earth.

Lenin said on December 5, 1919, after he had been exercising power

for two years: "Dictatorship is a harsh, heavy and even bloody word."
And a year later, on October 20, 1920, he explained with precise pedantry to doubting democrats: "The scientific concept *dictatorship* means
nothing more nor less than unrestricted power, not limited by anything,
not restrained by any laws, nor by any absolute rules, and resting directly
on force, *that, and nothing else but that*, is the meaning of the concept
dictatorship."

In short, all limitations, constitutional, traditional, legal, or moral,
were ruptured. Having taken power by force in the name of their blueprint, the dictators were to apply their blueprint without accepting any
restraint upon the use of force. For such a regime, though it last half a
century, no legitimacy is sought nor possible.

True, there were four pieces of semantic sleight-of-hand employed
by Lenin, but these were only meant to paralyze the enemy and lessen
opposition.

The first is the confusing of the proletariat with the people. The second
is the confusing of the party with the proletariat. The third is the confusing of the party machine (Central Committee, Politburo, Presidium,
Secretariat, *Apparat*) with the party. The fourth is the confusing of the
vozhd or leader or boss with the party machine. All four of these semantic
tricks are inventions of Lenin. As hypocrisy is said to be the tribute that
vice pays to virtue so these subterfuges are the tribute that dictatorship pays to democracy. They have grown stale by endless repetition
but Lenin's heirs do not dare dispense with them lest their world come
tumbling down.

As we probe the fictions, they dissolve before our eyes. The party is no
party, for a party means a part and where there are no contending parties,
life dies out in the single party.

From her prison cell Rosa Luxemburg admonished Lenin:

> Freedom for the supporters of the government alone, freedom
> only for the members of one party—that is no freedom at all. . . .
> All that is instructive, wholesome, and purifying in political freedom
> depends upon this essential characteristic. . . . With the repression
> of political life in the land as a whole, life in the Soviets must
> also become more and more crippled. Without general elections,
> without unrestricted freedom of press and assembly, without a free
> struggle of opinion, life will die out in every public institution. . . .
> Public life gradually falls asleep, a few dozen leaders . . . direct
> and rule . . . an elite of the working class is invited from time to time
> to meetings where they are to applaud the speeches of the leaders
> and approve resolutions unanimously . . . not the dictatorship of the

proletariat but of a handful of politicians, a clique. . . . Such
conditions must inevitably cause a brutalization of public life:
attempted assassinations, shooting of hostages, etc.

How grimly has history confirmed her prophetic vision! What she did
not foresee, however, was that Lenin himself would finally drain his own
party of all political life by prohibiting groupings, and that his successor would kill more members of his own party than all the enemies of
communism in the world put together.

Where then shall legitimacy lodge? There is no provision in statutes or
constitution for an infallible leader, yet an infallible doctrine in the long
run requires a single, infallible interpreter. If there are a number of
conflicting interpretations the doctrine loses its "scientific" and "infallible" character, and the voiceless people may make one of the rival
factions its mouthpiece, so that pluralism will break out in the monolith.

When a leader dies, who shall name his successor? The Soviets have
been drained of life, the party has been drained of life, the unions have
been drained of life, the Central Committee has been replaced by the
Politburo or Presidium, and that by the Secretariat. Only a "little clique
of leaders," as Rosa Luxemburg termed it, can proclaim its collective
dictatorship, and conceal its internal differences until a new dictator
emerges to declare his rivals to have been anti-party or enemies of the
people. Given the law of diminishing dictators, given too the muted
discontent and pressure within, and the external pressures without, there
is no telling how long this "system" will endure, but one thing is certain,
within it there inheres no true legitimacy nor any intention of seeking it
from a free discussion and vote of its people or a free functioning of its
"public" bodies. What I wrote on this ten years ago I am afraid is still
true:

> As long as collective leadership does not swiftly and deter-
> minedly broaden itself instead of narrowing; as long as it does not
> openly treat itself as 'pre-legitimate' in the sense of aiming to replace
> itself by a broader, non-dictatorial organization of power; as long
> as power does not flood down into the basic units of the party
> (where it did not inhere even in Lenin's best days), and as long as
> it does not then overflow the party dikes and spill out into self-
> organizing corporate bodies independent of the state and party; as
> long, in other words, as there develop no organized, institution-
> alized checks upon the reflux of power to the top, not a mere
> slowing but an actual reversing of the whole trend of totalitarianism
> —there is no reason to regard any directory or collective leadership

as more than a mere interregnum between dictators . . . and there will be no legitimacy to provide a lawful succession.

And at this moment I cannot imagine any faction in the Communist party that would make as its program the devolution of power to the limbs and parts of the body politic, or a genuine consultation of its people to establish a new democratic legitimacy. Nor can I presently imagine such a set of circumstances as might engender such a faction.

18

A Historian
Looks at the
Convergence Theory

Recently, when John Kenneth Galbraith departed for a trip to the Soviet Union, he sent a message to his friend Sidney Hook, "Tell Sidney not to worry, I won't come back a Communist." To which Hook retorted, "I'm not worried that he'll come back a Communist; I'm afraid he'll come back saying that *they* aren't Communists." Galbraith returned to add the weight of some four hundred pages of his wit and learning to the already fashionable convergence theory. This is fortunate for the present writer since it excuses me from trying to expound in my own words a theory to which I would find it difficult to do justice. Indeed, Galbraith also supplied a timely five-hundred-word résumé of his viewpoint in the course of an interview with the *New York Times*'s crack reporter, Anthony Lewis, who tape-recorded it and published it in full in the magazine section of Sunday, December 18, 1966. The interview concluded with the following exchange:

> GALBRAITH: The nature of technology—the nature of the large organization that sustains technology, and the nature of the planning that technology requires—has an imperative of its own, and this is causing a convergence in all industrial societies. In the Eastern European societies it's leading to a decentralization of power from the state to the firm; in the Western European [and American] industrial societies it's leading to *ad hoc* planning. In

This essay was published in *Sidney Hook and the Contemporary World: Essays on the Pragmatic Intelligence*, edited by Paul Kurtz (New York: John Day Co., 1968).

fewer years than we imagine this will produce a rather indistinguishable melange of planning and market influences.

The overwhelming fact is that if you have to have a massive
technical complex, there will be a certain similarity in the
organization, and in the related social organization, whether that
steel complex is in Novosibirsk or in Nova Huta, Poland, or in Gary,
Ind.

LEWIS: *Are you suggesting that as the two societies converge,
the Communist society will necessarily introduce greater political
and cultural freedom?*

GALBRAITH: I'm saying precisely that. The requirements of deep
scientific perception and deep technical specialization cannot be
reconciled with intellectual regimentation. They inevitably lead
to intellectual curiosity and to a measure of intellectual liberalism.

And on our side the requirements of large organization impose
a measure of discipline, a measure of subordination of the individual
to the organization, which is very much less than the individualism
that has been popularly identified with the Western economy.[1]

There are fashions in theories as in clothes. Just now it is the fashion
among many political scientists, sociologists, sovietologists, and economists to speak of convergence when they write about the Soviet Union, or
discuss relations between the Russian government and the American.
Though it has only now attained to high fashion, in one form or another
the theory has been around for some time. Thus in the diary of Lady
Kennet of the Deane, made available to me while living in Lord Kennet's
home in London, I found this entry for a date in late May 1921: "Nansen
was here to tea and gave me the reassuring news that our troubles with
Russia are over. Lenin is introducing a New Economic Policy which
restores a free market and represents a return to capitalist exchange of
goods in Russia." Such wishful thinking is one of the perennial springs
that has fed the current of the convergence theory.

In 1932 and 1933 there was a spate of books on technocracy, all
assuring us that the United States and the Soviet Union were converging
towards a common industrial and political system in which technologists
or technocrats would determine policy and set the basic standards for
social and economic life. In 1941, James Burnham published his *Managerial Revolution*, extrapolating one of the complex curves in modern
industrial life in a tangent into outer space. His book was a confident
prophecy that in all advanced industrial lands:

Institutions and beliefs are undergoing a process of rapid transformation. The conclusion of this period of transformation, to be

expected in the comparatively near future, will find society
organized through a quite different set of major economic, social
and political institutions and exhibiting quite different major
social beliefs or ideologies. Within the new social structure a different social group or class—the managers—will be the dominant
or ruling class. [These changes] will constitute the transformation
of society to a managerial structure. . . . The theory of the managerial revolution is not merely predicting what may happen in a
hypothetical future but is an interpretation of what *already* has
happened and is now happening. Its prediction is that the process
which has started and which has already gone a great distance will
continue and reach completion.[2]

When Hitler "perfidiously," as the Russian textbooks say, double-
crossed his ally, Stalin, during World War II forcing him into the camp of
the democracies, the convergence theory took on somewhat different
forms. There were two new variants, one a popular view, the other a
product of the wishful thinking of homesick, exiled Russian intellectuals
who in the twenties had found refuge in America and made a place for
themselves in our academic life.

The popular variant sprang from the naive crusading nature of American wars with our ingrained tendency to envision our enemies as devils
and our allies as knights in shining armor. Hitler's deeds gave plenty of
material to justify the devil theory, but we tended to extend it throughout
the history of Germany, to every living German, and to generations yet
unborn, while we seemed to regard the Japanese people, their leaders and
their sovereigns as villains rather than monsters. The Russian armies
fought valiantly as they suffered the brunt of German attack and invasion, which gave us a sense of moral debt, a feeling that was promptly
put to use by Stalin and his apologists to obscure the moral issues of the
peace. This popular version of the convergence theory said:

The Russians are much like people everywhere and want what
we want. [The people of Germany and Japan seemed to be
subhuman exceptions, but for various reasons, we were more
indulgent toward the Italians]. Since people everywhere want the
same things, it will be easy to build "one world" with a sobered
and friendly Joseph Stalin after the war is over. He now knows the
value of democracy, who his friends are, and how destructive war
is, so the Grand Alliance will continue into the peace; together
we will build a world in which the peace-loving countries will
become steadily more like each other and come ever closer
together.[3]

A more sophisticated theory came from the Russian intellectuals who had been exiled or had fled from Russia in the twenties and become important writers and teachers in sociology or political science in the United States, always retaining a deep emotional attachment to the land of their birth, such men, for instance, as N. S. Timashev and Pitirim Sorokin. Professor Timashev delivered a series of wartime lectures on this theme, then published them as *The Great Retreat* in 1946. Professor Sorokin toured the country lecturing on the convergence theory in 1942 and 1943 and in January 1944 published a book in which all his knowledge of the two lands was brought into play, along with his favorite sociological, cultural, and ethical generalizations. His *America and Russia* proved enormously popular, running through a number of printings in the first year of its publication, and was reprinted in revised form as late as 1950.

Joseph Stalin did not make things easy for its thesis, for within the next few years, every land that his troops occupied alone was endowed with a "people's democracy" and a purge of democrats, liberals, conservatives, national patriots, and "national Communists," while lands like Germany and Austria that underwent dual or tripartite occupation had a line cut right across them wherever the Russian troops held sway. This seizure of "liberated" lands was followed by the rejection of Marshall Plan aid, the Zhdanov attack on "kowtowing to the West" and "rootless cosmopolitanism" in the arts and sciences, along with other despotic barbarities too blatant to be ignored. But Professor Sorokin was not to be put off in his hopes and creed, for in 1950 he published his revised edition, in which he took account of the "Cold War" to minimize and explain away the resultant "incompatibilities." The "seemingly conflicting values [he wrote] . . . are so insignificant that their 'incompatibility' amounts to no more than the 'incompatibility' of the advertisements for this or that brand of cigarettes, each claiming superiority over all others."[4]

Professor Sorokin's study is of special interest because of the broad scope of his analysis of the "spiritual, historical, and sociocultural compatibilities" of the two nations, because of his influential position as a professor of sociology first in Saint Petersburg and then at Harvard, because he is the acknowledged or unacknowledged source of many of the more limited variants of the convergence theory, and because of his deep attachment to both America and Russia and his singular Russian talent to suffer and forgive, and one is tempted to add, to forget.

In Russia Sorokin had been a professor of law and sociology: a secretary in Kerensky's cabinet, editor of the Socialist Revolutionary daily, *Volya Naroda*, which Lenin shut down in February 1918; delegate to the Peasant Soviet, which Lenin submerged in the Soviet of Workers and

Soldiers Deputies; delegate to the Constituent Assembly, which Lenin dispersed by force after its first session. On November 22, 1922, Sorokin sent a letter to *Pravda* in which he renounced all political activity and declared his intention to limit himself to teaching and scientific work. Lenin welcomed his "straightforwardness and sincerity," but, in accordance with the Leninist tendency to politicize everything, added a warning to Sorokin that teaching and scientific work could also be "politically reactionary." Shortly thereafter the professor lost his chair and his right to teach. When he ventured to publish a study of the breakdown of marriage under the influence of war and revolution and the postcard divorce system, Lenin labeled him a "diplomaed flunkey of clericalism," and announced the intention to "politely dispatch him," i.e., exile him, to "some country with a bourgeois democracy, the proper place for such feudalists."[5] That is how Sorokin found his way, alive, to America and to Harvard. By the time he wrote *America and Russia*, Professor Sorokin had not only forgiven the fact that Lenin stopped him from writing, teaching, engaging in political activity, and living in the land of his birth, but he seemed to forget that Stalin, less "polite," would have taken his life along with his honor. Indeed, Sorokin wrote of the purges as if they were themselves nothing but a great and historically foreordained step foward toward convergence:

> The cycle of the Russian Revolution is clearly demonstrated by the purges of Communist leaders. . . . By whom? Not by counter-revolutionists or anti-Communists. No. They are executed, imprisoned, banished, or excommunicated by Stalin and the Communist Party itself. To these should be awarded the first prize for the mortal blow dealt the Communist phase of the Revolution. . . . Stalin won because he *moved with the current* of history and *not against it*. . . . Those who were purged were purged because they sought to stem the tide of historical destiny. . . . If in the future Stalin and his followers should try to revive Communism as it existed in the first stage of the Revolution, seek to stem the tide of historical destiny, they would be liquidated as inexorably as Trotsky and his adherents. That is why I do not worry about what Stalin or any other leader may think or do. . . . [6]

Sorokin found it possible to speak of the period of the purges as one of the "*restoration of law* and *government by law*," and as the period of the "new Constitution":

> The profound change which the *structure of the central govern-ment* has undergone is marked by the new Soviet Constitution of

1936. In all its essentials the structure of the government under this
constitution is explicitly democratic. . . . To be sure, the new Constitution has remained largely a theoretical reform; its provisions
have been realized only in part, owing to the short period that
has elapsed since its enactment.[7]

"Its provisions have been realized only in part" is a masterpiece of
understatement. It is hard to believe it could escape Sorokin's notice that
the great blood purges began precisely at the moment of the adoption of
the new Constitution with all its "guarantees of rights," and that one of
the victims was the very author of the document, Nikolai Ivanovich
Bukharin.

From arguments for convergence in the fields of spiritual, historical, and sociocultural "compatibilities," Sorokin proceeds to his final
clincher, the sphere of economic convergence:

In the economic field we observe the decline of the Communist system [he wrote in 1943]. Regardless of the personal predilections of
the Communists and capitalists, there is no impassable gulf between
the present economy of Soviet Russia and the United States. Each
has evolved a similar system of so-called "planned economy" with
supreme control vested in the government, and with a managerial
corporation bureaucracy that is progressively driving out the old-
fashioned capitalist owners. A like change has taken place in
virtually all the other highly industrialized countries. Actually,
economically and politically, the two nations have been steadily
converging toward a similar type of social organization and
economy.[8]

In this thesis it is impossible not to notice the line that leads from the
technocrats through Burnham to Galbraith. Sorokin's theory is much
wider including all aspects of the life of the two peoples, geopolitics,
history, traditions, culture, "socio-cultural creativeness," the life of the
spirit and the spirit of life, all of which are presented as having elements
of fundamental identity and as converging towards a common character
and fate. Hence Sorokin's may be termed the general theory of convergence while the others follow only one line of his thought and may be
regarded as special cases or varieties of economic determinism.

Thus Galbraith, the most sophisticated proponent of convergence
determined by economic forces, writes:

To consider the future of [our] industrial system would be to fix
attention on where it has already arrived. Among the least
enchanting words in the business lexicon are planning, government

control, state support, and socialism. To consider the likelihood of these in the future would be to drive home the appalling extent to which they are already a fact . . . to emphasize the convergent tendencies of industrial societies, however different their popular or ideological billing. . . . Convergence begins with modern, large-scale production, with heavy requirements of capital, sophisticated technology, and elaborate organization. These require control of prices and, so far as possible, of what is bought at those prices. This is to say that planning must replace the market. In the Soviet type economies, the control of prices . . . and the management of demand . . . is a function of the state. With us this management is accomplished less formally by the corporations, their advertising agencies, salesmen, dealers and retailers. But these obviously are differences in method rather than purpose. Large-scale industrialism requires, in both cases, that the market and consumer sovereignty be extensively superseded. Large-scale organization also requires autonomy. The intrusion of an external and uninformed will is damaging. In the non-Soviet system this means excluding the capitalist from effective power. But the same imperative operates in the socialist economy . . . to minimize or exclude control by the bureaucracy. . . . Nothing in our time is more interesting than that the erstwhile capitalist corporation and the erstwhile Communist firm should, under the imperatives of organization, come together as oligarchies of their own members. Ideology is not the relevant force.[9]

Nowhere does Galbraith indicate any awareness of the role played by public opinion, which he portrays as manipulated by the "techno-structure" for its purposes, of the role of consumers' choice, which he also portrays as manipulated by the technostructure, of nongovernmental organizations, of a free press, the separation of powers into legislative, executive and judicial, government regulation, which is also portrayed as an arrangement of the technostructure, of the multiparty system, or any other of the institutional arrangements by which a free society preserves its freedom. He makes one exception to his crude picture of the pre-dominance of the technostructure over every aspect of modern life, and that exception is the "class" to which he belongs and to which he appeals to follow his lead in exposing and reducing this evil dominion, namely, the intellectuals. The industrial system, it seems, needs, demands, and "brings into existence" great numbers of intellectuals. If they listen to him, they can free themselves from the superstitious belief in the system which it inculcates in them, and then they can cut their progenitor down to size. This is his one exception to the assertion that all our institutions and traditions are hollow, outmoded, and manipulated. After all, he is happily aware that he can write this book and get it published, that he can say what he pleases and if he says it strikingly enough, get it quoted. He is able to criticize the president and strive to prevent his reelection, to oppose the foreign policy of the administration, to make his critique of the technostructure. "None may minimize," he concedes at this point, "the differences made by the First Amendment." But if all this amounts to is a pious declaration made in one or a dozen amendments called the Bill of Rights, wherein are we any better off than intellectuals in Russia? The Soviet constitution has many more "guaranteed rights" than ours, but since there is no pluralism, no separation of powers, since there are no nongovernmental organizations, no independent press, no parties, in short, no institutional arrangements to guarantee a First or a Tenth Amendment, writers at this moment are being expelled by "their" writers' union, imprisoned, sent to concentration camps in the Arctic circle, committed to insane asylums, denied publication or a chance to state their case, for the crime of taking seriously the rights "guaranteed" under their equivalent of the First Amendment and the other amendments that make up our Bill of Rights.

This appeal to the intellectuals who are created by the industrial system constitutes the one hope Galbraith offers his readers. It is succinctly stated in the final paragraph (three short sentences) of the final chapter of his book. "Our chance for salvation lies," he writes, "in the fact that the industrial system is intellectually demanding. It brings into existence, to serve its intellectual and scientific needs, the community that, hopefully, will reject its monopoly of social purpose."

But it is the essence of his theory of the convergence of the two new industrial states that this self-same type of intellectual community is demanded and required by the intellectual and scientific needs of the Soviet state, for it too is one of *The New Industrial States* that give his book its title. Indeed, this is what his convergence theory and his book are about, and it is towards precisely this that "hopefully" the two great industrial societies are converging. Hence, when Anthony Lewis asks him the crucial question, "*Are you suggesting that as the two societies converge, the Communist society will necessarily introduce greater political and cultural freedom?*" with no ifs and no buts Galbraith answers, "I'm saying precisely that."[10]

Thus the convergence theory in both its simple and its sophisticated variants has as its core the thought that as soon as the Soviet Union approaches the United States as a "mature" industrial society, develops, as it surely has, a large stratum of managers, industrial bureaucrats, engineers, and technologists (and perhaps, as the more exigent may insist, as soon as it goes from words to deeds in producing a decent quantity and quality of dwelling space and consumer goods), then the differences between the two societies will have become minor and may for all practical purposes be abstracted from or ignored. "The future is not discussed [in America]," declares Galbraith, "because to fix attention upon the future would be to bring home the extent to which [its key features] are already a fact." "The theory of the managerial revolution," wrote Burnham "is an interpretation of what *already* has happened and is now happening." "Any sane person pays no attention to the remaining incompatibilities. . . . Communism and the destructive period of the Revolution are already corpses, and only political scavengers can be interested in their revival," proclaims Sorokin.[11] In short, the two societies as they approach each other economically or "industrially," are converging as societal systems developing similar institutions, outlooks, customs, ways of life, becoming mirror images of each other, and only the cultural lag that is natural to ideologically conservative Homo sapiens prevents the two peoples from realizing how like each other they have become.

One examines the history of mankind in vain for confirmation of such simplicities. Thus one can speak loosely of "the Ancient World" or "Ancient Society," but only until one begins to examine the history, culture and traditions of some "ancient civilization." Then how different does Athens appear from Sparta; how different the lands of the Hellenic peninsula from the Hellenic world of Alexander of Macedonia; how remote all these from the ancient civilizations of Mesopotamia, Persia, Babylonia, Egypt, India, and China; and each of these in turn from the others. Only a "terrible simplifier" like Karl Marx could write such a sentence as, "In broad outlines we can designate the Asiatic, the ancient, the feudal, and the modern bourgeois methods of production as so many epochs in the progress of the economic formation of society."[12]

And in this same book from which this passage was taken by subsequent vulgarizers of Marx to construct simplistic unilinear pictures of economic determination of historical development, one finds an intended introduction, published only posthumously, in which Marx consciously complicates all that he has here appeared to simplify. In the posthumously published "Introduction" he speaks of "accident, *varia*, freedom; . . . certain facts of nature, embodied subjectively and objectively in clans and races," the problem of Roman law's proving compatible with modern production; the complex and infinitely varied flowering of the human spirit in art:

> It is well known that certain periods of highest development of
> art stand in no direct connection with the general development of
> society, nor with the material basis and the skeleton structure of its

organization. Witness the example of the Greeks, or even Shakespeare. As regards certain forms of art, as e.g. the *epos*, it is admitted
that . . . in the domain of art certain important forms are possible
only at a low stage of its development. . . . Greek mythology was not
only the arsenal of Greek art, but also the very ground from which
it sprang. . . . Egyptian mythology could never be the soil or
womb which would give birth to Greek art. . . . But the difficulty
is not in grasping the idea that Greek art and *epos* are bound up
with certain forms of social development. It is rather in understanding why they still constitute a source of esthetic enjoyment and
in certain respects prevail as the standard and model beyond
attainment. . . . [13]

So one can speak, as Marx does, of "the feudal and the modern bourgeois methods of production" and feel comfortable doing so only until
one actually approaches the history and institutions of some individual
country of "medieval" Europe or Asia or Africa. When medievalists get
together to discuss their specialties, the lands break apart like blocks of
ice in a spring flood. As we turn to medieval England or France or
Germany or Poland or Italy or Russia, we find the most diverse traditions, institutions, attitudes, forms of mutual obligation or lack of mutuality in various latifundial lands, varying degrees of persistence of Roman
forms in one land, German customary law in another, Byzantine plus
Mongol plus Slav heritages in a third. How could Italy, for example,
develop anything meaningfully called "feudalism" in view of the persistence of the Roman *municipium*, the city states, the ghost of the Roman
Empire in the form of the church, the continued existence of the Mediter-
ranean and the Adriatic as lanes of overseas trade? And which "medieval
England" are we talking about, the Anglo-Saxon with its customary
common law? The Norman French that attempted to introduce the feudal institutions of northern France but with the conqueror maintaining
a strong monarchy, an institution that is the very antithesis of feudal
power dispersion and "immunities"? Or the later medieval England that
emerged from the fusion of centralized monarchy with fragments of
French feudalism and Anglo-Saxon common law? Or if we take the three
centers of the Slav world, Kievan Rus with its Byzantine heritage and its
river trade routes; Moscow at the other edge of Russia borrowing institutions and deriving strength from serving the Tartar conquerors; Poland
with its face turned toward Rome and its anarchic *liberum veto*—how
varied are the pictures we get. And how far the Russian peasant is from
feudal tenure with his allodial and not fief ownership of his land, with his
freedom each year on Saint George's Day to change overlords and take
his land with him from one patron to another. The feudal system, insofar

as there ever was in northern and central France something that might be called "a system," was the result of the decline of the central government and the absence of free land. In Muscovite Russia on the other hand there was always free land to escape to, a free peasantry with allodial landownership and both physical and institutional mobility until the later seventeenth century when fixity, serfdom, or bondage, and not "feudal mutualism," was decreed by ukaze because of the depopulation during the "Time of Troubles" and so that the recruiting sergeant and the tax collector might find every soul in his place for the great armies required by the Russian tsar, the first great armies since the decline of the Roman legions. Only in Russia where it is at present obligatory to find "feudalism" everywhere could it occur to the serious medievalist to speak of this as feudalism.

In the later forties of the present century, under the influence of Arnold Toynbee's assumptions concerning repetitive uniformities in history, a group of our sociologists, anthropologists, philosophers, sinologists, orientalists, and historians, with the support of the Rockefeller Foundation and the American Council of Learned Societies, formed a Committee on Uniformities in History, then looked around for some historical theme or field in which there might be some hope of finding uniformities to explore. Feudalism seemed to offer the most hope, so eight specialists in the history of ancient and medieval lands prepared papers on the existence, nonexistence, or pseudoexistence of something that might be called feudalism in the lands they knew best. When the papers were in, the Committee on Uniformities called a Conference on Feudalism at Princeton University.[14]

The reader who turns to the resulting study in the hope of finding a number of patterns repeating themselves, or a single clear pattern he can store in his mind and henceforth call feudalism, is doomed to disappointment. Indeed, he will carry away a far greater uncertainty as to what feudalism "is," and a deeper awareness of the variety, complexity, and disconcertingly multidetermined and contingent nature of human history.

From the "Introductory Essay" by Strayer and Coulbourn he will learn that "feudalism is primarily a method of government, not an economic or a social system . . . a method of government in which the essential relation is not that between ruler and subject, nor state and citizen, but between lord and vassal . . . the performance of political functions depending primarily on personal agreements between a limited number of individuals [in which] political authority is treated as a private possession. . . ."

He will learn that great estates (latifundia) can exist without feudalism, that "the existence of private armies in the services of great men" makes feudalism possible, but if "things do not go much beyond this stage," feudalism remains a mere possibility and a "feudal regime more than doubtful."

As for the "idea of feudalism" it is "an abstraction derived from some of the facts of early European history but it is not itself one of those facts." The term itself was invented by scholars of the eighteenth century after most of the institutions and "the system they postulated" were in desuetude or had vanished. The term is derived from the word *feudum* or fief, "but we should remember that the word comes long after the fact and that the emphasis it put on the fief may be misleading." As with private armies and latifundia, "the fact that one man holds land of another does not inevitably create a feudal relation, and the powers of a feudal lord are not a mere extension of the powers of a landlord. . . . On the other hand, the lord retainer relationship may be of great importance in a society which is not at all feudal. . . . Serfdom was most oppressive when a strong central government controlled lords and peasants alike," a state of affairs such as prevailed in Muscovy that may be described as *servage*, fixity (*krepost*), serfdom, or bondage, but is lacking in such essential elements as the dispersion of political power and the mutualism that characterized feudal institutions.

All these complications of the simple high-school textbook definition we once so comfortably memorized are in the first seven pages of the "Introductory Essay" by Strayer and Coulbourn. The actual studies of particular countries and epochs (with the exception of the "model" area of Western Europe and in Asia the millennially isolated islands of Japan) serve only to complicate the picture further or to make some progress in proving a negative, namely that the sought for uniformities do not appear in the lands and times studied and that the term feudalism as thoughtfully defined in the "Introductory Essay" does not apply to the individual histories studied.

Thus Derk Bodde, eager though he is to broaden the definition of feudalism given in the introductory essay so that he can find more "feudal features" and semi-feudal periods in the long history of China, winds up with a problem of a "managerial society" or a "bureaucratic-gentry form of society" distinct from the nonbureaucratic feudalism of Western Europe.[15] Burr C. Brundage, writing on "Feudalism in Ancient Mesopotamia and Iran" and accepting the definition of feudalism as "essentially a political phenomenon," finds that "on the subject of political relationships the texts are singularly silent. . . . As for the attempt to visualize feudalism in the ancient Near East as a process, our meager documentation does not permit us that luxury."[16] The Egyptologist, William F. Edgerton, writes that those of his colleagues who "have applied the term feudal to certain periods of Egyptian history have not had in mind such a substantive concept of feudalism as is put forward in the 'Introductory

Essay'. . . . It may be suggested that the institutions described in the body of this essay [on Egypt] were not truly feudal."[17] The paper on "Feudalism in India" by Daniel Thorner ends with these words: "Using feudalism in the sense of a method of government as indicated in the Introductory Essay, we have to conclude that neither the Rajput States nor the Muslim regimes of northern India were feudal." The essay on " 'Feudalism' in the Byzantine Empire," by the late Ernst H. Kantorowicz of Princeton puts the very word *feudalism* in quotes in his title, begins with some elementary semantics for historiographers, then warns the conference that "nothing comparable to the peculiar conception of the world and the complexity of Western feudal society . . . ever existed in the Byzantine Empire" though after the Frankish conquest of 1204 some features of Western feudal organization were grafted onto favorable root-stocks in the prior Byzantine setup.[18] Finally, Marc Szeftel, the specialist on Russian medieval institutions, finds that in the Kievan period and in the dominion of Novgorod the Great, trade with Byzantium, the Near East, and the Northern Baltic gave political predominance to the big cities and the merchant population, whereas in the Muscovite period the enormous extent of free land and the competition among princes for tillers of the soil enabled "both military servants and settlers" to change their allegiance without losing their landed property, their property being "an allod not a fief." In the case of land that could not be transferred, "the settler had complete freedom to relinquish his tenure and to change his master." Only with the growth of the central imperial power and the requirement of great armies was fixity created by successive ukazes. This bondage was peculiarly Russian, so that Professor Szeftel, though he obligingly wrestles with such terms as "semi-feudalism, quasi-feudalism, para-feudalism and abortive feudalism," finds that "the context being different, the similarity with early feudal development in the West is not more than superficial" and that "all Muscovite institutional changes were results of the action *from above* of a 'liturgical' state, representing not stepping stones in the direction of a feudal system, but as many measures leading from it toward an extreme centralization of all national life."[19]

In short, the fact that men lived for centuries or millennia primarily by tilling the soil supplemented by warfare and plunder does not signify that they developed similar institutions, outlooks, religions, cultures, traditions, or even similar systems of tilling and occupying the soil. Vulgarized Marxist unilinear and determinist simplicities will find scant comfort in this quest of a number of learned men for "uniformities." At most they will find occasional analogies that dissolve into differing contexts as soon as individual regions and periods are examined.

If the historian studies the rapid industrialization of Germany, the

United States, and Russia in the closing decades of the nineteenth century, when they were borrowing their technology from England and, in the case of the United States and Russia, had been getting much of their initial capital for industrialization from England too, he does not find that the growing convergence of technology and gross national product caused their cultural, institutional, and political differences to become nugatory. Indeed, between 1870 and 1914, as Germany pulled abreast of England economically and technologically, politically, culturally, institutionally, England and Germany became less like each other. Germany became a unified land empire with an autocratic emperor who had the power to appoint the chancellor and the high command of the army, possessed twenty votes and decisive power in the Bundesrat, an absolute veto over all proposals to change army, navy, taxes, or the form of government. Prussia dominated the Reich and, by a system of plural voting, the Junkertum and the emperor with his absolute powers dominated Prussia. Heavy industry was tied in ideologically and physically with militarism and a well-drilled, superbly equipped conscript army. England for its part contented itself with a small volunteer army and the self-assurance that Britons never would be slaves so long as Britannia ruled the waves; Englishmen gloried in their ancient charter of liberties wrung by an aristocracy from the monarch, then broadened to universality as every man's house became his castle; they celebrated liberty under law, the supremacy of Parliament, and the steady reduction of the powers of the monarch until he became little more than a cherished symbol. The mood of Germany found its expression in "expressionism" in painting, a form that had no analogue in England, or the United States, or Russia, or France, or Italy. In 1914 when they crossed swords with each other, the two greatest industrial powers in Europe were poles apart. The "common" experience of two total wars has made them still more unlike each other. In matters of the history and national character of a country, its traditions, attitudes, philosophy or philosophies, institutions, values, we must hold with the maxim of Aristotle, "Differentiation is the beginning of wisdom." To note the ways in which a given country fits into some generalized pattern is barely to begin the study of that nation. After putting it into a general class, the real work begins in examining the *differentiae* that distinguish it from the other nations in that general class. To note resemblances in some economic or institutional feature is barely to begin the study of a nation. To stop there is to abstract from all the things that give color, flavor, distinction to each people in its life and history.

Even when nations seek to borrow some institution from a "model" country, as nations borrowed the idea of a parliament from England, "the mother of parliaments," they transform what they borrow into something else that fits more nearly into their own heritage and condition. How different are the "parliaments" of England's colonies and ex-colonies from that of the mother country. The American colonies modeled their colonial legislatures, their continental congress, and federal congressional system on England's Parliament, but as we examine our division of powers, our cabinet, our president, our constitution, our supreme court, we realize that they are other institutions engendered in another world. If we move from these to the French Chamber of Deputies, the German Reichstag and Bundestag, the Cortes of Alfonso XIII and the Cortes of Franco, the "Soviet Parliament," the "guided democracy" and handpicked parliament of a Nasser or a Sukarno, the What-you-may-call-it, of a Hoxha, we realize that they are all quite different institutions. To lump them together as "deliberative bodies" is only to begin, or perhaps to hinder, the work of studying each of them in its own nature. As Pascal said of hypocrisy that it was the tribute that vice pays to virtue, so we can say of the Soviet, the Sukarno, and the Franco "parliaments" and "elections" that they are part of the tribute that dictatorship pays to democracy. It is one thing to import and copy technical devices, or the names and external forms of institutions, and quite another to import the cultural climate that engendered them.

Joseph Stalin once charged this writer with being "an American exceptionalist." The more I considered his curious charge, the more convinced I became that I was guiltier than his indictment suggested, for I realized that I was an "exceptionalist" not only for America, about which we were then arguing, but for all the lands on earth. I thought for instance of India and China and wondered how one could be content to lump them together under the single rubric of "Asiatic lands," without losing all sense of difference in their spiritual and intellectual life, their social structures, literatures, arts, philosophies, faiths, dreams—all the qualities of life that made these two Asiatic lands more different from each other than England from France or Germany. During that wide-ranging debate with Joseph Stalin I became aware of what I had long sensed, that every land moves toward its future in terms of its own past, its own institutions and traditions. To abstract from those differences as Marx sought to, as Lenin did, and as Stalin was trying to persuade me to do, was to miss the essence of each country's life and history. In that moment of challenge to simplifying abstractions, I think a historian was born.

Latterly a new generation of simplifiers has appeared. It employs, perhaps unwittingly, a grossly vulgarized Marxist concept to the effect that economics determines politics and culture, that economics is "the foundation" and all the rest is a "superstructure" that reflects and is determined by the "foundation," or is just "ideology" in the sense of "false consciousness," "cultural lag," or "official myth." This vulgar Marxism I fancy would have made Marx wince and repeat his famous epigram, "If that be Marxism, then I myself am no Marxist."

It is terribly easy to forget that technology is neutral as regards freedom, that it may be used either to liberate or to enslave, to inform or to brainwash.

That was what troubled Alexander Herzen when he contemplated Russia's constant drives for industrialization and "modernization" from above, always "modernizing" Russia's technology and industry for the purposes of power and war, but not permitting development of an autonomous public life. In an open letter to Alexander II, Herzen wrote:

> If all our progress is to be accomplished only through the government, we should be giving the world a hitherto unheard of example of autocratic rule, armed with every thing that freedom has discovered; servility and force supported by everything that science has invented. This would be something in the nature of Genghis Khan with the telegraph, the steamship, the railroad, with Carnot and Mongé in the general staff, with Minié weapons and Congreve rockets, under the command of Batu.[20]

"Some day," Herzen wrote in fear, "Genghis Khan will return with the telegraph." "Hurrah!" cry our convergence theorists, "then he will cease to be Genghis Khan." Can we so soon forget that it was the technologically most advanced country in Europe, with the earliest and best social welfare laws, the highest degree of literacy, the model universities and greatest number of Ph.D.'s, that developed first one of the most extreme forms of militarism and then one of the most rabid forms of totalitarianism?

Are we to believe that when every man can read, it will no longer matter whether he lives under a system that gives him freedom to choose what he will read or under a system that gives him no such choice but determines what shall be printed and prescribes that he shall read only a single officially prescribed version of each subject and event, and shall read, see, and hear the same slogan at the same moment in the same controlled press, radio, television, and wall-space in every corner of the land?

Are we to believe that because there are mass-circulation journals, a television set in every home, and a loudspeaker in every public place, that it no longer matters whether there are many parties or one; rival programs or one incessant iteration of unassailable and unquestionable dogma; rival candidates to choose from or no choice at all; a chance to instruct, rebuke, tame, turn out one's rulers, or no such chance?

Is the presence of heavy industry supposed to make us forget that the central problem of politics is not, *Who rules over us?*, but *How do we choose our rulers?* and *How do we tame them?* and *How do we keep some ultimate control over them in our hands?*

Suppose it were true that there is no difference between the way the Russians run a railroad and the Americans; suppose airplanes were just as open to the people of Russia as to the "new class," and anyone could ride or fly from one end of Russia to the other without a *komandirovka* or internal passport. There would still be a simple human difference that technological similarities would leave untouched. Here is the difference as stated by two young Russian itellectuals, "*B*" and "*T*," interviewed by John Morgan for a British television program *This Week* (one of them consented only to be interviewed in a moving auto with his face covered but both expressed substantially the same thought on the technology and politics of freedom of movement):

—*Who are the privileged classes?*

B: The people who are allowed to go abroad. . . .

—*Are you proud of being a Russian?*

B: Yes, I'm happy to be a Russian. If I had to die for my Russia, I would easily do it, like two uncles of mine. . . .

—*Would you prefer to live somewhere else than in Russia?*

B: Yes, of course. I wouldn't even choose a country if you just offered me one, as long as it wasn't a communist-run country, I would willingly go there.

T: In England you may be faced with a hundred political problems, in Russia one single one. "Is it possible to get out of Russia?" No, it is not possible. You cannot imagine what that means. In England you can either solve your problems or not solve them, and leave the country, and say "No" to England. . . . A Russian doesn't have such an opportunity open to him. He is forcefully kept inside this country. It is forbidden to leave it. You are locked in here. Therefore all politics is governed by this simple basic rule. A Russian and an Englishman work from different political axioms. In your conditions parallel lines don't cross, but with us all our lines cross at one point. It is difficult for us to understand each other in this matter. It is a basic condition of being a prisoner, of being surrounded. . . . The whole place is a prison. . . .

P: In spite of the huge territory, every one here realises that he has 11,000 kilometers one way, and 4,000 kilometers the other, and beyond that just barbed wire.[21]

All the technological similarities imaginable and all the Bills of Rights that paper will put up with will not alter the intellectual barbed wire represented by absolute monopoly of the means of communication and of all the devices, paper, presses, meeting halls, publishing houses, reviews, reviewers, formulations, even vocabularies, by which men communicate with each other and know each other and themselves. The rulers own and control the journals and organizations that might criticize their mistakes, their stupidities, and cruelties. Harvard professor Galbraith could not be a professor in a Soviet university, ADA leader Galbraith could not be a political leader, author Galbraith could not get a book published if it maintained that the two systems are getting to be indistinguishable. If he could steal a bit of paper and use an off-hour mimeograph machine to set down his views, he would be hauled into court for anti-Soviet propaganda, tried by a judge who knew in advance what the verdict was to be and how to make the crime fit the punishment. The courtroom would be packed with secret police masquerading as intellectuals and workingmen, who would testify that his views were intolerable to them, corrupted their children, endangered the public safety. He could not get friends, relatives, or admirers of his wit into the courtroom. The "audience" would drown the words of the accused and his witnesses with jeers and clamor for punishment. If he persisted he would run the danger of going to a sanitarium for the mentally deranged as has been the case with Yesenin-Volpin, Bukovsky, Tarsis, Batashev, Vishnevskaya, and General Grigorenko, whose madness has consisted in taking seriously the Soviet Constitution and its Bill of Rights and trying to act on the basis of the rights guaranteed therein.[22]

To sum up: the convergence theory will not stand up to examination in the light of history nor to an actual examination of the two countries that are supposed to be converging. The likelihood is that they will continue to move each toward its own future under the influence of its own heritage, its traditions, and its institutions, a heritage that will be both conserved and altered more by the actions of men than by the weight of things. Even the technical devices they borrow from each other they will use differently as they assimilate them into their differing ways.

Finally, there are two special matters that carry us beyond the usual framework of academic discussion of a tentatively advanced hypothesis.

The first concerns the inner health of American life. If our free institutions, our pluralism, multiparty system, right of dissent, complex of nongovernmental organizations, independent press and publishing houses, independent scholarship, freedom of literary and artistic creation, freedom of movement, of dissent, freedom of choice in the marketplace and the forum, have really been hollowed out and emptied of their meaning by manipulation by the technostructure, or if we are persuaded to this by technocrats, managerial revolutionists, and technostructural determinists, then we lose our perspective on what is worth defending in our society.

Conversely, the advocates of the convergence theory are presuming to speak for the silent in Russia, assuring us, and those struggling for freedom, that technological progress at a certain point brings freedom in its train and the human effort to secure such freedom is pointless or at best an unconscious reflection and epiphenomenon. The words of "B" and "T" to John Morgan, the efforts of Pavel Litvinov, Yesenin-Volpin, Bukovsky, Chukovskaya, Solzhenitsyn, Sinyavsky, Daniel, Brodsky, and countless other unsung heroes to be true to their vision, to awaken the conscience of the outside world and bring it to bear on their plight, are the best commentary on the notion that freedom comes out of the machine and the requirements of the technostructure and not out of the struggles of men longing to be free. Thus, it seems to me, there is mischief as well as error in the convergence theory.

19

The Totalitarian
Potentials in the
Modern Great-State
Society

War Is the Health of the State

The power of the state, measured by the fields it embraces, the degree of its authority in those fields, the amount it can take for taxes and for war, and the emotional loyalty it commands, has increased steadily during the past eight or nine centuries.

In the mercantilist period, as now in the post–laissez-faire period, the fostering and regulation of commerce and industry and the assumption of new economic functions, have had their share in the enlargement of that power. For more than three-quarters of a century, now, there has been a continuous growth in the education, welfare, and social security functions of government. But, during nearly a millennium of steady growth of power, the major demiurge has been and remains the growth in the scale, scope, and technique of war.

If we go back to the beginning of this millennium, we find armies diminutive, unstable, mustered but for a single campaign or a period of perhaps forty days, paid for out of the private resources of the king, who was but first among his peers. If he needed to increase his royal forces, he had to win the support of the peers and their diminutive armed retinues,

This essay was read at the Milan Congress on the Future of Freedom as part of Point 3, "Threats to a Free Society," September 12–17, 1955, Milan, Italy.

a support which had to be bargained for by concessions and which could easily again be withdrawn.

War lacked scope then, since power lacked scope. It could neither impose taxes, nor conscript men. Indeed, the parliamentary-representative system arose primarily out of this need to get the consent of the estates, and later of the towns, to levies of men and money, which levies had to be approved as to purpose, size, and utilization before consent was given, and again when consent was renewed or extended.

Slowly, in the course of centuries, monarchs centralized their domains and enlarged and rendered more permanent their powers, granting charters of liberties to the towns in return for their support against aristocratic liberties, privileges, and decentralized power. Therefore, some have held with Tocqueville and Jouvenel that liberty itself is aristocratic in its origins and sources of support, and that lands without a strong aristocracy have never succeeded in curbing the centralizing sovereign power or establishing a secure framework and tradition of freedom. They contend that English freedom was extended to the plebeians by "levelling upward" and making every man's hut "his castle."

On the other hand, many monarchist theorists, the latest being a Kuehnelt-Leddihn nostalgia for the Hapsburg Danubian monarchy, have deduced from a review of the same processes that it is the monarch, patriarchal in his attitude towards his subjects, impartial to minorities and to the least of his children, that has served as a bulwark against the centralizing tyranny of majorities, and thus the true fountainhead of freedom.

Both these schools unite in regarding democracy as the great driving force for conformism, centralization, and the undermining of liberty. Without at this point trying to assess either theory, it would be well for us to bear in mind that the earliest and greatest medieval charter of liberties, the Magna Carta of England, was actually wrested from an arbitrary and despotic king by a combination of the dignitaries of the church, the nobles of the realm, and the burghers of London. The charter's first liberty provides "that the English church shall be free, and shall hold its rights entire and its liberties uninjured." A number of the charter's safeguards apply "to all free men." Some, like the fortieth, would appear to apply to all men regardless of estate. And the forty-first applies specifically to merchants, whether Englishmen or merchants from abroad.

When the monarch had so far centralized his realm that he could impose regular taxes, he set up a regular or standing army. But, as modern critics of democracy have pointed out, so long as monarchy lasted, it never ventured to attempt the conscription of men.

It took the great French Revolution, which overthrew the monarchy, to complete the latter's task of centralizing France, rendering it uniform, sweeping aside all private interest, all the privileges and liberties of the estates, all local jurisdictions and loyalties, all nonstate organs and organizations, all social authorities, all church rights, all barriers of jealously guarded charter, status, autonomy or privilege, the whole pluriverse of organically nurtured and time-engendered medieval forms, in favor of the centralized, unitary, wide-powered modern bureaucratic state.

And it took the French Revolution's cry, "The Republic is in danger!" to introduce the first conscription of the manpower and resources of the nation for the armies of Carnot and Napoleon.

It was the latter, true son in this respect of the revolution, who introduced the concept of national responsibility, collective hatred of the enemy, and of the "enemy alien," into a world which had hitherto been at once more parochial and more cosmopolitan. It was Napoleon who ordered the press to attack Britain as a collectivity, British manners, customs, constitution, and "way of life." Some ten thousand British subjects were interned as "enemy aliens." Prior to the French Revolution, such an attitude was unknown. Thus the novelist Laurence Sterne continued to be feted by the court of Versailles while British and French soldiers were fighting on the battlefields of North America.

The underbrush of medieval autonomous growths having been hacked away by the great machete of revolution and the stubble leveled by the cannon of the empire, the centralized state grew rapidly. The cutting up of the tangled medieval map into orderly squares called *départements* was accompanied by the bureaucratization and centralization of all social and political functions. The subject became the citizen, the citizen the voter, and the voter the soldier. Uniformity and the uniform burgeoned together, so that "medieval survivals" began to seem anachronistic and faintly ridiculous.

How this looked to some of the more prescient and pessimistic thinkers of the nineteenth century can be presented in representative fashion in the words of Hippolyte Taine (easily matched in the writings of Burckhardt, Tocqueville, and a dozen other prophets of gloom in the midst of the universal optimism):

> The people conceived of conscription as an accidental and temporary necessity. But it became permanent and established when, after victory and peace had been achieved, the people's government continued it. Thus Napoleon continued it in France after the Treaties of Lunéville and Amiens, and the Prussian government kept it in Prussia after the Treaties of Paris and Vienna.

From war to war this institution has grown; like an infectious disease it has propagated itself from state to state; at present it has got hold of all continental Europe, and it rules there together with the natural compassion which always precedes or follows it, its twin brother, universal suffrage . . . , both blind and formidable leaders and regulators of future history, the one of them placing into the hands of every adult a ballot, the other placing on the back of every adult a knapsack.

With what promises of massacre and bankruptcy for the twentieth century, with what bitterness of revenge and international hatreds, with what waste of human labor, with what perversions of productive discoveries, with what perfecting of the means of destruction, with what retrogression towards inferior and unhealthy forms of past militarized societies, with what backsliding in the direction of egoistic and brutal instincts, of feelings, manners and morals, which characterized antiquity and tribal barbarism, we know only too well.

Yet the nineteenth century was one of peace and progress and well-nigh universal optimism. Historians will count that century not in the round numbers of the Gregorian Calendar but as the hundred stable years between the fall of Napoleon in 1815 and the fall of peace in 1914. Between those two dates there were wars enough, but they were brief, localized, limited, and for much of the century fought once more with small professional armies. They were regarded as disturbances of the normal state. In all of them the basic political and geographical arrangements of Europe suffered only minor modification.

In the sixties, Prussia reintroduced universal conscription, "the nation in arms," into Europe, and the contagion spread rapidly. It was not democracy, as its irreconcilable critics declare, but the more explosive force of nationalism which brought this second round of conscription into being. And the die-hard critics of democracy in the name of aristocratic and monarchical limited war have always ignored the serfdom-fixity-conscription system introduced into Russia by powerful monarchs before either of these related "isms" was born.

Still, the wars for the unification of Germany and Italy were limited wars. But now arms piled up, technology began a mad race between armorplate and armor piercers, and the next nationalist conflict (basically between the South Slavs fighting for national unification and the Danubian Empire fighting for survival) spread irresistibly into general, universal war.

Now it was possible to see how the monster had grown. At the end of the Napoleonic world wars, all the nations of Europe together had a total of three million men under arms. A century later, the killed and wounded alone in World War I was approximately five times that many! And World War II, which was openly recognized as total, involved the total conscription of labor and manpower and resources and the total annihilation of all the centers of industry and population of the enemy that could be effectively reached with bombs. The century which Raymond Aron had analyzed as the "Century of Total War" saw the "normalization" of unrestricted submarine warfare, demolition bombing, distance bombardment of "open" cities by "Big Bertha" (World War I), by buzz and rocket bombs (World War II), the deportation of civilians, conscription of one's own workers and of enemy workers in occupied territory, death camps, factorial or multiple reprisal shooting of hostages, and, as the curtain fell on World War II, the atomic bomb.

Thus the power of the state has increased steadily with the scope of war. And with the scope of the crises produced by war. Power tends to swell after wars as mushrooms after rain. Again to give the floor to an irreconcilable critic of democracy:

> Popular representations, resting on the comfortable fiction that
> the parliaments are "us, ourselves," control the private lives
> of "citizens" to a far greater extent than the monarchs of the past
> would ever have dared to regulate the doings of their "subjects."
> Even a Louis XIV, autocratic, centralist and breaker of many of the
> best traditions as he was, would hardly have ventured to exercise
> three prerogatives which "progressive democracies" have claimed
> and do claim without batting an eye: prohibition of alcoholic bever-
> ages, conscription, and an income tax involving annual economic
> "confession" to the State . . . not to mention "nationalization"
> which is a special form of theft.[1]

The Anglo-Saxon democracies, resting as they do in theory on the maxim that there should be constitutional and traditional restraints on the power of the state and that "that government is best which governs least," nevertheless have developed enormous budgets and bureaucracies along with aspects of the garrison-plus-welfare state. England has finally introduced peacetime conscription, and the United States a minor reserve draft as a supplement to its standing volunteer army. Each year the Congress gets, and kills by pigeonholing, a bill for universal military training, but it is hard to believe that it would not pass if a sufficient army could not be otherwise recruited for our time of cold war and limited hot wars.

Indeed, it is the United States, perhaps because it has most to spend and has been thrust into the position of the first world power of the free world, that is spending most and undertaking most. Its federal, state, and local governments spend more money, and carry more debt, than all the governments of the rest of the free world combined. It is less centralized than any other great state, but its federal government is outdistancing the state and local governments in expenditures and becoming the prime stimulator of many of the state and local expenditures in such fields as housing construction, social security, unemployment insurance, and is now entering as a stimulator or pump primer into state and local civil defense and road building, and flirting with federal aid in education and health insurance.

Last year the American federal government employed 2.4 million civilians; the state and local governments 4.5 million. Combined, this adds up to 6.9 million, or more than one person in every twenty-five of the population. If indirect employment through government contract to private firms, and if military employment is added, the ratio is one to sixteen.

Or if we compare the ratio of government workers to gainfully employed, we get the following table of growth. In 1900 1 worker out of every 24; in 1920 (after World War I) 1 worker out of every 15; in 1940 (after the Depression) 1 worker out of every 11; and in 1948 (after World War II) 1 worker out of every 8 or 9, was on some public payroll—national, state, or municipal. In the half century involved, while private employment in the United States increased 100 percent, government employment increased by close to 500 percent. The civilian and military personnel employed in the military establishment increased from 160,000 in 1900 to 350,000 in 1925 and 2,300,000 in 1949. Such is the price America has had to pay for abandoning its traditional isolation. To the traditional federal government activities of national defense, control of currency, and regulation of interstate commerce, it has added new foreign military and economic aid programs, and new domestic programs in health, social welfare, power development, scientific research, agricultural and business subsidies, housing, banking and education. One-quarter of America's enormous national income is now collected by the three types of government as taxes, and one-third of all income expended, which means a mounting debt. All its governments are collecting over $85 billion (1954), spending over $100 billion and engendering a deficit of over $15 billion to be added to a debt of over $300 billion. That sum, however, is less than a single year's income at the present rate of American production.

In the past quarter century, revenues have increased by 700 percent, expenditures by 900 percent, deficits by 1,400 percent, and the public debt by 900 percent. During the same period the population has increased by a mere 30 percent, the personal income by 235 percent, the gross national product by 260 percent; the production index has risen from 110 to 241. Thus government expenditure is gaining rapidly on population growth, income growth, and growth in productive power.

I have chosen the United States because it is my own country and I know it best, because observation of these phenomena, like charity, should begin at home, and, above all, because it is generally regarded as the land of antisocialism and "free enterprise." Actually it is a land of "mixed economy" like Laborite England, Social Democratic Scandinavia or any other except the totalitarian states. To me it seems that the historian of the future will find faintly ludicrous the idea that the central issue of our time was capitalism versus socialism or, for that matter, monarchism versus republicanism. He will note that the lands which seemed to have the most orderly governments—England, Norway, Sweden, Holland, Belgium—were all monarchies, and that the land which most protested its adherence to "free enterprise" had engendered a welfare state. The central issue of our time will seem to him to have been the issue not of capitalism versus socialism or monarchy versus republic, but of limited state versus total state. To paraphrase an old theological saying, Do the people exist for the Sabbath or does the Sabbath exist for the people, he will see the issue as one which asked: Does the state exist for its citizens or do the citizens exist for the state? Or, would the garrison-plus-welfare state be able to enlarge its functions and still be controlled by the society which it was supposed to serve?

Our Time of Troubles

On August 3, 1914, Sir Edward Grey stood looking out of his chancellery window at the settling night. "The lights are going out all over Europe," he said, "never to be rekindled again in our generation." Before he died, in 1933, he knew that it was for more than his generation. Ending that August night was the bright dream that the twentieth century was "too civilized" for general war. With it were shattered many other noble dreams to which the eighteenth century had given such hopeful and rational form, and the nineteenth had seemingly made such progress in realizing: dreams of cosmopolitanism and internationalism; of the freedom of movement of men, goods, and ideas in an ever more open society; dreams of a limited state with increasing control from below and ever stronger curbs upon dictatorial and autocratic power; dreams of the conquest of nature and the triumph over scarcity, disease, distance, and all man's physical limitations; dreams of the final abolition of serfdom, chattel slavery, and all forms of involuntary servitude; of a greater respect for human life and human dignity, of gentler and more just laws, diminishing in scope, and binding alike on all and equal for all; dreams of liberty, equality, and brotherhood, and the creation of a new humanity, free in spirit and intelligence, free in critical inquiry, master to an ever greater extent of nature, his own nature, and his social institutions. As in a nightmare, we make actual progress on the paths that lead towards the realization of all those dreams, yet they seem to recede as we approach them.

How remote now seems that old world of 1913, in which one could go to a ticket office and buy a ticket to anywhere on the face of the earth—except Turkey or Russia—without visa or passport. In those days a passport was the privilege of the envoy or wealthy traveler, not a necessity for the ordinary citizen or the refugee seeking somewhere on the planet where he might come to rest. The very term *refugee*, applying to countless millions uprooted from their native soil, expelled from society, is a twentieth-century phenomenon.

Before 1913, one's existence could be attested by mere physical presence, without documents, forms, permits, licenses, orders, identity cards, draft cards, ration cards, passports, visas, reports in multiplicate, or other authentications of one's birth, being, nationality, status, beliefs, right to enter, move about, work, trade, purchase, dwell.

True, there were more documents in 1913 France than in England or America, more documents in Germany than in France, and more documents in Russia than anywhere else on earth. But even in Russia the organs of bureaucratic domination and the fixation of every man to his place and status had been withering away for more than half a century, and were becoming mere vestigial appendages. In 1861 Russia abolished serfdom. In 1907 it cut the bonds that tied the peasant to his village and communal mir. In March 1917, it proclaimed all the freedoms which men had won in the West, or dreamed of winning. "The freest country on earth," Lenin called his homeland when he returned to it in April 1917.[2]

But alas for Russia, it was her fate to complete her century of struggle for the "loosening of the bonds" (*razkreposhchenie*) at the very moment when the first total war had engulfed Russia and the world, and when in the West itself the dreams of an open society and democracy were being called in question. That war "to make the world safe for democracy" had been brought to a victorious end; three of the most autocratic and authoritarian regimes, those of Russia and Germany and Austria-Hungary, had fallen. But the very victory of democracy in Germany and Russia seemed to bring about its downfall. Before long, Germany was to be under Hitler's boot, and Russia to know a new fixity of every man to his job and his place; the peasant was to be attached to the state-controlled land, the worker to his job and workbook and by a chain of penalties in the criminal code; Russia was to be surrounded by a wall for which the words "Iron Curtain" are too weak, and to go abroad, except on business of state, would become an act of treason punishable upon the bodies of innocent relatives. Paper and paperwork would reproduce and multiply faster than crops or goods or men, until Khrushchev himself would complain that agriculture "was drowning in a paper sea."

At the other extreme, America, classic land of free movement and free immigration, has begun to surround itself with an ever loftier wall of restrictions, screenings, immigration quotas. The two total wars and the intervening periods of false peace (cold war, limited hot wars), the mounting burdens assumed by America as a world power obligating itself to aid recovery and defend the free world wherever it is threatened, the burgeoning state intervention into new fields of economic life, have brought America, too, a slow but inexorable accumulation of bureaucratic hindrances, reports, regulations, administrative decisions, documents and forms.

If the nineteenth century was the world's great age of free movement of men, the twentieth has so far been distinguished by a new fixity—except where millions are being transported for war or occupation and other millions are in disorderly flight into stateless misery, or are being exchanged, deported, handed over with or without the land, from state to state, like bundles of faggots or lumps of coal.

The Triune Revolution

Three great revolutions—not in the sense of changes in regime or political structure but in the deeper sense of changes in outlook and way of life— can be seen in retrospect to have led to our present "time of troubles," with its total war breaking down into political revolutions and the revolutions building up into greater total wars. They are the related revolutions summed up in the terms, industrialism, nationalism, democracy.

The Industrial Revolution presented itself as the great unsettler of the ancient ways. It brought the momentum of dynamic technological change, the shrinkage of the globe, the hypertrophy of the implements of war, and the scope and inclusiveness of war. It stirred Eastern Europe and the Balkans, awakened Asia from millennial slumber, broke up the old regimes and the old traditions everywhere.

The pull of the new factory towns uprooted the villager, unsettled his ancient ways and faiths, cut him off from community tutelage and guidance and solidarity, dissolved all time-tested traditions, left a vacuum into which could rush the new secular pseudoreligions of worship of science, the nation, the race, the state, the party, the Führer, Duce, or *vozhd*. Factory and slum and occasions of anonymous vice in the new megalopolis presented a suddenly atomized villager with bewildering, unprecedented problems, and hastily improvised "solutions."

In some countries, socialist and labor movements made a try for the total organization of the life of atomized and urbanized man in insurance and medical care societies, dramatics, music listening and music making, choral societies, hiking, rifle clubs, gymnastics, adult education and indoctrination, and other multitudinous associations for every impulse and need.

Far more rapidly, the national state enlarged its functions to include the education of the citizen from his first letters and national language to training in a trade or profession and regulation of its exercise. It assumed responsibility for his social security from womb to tomb. It aspired to regulate his conduct, public and private, within a unified system of laws and administrative decrees. In this is contained the danger that the state, which compels all to go to school and runs all schooling, prescribing curricula, teaching standards, selection of teachers, may also inculcate doctrine to the point of making the cult of the state itself, or of its dominant party or leader, into the central objective of education, which thereby becomes mere indoctrination.

Democracy and universal literacy and universal military service have brought inexperienced new millions into the arena of response to and influence on foreign policy and domestic. Their "entrance into history" has been accompanied by terrible simplifications of complicated matters, scare headlines, yellow journalism of Right, Left, and gutter and boulevard press, intensified propaganda by parties and governments, wooing and cajoling and stirring and coercing by the "terrible simplifiers" whom Burckhardt had foreseen.

Inevitably, with such a mass audience and mass participation, foreign policy suffered a kind of hypertrophy. Governments felt impelled to be either too intransigent or too appeasing in negotiation, "too pacifist in peace and too bellicose in war."

The French Revolution having introduced the conscription of the citizen-soldier and the Prussian drive for German national unity having developed this into the nation in arms, thereafter governments were concerned not with the mobilization of specialists, mercenaries, or volunteers, but of whole populations, while the Industrial Revolution contributed ever new and more efficient weapons with an ever vaster range and inclusiveness, on a swiftly obsolescing and gigantean technological basis.

As Raymond Aron has shown, World War I was still entered into by governments that imagined they were entering into a brief, limited war, with limited objectives: but the new technology, the stalemate, the frightful costs in wealth and human lives and the mobilization of entire populations compelled the introduction of ideological objectives and the struggle for a victory which, by its unlimited sweep and its promise of "a world fit for heroes to live in" would "justify" the frightful losses and costs. Thus the war became total, and the peace that came out of it a false peace which inevitably begot a second world war. This in turn was consciously total and by its course, and the mistakes of some of its leaders, automatically begot the conditions for a third world war which both sides have so far agreed to limit to cold and limited hot war. This "semi-war requires semi-mobilization" and, if it can be kept from becoming total, still promises to last for decades and require decades, even in the democracies, for the semigarrison state. The problem arises: How far is the garrison state compatible with limited and liberal democracy?

The Fourth Revolution

Out of the triune revolution, industrialism, democracy, and nationalism, has sprung yet a fourth revolution: totalitarianism. Is this the image of all our futures, as its spokesmen assert? Is this where the semigarrison state, where swelling state intervention, where democracy and the welfare state, are leading us all at varying tempos and by varying paths? Is this the wave of the future?

Mussolini is dead; Hitler is dead; but bolshevism, which like them grew out of World War I expanded in World War II to rule over one-third of the inhabitants of the globe, and is committed by both its offensive actions and its calculatedly disarming slogans to complete the conquest of the globe. It is well to remember, as the enemies of democracy assert, that totalitarianism is in a certain sense democracy's child. Hitler called himself "an arch-democrat" (*Völkischer Beobachter*, November 10, 1938); called National Socialism the "truest democracy" (ibid., January 31, 1937); called the National Socialist Constitution democratic (ibid., May 22, 1935); and in *Mein Kampf* wrote of "the truly Germanic democracy with the free election of the Leader, who is obliged to assume full responsibility for all his actions." Goebbels called national socialism "the noblest form of European democracy" (March 19, 1934). Hess called it "the most modern democracy in the world, based on the confidence of the majority." Mussolini proclaimed that "Fascism may write itself down as 'an organized, centralized, and authoritative' democracy." The words, *organized, centralized, and authoritative,* are well chosen to fit Nazism and bolshevism as well; just as Mussolini's "all for the State, all through the State, nothing against the State, nothing outside the State," is tailored to fit all three and provide a working definition of totalitarianism itself. As for bolshevism, Lenin proclaimed the soviets a "higher form of democracy" before he gutted them of their powers, while Stalin announced that his "constitution" was "the most democratic constitution in the world," even as he was killing fourteen out of thirty-four of its authors in the blood purges, insisting on the worship of his person like the cult of a living god, and herding his subjects by police methods to the "polling" places for the mockery of elections which he called "the most democratic elections in the world."

In part this is merely the infected lexicon of Newspeak, in which dictatorship is called democracy, perpetual purge is called collective leadership, war is called peace, conquest is called liberation, and freedom is called slavery and slavery freedom.

But we must own that it is not merely semantic poison. As Bernanos has written, "Every democracy can at any moment have an acute attack of dictatorship, as one has an acute attack of appendicitis." Against these attacks, especially in our time of edema of the state, systematic safeguards are needed. The problem, which it is the task of this Congress to examine, is how to safeguard *liberal* democracy and *limited* state against the danger endemic in our modern great-state society, in industrialism, urbanism, nationalism, socialism, total war. The problem of how the democratic state, in the very act of defending itself against totalitarian conquest, can still be kept a limited, albeit an expanding state. And the related problem of how it can watch over the welfare of its citizens in a time of troubles without the hypertrophy and the corruption or coercion of its beneficiaries which will render them unable to watch over and control it. Along with all these, and in a sense containing them all, there is the problem of how democracy in the Rousellian sense of "the general will" can be prevented from voting itself out of existence and voting the dictator and totalitarianism in. How the "general will" can be induced to and how it can contrive to set limits upon itself in the interests of minorities, of the individual, of the right of opposition, of the permanent two-party or multiparty system, how it can protect dissent and heresy while defending itself against the conspirators who aim to use its freedoms to destroy it and then root out all dissent, heresy and freedom in purges, inquisitions, concentration camps, and bullets in the base of the dissenting brain. The purpose of the present paper has been to illuminate the urgency of these problems by suggesting how the germs of totalitarianism are endemic in the modern great-state society, the triune revolution that brought it into being, and the total wars which afflict our age.

Notes

1. Backwardness and Industrialization in Russian History and Thought

1. An excellent study of the meaning for Russian Socialist thought of *stikhiinost'* [spontaneity] and its supposed opposite, *soznatel'nost'* [deliberateness] is in Leopold H. Haimson, *The Russian Marxists and the Origins of Bolshevism* (Cambridge, Mass., 1955).

2. General Cavaignac, Minister of War in the French Provisional Government set up by the uprising of February 1848, put down the uprising of the Paris workingmen in June of the same year. Lenin applied the epithet now to the generals of the army, now to the Kadets, now to Kerensky. Characteristically, he expected his readers to know who Cavaignac was, and since polemics were largely addressed by intellectuals to each other and not to the workers or peasants, his readers, living in the same French dream as he, knew.

3. Versailles had been the headquarters of the Republican government of France which, in 1870, attempted to disarm the National Guard of Paris. Resistance to the disarming was the beginning of the uprising of the Paris Commune.

4. Actually the Paris Commune was an emergency city government, while the soviets of 1905 (imitated in 1917) were an emergency general-strike committee. Marx's final verdict on the Paris Commune, written in a letter to Domela Nieuwenhuis on February 22, 1881, said: "The Commune was merely the rising of a town under exceptional circumstances; the majority of the Commune was in no sense socialist nor could it be. With a small amount of common sense, they could have reached a compromise with Versailles." Lenin read this letter when he was preparing *State and Revolution*, but studiously ignored it.

5. Preface to *A Contribution to the Critique of Political Economy*, in Karl Marx and Friedrich Engels, *Selected Works in Two Volumes* (Moscow, 1962), 1:363–64. The passage reads: "In broad outlines Asiatic, ancient, feudal, and modern bourgeois modes of production can be designated as progressive epochs in the economic formation of society. The bourgeois relations of production are the last antagonistic form of the social process of production . . . at the same time the productive forces developing in the womb of bourgeois society created the material conditions for the solution of that antagonism. This social formation brings, therefore, the prehistory of human society to a close." Professor Karl Wittfogel has suggested in his *Oriental Despotism* that Marx's "progressive" epochs here do not constitute a *developmental* scheme, but rather a *typological listing* of "antagonistic" societies. This is no doubt so. However, a total reading of Marx's work makes it clear that he frequently made a mental switch from "typology" to "inevitable succession," at least when he was thinking of three of these types, namely, feudalism, capitalism, and socialism. When the peasants and artisans are

"expropriated" and thrown on the labor market, feudalism "leads into" the bourgeois order. And the bourgeois order, by its very nature, is pregnant with the seeds of the socialist order. Thus the passage from *Zur Kritik* quoted above begins with typology but ends with the idea of "pregnancy," with its strong suggestion of inevitability.

6. Quoted by Marx from the first French edition of his own *Das Kapital*, in a letter written in 1877 to *Otechestvennye zapiski* [Notes from the fatherland]. This letter, in the original French, is in Karl Marx, *Ausgewählte Briefe* [Selected letters] (Berlin, 1953), pp. 365–68, and in Russian translation in *Perepiska K. Marksa i F. Engel'sa s russkimi politicheskimi deiateliami* [Marx and Engels' correspondence with Russian political activists] (Moscow, 1957), pp. 177–80.

7. Marx, *Ausgewählte Briefe*, p. 366, where the sentence is quoted in Russian from a review by N. Mikhailovskii entitled "Karl Marx devant le tribunal de M. Joukovsky."

8. Friedrich Engels, *Anti-Dühring*, 2d ed. (Moscow, 1959), p. 250.

9. Marx, *Perepiska*, p. 242, in a letter to Vera Zasulich.

10. Marx, *Ausgewählte Briefe*, p. 366.

11. Though Vera Zasulich, when she wrote her letter to Marx, still believed that the *obshchina* might serve as a shortcut to socialism, her letter speaks of the necessity of first "freeing it from excessive taxes, redemption payments, and police arbitrariness" (*Perepiska*, p. 240). Marx did not touch these points in his answer. See Michael Karpovich: "The prevailing opinion among the authorities tends to view the most characteristic features of the rural commune in modern times as a product of comparatively late historical development." The periodic redivision of the land arose in the eighteenth century, likewise the strip system and the compulsory course of husbandry (W. H. Bowden, Michael Karpovich, and Albert Payson Usher, *An Economic History of Europe since 1750* [New York, 1937], pp. 296–97. The sections on Russia are by Professor Karpovich). In the Emancipation of the serfs by Alexander, wherever communal landholding prevailed, allotments were turned over to the village to distribute (and redistribute) according to the fluctuating size of the household (ibid., p. 600). Florinsky writes: "The Emancipation Acts of 1861, granting personal freedom to the former serfs, created at the same time a highly complicated system of economic and legal relationships which amounted, in the last resort, to the establishment of a new bondage for the now 'free' tiller of the soil, his bondage to the land commune. Established primarily for fiscal reasons—in order to secure the collection of redemption payments imposed on the liberated serfs in exchange for the parcels of land transferred to them on their emancipation—the land commune became one of the chief obstacles to the economic development of the country. Not only did it prevent any improvement in agriculture, but it also greatly hindered the formation of a permanent class of hired labor, of a town proletariat, which is one of the indispensable conditions of industrial progress. . . . It was not until the shock of the Russo-Japanese War and the terrible agrarian disturbances which followed it that the Government [under Stolypin] undertook a radical agrarian reform [of the communal village]" (Michael Florinsky, *The End of the Russian Empire* [New York, 1931], p. 15).

12. Marx, *Ausgewählte Briefe*, pp. 367–68.

13. *Perepiska*, pp. 241–42.

14. The articles which are here summarized are programmatic. Their main formulator was presumably N. Morozov, but they represent the views of the little circle of leaders of the group that published them. I have followed the summary by Franco Venturi in *Roots of Revolution* (New York, 1960), pp. 667–68. They are excerpted from *Narodnaia volia* [People's Will] nos. 1–3 (1880), which were reprinted in *Literatura partii 'Narodnoi voli'* [The literature of the People's Will party] (Moscow, 1906). See also L. Tikhomirov, *La Russie politique et sociale* (Paris, 1886), p. 206.

15. Alexander Gerschenkron, *Economic Backwardness in Historical Perspective* (Cambridge, Mass., 1962), pp. 14, 21.

16. V. I. Lenin, *Sochineniia* [Works], 4th ed. (Moscow, 1949), 26:82; (1951), 33:68.

17. Joseph V. Stalin, *Sochineniia* [Works] (Moscow, 1951), 13:38.

18. Karl Marx and Friedrich Engels, *Werke* (Berlin, 1960), 9:116; quoted in Marx and Engels, *The Russian Menace to Europe*, ed. Paul W. Blackstock and Bert F. Hoselitz (Glencoe, Ill, 1952), p. 141.

19. Gerschenkron, *Economic Backwardness*, pp. 22–29.

20. And not only Marxists. Today the idea that heavy industry is the measure of a state's progress and greatness is widespread among new nations and among older nations faced with the possibility of total war. The idea of Denmark that it can remain a prosperous, modern, progressive, and happy land, on the basis of intensive agriculture and dairy farming for the markets of more heavily industrialized countries, is rare indeed.

21. *Sovetskaia Rossiia i kapitalisticheskaia Frantsiia* [Soviet Russia and capitalist France] (Moscow, 1922), p. 21, as quoted in B. B. Grave, "Byla li tsarskaia Rossiia polukoloniei?" [Was tsarist Russia semi-colonial?] in *Voprosy istorii* [Questions of history], no. 6 (June 1956): 65–66. Pavlovich compared the Russian army to the black-skinned troops who also had to die for the glory of the "French Shylocks."

22. Quoted in Grave, "Byla li tsarskaia," pp. 65, 67.

23. These views of Stalin are to be found in *Sochineniia*, 6:75; *Istoriia Vsesoiuznoi kommunisticheskoi partii (b): Kratkii kurs* [The history of the Communist party of the Soviet Union: a short course] (Moscow, 1938), p. 156; and "O stat'e Engel'sa 'Vneshniaia politika russkogo tsarizma,'" *Bol'shevik* [On Engels' article, "The foreign policy of Russian tsarism"] no. 9 (May 1941): 4. Stalin's article in *Bol'shevik* was originally a letter sent by him to the editors of that journal in 1934, when he ordered them not to publish Engels's article in their issue commemorating the twentieth anniversary of the outbreak of the world war in 1914. His letter and his order to suppress Engels's article were kept secret until their publication during World War II.

24. Grave, "Byla li tsarskaia," p. 66.

25. It is frequently forgotten that tsarist Russia also led the world in book publishing with 34,000 titles in 1914.

26. For these comparative figures, as for much of the statistical material in the present article, I have drawn on Alexander Gerschenkron's ground-breaking study, "The Rate of Industrial Growth in Russia since 1885," *Journal of Economic History* 7, supplement 7 (1947): 144–74. Gerschenkron's comparative tables include Sweden, whose rate of growth during the same decades surpassed even Russia's, without either government subsidies or a lowering of living standards. Sweden, like the United States, suggests how widely methods of industrialization may differ, according to differing situations, traditions, outlooks, and institutions.

27. Gerschenkron, *Economic Backwardness*, p. 10.

28. "Taxation by price" was what Preobrazhenskii called it when in the 1920s he proposed the development of Soviet industry through "primary socialist accumulation." And "taxation by price" has been the method of pressing out of the masses the sums for Soviet industrialization. The turnover tax has been levied and is still levied on articles of mass consumption on a scale which would have shocked Vyshnegradskii and Witte, as well as Marx and Engels.

29. Lenin, *Sochineniia* (1947), 15:30–31.

2. The Reign of Alexandra and Rasputin

1. Pierre Giliard, *Thirteen Years at the Russian Court*, 4th ed. (New York, n.d.), p. 52. The material on Rasputin is so voluminous that the present essay will not undertake to document every statement in detail. Some of the principal sources used are the letters of the tsaritsa and the tsar to each other; various letters of other members of the royal family; the diaries and memoirs of high officials of the tsar's government and household and of the Duma; police records and memoirs of police officials; the testimony of officials and members of the court before the subsequent Extraordinary Investigating Commission of the Provisional Government, which has been published in the seven volumes of verbatim reports now known as *Padenie tsarskogo rezhima* [The fall of the tsarist regime] (Moscow, 1924–27); the memoirs of Rasputin's secretary, Aron Simanovitch; of Rasputin's daughter, Maria; Sir Bernard Pares's classic, *The Fall of the Russian Monarchy*; and numerous special accounts of Rasputin's life. Where documents and memoirs and official testimony are in substantial agreement, there is no annotation. Where a specific source is being quoted, this is indicated. Where Rasputin's daughter, who wrote to vindicate her father's holiness and his name, acknowledges some failings of her father, this is particularly noted, for, wherever she can, she justifies, glorifies, adorns, and conceals. For the single most dependable and best-documented secondary account, see the above-named work of Bernard Pares.
2. From the fourth chapter of *The Brothers Karamazov*, entitled "Startsy [The elders]." I have followed the translation of Constance Garnett (New York, 1945), p. 27, but I have retained the word *starets* (plural *startsy*) where she uses "elder."
3. A number of upright people have left records of his attempts to hypnotize them. When Stolypin's children were injured by a bomb intended for him, the tsar sent Rasputin as a "healer" and Stolypin told Rodzyanko later that Rasputin had tried to hypnotize him. Count Kokovtsev writes in his memoirs *Out of My Past* (Stanford, 1935): "When Rasputin entered my study I was shocked by the repulsive expression of his eyes, deep-set and close to each other, small, gray in color. Rasputin kept them fixed on me for some time, as if he intended to hypnotize me. . . ." Kokovtsev rated him "a typical Siberian tramp, a clever man who had trained himself for the role of simpleton and a madman who played his part according to a set formula . . . [and] had trained himself to certain mannerisms . . . to deceive those who sincerely believed in all his oddities (p. 296)." To say no more than this, however, is to underrate both his real piety and the depths of his nature and his power.
4. Maria Rasputin, *My Father* (London, 1934), pp. 29–30; on *khlysty* and mixed bathing, see ibid., p. 117.
5. Ibid., pp. 88–91.
6. Bernard Pares, *The Fall of the Russian Monarchy* (New York, 1939), p. 142; Vladimir Nikolaevich Kokovtsev, *Out of My Past*, p. 296; Rodzyanko, *The Reign of Rasputin* (London, 1927), pp. 23–27, 76–77.
7. Giliard, *Thirteen Years*, p. 52.
8. Aron Simanovitch, *Rasputine*, 10th ed. (Paris, 1930), pp. 23–24.
9. Pares, *Fall of the Russian Monarchy*, p. 133.
10. Maria Rasputin, *My Father*, pp. 61–62.

3. Gapon and Zubatov: An Experiment in "Police Socialism"

1. Vyacheslav Konstantinovich von Plehve, Minister of the Interior and one of the spiritual authors of "police socialism," assassinated on July 15, 1904, in a plot organized by Yevno Azev, one of his own spies whom he had planted in the Social Revolutionary party.
2. Count Sergei Yulievich Witte, Minister of Finance, Commerce, and Industry from 1892 to 1903, whose regime was accompanied by a 114 percent increase of state revenues and the construction of the great Trans-Siberian Railroad. He became premier in 1905, but was dismissed from political life in 1906.
3. The nineteenth-century conspiratorial terrorist Party of the People's Will or People's Freedom which managed the assassination of Alexander II in 1881 and then was crushed by the police with the aid of agents who penetrated and then betrayed the movement.
4. In 1897 the local social democratic organizations attempted to form a nationwide organization at a congress held in Minsk. All but one of the delegates were caught by the police.
5. The first real congress of the Social Democratic party, held in London in 1903, was officially known as the Second Congress, in recognition of the abortive "First" Congress held in Minsk in 1897.
6. The full story can be found in Boris Nicolaevsky, *Aseff, the Spy* (New York, 1934).

4. War Comes to Russia

1. S. I. Shidlovsky was a well-to-do liberal landowner, a zemstvo leader, an ardent advocate of peasant reform, chairman of the Land Commission of the Third Duma. Later he became chairman of the Progressive Bloc. It was his theory, as it was Stolypin's and Lenin's, that the Stolypin land reform if carried out over a decade or two would solve Russia's agrarian problem, and modernize and liberalize Russia. Lenin wrote that its success would make a "bourgeois revolution" impossible, "not only the present revolution but any possible democratic revolution in the future" (*Sochineniia* [Works], 5th ed., 13:419, 15:30). See also "Lenin and Stolypin," chap. 21 in *Three Who Made a Revolution*, and Bernard Pares, *The Fall of the Russian Monarchy* (New York, 1939), pp. 113–14, 238.
2. Premier Stolypin wrote this to A. P. Izvolsky, Russian ambassador in Paris, on July 28, 1911. Thoroughly at home in domestic matters, Stolypin was lost in foreign affairs and fearful lest Russia's alliance with France might get her into a war before agrarian reform, democratic parliamentarianism, and an enlightened and patriotic public opinion, had had time to develop. Izvolsky as Foreign Minister had favored the Franco-Russian Treaty. To win Stolypin's confidence, he had appointed Sazonov, Stolypin's brother-in-law, Deputy Minister. Then he resigned in Sazonov's favor in order to get the ambassadorship to Paris, where he could further cement the alliance. He was ambassador to Paris from 1910 to 1917, and one of the leaders of the pro-French wing of the Russian bureaucracy. Other interesting sentences in Stolypin's letter read: "Every year of peace fortifies Russia not only from the military and naval point of view, but also from the economic and financial. *Besides, and this is the most important, Russia is growing from year to year; self-knowledge and public opinion are developing in our land. One must not scoff at our parliamentary institutions.*" The letter is in Alexsandr Fedorovich Kerensky, *The Crucifixion of Liberty* (New York, 1934), p. 188n., who was permitted

by Izvolsky's daughter to copy it. I do not know whether the italics were in the original or have been added by Kerensky.

3. P. N. Durnovo was Director of Police, then Minister of the Interior (under Witte). His secret report to the tsar, dated February 1914, was inspired by the near outbreak of war between Russia and Austria-Hungary during the Balkan crisis of 1912 and 1913. If Marxism, as Stalin has written, really gives "the power to find the right orientation in any situation, to understand the inner connections of current events, and to perceive not only how and in what direction they are developing, but how and in what direction they are bound to develop in the future," then there was no better "Marxist" than this ex-police director and Minister of the Interior. The entire report is fascinating in the clarity of its analysis and pre-vision. It is in *Krasnaya Nov'* 6 [Red virgin soil] (November–December 1922); in English in Frank A. Golder, *Documents of Russian History, 1914–17* (New York, 1927), pp. 3–23.

4. Rasputin, wounded by Guseva, one of the victims of his lust, was recovering in a hospital when the war began. Anna Vyrubova was a lady-in-waiting to the tsaritsa. The telegram is in Vyrubova's *Souvenirs de ma vie* (Paris, 1927), p. 49. A slightly different text is given by Lili Dehn's *The Real Tsaritsa* (London, 1922). She makes it read: "The war must be stopped—war must not be declared; it will be the end of all things" (p. 106). Vyrubova's version seems closer to the style of Rasputin.

5. A. F. Ilyin-Genevsky, *Between Two Revolutions* (Moscow, 1931); Théodor Dan, *Die Sozialdemokratie Russlands nach dem Jahre 1908* (Berlin, 1926), p. 273; Maurice Paléologue, *An Ambassador's Memoirs* (New York, 1925), p. 56; Sir George Buchanan, *My Mission to Russia*, cited in Leon Trotsky, *My Life: An Attempt at an Autobiography* (New York, 1930), p. 233; Bernard Pares, *The Fall of the Russian Monarchy* (New York, 1939), p. 187; M. V. Rodzyanko, "Gosudarstvennaya Duma i Fevralskaya Revolyutisa" [The state Duma and the February Revolution] in *Arkhiv Russkoi Revolyutsii* [Archive of the Russian Revolution] (Berlin, 1922), 6:16–17. Rodzyanko reports that "agrarian, and indeed all manner of disturbances in the villages, suddenly ceased."

6. Brother of the well-known Bolshevik, Vladimir Bonch-Bruevich. Tsarist justice did not persecute innocent members of a family for the political or common crimes of the guilty member. His brother's activities were no obstacle to his advancement in the tsar's service, but of great help to him under the Bolsheviks. He served the latter just as faithfully as he did the tsar, but the passage quoted here suggests a deep nostalgia for the "good old days."

7. Memoirs of General M. D. Bonch-Bruevich, *Vsya Vlast Sovetam* [All power to the soviets] (Moscow, 1957), pp. 11–13.

8. The Miliukov statement, and that of Kokovstev, are both from P. N. Miliukov, *Vospominaniya* [Memoirs] (New York, 1955), 2:183–84; cf. Kokovtsev, *Out of My Past* (Stanford, 1935), p. 388.

9. Sociologist and philosopher of the school of Soloviev.

10. Fedor Stepun, *Byvshee i Nesbyvsheesya* [What was and what wasn't] (New York, 1956), 1:334–35.

11. W. S. Woytinsky, *Stormy Passage* (New York, 1961), p. 223.

12. It is a puzzle for the historian or political scientist to translate the word *obshchestvo* or *obshchestvennost'* as it is used so often in Russian political and sociological writing. Literally it means *society*, but that word in English carries either too all-inclusive or too upper-crust flavor. It usually refers to the circle of educated, articulate, and "advanced" people of Russia, including the intelligentsia and the politically or socially active elements, who read, wrote for, and published the newspapers, journals, and books, became the activists in the political parties, helped to form and sought to give voice to

public opinion, taught and studied at the universities, constituted the more educated and thinking sections of the bureaucracy, and participants in and employees of the rural *zemstvos*—in short, all those who, as audience or speakers or both, engaged in the great theoretical disputations and controversies and professed to speak for Russia. Through the political parties and *zemstvo* workers its influence extended into the working class and peasantry, but *obshchestvo* is not normally used to include these classes as a whole. At the other end of the social spectrum it reached into the nobility and even the reigning house, for at least one of the grand dukes enjoyed a reputation as a historian and several as liberal thinkers and thus part of the *obshchestvo*.

13. It is worthy of note that Nicholas did not find it necessary to imprison or deport the Baltic or Volga Germans, as Stalin did in World War II.

14. For the tsar's Manifesto, Rodzyanko's, Miliukov's, Friedman's, and Kerensky's declarations, see Golder, *Documents*, pp. 29–37.

15. General Dzhunkovsky, humane and honorable, had just been put in charge of the police. He withdrew the police spies from the army and the schools and, when he discovered that there was a police agent in the Duma, he informed the Duma chairman of that fact. For his own account of these matters, see his testimony in *Padenie tsarskogo rezhima* [Fall of the tsarist regime] (Moscow, 1926), pp. 68 ff.

16. We shall hear of him again in 1917 when he plays a significant role in the formation of the Petrograd Soviet and in the writing of the military "Order No. 1."

17. For the Bolshevik version of the drafting of the joint declaration, see Badayev, *The Bolsheviks in the Tsarist Duma* (New York, n.d.), pp. 199–200. Written in 1929 when it was regarded as shameful to have agreed with the Mensheviks on the war, Badayev's account contains a number of evasions. Thus on page 199 he acknowledges that there was a joint declaration, but on page 200 he resorts to the passive voice ("was read") to avoid stating that the Menshevik deputy, Khaustov, read the declaration, and he has the Bolsheviks march out of the chamber alone, with no mention of the Mensheviks and Trudoviks who marched out with them. A Menshevik account of the matter is in Dan, *Sozialdemokratie Russlands*, p. 282. Boris Nikolaevsky gave me the information concerning the role of Garvy, Ehrlich, and Cherevanin in the preparation of the document and showed me unpublished materials confirming his version. The text of the declaration is in Fedor Ivanovich Kalinychev, *Gosudarstvennaya Duma v Rossii v Dokumentakh i Materialakh* [The Russian state Duma in documents and texts] (Moscow, 1957), pp. 595–96. The fact that it was a common declaration of Bolsheviks and Mensheviks is concealed here, as it has been in all party histories from Zinoviev's in 1923 to Stalin's "Short Course." The new *Istoriya Kommunisticheskoi partii Sovetskogo Soyuza* [History of the Communist party of the Soviet Union] (Moscow, 1959) suggests that the Mensheviks made a show of not being for the war as a "maneuver caused by the fear of losing all influence whatsoever in the working class," but it says nothing about the joint declaration of Bolsheviks and Mensheviks.

18. In Germany, too, one Reichstag deputy, Kuhnert, had walked out to avoid voting. Since it was only a single deputy, his absence was not even noticed until he himself reported it a few months later.

19. Because of this "special set-up" for a police raid, many Old Bolsheviks have thought that Muranov was a police agent. One of those who believed him to be a police agent was Alexander Orlov. While this is possible, plain stupidity should not be neglected as a more likely explanation.

20. A Socialist journalist who testified in court that Kamenev had provided for an article of his the title: "Let There Be Victory."

21. For Lenin's discussion of the conduct of the Duma deputies, see his *Sochineniia*, 5th ed.,

21:149–54, 290–93. In the latter account (in his pamphlet, "Socialism and War"), Lenin wrote of the two attitudes toward parliamentary activity, that of the opportunities of Germany, France, and Italy and of "Chkheidze and Plekhanov" and the Menshevik fraction, on the one hand, and that of the Bolshevik fraction on the other. "The parliamentary activity of the former leads to ministerial chairs, the parliamentary activity of the latter leads them—to prison, to exile, to penal hard labor. The one is socialist-imperialist. The other is revolutionary Marxist." The distinction is something less than candid.

For a discussion of Kerensky's intervention on behalf of the Bolshevik Duma deputies, see Pares, *Fall of the Russian Monarchy*, pp. 333, 347, and Kerensky, *Crucifixion of Liberty*, pp. 250–52. That Kerensky was concerned with the fate of the Bolshevik Duma deputies is proved by the fact that in 1916, when an upright man, A. A. Khvostov, became Minister of the Interior, Kerensky petitioned Khvostov to do justice to the exiled deputies by granting a free pardon. The minister offered to forward Kerensky's appeal with its legal documentation to the tsar, but as Khvostov lasted only two months, nothing came of it. On this see Khvostov's testimony in *Padenie Tsarskogo Rezhima* [Fall of the tsarist regime], 5:454.

5. Autocracy without an Autocrat

1. Konstantin Pobedonostsev was a man of learning, of strong intellect, unimpeachable honor, devotion to his country and his sovereign. Like so many Russian intellectuals he held his dogmas in extreme form, to the exclusion of all doubts, shadings, intellectual humility. If one examines the way in which Russian conservative Slavophile thinkers held their dogmas, even in many respects what dogmas they held, one often finds a startling resemblance between a Lenin, say, and a Konstantin Nikolaevich Leontiev or a Konstantin Petrovich Pobedonostsev.

Pobedonostsev had a deep distrust of human nature, especially of the mind and moral depths of the *meshchanin*, the ordinary, average, "middle" or "mediocre" man. Like the radical intelligentsia he used the word with aversion to mean "philistine," "petit-bourgeois." For him wisdom was conferred upon the autocrat by God, by virtue of his divinely appointed station. As long as it was "uncontaminated" by the ideas of the average urban citizen (philistine), the folk (*narod*) was endowed by God with wholesome instincts—the instinct to obey, revere and love the proper authorities and to follow them in all things.

Having tutored both Alexander III and Nicholas II, Pobedonostsev did not think too highly of either as ideal types of the species autocrat, but he felt that they could remedy their weaknesses by listening to the advice of sound counsellors, of which he never doubted that he was the soundest. It was he who had won the future Alexander III for the conservative faction in the court of the Emancipator Tsar (Alexander II). When the latter died with the draft of a shadowy constitution on his desk about to be promulgated, he persuaded his charge that he was not required by filial piety to follow his father in this. So, too, he would persuade Nicholas II to repulse the zemstvo liberals upon his accession to the throne, and, in the early 1900s, to reject all projects of constitutional reform, which the tsar at times considered under the influence of more liberal advisers. When the storms of 1905 finally forced Nicholas to part with his mentor, he seemed to do so readily, without any outward show of feeling, only to replace him in the long run by shallower, mentally and morally weaker advocates of unyielding autocracy.

Pobedonostsev's writings show that he (like Lenin) had a deep distrust of "spontaneity," democratic parliamentarism, free press, free political debate, and "western" democracy. A free press would confuse and corrupt the popular mind. Parliament was "the great falsehood of our time." The independent politician was necessarily a careerist and a demagogue. Western democracy was rotten to the core, productive only of evil in the body politic. Society had to be guided, directed, led properly, firmly, and with a design. This required an autocrat who must be the father of his people, always seeking and encompassing their goodwill and sternly exacting obedience. The people had as its first duty love for its leader and obedience to his wisdom. To protect his flock, the village priest should be a kind of spiritual policeman, suppressing divisive heresies or dark, spontaneous, anarchistic variants of Christianity, dissent, priestlessness, disobedience to constituted authority, or other devilish doctrine. The parish priest should not only lead his flock, perform for them the sacred rites, preach to them and sanctify the central experiences of their lives: he should also inculcate obedience and love for the tsar, and report any politically untrustworthy elements to the police. As there was only one proper doctrine, so there was only one proper state structure, only one true orthodox faith. Toleration of dissent should be shunned as an evil, and the dikes kept strong against the winds and waters of subversion which might erode Russia's unique structure, spiritual unity, sacred institutions, and orthodoxy.

With such ill-fitting armor the weak Nicholas II faced a world that was changing rapidly and begetting new forces that could find no place in Pobedonostsev's system, a world that was growing and beginning to prosper. Revolutions do not come, as so many imagine, in times of universal misery, but rather in times of rapid social progress which meets unyielding walls with no spillways to permit peaceful overflow. Next to the weakness at the head of the state the chief source of rebelliousness was to be the "strength" of the unyielding doctrine accepted by Nicholas, a doctrine as inappropriate to his nature as to the times. Pobedonostsevism was bad enough with a Pobedonostsev as counsellor; with an Empress Alexandra as its Pobedonostsev, it was an impossibility.

In 1905, Pobedonostsev was dismissed when the Witte cabinet came in; two years later the old man died. He had been Chief Procurator of the Holy Synod from 1880 to 1905, a quarter of a century. The church was not to have a stable government again. Pobedonostsev's first successor was Prince A. D. Obolensky, older brother of the Prince Obolensky who had been one of Nicholas's traveling companions on the grand tour. A. D. Obolensky was a provincial liberal, an admirer of the religious philosopher Soloviev, a muddle-headed man in whose head, to quote Pobedonostsev, "three cocks were always crowing at once." He lasted until early 1906. Next came Prince A. A. Shirinsky-Shikhmatov, who lasted only a few months; then P. P. Izvolsky, whose chief qualification was that he was the brother of the Foreign Minister. The growing influence of Rasputin brought V. K. Sabler, one of his pliable tools, to the head of the church from 1911 to 1915. His administration was surrounded by scandal, church dignitaries being promoted and demoted according to the wishes of Rasputin. In 1915 the scandal had grown so great that the tsar replaced Sabler by the upright, extreme conservative, A. D. Samarin, but Samarin, under the hostile fire of the empress and Rasputin, did not last three months. Alexander N. Volzhin then filled the post without distinction until the shakeup that followed Rasputin's murder. He had survived by trying neither to cross Rasputin nor to have dealings with him. He was followed, at the end of 1916, by N. P. Raev, a creature of Rasputin, whose candidacy was urged upon Nicholas by the empress, and who did not have time to make his mark before he fell along with the tsar. Not one of the successors of Pobedonostsev was capable of filling the old man's place as philosopher of conservatism or as the energetic, if not top, wise adviser of the emperor, while his place in the Holy Synod was never decently filled at all. The consequent decay in the church played a large part in weakening the throne and alienating from the tsar the support of decent conservatives.

2. Throughout his reign Alexander III wavered between dislike of Austria as oppressor of the Balkan Slavs, and dislike of France as a republic. Gradually, Wilhelm's closer relations with Austria drove him into reluctant relations with France. In 1888 Russia placed large orders for rifles in Paris and in 1889 began to float a loan in France. A military agreement between the two general staffs was signed on August 17, 1892 (New Style). By an exchange of letters, that of the French ambassador being dated January 4, 1894, the agreement became binding during Alexander's last year. The heir was told nothing of all this, but as a matter of piety (fortified by a personal dislike of his cousin Wilhelm II), he upheld the agreement, as he did other parts of his inheritance from his father. The alliance of autocratic Russia with republican France was to prove as fatal to imperial Germany as to imperial Russia. (For a discussion of the steps in this alliance, see Michael T. Florinsky, *Russia: a history and an interpretation* [New York, 1953], 2:1124–40.)

3. The diary of Nicholas II exists in many editions, in Russian, French, and German, but as they are not uniform and none is complete nor widely available, I have given journal dates rather than page and edition. The dates are Old Style. The diary as a whole is still unpublished. It fell into the hands of the Bolsheviks when they executed the tsar in Ekaterinburg. From time to time they have published parts of it. How much they may have tampered with it by suppression it is impossible to say, but the excerpts actually published seem genuine and accord with the tsar's nature as revealed in his letters and other sources. They have been accepted as genuine alike by Russian monarchists and by scholars. The first publication was "Dnevnik Nikolaya Vtorogo" [The diary of Nicholas II], *Krasnyi Arkhiv* [Red archives], 20–22 and 27. It was published in book form in Russian in Berlin, 2 volumes, 1923, under the title *Dnevnik Imperatora Nikolaya II* [The diary of Emperor Nicholas II]; and in German, with an introduction by S. Melgunoff (Melgunov), *Das Tagebuch des letzten Zaren von 1890 bis zum Fall, nach den unveröffentlichten rüssischen Handschriften herausgegeben*. This edition ended, with great literary fitness, with the entry of December 31, 1917, which reads: "Not a cold day, but a cutting wind. In the evening Alexei got up, since he could put on his boots. After tea we separated without awaiting the New Year. Lord, My God, save Russia!" But alas for literary fitness, Moscow then published an anticlimactic version which began with July, 1914, and ran into July, 1918. The last entry for 1917 in this edition omits the prayer to God to save Russia, undoubtedly in the diary. The final entry, dated June 30, 1918, reads: "Alexei took his first bath since Tobolsk; his knee is better but he cannot yet bend it completely. The weather is gentle and agreeable. No news from outside." Then the diary stops, for on the night of July 3, the tsar, his wife, his son, his four daughters, his son's doctor, the remnants of his staff, and his servants, were killed in the cellar of their prison. What happened between June 30 and July 3 Nicholas did not record, or it has not been printed. Besides the Russian and German editions, there are two French versions: *Journal Intime de Nicholas II*, Paris, 1925, and *Journal Intime de Nicholas II (Juillet 1914–Juillet 1918)*, Paris, 1934. The latter follows *Krasnyi Arkhiv* in its later installments.

4. The entry signaling his mother's birthday and the twenty-third anniversary of his marriage is dated 14 November. Tuesday. He had been in prison eight months.

5. In her letters Alexandra repeatedly refers to her spouse as "Little Boy Blue" and once or twice he uses the same appellation for himself.

6. "Uncle Nizi" should probably be "Uncle Niki."

7. His companions were his younger brother Georgi, the princes Baryatinsky, Kochubey,

Obolensky, the Hussar Guard Volkov, and Prince Ukhtomsky. In Athens they were joined by the older son of the King of Greece, the Prince George who saved the life of Nicholas in Japan.

8. Egyptian dancers who chant as they dance. Nicholas russifies the word. The Russian does not make clear whether the Orientalist, Ukhtomsky, engaged in dance steps with them or whether they played "all kinds of tricks" with him, since the word, *shtuki*, could have either meaning.

9. On Kshesinskaya, see *Journal Intime de Nicholas II*, p. 31, n. 1; V. I. Gurko, *Features and Figures of the Past*, pp. 99 and 623; *Letters of the Tsaritsa to the Tsar, 1914–16* (London, 1923), pp. 112 and 450; and *Dancing in Petersburg: The Memoirs of Kschessinska*, by H. S. H. The Princess Romanovsky-Krassinsky (New York, 1962). The princess who writes the book is the dancer herself, for she bore a child by Grand Duke Andrei Vladimirovich, and after the revolution they fled abroad and were married in Paris, where she established a school and trained some fine ballet dancers. Now in her nineties, she is proud of her triumphs in the dance but prouder of her connections with royalty. She boasts that whenever her plans were thwarted, or she did not receive a role she coveted, she had always been able to get word to her first royal lover, the tsar, and he would see that "justice" was done.

10. In his letters to his wife from 1914 to 1917, when Japan was an ally, his reference to Japanese liaison officers is invariably correct and friendly.

11. Fedor I. Rodichev, a Westerner and a Liberal on the English model, was a member of the bar and a leader of the Zemstvo of Tver, which played a leading role in the zemstvo movement. He had already been the author of two manifestoes addressed by the Tver body to Alexander II. The murder of the Tsar Emancipator had made the zemstvo movement passive, but with the death of Alexander III, these loyal men, monarchists all, had hope that the young Nicholas might resume the evolution of the monarchy in the direction of a moderate constitutionalism. The success of the old reactionary counsellor, Pobedonostsev, in persuading the young tsar to see in this modest address a "senseless dream" marked Nicholas's first step on the road which would separate him from the liberal zemstvo leaders and drive them increasingly in the direction of flirtation with revolution. Rodichev became a leader of the Kadets in the Duma, and then of the Progressive Bloc. A founder of the Kadet party, he was on its Central Committee, represented it in all four Dumas and in the Provisional Government. He was that government's Commisar for Finland, fled abroad after its fall, and died in exile in 1933. The text of his address to Nicholas and the tsar's reply are in A. Kornilov, *Modern Russian History* (New York, 1917), 2:276–78. For Pobedonostsev's explanation to the tsar that the address must be rejected, see Pares, *Fall of the Russian Monarchy* (New York, 1939), pp. 56–57.

12. *Opapa* is baby talk for his maternal grandfather, Christian IX of Denmark. One of Christian's sons was King of Greece; one of his daughters, the future Queen Alexandra of England, was married to the Prince of Wales; his other daughter, Dagmar, had married Alexander III of Russia and adopted the Russian name, Maria Fyodorovna. The diary as printed in Russian says "Apapa," but this is a mistake, Opapa being a corruption of Grosspapa or Grossvater. When Nicholas II's bride writes him letters in English, she refers to Christian IX as *Anpapa*, which is English baby talk for grandpapa or grandfather. This use of baby names for many of his older relatives, and even for some of his contemporaries (e.g., he calls the Vorontsev girls "kartoffeln") is one of the childlike characteristics of this grown man's diary.

13. This fight for a responsible cabinet continued with fluctuating intensity until the tsar's downfall.

14. Pobedonostsev's language in this passage is strikingly reminiscent of the language Lenin used to characterize an "opportunist." Beginning with the words, "only understands . . .", it coincides almost word for word with a passage from Lenin.

15. "Dnevnik A. A. Polevtseva," *Krasnyi Arkhiv*, no. 46 (1931) and no. 67 (1934).

16. V. I. Gurko, *Features and Figures of the Past* (Stanford, 1939), pp. 221–22; p. 493.

17. Contrary to the widely held notion, there was a kind of "constitution" and "constitutional logic" in nineteenth-century autocracy. From the moment when Speransky codified the laws of Russia under Nicholas I, the emperors and their officials felt that they too were bound by the law as it existed. The emperor as autocrat had the power to *change* the law but not to *ignore, violate* or *circumvent* it. When the emperor, after duly consulting his council, promulgated a new law, he could follow his own will in fashioning it. But while the old law prevailed, he and his ministers treated it as the law. This was true of Nicholas I, Alexander II, and Alexander III. It remained for Nicholas II and Alexandra, his empress, to adopt the popular notion that the tsar without a fresh *ukaz* or law could ignore his own statutes at will. Most of the deepest misunderstandings between Nicholas and his ministers, and between Nicholas and the State Council, arose from petty matters in which he intervened arbitrarily to violate some existing law which his father, or he himself, had promulgated. It was this which gave his gentler reign the air of arbitrariness and his father's more despotic and sterner rule the air of stable lawfulness. For an analysis of this type of misunderstanding, and a citation of some of the petty instances in which the tsar and the tsaritsa violated even the lawfulness of autocracy, see V. I. Gurko's monograph, *Tsar i Tsaritsa* [The tsar and tsaritsa] (Paris, 1927), particularly pp. 34–40.

The present essay owes a large debt to Gurko's monograph, and to Sir Bernard Pares's classic, *The Fall of the Russian Monarchy*.

18. When the State Council, consisting entirely of elder statesmen who had long and faithfully served the tsar or his father and then been named to the council as their reward, sent him a respectful suggestion in connection with some matter he had put before them, in which they expressed the desire that he abolish the right of the Volost courts to condemn peasants to corporal punishment, he wrote testily on their communication: "This will be when I happen to want it" (*Éto budet togda, kogda ya ètogo zakhochu.*) This was a needless slap in the face delivered to the most important of all the institutional supports of autocracy, and but one of the instances which, when multiplied, gradually undermined the supports of the tsar and surrounded his power with a vacuum. (See Gurko, *Tsar i tsaritsa*, pp. 14, 39.)

19. Nicholas II to his uncle, Grand Duke Vladimir Alexandrovich, November 26, 1896, *Krasnyi Arkhiv*, no. 17, 1926, p. 219.

20. It is indicative of the growing decay in the tsarist regime that the police agent, Azev, was head of the terror section of the Socialist Revolutionary party, and, knowing of Kalyaev's plan to kill the tsar's uncle, did not forestall it. Similarly the police were privy to the murder of Stolypin in 1911, undoubtedly the best adviser Nicholas ever had. It is no less bewildering to learn that D. F. Trepov, put at the head of St. Petersburg to suppress the disorders called forth by the firing on Father Gapon's procession, was one of the founders and sponsors of that peculiar "police socialism" which brought into existence Gapon's organization. (For an analysis of "Police Socialism," see the chapter by that title in *Three Who Made a Revolution*.)

21. A. A. Mossolov, *At the Court of the Last Tsar* (London, 1935), p. 90.

22. *Letters of the Tsaritsa to the Tsar*, Intro. by Sir Bernard Pares (London, 1923), p. xx.

23. Ibid.

24. Letter of November 7, 1916, *Lettres des Grands-Ducs à Nicolas II* (Paris, 1926), p. 31. Other letters of Nikolai Nikolaevich to his imperial cousin are equally warm.

25. *Out of My Past: The Memoirs of Count Kokovtsev* (Stanford, 1935), pp. 7 and 11.

26. This is only one of a number of signs that both her influence and Rasputin's possessed a hypnotic aspect.

27. Ibid., p. 478; Pares, *Fall*, p. 414.

6. Lenin and Inessa Armand

1. The principal sources of information on Inessa Armand used in the present article are: Krupskaia's references to her in *Vospominaniia o Lenine* [Memories of Lenin] (Moscow, 1957); the reminiscences of Krupskaia and others in *Pamyati Inessy Armand, Sbornik pod redaktsiei N. K. Krupskoi* [In memory of Inessa Armand] (Moscow, 1926); the letters of Lenin to Inessa as published in censored form in Lenin, *Sochineniia* [works], 4th ed. (Moscow, 1941–52), p. 35; reminiscences of Angelica Balabanoff communicated orally to the writer; reminiscences of Marcel Body, who was recounting both what he himself knew (he was a member of the League of French Communists in Russia formed by her in 1918), what Alexandra Kollontai told him (he was an aide in her embassy and her confidant for many years), which he later published, and matters communicated by him in a letter to the writer; *Inessa Armand: Une Grande Figure de la Révolution Russe* (Paris, 1957) by Jean Fréville, who was permitted to examine materials concerning her in the archives of the Marx-Lenin Institute (he has refrained from quoting, or was forbidden to quote, any key passages from her letters to Lenin, although he makes it clear that he was permitted to read them; his book is more pious hagiography than biography); an obituary notice in *Pravda* on the occasion of Inessa's death, signed by Krupskaia; an article on her in the *Bol'shaia sovetskaia entsiklopediia* [Great Soviet encyclopedia]; a discussion of her relations with Lenin in N. Valentinov, *Vstrechi s Leninym* [Meetings with Lenin] (New York, 1953), pp. 97–102. Gérard Walter, *Lénine* (Paris, 1950), pp. 204–5. These various accounts contain some discrepancies, many reticences, in some cases palpable inaccuracies. For example, most of the accounts give the first name as Inessa, not Elizabeth, omit her maiden name or give it wrongly as Petrova, Petrovna, or Stephanie, and set her date of birth as 1875 instead of 1879. Gérard Walter has examined the original French documentary sources to establish her first name, father's name, maiden name, real age, and so forth, using among other documents Lyonnet's *Dictionnaire des Comédiens français*, which gives biographical data on her father in vol. 2, p. 513. According to Walter, the errors concerning Inessa Armand in the *Bol'shaia entsiklopediia* were in large measure corrected in the *Biograficheskii slovar'* [Biographical dictionary] published by the Society of Former Exiles and Political Prisoners (Moscow, 1931), vol. 5, pt. 2, cols. 127–29, which I have not had an opportunity to consult.

2. In 1952, twenty-four of his letters to her—manifestly somewhat cut and usually deprived of their salutation and complimentary closing—were published in vol. 35 of Lenin's *Sochineniia*.

3. This is testified to by every mention of Martov in the two volumes of Krupskaia's *Vospominaniia* [Memories] and by M. Gorki, *V. I. Lenin* (Moscow, 1931), p. 43. Krupskaia relates that when Lenin felt his end was near, one of his last utterances was a mournful query: "They say that Martov is dying, too!"

4. Lenin, *Sochineniia*, 34:117–18 (the *ty* letter), and p. 146 (the first *vy* letter). Between

the two letters, seven months apart, had come the fateful disagreement on the definition of a member and on the composition of the *Iskra* editorial board.

5. Lenin, *Sochineniia*, 34:113–14, 127, 186–88; 35:370–71, 375–76, 397, 399, 400, 405, 406–7, 409–10, 414, 415, 422, 423–34, 456, 472. All the letters in vol. 35 use *vy*.

6. The last letter using *ty* is dated July 15, 1914. The first wartime letter is dated by the Marx-Lenin Institute as "written in September 1914." One cannot tell whether Lenin thinks of her as *ty* or *vy* because, for the first time in his life, Lenin tries to write the whole letter, except two impersonal sentences, in English. It remained unpublished until 1960, when a Russian translation (with no original) was published in *Voprosy istorii KPSS* [Questions on the history of the Communist party of the Soviet Union], no. 4 (1960): 3–4. Then there were no letters until the war was five months old because Inessa joined Lenin and Krupskaia in Berne as soon as they got to Switzerland. But when they separated and there was occasion to write her once more, on January 17, 1915, Lenin wrote *vy*.

7. "Inessa," by N. Krupskaia, in *Pravda*, October 3, 1920.

8. A common bond between Lenin and Inessa Armand on their first meeting was their shared admiration for Chernyshevsky's novel. This novel, which took the Russian intelligentsia by storm with its image of the "new men," also contained a "new woman," its heroine, Vera Pavlovna. The American anarchist Benjamin Tucker, who translated it into English, wrote of the novel: "The fundamental idea is that woman is a human being and not an animal created for man's benefit, and its chief purpose is to show the superiority of free unions between men and women over the indissoluble marriage sanctioned by the Church and State" (Preface to the 4th ed. [New York, 1909], p. 3).

If Lenin was attracted by the vision of the "uncommon men" and their "rigorist" leader concerning utopia, Inessa was attracted by the deeds and views of the novel's heroine. In *Pamyati Inessy Armand* Krupskaia wrote: "Inessa was moved to socialism by the image of woman's rights and freedom in *What Is to Be Done?*" Like the heroine, she broke her ties with one man to live with another, concerned herself with good deeds to redeem the poor female and the prostitute, tried to solve the problems of woman's too servile place in society. Indeed, whole generations of Russian radicals were influenced by Chernyshevsky's many-sided utopian novel and were moved to imitate its "uncommon men and women." Just as Marx could be the spiritual ancestor of people as various as Bernstein, Kautsky, Bebel and Luxemburg, so Chernyshevsky was a formative influence for the two men who in their persons incarnated the two opposing poles of socialism in 1917: Tsereteli and Lenin. If Inessa found in the novel her image of woman's rights and freedom in love, and Lenin the prototypes of his vanguard and his leadership, Tsereteli found there his ideal of service to the people. Men who are big enough to have spiritual progeny are likely to be thus many-sided and complicated, while each "descendant" finds in his "ancestor" that which enlarges and reinforces what already exists in him.

9. *Pamyati Inessy Armand*, p. 7.

10. The one exception is Angelica Balabanoff, who got to know her five years later through their joint work in the Zimmerwald and Kienthal wartime conferences, and the International Woman's and Youth's meetings. Dr. Balabanoff told me: "I did not warm to Inessa. She was pedantic, a one hundred percent Bolshevik in the way she dressed (always in the same severe style), in the way she thought, and spoke. She spoke a number of languages fluently, and in all of them repeated Lenin verbatim."

11. For this controversy, see my *Three Who Made a Revolution*, chap. 29.

12. Valentinov, *Vstrechi s Leninym*, p. 99.

13. The quotations from Krupskaia, here and throughout the article, are either from her ac-

count in *Pamyati Inessy Armand* or from vol. 2 of her *Vospominaniia*. In the English-language edition, *Memories of Lenin* (New York, 1930), they are quoted from pp. 58, 66, 67, 73, 84, 90, 121, 123, 124, 125, 126, 128, 130, and 150. Where the translation seemed poor, I have retranslated from the corresponding pages of the 1957 Russian edition.

14. The Kamenevs lived on an upper floor in the same building as the Ulianovs.

15. See n. 13 above.

16. *Lenin i Gorki: Pis'ma* [Lenin and Gorky: correspondence] (Moscow, 1958), pp. 251–52. An English translation is in Maxim Gorky, *Days with Lenin* (New York, 1932), p. 52.

17. Lenin, *Sochineniia*, 37:430.

18. Fréville, *Inessa Armand*, p. 90.

19. See n. 13 above.

20. Lenin, *Sochineniia*, 35:232.

21. Ibid., p. 96.

22. Krupskaia, *Vospominaniia*, English ed., pp. 188 and 197; Russian ed., pp. 264–65 and 271. Lenin, *Sochineniia*, 35:167.

23. Lenin, *Sochineniia*. 35:209.

24. This did not prevent Lenin from writing out for her every word she was to say, and supplementing this with four sets of *zametki privées* (private notes). The report and instructions he wrote for her take up forty pages in vol. 20 of his *Sochineniia*.

25. Lenin, *Sochineniia*, 35:108–10; 20:463–502.

26. All passages in italics are underlined by Lenin in the original; an asterisk (*) after them indicates that they are in English or French or some language other than Russian. The first two paragraphs are in what Lenin believes to be English, the third in Russian except for the word *contrepropositions*.

27. I am indebted to Vera Alexandrova for identifying the novel as the only one of Vinenchenko's works that fits Lenin's "critique."

28. English in the original. Where the editors have not omitted the salutation and closing, Lenin generally writes *Dorogoi Drug* (Dear Friend) and closes with "firmly [or "firmly, firmly"] I press your hand." In one letter he tries to put this into English as "Friendly shake hands!"

29. Lenin, *Sochineniia*, 35:107.

30. Ibid., pp. 137–38. This is the letter which closes with the English "Friendly shake hands!"

31. Ibid., pp. 139–41.

32. Marcel Body, "Alexandra Kollontai," in *Preuves* (Paris), April 1952, pp. 12–24. Body was a French workingman, a printer in Limoges. Mobilized in 1914, he was sent to Russia with a French military mission to the Russian army. Like a number of other men of that mission (Captain Jacques Sadoul, hitherto a Right Socialist, for example), he sympathized with the February and October revolutions. Remaining in Russia, he joined first Inessa's group of French Communists in Moscow, then the Russian party, and served the Soviet government in various capacities. When Kollontai arrived in Oslo as the world's first woman ambassador in 1922, a kind of honorific exile by Lenin for her activity in the Workers Opposition, she found Body there as secretary to Ambassador Suritz. His friendship with her and his service under her began then and lasted until her death. Sickened, as she was too, by Stalin's purges, he did not return to Russia and now lives in Paris.

33. "Kolosov" is the hero of a short tale by Turgenev, which Lenin cherished as a discussion of the proper attitude of the "uncommon person" toward love. Krupskaia told Valen-

tinov that when they were in Siberia, she and her husband translated several pages of the tale into German. (This was Lenin's method of improving his German and at the same time becoming more deeply acquainted with some of his favorite pages from literature.) Kolosov, the narrator of the tale says, fell in love with a girl, lost his love for her, and left her. In this there was nothing "unusual." Unusual was the resoluteness with which he broke with her and with his whole past as tied up with her: "Which of us would have been able to break in good time with his past? Who, say, who does not fear reproaches—not, I say, the reproaches of the woman but the reproaches of the first stupid bystander? Which of us would not yield to the desire to play the magnanimous, or egotistically to play with another devoted heart? Finally, which of us has the strength to oppose petty selfishness, petty proper feelings: pity and remorse? Oh, gentlemen, a person who breaks with a woman once loved, at that bitter and great moment when he involuntarily realizes that his heart is no longer entirely filled by her, that person, believe me, better and more deeply understands the sacredness of love than do those faint-hearted people who from tedium, from weakness, continue to play on the half broken strings of their flabby and sentimental hearts. We all called Andrei Kolosov an uncommon man. . . . In certain years, to be natural means to be uncommon" (cited by Valentinov, *Vstrechi*, pp. 92–94).

34. Body, "Alexandra Kollontai," p. 17.
35. O. H. Gankin and H. H. Fisher, *The Bolsheviks and the World War* (Stanford, 1940), pp. 301–8.
36. The writer interviewed Angelica Balabanoff many times concerning Lenin during her years in America, but she never hinted at the Inessa affair until I said to her in Rome that I had learned of it from Marcel Body. Then she told me the above, permitting me to take notes as she talked.
37. Singularly, all of the Ulianov family of Lenin's generation, his sisters Anna and Maria, his brother Dmitri, and Lenin himself, remained childless.
38. On this, see Ypsilon, *Pattern for World Revolution* (Chicago and New York, 1947), p. 68. The writer interviewed both of the anonymous authors of Ypsilon on Eberlein's marriage and Inessa Armand. [Ypsilon was a composite pseudonym for two writers who did not wish to use their real names. The Wolfes knew both writers.]
39. For Lenin's appreciation of John Reed's book, see Lenin's Foreword to *Ten Days That Shook the World* (New York, 1960), p. xlvi. Lenin's note to Kobetsky is not given in any edition of his *Sochineniia*, but was printed by *Inostrannaia literatura* [Foreign literature], no. 11 (1957), in an article on "Lenin and Foreign Writers," in the commemorative number for the fortieth anniversary of the October Revolution.
40. Fréville, *Inessa Armand*, p. 180.

7. Krupskaia Purges the People's Libraries

1. For Gorky's letter to Khodasevich and Khodasevich's notes thereon see "The Letters of Maksim Gorky to V. F. Xodasevich, 1922–1925. With Notes by V. F. Xodasevich and an Introduction by Sergius Yakobson, translated and edited by Hugh McLean," *Harvard Slavic Studies* 1 (1953): 306–7, and Bertram D. Wolfe, *The Bridge and the Abyss* (New York and London, 1967), pp. 143–45.
2. In 1929 Krupskaia took a backward glance at the library situation at the end of the civil war in a little book entitled *Chto pisal i govoril Lenin o bibliotekakh* [What Lenin wrote and said about libraries]. In her introduction she pictures Lenin as personally turning his attention to the rebuilding of the libraries, proposing the organization of volunteers

(*subbotniki*) to catalog a million or so uncataloged books in the Rumyantsev (today the Lenin) Library; ordering the restoration of the library of the Academy of Sciences, etc. "If his intervention was necessary to clear the premises of the Academy of Sciences [it had been turned into a field hospital], one can imagine the state of ordinary libraries. Libraries had to be purged of narrow-minded and religious books, and in the process the shelves of old-established libraries were almost denuded. . . . There was no lack of good intentions [locally], but little common sense." He worried about "Soviet bureaucrats who grab books and newspapers" and proposed to requisition them for the libraries, he worked out decrees on the requisitioning of books, the "punishment for concealing collections of books and other printed matter," the conditions and places in which "White Guard Literature" should be available for public use, the organization of bibliographies, the preservation of newspapers in reading rooms so that they would last longer, and countless other details, with his usual meticulous precision. In 1936 Krupskaia told an All-Union Conference on Library Work: "In our library section of the cultural front things are made significantly easier by the fact that we have the sufficiently detailed directions of Vladimir Ilich, who always paid the most thorough attention to the work of the libraries." As far as temperament and memory permitted, she tried to follow his indications when he was no longer there to be consulted. On this, see her booklet *What Lenin Wrote and Said about Libraries*, and the subsequent compendium, *Lenin o bibliotechnom dele* [Lenin on library work] (Moscow, 1960), an anthology of some 180 pages.

3. The *Pravda* article is entitled " 'Ogrekhi' Glavpolitprosveta" [" 'Defects' of the Bureau of Political Education"—*Ogrekh* is an archaic word referring to a slip made by a plough when trying to plough a straight furrow]. The article is reprinted in N. Krupskaia, *Pedagogicheskie Sochineniia* [Pedagogical works] (Moscow, 1960), 8:78–80.

4. That issue of *Krasny Bibliotekar'* [Red librarian] is in the Slavonic division of the New York Public Library. I owe my copy to the kindness of Anna M. Bourguina who had a photostat made for a study of Soviet cultural controls on which she was engaged. To her also as curator of the Boris I. Nicolaevsky Collection in the Hoover Institution, I owe the opportunity to photograph the hard-to-come-by original of Krupskaia's Second Circular, the one referred to by Maxim Gorky in his letter cited above. As far as I have been able to ascertain, the Nicolaevsky Collection contains the only copy now extant outside of secret archives in Russia. S. G. Sumski-Kaplun showed the circular to Gorky, used it for an article (unsigned), in *Sotsialisticheski Vestnik* [Socialist Herald] of 27 November 1923, and then may have given the same copy to Boris Nicolaevsky.

5. The letter is cited and discussed in Wolfe, *The Bridge and the Abyss*, pp. 50–51; the Russian text is in Lenin, *Sochineniia* [Works], 35:89–91. (Except where otherwise indicated, all references in this article are to the fourth Russian edition of Lenin's *Works*.) A corrupt and bowdlerized English translation of the fourth edition is available. A good example of the bowdlerization is to be found in this very letter where "seducing little girls" becomes "corrupting" them and where *trupolozhestvo* (copulation with a corpse) becomes necrophily (*sic*!).

6. On this, see N. Krupskaia, *Izbrannye Pedagogicheskie Sochineniia* [Selected pedagogical works] (Moscow, 1958), pp. 248–49, and Krupskaia, *Memories of Lenin* (New York, 1930), 1:3.

7. Part of this search had to be undertaken with the help of a long-distance phone call to New York where the only set of *Krasny Bibliotekar'* for those years is to be found in the Slavonic division of the New York Public Library. I want here to express my thanks to Avrahm Yarmolinsky, who for many years directed and built up the remarkable collec-

tion of Slavonica in that library, and one of his assistants, now also retired, whose name Mr. Yarmolinsky did not forward to me, for their prompt and generous help in searching through the issues of the magazine. From Anna M. Bourguina, I got some of the evidence that appears below, showing that somehow the lists did indeed reach their destination.

8. For the evidence, see "Part V., The Conditioning of Culture" in my *An Ideology in Power: Reflections on the Russian Revolution* (New York, 1969), particularly chaps. 1 and 3.

9. In a totalitarian single-party regime where the party uses the state as its major transmission belt, the separation between government and party is a fiction to bemuse the governments and public opinion of other countries, but the fiction makes *Izvestia* the official journal of the state, and *Pravda* the official journal of the party. The purge of libraries was thus treated as a state matter rather than a party matter for, as far as I could find, *Pravda* had nothing to say on truth in libraries.

10. In *Kommunisticheskoe Prosveshchenie* [Communist enlightenment], no. 4 (1926): 161–63.

11. Dikshtein is Szymon Diksztein, a Polish socialist who popularized Karl Marx and whose *Who Lives by What* was regarded as a socialist classic. Antonio Labriola was a leading Italian Marxist theoretician of the early twentieth century. Dmitri Andreyevich Koropchevski, editor of *Znanie* and *Slovo*, was a popularizer of anthropology; under the pseudonym G. Taranski he also wrote in the field of fiction. Marek Konkol's work dealt with the Paris Commune.

12. Both Baturin and Kerzhentsev were Leninists, the former being an editor of *Pravda* and *Zvezda*, and the latter a future biographer of Lenin and an agitprop director under Stalin. Gorky's *Song of the Stormy Petrel*, of which he himself got tired of hearing the praises, was regarded by revolutionaries as a remarkable prophecy in verse of the coming revolution.

8. Soviet Party Histories from Lenin to Khrushchev

1. G. Alexandrov, "Concerning the Present and the Future," *Literaturnaya Gazeta,* January 1, 1952.

2. *Pravda,* no. 17, July 1960.

3. *Voprosy istorii KPSS,* no. 5, 1960, p. 172.

4. Ibid., no. 8, August 1960, lead editorial.

5. Ibid., no. 5, 1960, p. 157.

6. The most ambitious Populist attempt is Ivan-Razumnik's *Istoriya Russkoi obshchestvennoi mysli* [The history of Russian social thought] (St. Petersburg, 1908).

7. Today most easily available in German with Dan's updating of the history of the movement from 1908, where Martov left off, to 1925 (Berlin, 1926).

8. Lenin, *Sochineniia* [Works], 10:7. How literally Lenin took History's support is suggested by the style of this obiter dictum: "ibo za nashi vzglyady vstupaetsya sama istoriya, vstupaetsya na kazhdom shagu deistvitel'nost" [Thus History personified has enlisted in the fray on our side while Reality stands shoulder to shoulder with her in the combat].

9. The Russian reads "poshlyi, meshchanskii radikalizm." This analysis first occurs in Lenin, *Sochineniia,* 1:246, but never one to waste a good epithet, Lenin uses it again and again whenever he returns to the subject.

10. Significantly coinciding in dates with the period when Lenin was in Siberia and unable to keep the movement on the right course.

11. See, for instance, "Nekotorye voprosy istoriografii partii" [Some questions of party historiography], in *Voprosy istorii KPSS*, no. 5, 1960, pp. 156–72.

12. All these questions are taken from ibid. The numbering and ordering are my own.

13. There was also a "Sketch of the History of Social Democracy in Russia," by N. N. Baturin (N. N. Zamyatin), who in 1912 was a member of the editorial board of *Pravda*. Though it was reprinted eleven times after 1917, I could not learn the date of original issue, nor secure a copy.

14. Reprinted in German, Leipzig, 1921, in the Kleine Bibliothek der Russischen Korrespondenz.

15. *Voprosy istorii KPSS*, in its lead editorial, "Towards a New Ascent (pod"em) of the Science of Party History," (no. 5, 1960, pp. 1–20) recognizes the following as "scientific works and systematized textbooks of party history" which in their time represented "significant material of scientific investigation . . . but contained many methodological and theoretical errors": Lyadov and Baturin for the pre-1917 period, and A. S. Bubnov, "Fundamental Problems of the History of the RKP," 1924; V. I. Nevsky, "Outlines of the History of the Russian Communist Party," pt. 1, 1923; N. N. Popov, "Outlines of the History of the Communist Party of the Soviet Union," in 16 editions, 1925–35; V. I. Nevsky, "History of the RKP (b), Short Outline," 1925 and 1926; Em. Yaroslavsky, "Short Outlines of the History of the VKP (b)," in two parts, pt. 1, 1926; a collective work under the editorship of Em. Yaroslavsky, "History of the Communist Party of the Soviet Union," in 4 vols., vol. 1, 1926, vols. 2–4, 1929–30; P. M. Kerzhentsev, "Pages of the History of the RKP (b)," 1925; D. I. Kardashev, "Fundamental Historic Stages and Development of the VKP," 1927; "History of the VKP (b) in Congresses," under the editorship of P. N. Lepeshinsky, 1927; A. S. Bubnov, "VKP (b)," in 2 vols.; Em. Yaroslavsky, "History of the VKP (b)," pts. 1–2, 1933 (reissued until 1938); "Short History of the VKP (b)," under the editorship of V. Knorin, 1934; *History of the VKP (b), Short Course*, under the editorship of a commission of the CC of the VKP (b), 1938 and a series of other editions. The rather chaotic chronological order is theirs. The fact that a historian starts a two-volume work and publishes only the first part, then starts a new one, is a sign of the high mortality rate in these histories. There are other editions of works by Yaroslavsky and Bubnov which *Voprosy istorii KPSS* has chosen to ignore, as they have such histories as Zinoviev's. The last work mentioned in the list is, of course, the one known as Stalin's *Short Course*.

16. I have seen a number of Yaroslavsky efforts which are not mentioned in *Voprosy istorii KPSS*'s bibliographical note.

17. See *Soviet Survey*, April-June 1960.

18. The book was published in 1938. The *Pravda* quote was published twelve years later on the occasion of its anniversary. Whether Stalin wrote it, or wrote only parts of it, making emendations on every page, it bears the unmistakable imprint of his unique temperament. It will hereafter be referred to as Stalin's *Short Course*.

19. The Politburo decision was adopted on August 5, 1938, but was kept secret for twenty years. See *Spravochnik partiinogo rabotnika* [The party worker's handbook] (Moscow, 1957), p. 364.

20. *The Communist Party of the Soviet Union* (New York, 1960), pp. 471–72.

21. Three days after the *Pravda* "Theses" appeared, the present writer prepared a paper for the American State Department which said: "No living name is mentioned because a struggle goes on for the succession. He who yesterday praised Beria is a dead duck. He

who today praises Malenkov or Molotov or Zhukov may be doomed tomorrow. Thus the ultimate in the depersonalization of history is the blank space, the anonymous 'party and government,' the standardized replaceable parts."

22. Even the delicate allusions and sporadic rehabilitations permitted to serious historians ("archive rats") during the "thaw" after 1956 are not for this "popular textbook." As archives were published and memoirs, long suppressed, were republished with excisions, footnotes were permitted concerning the dates of birth and bureaucratic posts of some of the purged. The climax of refinement came in the formula used in the biographical notes on twelve purged memorialists in vol. 2 of *Memories of Lenin* (1957), of whom it was said: "In 1937, he became a victim of enemy slander; later rehabilitated." But such refinements are not for this work intended for general reading.

23. Judging from the proceedings of the Twenty-first Congress, Peruvkhin and Saburov are also slated for historical oblivion.

24. *Voprosy istorii KPSS*, no. 5, 1960, p. 11.

25. Ibid., p. 13.

26. The other reports are purely technical: A Report of the Central Control Commission (or, as it is now called, "Revision Commission") by the minor figure, A. F. Gorkin, and a report on "Changes in the By-Laws or Statutes of the CPSU," with Kozlov as reporter.

27. *Pravda*, April 19, 1959.

28. On this, see Herbert Ritvo, "Twenty-first Congress—Before and After (Part One)," in *American Slavic and East European Review* (April 1961): 208, and W. Ulbricht, *Einheit* (April 1959).

29. Issue of January 24, 1959.

30. *Voprosy istorii KPSS*, no. 12, 1960, p. 113.

31. Ibid., no. 5, 1960, p. 14.

9. A Party of a New Type

1. *Charismatic attributes.* In this essay, as in my *Communist Totalitarianism*, I have used the term *charismatic* in the sense given to it by Max Weber in "Die drei reinen Typen der legitimen Herrschaft."

In its original sense, *charisma* meant the grace of God, manifested by prophets, priest-kings, divinely inspired rulers and leaders, upon whom God has conferred his grace or guidance. In the course of history many peoples have held their rulers to be divine, or divinely inspired, chosen, guided, or otherwise endowed with magical or transcendentally derived qualities. The "Divine Right of Kings" and the sovereign who is head of the church of his realm (*rex et pontifex maximus*) are survivals into recent times of charisma in this primary sense.

The great service of Max Weber has been to call our attention to a nonrational and nonbureaucratic element in the leadership and rulership of some who do not think of their powers as derived from a transcendental or a magical source. He has extended the term *charismatic* to qualities and dimensions of leadership and rule in societies which consider themselves "modern," "rational," bureaucratically or constitutionally regulated. As used by him, the term serves as a distinction between two basically different types of leadership and rule in modern movements and great-state societies. On the one hand, there are the ordinary rulers, leaders, and officials who hold their places by virtue of some established procedure or practical qualification, and who display in general the "rational" and workaday talents which ordinarily go with men in such offices. On the other hand, there are those leaders and rulers who—however they acquire their position—exhibit in their leadership an added dimension which is nonrational (or supra- or infrarational), depending on some quality in their persons which is felt as magnetic, contagious, stirring, overpowering, a quality which inspires in their followers powerful emotions and fanatical devotion. There is something about the latter type of ruler or leader which, whether for good or evil, surpasses the common light of every day, makes incandescent the multitudes listening to his word, calls forth unquestioning and fanatical obedience to commands, induces a surrender of individual reason and the normal moral code of the individual in favor of the reason and the code proclaimed by the charismatic leader or ruler. It is a quality which makes for disciples rather than mere attentive subordinates and fuses around the person of the charismatic leader a *movement* of followers and idolizers. Max Weber thus finds charisma not only in prophets but also in fanatically followed and idolized war leaders and in urban "great demagogues."

Weber's extension of the term *charisma* and the adjective *charismatic* to types of leadership and rule (*Fuehrerschaft und Herrschaft*) whose possessors do not feel that the source of their powers is transcendental and whose followers do not feel it to be transcendental either, has evoked critical reactions in those who (like Professor Carl J. Friedrich of Harvard) find the extension improper, not to say blasphemous. Such objectors would allow charisma to Jesus and His disciples, to the prophets and the saints, and perhaps to some of the successors of Peter. Not to be parochial, they would allow it to a Mohammed, too, since he and his followers believed that his powers of prophecy, prescription, command, and leadership in war and statecraft came from Allah. But they would deny the term to a Lenin or a Hitler, the first of whom surely, and the second presumably, believed neither in God's grace nor in God.

Max Weber, who bluntly, even proudly, proclaimed that he was tone deaf in religion as others are tone deaf in music, did not ease matters any when he wrote: "It is clear that the expression *charisma* is here used in an entirely value-free sense. The manic seizure of rage in the Nordic Beserker, the miracles and revelations of any hole-in-the-corner prophet, the demagogical gifts of a Cleon, are to sociology as much 'charisma' as the qualities of a Napoleon, a Jesus, a Pericles."

To the religiously sensitive, the second triad (Napoleon-Jesus-Pericles) is likely to be as offensive as the first.

However provocative or Puckish this juxtaposition may seem, there is need in sociology, history, and political thought for a term both to cover and to call our attention to that special dimension in some leaders and rulers not to be found in functional, bureaucratic, practical, prosy, uninspired and uninspiring, sometimes competent and sometimes bumbling, everyday leadership and rulership. Weber has given us such a term, serviceable in social and political analysis and historiography. We must be careful to indicate its different varieties and different approaches to itself, and be aware that it is not an absolute but a matter of more or less; we must perforce leave it to theology and religious feeling to decide whether in a given case its source is transcendental. Nor can one (as Dr. Friedrich has suggested to the writer) content oneself with a diversity of special terms for each special case: "military leadership," "demagogic leadership," "totalitarian leadership," "demonic leadership." For despite the illusions of our age concerning its "rationality," there appear today, with increasing importance, leaders and rulers who have this special irrational dimension or quality for which some special term is needed.

What, for instance, shall we say of a Gandhi, who did not himself claim that his gifts were from God, but whose simple journey to the sea clad in a homespun loincloth and armed with a ladle to scoop out one spoonful of water from the sea and wait for the sun to turn it into salt, could arouse an entire people to a frenzy?

Or what shall we think of a Shamyl, leading from his mountain peaks and deep ravines his little band of Moslem tribesmen in a war which held off the armies of mighty Russia for three decades (1830–61)? He believed in his own transcendental charisma, as did his followers. He thought of himself as the next great prophet after Mohammed, invincible, invulnerable, obligated to enforce his rule with ruthless severity since through him Allah spoke. Even outsiders wrote that he "exuded a mystical aura of leadership." Men—and women and children—died willingly in his Holy War, confident that they would awake that very day in Paradise. But to the Russian armies hunting him down like a wild beast, he was not even one of Weber's "hole-in-the-corner prophets," only a guerrilla leader, a mountain bandit, an enemy of the true faith and the truly charismatic Sovereign, Autocrat by divine right, by sacred charismatic inheritance through the royal blood, by holy anointment and patriarchal coronation, Defender and Head of the True Faith and dread absolute ruler over Holy Mother Russia. Yet Nicholas I did not possess charisma in Weber's sense and Shamyl did.

In the present work I have further extended the term as used by Weber. He used it to cover three types (the religious leader and prophet; the warrior leader; and the "great Demagogue"). But as the present essay suggests, modern total war called for and elevated to leadership a new type of war leader who is no warrior, no leader of armies in the field, but a *civilian* war leader. He sweeps aside the everyday politician when the latter proves incapable of developing the high emotion and energy, and inspiring the fanatical devotion, which total war requires. A Lloyd George replaces an Asquith; a Clemenceau takes over from a succession of Vivianis, Ribots, and Painlevés; a Churchill supplants a Chamberlain; a de Gaulle seizes the standard from the feeble hand of a Pétain or a Darlan, who does not know how to raise it high enough to gather Free France around it. This replacement is not necessarily a matter of greater competence or even greater energy, though of course competence and energy help. It is primarily a matter of greater "appeal," a stronger belief in one's "mission," somehow communicated to multitudes.

Since for millions nationalism has been an *ersatz* or *quasi* religion, and for other millions Marxism has served as a surrogate for a lost transcendental faith, while for yet other millions this function has been fulfilled by a mixture of nationalism and Marxism called national socialism or national communism, it is not surprising that these movements have tended to invest their leaders with an aura of quasi-religious feeling. There is no more difficulty here in the use of the word *charisma* than there is in the use of the word *religion* for the prefix *quasi* is as readily understood in the one case as in the other, and the attributes of charisma, though hard to define, are not difficult to perceive in their possessor.

When the Leader of such a movement dies, a special problem arises which does not exist for ordinary "rational" organizations, everyday political parties or ordinary legitimate governments—the problem of the succession. When a charismatic Leader dies, a vacuum remains at the heart of his movement and his state until the problem of the succession is solved. Thus these movements and institutions which already exhibit so many quasi-religious features have now to develop yet another feature: namely, a sort of apostolic succession. In the first chapter of *Three Who Made a Revolution* I noted among these quasi-religious features: singleness, exclusivism, dogma, sacred and infallible doctrine, orthodoxy, heresy, renegacy, schism, inquisition, purge, confession, excommunication, prophesy, prophets, disciples, vocation, asceticism, chiliastic expectation, redemption, the readiness to suffer all things for the sake of the faith.

But what if no other charismatic person be at hand among the disciples or lieutenants? For a movement whose members are sufficiently close in their banding together and in their separateness from the rest of society and its criticism, any successor, by the mere fact of his reaching the vacant post, may be made to appear to possess some semblance of the necessary attributes. Or else there may be a struggle for the succession until another such Leader appears, or until the movement is fragmented and disintegrates.

For a movement-in-power there is a special means employable to fill the gap, when a suitable charismatic successor is lacking. Since its monopoly of power and of doctrine gives it a monopoly of all the springs and levers of organization, communication and manipulation of public feeling and thought, it has proved possible for such a movement-as-state to manufacture a synthetic pseudo-charisma in a successor who, until he came to power, may have seemed to the masses and even to his close associates to be no more than "a grey blur." If the genuine Leader may be said to possess only *ersatz*-charisma in the transcendental sense, then this synthetic fabrication is *ersatz* to the second power.

Since one of the laws of a dictatorship-in-permanence seems to be that the Dictator normally surrounds himself not with original thinkers and questioners or men of independent intellectual and emotional force, but with disciples, faction lieutenants, yesmen, able but faithful executors of his will, the constantly recurring need to build up some hitherto colorless lieutenant into another Leader of more than natural size and attributes, another master of everything and infallible interpreter of infallible doctrine, becomes an ever more difficult task. There seems to be a built-in tendency to a downward trend in the charismatic or demonic attributes: after a Lenin comes a Stalin, after a Stalin a Khrushchev, after a Khrushchev . . . ?

2. The tragedy of Russia in wartime came not so much from the fact that the tsar, under the influence of the empress, persisted in selecting for the symbolic "leadership of the nation" a doddering Goremykin and then a contemptible Stuermer, men who lacked not merely magnetism but elementary competence, and in Stuermer's case even common honesty. Much more serious was the fact that both the empress and Nicholas himself were convinced that the tsar possessed charisma in the primary, sacred sense—the grace hereditary in the royal blood, in the divine guidance of the autocrat of Holy Russia, in the leadership of the true faith, and the literal love and reverence of his people. This was augmented in their eyes by Alexandra's certitude of a special divine guidance vouchsafed through the "Man of God," Rasputin. Neither the "public," nor the other members of the royal family, nor the more serious cabinet ministers, nor the Duma, nor the urban crowd, nor, as it turned out in the end, even the peasants, felt in Nicholas any charismatic spark. There were some at court who felt the "charisma" of Rasputin, but many more thought of him as demonic, or merely dissolute, and an unexplainable evil influence on the sovereigns.

3. V. I. Lenin, *Sochineniia* [Works], 9:111. From 1905 to 1907 and again during the war, Lenin's writings abound in hymns to force (the official English translation usually says "violence") and terror. The passage cited appears again and again in varying contexts but always with a touch of exultation. Lenin manifestly rejoices that the Russian autocracy has "put the bayonet on the order of business." He foreshadows his boycott of the Duma elections and his future dispersal of the Constituent Assembly by expressing relief that "constitutional illusions and school exercises in parliamentarism are becoming

only a screen for bourgeois betrayal of the revolution. . . . The really revolutionary class must then specifically advance the slogan of dictatorship" ("Dve taktiki sotsialdemo-kraticheskoi i demokraticheskoi revolyutsii") [Two tactics of the social-democratic and democratic revolution], 8:120. One interesting variant reads: "A revolutionary army is necessary because only by *force* can great historical questions be decided, and *the organization of force* in the contemporary struggle is a military organization (ibid., 8:527).

4. V. I. Lenin and A. M. Gorkii, *Pis'ma, Vospominanliia, dokumenty* [Correspondence, memoirs, documents] (Moscow, 1958), p. 91 (hereafter cited as Lenin and Gorky).

5. Again we catch a note of exultation. The passage reads: "If it was still possible to be satisfied with thin and weak soles when it was a matter of walking on the cultured sidewalks of a little provincial city, it is impossible to go without heavy, hob-nailed soles when you are marching into the mountains. Socialism in Europe has left the state of comparatively peaceful and narrow national limits" so that it is now "impossible to tolerate opportunism" in the day of the "hob-nailed soles." This passage leaves no doubt as to which era and way of struggle Lenin found more congenial (*Sochineniia*, 21:222).

6. Lenin is considered at length in *Three Who Made a Revolution*. Here only such features are touched on as seem most significant for an understanding of his role in the war and the October Revolution.

7. This and subsequent passages from Potresov are from the latter's article, "Lenin," in *Die Gesellschaft* (Berlin, 1927). For a Russian translation, see B. Nikolaevsky, *A. N. Potresov: Posthumous Collection of His Works* (Paris, 1937).

8. For letters to Krzhizhanovsky addressing him with the intimate pronoun, *ty*, and employing the pseudonymous title *Starik*, see Lenin, *Sochineniia*, 34:113–14, 127, 186–88. One letter is extant showing that for a brief period Lenin also felt close enough to Martov so that they addressed each other as *ty*. But with their first political disagreement, Lenin switched to the formal *vy*. There was only one other Bolshevik besides Krzhizhanovsky (we must, of course, except the members of his immediate family, two sisters, a brother, and his wife) to whom Lenin was to write *ty*, namely, Inessa Armand. But by that time he had had a difference with Krzhizhanovsky (in 1904 over the question of splitting the party). Thereafter, though the latter remained his faithful follower and Lenin wrote notes to him almost daily when he made Krzhizhanovsky the chairman of the State Planning Commission, the "Old Man" never used *ty* to him again. Once you had differed with Lenin on a political matter, all intimacy was at an end.

9. For a discussion of the overtones of the use of *Ilyich* and *Starik* as they affect a sensitive Russian ear, see N. Valentinov, *Vstrechi s Leninym* (New York, 1953), pp. 71–73.

10. Lenin, *Sochineniia*, 5:390, 435; 7:338-39.

11. *Leninskii Sbornik* [Collected Leniniana], 6:134 and 137; *Vtoroi ocherednoi s"ezd* [The second regular congress] Geneva, 1903), p. 241. *Leninskii Sbornik* wrongly ascribes the speech to Rozanov instead of Popov. The *Sbornik* is illustrated with a reproduction of the handwritten notes which Lenin used for the interruption and for his subsequent speech. When a delegate spoke of the rights of party members, Lenin wrote in his notes, "*There are no rights* in party membership. RESPONSIBILITY." But the minutes show that he softened this when he said, "Independent even of rights, we must not forget that every member of the party is responsible for the party and *the party responsible for every member*" (*Vtoroi s"ezd* [Second congress], p. 254).

12. Lenin, *Sochineniia*, 6:211-15.

13. Ibid., 4:273.

14. There is an ambivalence about leadership and its functions even in democratic societies: how far shall the leader follow his followers, and how far seek to lead them? Perhaps in

all Marxists, beginning with Marx himself, because they think they know what path and what doctrine the working class *must* choose, there is an unconscious germ of authoritarianism, an intention to indoctrinate, enlighten, instruct, and direct, according to a preconceived formula. But most Marxists, again beginning with Marx himself, rejected any intention to dictate to the working class. They expected the working class to arrive at its own "consciousness" out of its own experiences, form its own mass parties, select its own leadership, write its own programs. At most the Marxists hoped consciously to serve as informed experts and thus reach official position and the chance to give leadership by virtue of such selection. It was the opponents of Marx, notably the Pole Makhaiski (Machajski) and the Russian Bakunin, who charged that Marxism aimed at a dictatorship by the intelligentsia, a new official class. Among Marxists, however, Lenin was unique in developing this authoritarian germ to full flower, unique in taking pride in it. It was only gradually in the development of their struggle with Lenin and Leninism that the more democratic socialists came to reject the authoritarian strain in the doctrine they had accepted. At the opposite extreme of the spectrum from Lenin was Axelrod, whose organization doctrine genuinely anticipated the dissolution of the "elite party" in the future mass party of the working class.

15. Lenin's "rages" are discussed from time to time in Krupskaia's letters to his family as if they were a familiar thing to them. They are several times hinted at in her memoirs, where she describes how they are followed by periods of complete exhaustion and a desire only to doze or find solitude in mountain walks. The best analysis of these seizures of rage alternating with depressed exhaustion is to be found in Valentinov, *Vstrechi s Leninym* [Meetings with Lenin], pp. 182 and 210–12. Lenin acknowledges that he was "possessed" by such a "rage" during the controversies with his fellow Iskrists at the Second Congress. He writes of it apologetically in a letter to Potresov, dated Sept. 13, 1903 (Lenin, *Sochineniia*, 34:137–39). He also speaks of the rages which "possess" him in several letters to Gorky. In one such letter he angrily denounces Gorky for "God-constructions" ("Every God-worship is copulation with death"). Because it was Gorky, whom Lenin pardoned for many things and treated with special consideration as a writer useful to the cause, he delayed the sending of the letter until he had cooled off. Nevertheless, he sent it, with a lame apology, for Lenin by no means repudiated in his cooler moments the things he said in his rages. The admission and apology were omitted from the 4th edition of Lenin's works but may be found in Lenin and Gorky, pp. 105–9.

16. *Iskra* ("The Spark") was the name he had chosen for the journal.

17. And Lenin did not mean the word *military* to be merely figurative.

18. Lenin, *Sochineniia*, 5:8–12, 346–50, 355–56, 400–401, 410, 421–22, 431, 440–41, 442–44, 481.

19. Lenin, *Sochineniia*, 36:80.

20. The verbal difference was trivial, but actually Lenin's definition envisaged a party of "professional revolutionaries" or a revolutionary vanguard elite, while Martov's was intended to be looser and more inclusive, making room for anyone who accepted the party's directives and the party's program. For an analysis of this point and other aspects of the congress, see *Three Who Made a Revolution*, chaps. 14 and 15.

21. The election of the members of the leading bodies.

22. Lenin's temporary majority elected Martov also to the editorial board, but he refused to serve because Axelrod, Zasulich, and Potresov had been excluded.

23. Ibid., 34:252.

24. Rafael Abramovich to the writer.

25. It was to remain the common *Program* of both Bolsheviks and Mensheviks until 1919!

26. Karl Marx and Friedrich Engels, *Ausgewaehlte Werke* (Berlin, 1958), 1:360; 2:8.

27. Leon Trotsky, *Lenin* (New York, 1925), p. 43. But when Lenin did not have a majority in the Central Committee, there was no room in his thoughts for the idea of the "subordination of the minority to the majority." Then he would threaten to resign, to mobilize the party against the Central Committee, or even, as in November 1917, to "go to the sailors," i.e., mobilize the unruly, nonparty masses against the party.

28. Lenin, *Sochineniia*, 5:448.

29. Ibid., 7:365–66.

30. *Vospominaniia o Lenine* [Memories of Lenin] (Moscow, 1956), 1:313.

31. Lenin to the Ninth Congress, April 1920; and "II Kongress Kommunisticheskogo Internationala, Stenograficheskii Otchet" [Second congress of the Communist International, stenographic account], p. 576.

32. Lenin, *Sochineniia*, 6:221-23; cf. ibid., 7:365-66.

33. Ibid.

34. Alfred G. Meyer, *Leninism* (Cambridge, 1957), p. 98. Better, a revolutionary with a bureaucratic-military mind.

35. Lenin, *Sochineniia*, 27:477.

36. Denikin, Kolchak, and Yudenich were leaders of the anti-Bolshevik armies that tried to overthrow Lenin.

37. Ibid., 4:343.

38. Ibid., 5:350 ff.

39. Ibid., pp. 347–48.

40. Ibid., p. 431.

41. Ibid., pp. 355–56.

42. Ibid., p. 392.

43. Ibid., p. 398.

44. Ibid., p. 410.

45. It is interesting to note that of the original *Iskra* six, four were from the hereditary nobility—Plekhanov, Zasulich, Potresov, and Lenin—while the other two, Axelrod and Martov, were *raznochintsy* from those "miscellaneous groups," neither noble, peasant, nor worker that did not belong to any of the basic classes or estates of traditional Russian society. All six were students when they became revolutionaries.

46. Lenin, *Sochineniia*, 5:441.

47. Ibid., 27:420. Lenin uses the term *katorzhno*, derived from the word *katorga*, hard labor in a juridical sense, i.e., penal servitude.

48. Ibid., 5:421.

49. Ibid., pp. 442–43.

50. Cf. "We must put the revolutionary party in the place that the mythical Tsar now holds in the eyes of our citizens" (*Zemlya i volya* [Land and liberty], April 1879).

51. Lenin, *Sochineniia*, 28:54; 32:222; 27:69.

10. The Split in the Socialist Parties

1. *The Communist International* (Petrograd), no. 3, July 1, 1919, p. 370.

2. Jindřich Veselý, *Entstehung und Gründung der Kommunistischen Partei der Tschechoslowakei* (Berlin, 1955), p. 95.

3. Eugen Prager, *Geschichte der USPD*, 2d ed. (Berlin, 1922), p. 222.

4. V. I. Lenin, *Polnoe sobranie sochinenii* [Complete works], 5th ed. (Moscow, 1963), 41:27.

5. *Entsiklopedicheskii slovar'* [Encyclopedic dictionary], Institut Granat, Moscow, 1926[?],

vol. 41, pt. 2, p. 168. In fact Radek arrived in Germany in September—and not in October as he wrote in 1926—as may be seen from an article he wrote in March 1923: "It was at the moment of our defeat in the war against Poland, at a time when the negotiations of Riga began. I was about to leave Russia and to see Lenin . . ." Now the Riga negotiations started on September 11, 1920. Cf. Radek's article on Lenin, *La Correspondance Internationale*, March 14, 1923, p. 152.

6. Arnold Struthahn (Karl Radek), *Die Entwicklung der deutschen Revolution und die Aufgaben der Kommunistischen Partei* (Stuttgart, 1919), pp. 52, 54.

7. *Der zweite Kongress der Kommunistischen Internationale*. Protokoll der Verhandlungen (Hamburg, 1921), p. 370.

8. G. Zinoviev, *Dvenadtsat' dnei v Germanii* [Twelve days in Germany] (Petersburg, 1920), p. 8.

9. Prager, *Geschichte der USPD*, p. 224.

10. G. Zinoviev, *Die Weltrevolution und die III. Kommunistische Internationale*. Rede auf dem Parteitag der USPD in Halle am 14. Oktober 1920. Verlag der Kommunistischen Internationale, 1920, p. 4.

11. Ibid. (The last sentence is incomplete in this brochure. The quotation is therefore taken from the minutes of the Halle congress: *Protokoll über die Verhandlungen des ausserordentlichen Parteitages in Halle* [Berlin, n.d.], p. 151.)

12. Zinoviev, *Dvenadtsat' dnei v Germanii*, pp. 14–16.

13. Ibid., p. 29.

14. Ibid., p. 54.

15. Ibid., pp. 180, 197.

16. Ibid., pp. 184–85, 187–88.

17. Ibid., p. 15. A position similar to Hilferding's, i.e., in favor of joining the Third International but against splitting the Socialist party, which was ready and willing to join, and against knuckling under to the Bolsheviks, would produce a similar cleavage in the SFIO in December and in the Italian Socialist party in January 1921, the Comintern's Russian leaders having already firmly made up their minds to bar from the future International any and all who criticized or questioned its internal organizational structure. To Lenin and Zinoviev, acceptance of the idea of a dictatorship by the proletariat (of which Hilferding expressed approval in his speech) was less important than acceptance of the Bolshevik scheme of organization (which Hilferding flatly rejected and which, as he made a point of stressing, Rosa Luxemburg had turned down as far back as 1904). Hilferding's attitude infuriated Zinoviev, who after the speech characterized him as a "petty shopkeeper" having "the mind of a worm" (G. Zinoviev, *Dvenadtsat' dnei v Germanii*, p. 22).

18. *Der Beginn der Krise in der KP Deutschlands* (Remshied, n.d.), p. 19. Levi added a remark about Zinoviev's behavior in Halle which highlighted the latter's typical volatility: "When comrade Zinoviev came to Germany—and this was not only my impression—he was completely different, and we, whom in Moscow he had regarded as more or less semi-independent, had to keep hold of his coattails so that he wouldn't run too wild" (ibid.).

19. *Die Rote Fahne*, no. 211, October 19, 1920, Berlin.

20. Zinoviev, *Dvenadtsat' dnei v Germanii*, p. 113.

21. Paul Levi, *Der Beginn der Krise in der Kommunistischen Partei Deutschlands* (Remschied, n.d.), p. 22.

22. *Bericht der Zentrale an den 2. Parteitag der VKPD vom 22. bis 26. August 1921 in Jena*, n.d., pp. 13–14.

23. *Journal du Peuple*, January 24, 1918.

24. *L'Humanité*, Paris, July 24, 1918.
25. A. Kemerer (V. Taratouta), "Brief an Jean Longuet und an das 'Komitee zur Wiederaufrichtung der Internationale,'" *Die Kommunistische Internationale*, no. 9, 1920, p. 1504.
26. *The Workers Dreadnought*, no. 41, January 3, 1920; also in V. I. Lenin, *Polnoe sobranie sochinenii*, 39:251.
27. Leon Trotsky, *Sochineniia* [Works] (Moscow, 1926), 13:144.
28. Lenin, *Polnoe sobranie sochinenii*, 40:135.
29. L. O. Frossard, *Le Parti socialiste et l'Internationale*. Rapport sur les négociations à Moscou (Paris, 1920), p. 5.
30. Parti socialiste, *Rapport du secrétariat au Congrès National Ordinaire du 25 décembre 1920* (Paris, n.d.), p. 8.
31. Der zweite Kongress . . . , pp. 263–64.
32. *Le Problème de l'Internationale*. Controverse entre les citoyens Cachin-Frozzard-Mayèras (Lille, 1920), p. 37.
33. *Manifestes, Thèses et Résolutions des quatre premiers congrès de l'Internationale communiste, 1919–1923* (Paris, 1934), p. 40.
34. Parti socialiste, *18ème congrès national tenu à Tours*. Compte rendu sténographique (Paris, 1921), p. 398.
35. Ibid., p. 486.
36. Zinoviev, *Dvenadtsat' dnei v Germanii*, p. 52.
37. *Le Phare*, no. 14, November 1920, Chaux-de-Fonds, p. 75.
38. Lenin, *Polnoe sobranie sochinenii*, 41:686.
39. Parti socialiste, *18ème congrès national*, pp. 312–13.
40. Ibid., pp. 585, 583.
41. Ibid., p. 447.
42. Letter from C. Zetkin to P. Levi, dated January 10, 1921 (in the author's possession).
43. Ibid. The initials refer to the following: Cachin, Vaillant-Couturier, Renand-René Reynaud, who enjoyed the confidence of the Committee for the Third International, and A. hides the pseudonym of Abramovich-Albrecht Zalewski.
44. Parti socialiste, *18ème congrès national*, p. 391.
45. Ibid., p. 419.
46. Ibid., p. 244.
47. Ibid., p. 246.
48. Ibid., p. 247.
49. Ibid., p. 255.
50. Ibid., p. 381.
51. Ibid., p. 488.
52. *Un an d'action communiste*, Rapport du Secrétariat générale (Courbevoie, 1921), p. 37.
53. G. Zinoviev, *Ce que a été jusqu'ici l'Internationale communiste et ce qu'elle doit être* (Petrograd, 1920), p. 15.
54. Parti socialiste, *17ème congrès national tenu à Strasbourg*. Compte rendu sténographique (Paris, 1920), p. 286.
55. A. Rossi, *La naissance du fascisme en Italie, de 1918 à 1922* (Paris, 1938), p. 62.
56. Serrati was not opposed in principle to the exclusion of Turati and the other reformists, but only to Moscow's procedure in this case. At the meeting of the Executive Committee of the Comintern, on August 11—that is, after the end of the Second Congress—the problem of the purge of Italian reformists was discussed in the following fashion: "Nobody opposed the exclusion from the party of people like Turati, Modigliani, d'Aragona, etc.; but the Italian comrades (Serrati) insisted that the exclusion should be

done in a way that would not alienate the masses" (*L'Internationale communiste*, September 1920, p. 2593).

57. Lenin, *Sochineniia* [Works], 3rd ed. (Moscow, 1929), 25:360.

58. *Die Kommunistische Internationale*, no. 13 (Petrograd, 1920), pp. 289–90.

59. Ibid., p. 294.

60. *L'Internationale Communiste*, no. 14, November 1920, pp. 2915–16.

61. *Le Parti socialiste italien et l'Internationale communiste*, Recueil de documents (Petrograd, 1921), p. 57.

62. Ibid., p. 97 (emphasis in the text).

63. *18ème congrès national*, pp. 398–99.

64. Rossi, *La naissance du fascisme*, p. 66.

65. *Umanita Nuova*, October 11, 1964, letter from Silone to A. Borghi.

66. *Le Parti socialiste italien . . .* , p. 100.

67. *Bulletin du IIIe congrès de l'Internationale communiste* (Moscow, June 29, 1921), no. 6, p. 9.

68. Lenin, *Polnoe sobranie sochinenii*, 41:418.

69. Ibid., pp. 418, 422.

70. V. Degot, *Pod znamenem bolshevizma* [Under the banner of bolshevism] (Moscow, 1927), p. 143.

71. *Le Parti socialiste italien*, p. 113.

72. Rede des Genossen Rakosi am 16. Februar 1921 (in the author's possession).

73. Bericht Genossen Paul Levi an das Exekutivkomitee der Dritten Internationale über den italienischen Parteitag, January 20, 1921 (in the author's possession).

74. Christo Kabakchiev-Bio-bibliographie (in Bulgarian) (Sofia, 1958), p. 39.

75. C. Zetkin's letter of January 10, 1921 (in the author's possession).

76. Paul Levi, *Was ist das Verbrechen? Die Märzaktion order die Kritik daran?* (Berlin, 1921), p. 42.

77. *Bericht des Genossen Paul Levi an das Exekutivkomitee*, p. 3. It is to be noted that Levi's report described the parts played by all the protagonists in the Leghorn drama, both those on the Soviet side (Rakosi and Kabakchiev) and those on the Italian side (Serrati, Bordiga, Bombacci, Graziadei), but that Antonio Gramsci was not present at this summit at which the fate of the Italian party was decided, his name never once appearing in Levi's account.

78. Paul Levi, *Der Beginn der Krise*, pp. 15–16.

79. *Bericht des Genossen Paul Levi.*

80. *Bulletin du IIIe congrès*, no. 4, June 25, 1921, p. 11.

81. C. Zetkin's letter.

82. Levi, *Der Beginn der Krise*, p. 16.

83. Sitzung der Zentrale mit dem Vertreter des Exekutivkomiteess für Deutschland, Berlin, Freitag, den 28. Januar 1921 (in the author's possession).

84. Levi, *Der Beginn der Krise*, p. 22.

85. Lenin, *Polnoe sobranie sochinenii*, 52:149.

86. *Le Parti socialiste italien*, p. 154.

87. Sitzung der Zentrale mit dem Vertreter. . . .

88. Degot, *Pod znamenem bolshevizma*, p. 146.

89. *Bericht des Genossen Paul Levi.*

90. Sitzung der Exekutive am 22. February 1921, Moskau (in the author's possession).

91. Rossi, *La naissance du fascisme*, p. 191.

92. Rapport du comrade B. Jilek sur le développement et l'état du parti communiste de Tchécoslovaquie. Second enlarged plenum. June 1922 (in the author's possession).

93. *Rude Pravo*, Prague, December 29, 1920. For the full text, see *Kommunisticheskii Internatsional* [Communist international], no. 16, 1921, pp. 3825–28.
94. *Acta Historica*, Budapest, vol. 6, nos. 1–2, 1959, p. 48.
95. *Kommunisticheskii Internatsional*, no. 16, 1921, pp. 3881–82.
96. Ibid., no. 17, 1921, pp. 4317–20.
97. Jindřich Veselý, *Entstehung und Gründung*, p. 188.
98. Ibid.
99. Report of Comrade B. Jilek to the enlarged second plenum, June 1922, p. 6. It was at its meeting of July 16, 1921, that the "little bureau" of the Executive Committee had decided to send an emissary to Czechoslovakia, but the assumed name "Comrade Carlo," and of course the identity of the assumer, remained secret.

11. Tito and Stalin

1. *Pravda*, October 20, 1920; Joseph V. Stalin, *Sochineniia* [Works] (Moscow, 1951), 4:351–63.

12. The Struggle for the Soviet Succession

1. The words were *razbrod i panika*. *Razbrod* means disarray or disorder. It is stronger and has a wider sweep than our word *confusion*. *Panic* has the same meaning in both languages.
2. He doubtless set up a smaller, extralegal body of men on the spot to consult with, not unlike the old Politburo.
3. The satellite and foreign Communist press also took it for granted that Malenkov was being made into a new Stalin. Typical is the American Communist journal, *Political Affairs*, carrying material prepared in early March for its April issue. Of the three funeral orations, *Political Affairs* found room only for Malenkov's. And William Z. Foster wrote the lead article under the title: "Malenkov at the Helm." In it eight separate passages indicated that Malenkov was regarded as the successor. A few quotes will show the spirit of the article: "The prompt election of Georgi Malenkov to Stalin's post. . . . This (Marxist-Leninist) training constitutes the best possible preparation for the heavy tasks of leadership that have now come to Malenkov. . . . His superb Marxist-Leninist training and his high natural ability will make him a giant. . . . Today as Malenkov becomes the outstanding leader of the Party and the Government . . . Malenkov at the head of the Government. . . ."
   By the May issue, prepared in early April, Mr. Foster had repented of his rashness to the extent that in an article titled "Stalin and the Coexistence of the U.S.S.R. and the U.S.A.," he does not even bring in the appropriate quotation from Malenkov's statement on Stalin's policy of "coexistence" in the funeral oration.

13. A New Look at the Soviet "New Look"

1. Lenin was born in 1870, Stalin and Trotsky in 1879, Zinoviev in 1883, Bukharin in 1888. Khrushchev was born in 1894, but did not join the Communist party until 1918, after it had taken power. Malenkov was born in 1902 and joined the Communist party only in 1920.
2. For many of the biographical details in this article, I am indebted to the researches and

reports of Lazar Pistrak, of the United States Information Library, and to Boris Nikolaevsky, who is at work on a study of Malenkov and his associates. Others come from wartime and postwar Russian refugees, and from Soviet documents.

3. Saburov is now deputy premier and was selected this year to make the November 7 address from the Lenin-Stalin tomb.

14. Stalin's Ghost at the Party Congress

1. On March 8, 1956, *Pravda* published an article by the aged G. I. Petrovsky, associate of Lenin who was released from a concentration camp and "rehabilitated" shortly after Stalin died. It was devoted to the Tenth Congress and said: "Lenin stressed that Party unity should become Party law. . . . Lenin could be merciless to enemies. The Tenth Party Congress adopted the Leninist resolution 'On Party Unity,' which condemned all opposition groups and banned all factions and groupings in the Party. . . . The Tenth Party Congress was an example of Lenin's style of leadership, *of Lenin's ability to work on a strictly collective leadership basis. . . .*" (emphasis added).

2. Solomon Schwarz, "Kompartiia na dvadtsatom sezde" [The Communist party at the twentieth congress], *Sotsialisticheskii Vestnik* [Socialist herald] (April 1956): 60–62.

15. The New Gospel according to Khrushchev

1. The book was published in 1938. The *Pravda* quote was published twelve years later on the occasion of its anniversary. Whether Stalin wrote it, or wrote only parts of it, making emendations on every page, it bears the unmistakable imprint of his unique temperament. It will hereafter be referred to as Stalin's *Short Course.*

2. The Politburo decision was adopted on August 5, 1938, but kept secret for twenty years. See *Spravochnik partiinogo rabotnika* [The party worker's handbook] (1957), p. 364.

3. "The Communist Party of the Soviet Union" (New York, 1960), pp. 471–72.

4. Three days after the *Pravda* "Theses" appeared, the present writer prepared a paper for the State Department which said: "No living name is mentioned because a struggle goes on for the succession. He who yesterday praised Beria is a dead duck. He who today praises Malenkov or Molotov or Zhukov may be doomed tomorrow. Thus the ultimate in the depersonalization of history is the blank space, the anonymous 'party and government,' the standardized replaceable parts."

5. The fate of Knorin was clarified in the April-June 1960 issue of *Soviet Survey.* This old Bolshevik Lett, who joined Lenin's party around 1912 or a little earlier, was arrested in 1937, accused of nationalist deviation, horribly tortured, and forced to confess that he had been a tsarist agent and then an agent of the Gestapo. He was shot within a year of his "confession."

6. Even the delicate allusions and sporadic rehabilitations permitted to serious historians during the "thaw" after 1956 are not for this book. As archives were published and memoirs, long suppressed, were republished with excisions, footnotes were permitted concerning the dates of birth and bureaucratic posts of some of the purged. The climax of refinement came in the formula used in the biographical notes on twelve purged memorialists in volume 2 of *Memories of Lenin* (1957), of whom it was said: "In 1937, he became a victim of enemy slander; later rehabilitated." But such refinements are not for this history textbook.

16. The Durability of Soviet Despotism

1. This comparison is a central part of Karl A. Wittfogel's *Oriental Despotism: A Comparative Study of Total Power* (Yale, 1957). His attention is centered on the countries in which "the state became stronger than society" because of the need to undertake vast state irrigation and flood control works by *corvée* organization of the entire population, with the consequent assumption of enormous managerial functions. But his study is full of insights into modern, industry-based totalitarianism highly suggestive for the purposes of our theme.
2. This does not apply to the Soviet empire but only to the Soviet Union. In general I have omitted any consideration of the empire here.
3. At the Oxford Conference to which this paper was presented, Leonard Schapiro offered a brief and simple criterion of distinction between within-system changes and changes in the system. He said: "Any changes which leave undisturbed the monopoly of power by the party and its leaders may be regarded as a 'within-system' change. Any firm limitation upon this monopoly of power would represent a 'change-in-the-system.'"
4. For a time Bulganin made the "purely" economic pronouncements, but that period seems to have ended with the Twentieth Congress.

17. Reflections on the Future of the Soviet System

1. From the Introduction to the fourth edition of *Three Who Made a Revolution*.
2. See the author's article based on the paper "The Durability of Despotism in the Soviet Union," *Russian Review* (April and July 1958), pp. 83–93, 163–75.
3. Lenin, *Sochineniia* [Works], (4th Russian ed.), 5:398.
4. Ibid., 26:303–4. The article was written on October 24 (November 6, New Style), 1917.
5. Ibid., p. 318. "Speech on the Question of the Constituent Assembly," *Pravda*, December 1, 1917.

18. A Historian Looks at the Convergence Theory

1. Emphasis here, as in all quoted passages, is in the original.
2. James Burnham, *The Managerial Revolution* (New York, 1941), pp. 74–75. Mr. Burnham has long since abandoned the prophecy, but the notion that managers and technocrats are running, or will soon run both societies is still a key element in the convergence theory, and central to John Kenneth Galbraith's *The New Industrial State* (New York, 1967). From Burnham to Galbraith, economic determinists and economists generally have found it hard to believe that politicians and governments keep such specialists on tap, but not on top.
3. These words are quoted from no one in particular but recurred in a thousand editorials and addresses, and with slight variations were to be heard almost everywhere. I heard them from many platforms on which I debated with Frederick Schuman, Henry Pratt Fairchild, Louis Dollivet, Joseph Barnes, Corliss Lamont, Isaac Deutscher, Vera Micheles Dean, Kirby Page, Sir Bernard Pares, and a wide range of other speakers. It is not my intention to lump these diverse people with diverse motives together in any way beyond the fact that they all advanced in more or less similar language the view expressed in this synthetic, generalized quotation.

4. Pitirim Sorokin, *Russia and the United States* (London, 1950), p. 176.

5. Lenin, *Sochineniia* [Works], 4th ed. (Moscow, 1949), 33:208–9. Sorokin was first condemned to death but the death sentence was then commuted on Lenin's order to exile and deprivation of citizenship.

6. Sorokin, *Russia and the United States*, pp. 195–96, 208.

7. Ibid., pp. 195–96.

8. Ibid., pp. 205–6.

9. Galbraith, *New Industrial State*, concluding chapter "The Future of the Industrial System," pp. 389–90.

10. Ibid., p. 399 and interview with Anthony Lewis cited above.

11. Ibid., pp. 388–89; Burnham, *Managerial Revolution*, p. 75; Sorokin, *Russia and the United States*, p. 208.

12. Karl Marx, *A Contribution to the Critique of Political Economy* (New York, 1904), p. 13.

13. Ibid., pp. 266–312. This intended Introduction to the *Critique of Political Economy* was left uncompleted by Marx, perhaps because it would have served to complicate the diagrammatic simplicities of the *Critique* as a whole. It was found among Marx's papers after his death and first published by Karl Kautsky in 1903 in the editions of March 7, 14, and 21 of the weekly *Neue Zeit*, then included in English translation as an appendix to the 1904 edition of the *Critique* from which I have been citing. It shows the richness of Marx's mind and his awareness that the history of actual peoples and civilizations was infinitely more complicated than the simple formulae of economic determinism and "inevitable social progression" that his book was intended to advance. No wonder he left it unfinished and unpublished. How else could he get on with the "cause" his writings were intended to serve? As I have suggested elsewhere, a similar awareness that actual social and economic life was more complex than the simplicities he was advancing made Karl Marx leave *Das Kapital* unfinished, or, in the words of Fritz Sternberg, a "mere torso." (See my *Marxism: A Hundred Years in the Life of a Doctrine* (New York, 1965), pp. 321–23 and 342–50; "Das Kapital One Hundred Years Later," *Antioch Review* (Winter 1966–67): 436–37; and Fritz Sternberg, *Anmerkungen zu Marx-Heute* (Frankfurt am Main, 1965), published posthumously.

14. The eight papers and the discussion of their meaning were published as *Feudalism in History*, edited by Rushton Coulbourn (Princeton, 1956).

15. Coulbourn, *Feudalism in History*, pp. 50 and 92.

16. Ibid., p. 93.

17. Ibid., p. 150.

18. Ibid., p. 152.

19. Ibid., pp. 167–82.

20. *The Bell*, no. 4 (London), October 1, 1857.

21. *Encounter* (London), February 1968, pp. 68–75. "P" is a third interviewee.

22. From dependable sources (which will have to be accepted or rejected on faith since I cannot name them), I have learned that there are now two lunatic asylums, one on the outskirts of Moscow and another near Leningrad, given over to "political lunatics" and a third of increasingly political character. In the whole history of tsarism there was one tsar, Nicholas I, who declared one philosopher, Peter Chaadaev, insane for critical remarks on Russia's cultural sterility, but he was not committed to an asylum, merely somewhat restricted in his freedom of movement and compelled to accept the indignity of daily visits from a doctor for one year, after which he apparently recovered his sanity. There were no political or literary or philosophical lunatics under Lenin or Stalin but an epidemic of such madness since Khrushchev at the beginning of the sixties declared:

"We have no more political criminals in the USSR. The only ones who oppose our system today are madmen." Yet the terms remain interchangeable. Yesenin-Volpin, for example, has spent four years in camps and two in asylums, and in February 1967 he was again declared insane for his activity on behalf of Sinyavsky and Daniel and his insistence that the Constitution's Bill of Rights be taken seriously by censors, courts, and police. His madness is evidenced in the appropriate fields of philosophy, mathematics, cybernetics, and concern with poetry and freedom. His *Leaf of Spring* was published in English in 1961. The president of the Academy of Sciences, Kaldysh, has more than once secured his release from jail or asylum by insisting on his importance in cybernetics and mathematics. I suppose the use of a madhouse instead of a bullet in the base of the brain may be set down as liberalism, or relaxation, or thaw.

19. The Totalitarian Potentials in the Modern Great-State Society

1. Kuehnelt-Leddihn, *Liberty or Equality* (Caldwell, Idaho, 1952), p. 281. It is interesting to note that there were centralizing monarchs in France before there was a centralizing republic, and bureaucratic centralization in Tsarist Russia before there was a Lenin and a Stalin, but both the French and the Bolshevik revolutions gave centralization an enormous booster charge. Interesting, too, to note that prohibition was introduced in America as a wartime measure to save grain for America's allies, but continued as a "moral" law in peacetime until the depression, when considerations of freedom combined with a need for finding a new source of taxation to bring repeal.

2. As late as 1928 the *Small Soviet Encyclopedia* under the heading "Passport" said: "The Passport system was the most important weapon of police activity and headtax policy in the so-called 'police state.' The passport system prevailed also in prerevolutionary Russia. Especially burdensome for the toiling masses, the passport system was also a hindrance to civilian movement in the bourgeois state, which abolished or weakened it. Soviet law knows no passport system. ... " In 1932 Stalin restored the internal passport system, giving it a scope and severity which it never had under the tsars.

Index